The Edge of Cymru

To Rob, for being with me all the way

The Edge of Cymru

A Journey

Julie Brominicks

SEREN

Seren is the book imprint of
Poetry Wales Press Ltd.
Suite 6, 4 Derwen Road, Bridgend, Wales, CF31 1LH

www.serenbooks.com
facebook.com/SerenBooks
Twitter: @SerenBooks

ISBN: 9781781727782
Ebook: 9781781726853

A CIP record for this title is available from the British Library.

The publisher acknowledges the financial assistance of the Books Council of Wales.

Cover image: Stuart Cambell Argue Photography
Printed in Perpetua by CMP.

CONTENTS

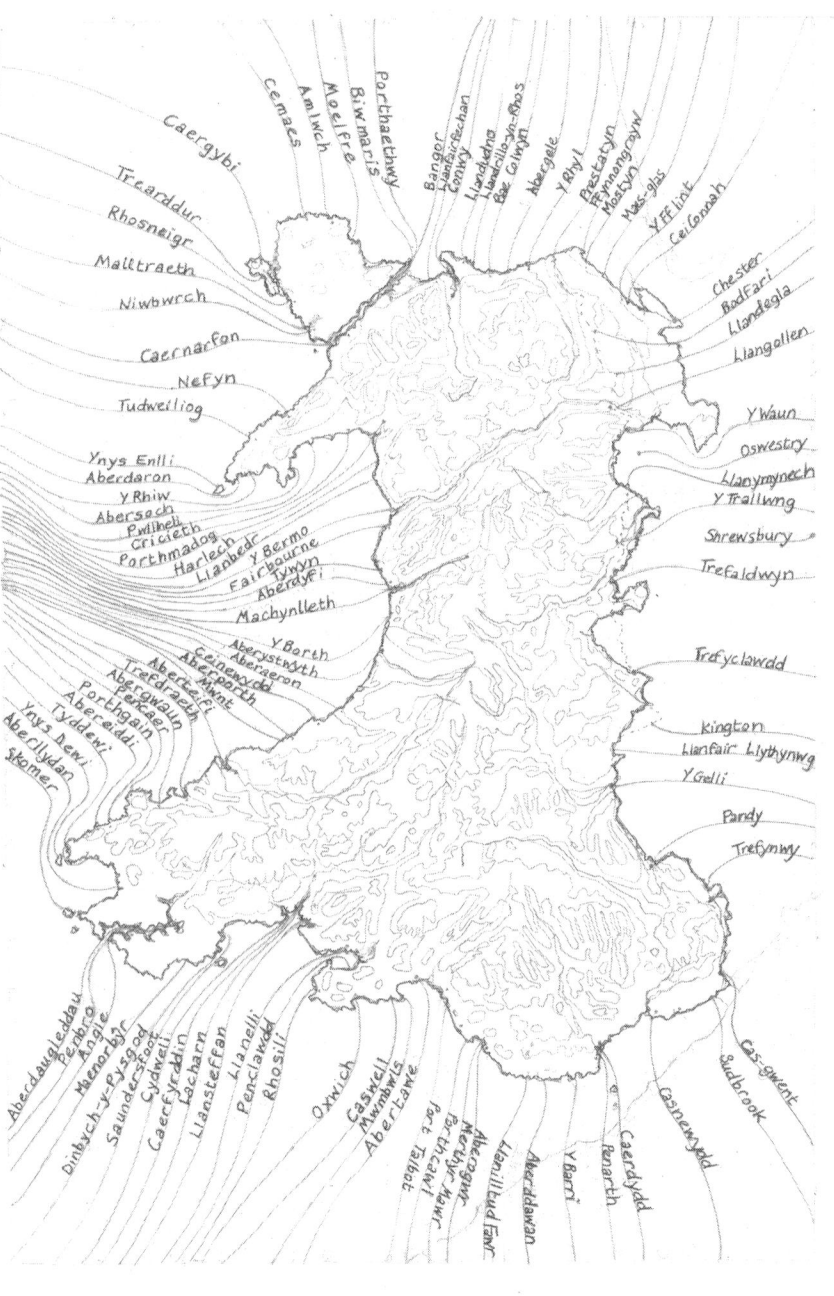

Caergybi
Trearddur
Rhosneigr
Malltraeth
Niwbwrch
Caernarfon
Nefyn
Tudweiliog
Ynys Enlli
Aberdaron
Y Rhiw
Abersoch
Pwllheli
Criccieth
Porthmadog
Harlech
Llanbedr
Y Bermo
Fairbourne
Tywyn
Aberdyfi
Machynlleth
Y Borth
Aberystwyth
Ceinewydd
Aberaeron
Aberarth
Aberporth
Trefdraeth
Abergwaun
Porthgain
Penfro
Abereiddi
Tyddewi
Ynys Dewi
Aberllydan
Skomer

Cemaes
Amlwch
Moelfre
Biwmaris
Porthaethwy
Bangor
Llanfairfechan
Conwy
Llandudno
Llandudno-Rhos
Bae Colwyn
Abergele
Y Rhyl
Prestatyn
Ffynnongroyw
Mostyn
Maes-glas
Y Fflint
Cei Connah
Chester
Bodfari
Llandegla
Llangollen
Y Waun
Oswestry
Llanymynech
Y Trallwng
Shrewsbury
Trefaldwyn
Trefyclawdd
Kington
Llanfair Llythynwg
Y Gelli
Pandy
Trefynwy

Abercastell
Aberdaugleddau
Penbro
Angle
Maenorbŷr
Dinbych-y-Pysgod
Saundersfoot
Cydweli
Caerfyrddin
Lacharn
Llansteffan
Llanelli
Penclawdd
Rhosili
Oxwich
Casllwchwr
Mwmbwls
Aberdawe
Port Talbot
Aberafan
Maesteg
Aberafan
Llanilltud Fawr
Aberddawan
Y Barri
Penarth
Caerdydd
Casnewydd
Cas-gwent
Sudbrook

NOTE ON LANGUAGE

I have (with the exception of Welsh Government which is Llywodraeth Cymru throughout), used English terms for organisations – so Natural Resources Wales rather than Cyfoeth Naturiol Cymru, and for manmade features – Pontcysyllte Aqueduct rather than Dyfrbont Pontcysyllte. I have also used English for places currently in England – Chester then, rather than Caer. But places are not simple. They have roots. Memory perhaps. So I've used Cymraeg for settlements and topographical features currently in Cymru. You'll find Casnewydd rather than Newport and Mynyddoedd Eryri rather than Snowdonia Mountains, despite my husband Rob expressing doubts. On reading my first draft he felt disoriented. Locations he knew had become unfamiliar.

I don't want readers to feel lost. But Rob had only just finished reading *China Road* which he'd enjoyed despite there being two or three place names new to him on every page. This, I hope, is the key – imagine you are meeting Cymru for the first time. Perhaps you are. I have used the standard forms recommended in the Welsh Language Commissioner's List of Standardised Welsh Place-names, found on the Commissioner's website.

You will also find

Cymru – Wales
Cymry – Welsh people
Cymraeg – Welsh (language)
Cymreig – Welsh (everything but language)

HOME

The stream is an elemental expression. An intervention of stone, a discussion of rain. Trees cast shady thoughts across it, bubbles invite light to its depths. It sounds like people brushing their teeth.

It is 2021, so I'm at home, though Covid restrictions are easing. The border is no longer in the news. There are no photographs just now, of road-signs advising travellers from England that 'Welsh lockdown rules apply'. No more stories of wives stowed away in car boots trying to get to their second homes, or of eBay purchases justifying journeys to Aberdyfi. But people have been reminded of Cymru's devolved government and I am pleased about that.

I have just finished writing this book. You could say I began it nine years ago, when Rob and I stood on a Portuguese track watching an old woman water vegetables with a can nailed to a stick – the precise moment I decided to quit my job. Financial disaster had finally winkled out the eco-centre where we both worked, and all of us there felt ship-wrecked. Stripping-down and upheaval would follow. But the introvert in me was also relieved because teaching had tired me out. I'd seen all those faces light up and felt my own spark fade. But now – now redundancies were up for grabs. Other decisions arrived, like birds. By the time we reached Muxia on the Spanish coast we'd decided to get married. But it was as we crept north along those white dusty Portuguese roads, that I made the decision to walk around the edge of Cymru and become a writer.

Why? Because the new Wales Coast Path was calling. I was already a hiker, so the question was when not if. I was not however, a writer. Writing was a fantasy that surfaced when travelling, then got buried back home, by work. I would make it my work.

But I didn't know what I'd write about. I didn't know the walk would lead to a deeper exploration of Cymru – the country in which I'd holidayed, studied, worked and now lived. And of my relationship with it. Or that the walk would inspire a second journey, into Cymru's history, that would result in this book. Or that I'd make peace with the environmental work I'd quit but could never shake off. I imagined I'd complete the walk in one go. That didn't happen. But that is the advantage of travelling where you live. You can be somewhere so strange and beautiful it shifts your life perspective, then hop on a bus and be home for dinner. The walk spanned a year in the end, from

September 2012 to September 2013, while the other journey, the research and writing it inspired – this book, is only just done.

I knew very little about Cymru when I started out. I did know that Cymru, like everywhere else (and particularly England from which data is not always easily separated) was implicated in global environmental collapse. But after so much teaching, I was pretty tired of thinking about all that. It took me some time to reconcile crisis with clarity and calm.

I lie back and listen to the stream, and it sounds like people scraping treacle out of tins.

DEVOLUTION; CYMRU TODAY

A lmost half of the population of just over 3 million live in towns or cities in the south-east. Grassland pasture accounts for 75% of the total land use, while 6 percent of the total is arable. Fifteen percent of land is woodland, with slightly more broadleaf than conifer. There are 24,000 kilometres of rivers and streams, 400 lakes, 150 reservoirs, and 136 mountains.

The National Assembly for Wales was created in 1999 with a Labour leader. In 2006 it became the first elected government in the world to have a majority of women members, though ethnic minority representation remains low. In a 2011 referendum following the One Wales coalition agreement between Labour and Plaid Cymru, 64 percent of the electorate voted for the Assembly to become known as Llywodraeth Cymru (Welsh Government). Llywodraeth Cymru is held to account by the Assembly which was renamed Senedd Cymru (Welsh Parliament) in 2020, and consists of 60 elected members. 'Senedd' also refers to Llywodraeth Cymru's main building in Caerdydd.

Llywodraeth Cymru is able to make laws for the areas it has responsibility for – urban and rural development, health and welfare, culture, education, transport, tourism and environment. But Cymru remains part of the UK with the King as Head of State and the Prime Minister as leader of His Majesty's Government. The UK Government retains control of law and order, tax and benefits, defence and foreign affairs. Currency and finance is organised by the Bank of England, and the British military trains troops and tests weapons in Cymru. Llywodraeth Cymru receives funding from the British Government and prior to Brexit, from the European Union (EU) which in 2016 a slim majority voted to leave. Cymru still sends MPs to Westminster, but they make up just 6 percent of the House of Commons and have little influence on UK governance. In 2014, the Yes Cymru non-party campaign for a fully independent Cymru was founded, and is gaining strength.

Prior to Brexit, inward and outward migration was roughly balanced with young people seeking work elsewhere while economic migrants and refugees arrived. In 2014, Polish-born people (particularly in Merthyr Tudful) represented the biggest overseas migrant community, while Caerdydd had the biggest population of non-UK born migrants. But most incomers, like Rob and myself were and remain English, accounting for 22 percent of the population. Many are retired, and settle in the countryside or on the coast. Immigration is not without impact. A 2015 report by the Welsh Language Commissioner found the number of people able to speak Cymraeg appeared to have increased to 23 percent (compared to 19 percent in the 2011 census) but that only half the speakers were fluent. Most fluent speakers lived in Gwynedd, Ynys Môn, Sir Gâr and Ceredigion. But a general decline in their numbers is being met by an increasing number of schools teaching through the medium of Cymraeg, particularly in large urban areas.

Rugby and football remain popular. Competitive eisteddfodau continue to cultivate Cymreig music and literature, as do media and social media, facilitated by a slowly improving broadband service. Religion is less influential than in previous centuries, though many people still have some alliance to Protestant churches or nonconformist chapels, and all religions are represented, particularly in Caerdydd, Abertawe and Casnewydd, with Islam the largest non-Christian faith.

Although unemployment rates have improved, Cymru is still one of the most deprived areas of the UK. Child poverty is particularly high, an above average percentage of people earn low or insecure wages and parts of the west and south have received significant EU developmental aid. Manufacturing, particularly in electronics, now accounts for about a third of the economy and the service sector (particularly tourism), about two thirds. Industries perceived to be traditional, such as coal mining, sheep farming and fishing, are economically negligible – agriculture, forestry and fisheries account for just 1.5 percent of the economy. Only eight working wool mills remain, and just a handful of mines and quarries still operate, the latter excavating mostly sand, gravel and limestone. But then you wouldn't expect coal mining with the climate tail-spinning into crisis and you wouldn't expect plentiful fish, with global biodiversity crashing.

As the climate destabilises, Cymru too is suffering – from increasingly savage storms, milder wetter winters and an increase of summer droughts, landslides and coastal erosion, and from floods that affect aquatic life. But urban expansion prevents the land's ability to absorb rain. Renewable energy still only accounts for just over 25 percent of total electricity production. Imported natural gas, coal and oil, still accounted for 75 percent of electricity generated in 2018. Half was produced by burning natural gas imported mainly from Qatar, Algeria, Egypt, Trinidad and Malaysia into deep-sea ports, particularly Aberdaugleddau. Although coal and nuclear plants have closed down, new nuclear has not been ruled out, and marine energy is hampered by lack of investment.

Air pollution from heating, transport and agriculture is unregulated, and soil health is decreasing. Although much is acidic due to underlying geology, neutral soils now receive more acidity than they can cope with, particularly from agricultural emissions of ammonia and nitrous oxide. Increased nitrogen in the atmosphere benefits plants like gorse and nettles which dominate sensitive plants – over 75 per cent of intensively-managed farmland is too acidic for optimum plant growth. The majority of raised bogs and fens are in a poor condition due to nitrogen deposition, drainage and eutrophication, compromising their biodiversity and ability to absorb and retain carbon.

Cymru (like the rest of the UK) is now one of the least wooded and most biodiversity-poor countries in Europe. Forty percent of the creatures that have disappeared since 1800 required woodland with mature trees, veteran trees and standing or lying dead wood, but large areas of woodland and connecting corridors of trees and hedges on which wildlife depends is *still* being lost to development and agricultural intensification. Meanwhile coniferous plantations on peat threaten natural carbon stores, and some native trees are suffering from being shaded out by rhododendron, browsing by grey squirrels, and tree diseases – with more expected to develop, due to warmer wetter winters.

Seventy per cent of land is grassland for sheep, beef and dairy cattle, and most is 'improved' – ploughed and reseeded predominantly with ryegrass and clover, to the detriment of other vegetation and necessary soil fungi. Only 9 per cent of grassland is semi-natural (has not experienced significant herbicide or fertiliser treatment). Inappropriate or inconsistent livestock grazing remains problematic. Numbers of sheep have increased by 3 per cent since the turn of the century, and numbered 10 million by 2017. In comparison to cows, which browse more lightly, sheep nibble plants to death and compact the soil unless moved on. Sheep intensity and overgrazing in the uplands over millennia, has transformed heath to species-poor grassland. But in other areas, where wild animals or small numbers of domestic stock once roamed, undergrazing is now a problem.

Fields are usually farmed to the very edges, with hedges removed to increase field-size, productivity and economic growth. Sensitive plants, associated invertebrates and birds have been lost. The EU has funded both intensification and better practice – which hasn't stopped the rapid decline of 54 per cent of arable-associated flora. Ninety-eight per cent of flower-rich hay meadows have gone. Farmland birds have declined by 15 per cent between 2003 and 2009. Populations of yellowhammers, lapwings, skylarks, curlews, hedgehogs and hares have plummeted. Pollinator bees have declined by 23 per cent from 1985-2005 due to habitat loss, chemical use and loss of food sources, and moths by 50 per cent in the last fifty years – rapid crop rotation means large insects no longer have time to complete their life cycles. Since the year 2000, though levels of agricultural nitrous oxide and methane have slightly reduced, they remain too high. Excess nitrogen from fertilisers not absorbed by plants is released as nitrous oxide – a gas with 300 times greater global warming potential than carbon dioxide. Pollution from slurry, fertilisers and pesticides as a result of intensification is increasing.

Meanwhile, micro-plastics have been found in 50 per cent of caddis flies and mayflies in Afon Taf, Afon Wysg and Afon Gwy. Numbers of fish such as salmon and eel are decreasing once more after a brief post-industrial recovery and sea fish populations remain dangerously low. Marine litter is a problem. And although 40 per cent of Cymru's territory lies under the sea, only a fraction is protected. Tidal reefs, mudflats, sandflats and sub-tidal areas of sand and gravel are deteriorating, but scallop-dredging, which damages sea-bed habitats, is allowed in a Special Area of Conservation in Bae Ceredigion – where the resident population of bottlenose dolphins is in decline. Horse mussels are in a poor condition, oysters rare, and seagrass beds remain vulnerable.

In short, Cymru's eco-systems are in a state as perilous as everywhere else, and its language is also at risk. But the Cymru I know, and already knew as I set out on my walk, is also spirited and lovely.

GWYNEDD

S torms and frost influence the biodiversity of the highest Eryri summits. Lichens, ferns, mosses, and Arctic-alpine relics like purple saxifrage, roseroot and Snowdon lily, survive on treacherous slopes. Twentieth-century conifer plantations creep across the hills, but steep gorges harbour Atlantic temperate sessile oak rainforest supporting rare bryophytes, lichens, ferns and fungi. Preserved since the end of the last Ice Age by their inaccessibility, they are hydrated by short, swift rivers. Meanwhile, low-lying Pen Llŷn with its patchwork of fields, has a mild maritime climate.

The air was ripe as old fruit the day I walked out of our valley to take the coast path which is forced twelve miles inland to cross Afon Dyfi at Machynlleth. It was 2012, the last day of August, and the larches were beginning to mellow. Across seething plantation forestry, the Tarrenau sprawled like brown lions. Water trickled faintly, wind stirred distant trees and I felt free.

There was no-one. Then at Pennal, two women on a bench with their legs stretched out in the sun. "How far is it to Machynlleth?" they sleepily asked. "Five miles," I said "ish," and they settled further into the bench. "Hmm." "Maybe not today." I tried the church door, but the vicar had taken early retirement following an incident in which he'd set fire to 'the nasty bits' of the bible, and it was locked, which was annoying, because I wanted to see its copy of the Pennal letter.

The original letter had been sent to Charles VI of France by Owain Glyndŵr in 1406, two years after he'd established a parliament in nearby Machynlleth and been crowned Prince of Cymru. Glyndŵr sought help from Charles, to liberate Cymru which was "oppressed by the fury of the barbarous Saxons; whence because they had the government over us... it seemed reasonable with them to trample on us." I knew that Cymru had been oppressed by England, and it made me uneasy, but that was about all I knew then.

It was the last day of the school holidays and the first hot one. Sheep sheltered in hawthorn shade and the hills thronged with families who'd driven up from Aberdyfi. Afon Dyfi shivered over estuary sand. Wedges of sea split the hills. Farms were secreted in valleys – I knew that Meinir, who I'd briefly worked with at the eco-centre, and her husband Dewi lived in one. Dewi's grandfather, a slate quarryman, had bought the farm after the war. In 2015 I would interview them about their wind turbine. "When people come up," Dewi would tell me, "we say 'have you noticed our turbine?' and they say 'no we haven't seen it at all'. We have to point it out to them." The turbine had reduced their bills. But the people who'd installed it, friends of mine, had decided not to put a logo on their van, because of anti-wind hostility in Y Drenewydd area. It's not easy being green. It is tiring to justify yourself. I wanted a break from it.

But that's not what I was thinking as the path dropped into Aberdyfi's steep back streets and I fell into step behind two plump girls in flip-flops pushing a buggy. I was enjoying the sun, the wetsuits hanging in open windows that wobbled light onto blue walls. I wasn't thinking about holiday homes. I didn't know that in 2013, Aberdyfi would be named the fourth most expensive community in Cymru for house prices – with sixty percent of them being English-owned holiday homes. Or that tourism is considered so important to the economy, that in January 2020, just before Covid, Visit Wales would announce a five-year tourism promotion plan worth £60 million. Tourism comes with a price. Local people can't afford homes. Jobs are seasonal – Aberdyfi is a ghost town in winter. But now the cafés and beach were crammed and the harbour was full of pleasure boats. I'd grown up being a tourist in Cymru. I was remembering the greengrocer who'd given me cherries to eat as a child, while we queued. Now I ate chips on a bench by some West Midlanders. "I know it's hot loik, but I'm cowd," said one. It was freezing. His mates ignored him. The greengrocer had long gone.

The wind blew desert storms round my ankles. I put up my tent in a dune slack, and waited for a man with a metal detector to finish digging his hole, before getting in. Later I woke shivering, and lay there missing Rob. This was my walk – Rob hadn't quit his job. But he would join me at weekends, tomorrow even, tomorrow being Friday, so missing him was ridiculous. After our holiday in Portugal and Spain, I'd worked three months' notice, signed on, and signed up for several writing courses funded by Llywodraeth Cymru (due to having been 'made' redundant). I'd improved my Cymraeg with a month-long language course. But preferring surprise to guidebooks, all I'd done in preparation for the walk was print out maps I rarely looked at from the Wales Coast Path website. I prefer not to plan. I hadn't planned on missing Rob. Now I tried to work out how many days it would take to walk 1,027 miles around Cymru's edge through sixteen counties – not including the English ones I'd weave in and out of on the border. I'd have to pop home sometimes (mainly to sign on), but assumed I'd finish by Christmas. Lying in the cold, it seemed like a bigger deal than I'd thought. Not thought. Cymru was big. Outside the sky was lilac. Sailing across it, a bright moon cast marram grass shadows on the cold lovely dunes.

Morning was crisp and clear. Oystercatchers paced up and down the strand-line and night rabbits had left tracks on the sand. Tywyn was on the horizon, where we'd holidayed every year as kids, in Granddad's static caravan. I'd been about four when I'd seen two head-scarfed women chatting over their shared garden wall in a language Dad said was Welsh. Wales, he said, was where Ifor the Engine lived. Tywyn was where I'd learned my first Cymraeg. 'Cymru am Byth' was written on the purse I bought. The shopkeeper told me how to pronounce the words and explained what they meant, but not in the indulgent manner that adults usually used. She imbued them with such significance I would never forget. Cymru am byth – Cymru Forever.

Tywyn was in my bones, but I'd not really noticed the new breakwater. Built in 2010 from 51,000 tons of rocks shipped from Penmaenmawr, Minffordd and Brittany, it formed part of 2 kilometres of defences against storms and rising sea levels. Scant else had changed. The seafront was still shabby. Buccaneer Amusements still lacked a few lightbulbs. But the prom no longer smelt of lollies and cigarettes.

Rob and I would get married here in March, on the Talyllyn Railway. We were so buzzed it would be months before we realised the irony of us environmentalists, chartering a coal-powered steam train. Built to carry slate from the Abergynolwyn quarries, Talyllyn claims to be the first narrow-gauge railway authorised to carry passengers, one of whom in the 1920s, was my granddad – little Ernie, despatched from Shrewsbury to visit an aunty on a farm up the valley. We'd just watched a documentary about the Talyllyn Railway. It had both inflamed my English guilt and begun to diffuse it. We learned that the railway had been restored by volunteers, some of whom had stayed on in Tywyn, and that most of them were English. The flickering footage of bearded men and long-haired women with wheelbarrows resembled the pioneers who'd built wind turbines and scratched gardens into the derelict slate quarry which became the environmental research, demonstration and education centre I'd just quit. The Talyllyn volunteers made me feel part of a bigger wave of settlers than the sustainability crowd I identified with, and my presence here more inevitable.

"You'll be going inland up the river now," said the catering manager after we'd discussed soup. "I rebuilt most of the stone walls around Tonfanau" he added wistfully. Despite his English accent, he was a Tywyn kid.

Englishness was contributing to an erosion of language, culture, and politics – Tory seats increasing in a Labour (and in Gwynedd, a Plaid Cymru) stronghold, and I felt guilty by default. But I was pretty sure Cymru like everywhere was built on immigration, and I believed in freedom of movement and refuge for refugees, so my guilt wasn't easy to justify. It was annoying and vague. English environmentalists had been moving in since the 1970s. At the eco-centre, we settlers varied in how we related to Cymru. Some had a global rather than national outlook, some were oblivious to Cymru's language and culture, some didn't stay long enough to find out. Many were like Rob – culturally concerned, technically gifted, linguistically lacking, and some were like me – prioritising environmental action above all else, but feeling guilty. We kept a low profile. We didn't want to be English oppressors. Others were timid because the first wave had been mocked and their kids bullied. But we all loved Cymru. And most (including Rob) had sent their kids to Cymraeg-medium schools, where some kids felt ostracised, while others became confidently bi-lingual. I didn't have kids so couldn't pass on the integration responsibility – it was up to me.

Being English bothered me. England was an imperial bully. I couldn't be Cymreig but at least maybe I could speak Cymraeg, preferably by osmosis, being allergic to evening classes, podcasts and textbooks. Despite my allergy, the month-long language course had bolstered me. I would travel as if overseas with eyes and heart wide open. I might even chat to people in Cymraeg. Here I am Cymru!

But there were no gossiping old women in their gardens, and small chance of practising Cymraeg with the Tywyn English who were not like Machynlleth English environmentalists or moneyed Aberdyfi second-home owning English. Most were retired, some perhaps were steam enthusiasts, but none, as they shuffled amiably down the high street, looked guilty. Later, it occurred to me that their sense of belonging stemmed from the Second World War when Tywyn had been stuffed with army camps for British servicemen, (and where later, refugees from the Ugandan Civil War had been warmly received). A sense of British comradeship was still palpable here, as it was across Britain, albeit distorted by time and the right-wing media into something ugly.

Some of the Wales Coast Path wasn't complete because its launch had been brought forward a year to (somewhat unfathomably) coincide with the London Olympics. The footbridge across Afon Dysynni had yet to be helicoptered in, so the path advanced inland towards Mynyddoedd Eryri. The mountains looked like a cardboard stage-set with shadows painted grainy-blue technicolour, and Craig Aderyn rising inky in a wash of misty hills. In the foreground, water-birds squabbled on Aber Dysynni and cormorants lined up like old priests on a spit.

Having crossed the river, I turned back to the coast on a lane that a moped was leaving. Its engine cut out, the driver planted his feet on the old tarmac and looked left and then right in a rich silence before spluttering on. It was all rich silence save for insects droning in honeysuckle. I ate sandwiches at a field gate feeling blissfully at large in the world. A Land Rover passed driven by a child on his father's lap. Later, alerted more by instinct than sound, I peered through a hedge and deciphered a farmer whispering commands to dogs silently whirling sheep into a pen. I knew a few farmers, but I didn't know their magic.

I was running late to meet Rob I realised, as I hurried to Llwyngwril, where there were hand-painted signs in the fields, 'Cau'r Ysgol, Dim Cymuned, Dim Dyfodol' (Close the school, No community, No future). I'd once given a workshop here to the primary school's thirty-five pupils. The older kids had held the little ones' hands. But small schools cost disproportionately more per pupil than large ones, and 157 across Cymru, would be closed in a decade. In 2013, this one would be merged into a new school of eighty-seven pupils nearly six miles away making me wonder if the big kids still held the little ones' hands.

I arrived at the station all sweaty. Rob stepped onto an almost empty platform like a scene from a film. We'd only been apart for a day but I felt almost shy. We grasped hands and strode into hills on which cloud descended, soaking our clothes and turning the landscape white. Deprived of distance our eyes were drawn to the reds and greens of moss and lichen on the wall, as we followed a cow gently butting her calf with tapered horns.

The mist cleared on a hill above Fairbourne and we camped by a stream. I watched Rob hang our clothes on a branch and cook curry and rice on the stove. Everything was perfect. Our tent was filled with soft filtered light, the canvas a damp skin over cool squishy earth.

Outside Golwern Quarry, vacant teenagers, high on something, sat wrapped in blankets around a burning tyre. We ducked into the quarry tunnel to see the blue lagoon which had replaced the slate, and when we came out the teenagers had gone and a man was bashing at the belching black smoke with a branch. "Bloody kids!" he shouted. "They're always up here! No purpose!"

Fairbourne lay frail and exposed between saltmarsh and sea, a scatter of white bungalows behind a shingle ridge on which concrete tank traps had been built in fear of Germans who never came. The invasion will come from climate-change associated tidal, river and groundwater flooding instead – Fairbourne has been identified as an area of managed retreat. In 2016, residents would declare they'd sue Llywodraeth Cymru over plans to 'decom-mission' their village. "They think they've been abandoned because they're English" an English friend (who lives safely up the hill) told us, but there is a Cymreig community in Fairbourne too. Thousands of refugees worldwide have already been displaced due to climate change. There will be millions more and the impoverished will suffer most. Britain with its comparatively wealthy population and northern hemisphere location, will be affected less. Scant consolation to the people of Fairbourne. A man sat outside the chippy with a red mug then sauntered back to his potato buckets, as we left for Y Bermo. Which was loud.

A man filled his jet-ski at the Birmingham Garage, holidaymakers milled about with fishing nets and shopping, and dripping families wearing race-numbers carried wet kayaks. A girl on her Dad's shoulders dangled an arcade teddy in front of his cigarette, a bored lifeguard leant against the paddling pool wall, a small boy rolled slowly around in a plastic zorb and the cater-pillar was like an old biscuit tin rattling round its tracks to a soundtrack of sirens and slot-machines. When at last the smiley-faced tooting train that had tailed us to the end of the prom turned back, silence filled its wake like a lake. A tattered yellow flag flapped above the car park café, a frontier to five miles of sand.

We squeezed past cars on the pavement to reach it, passing wedding guests in sunglasses gathering in nervous groups, backdropped by grey church and grey beach. The women smoothed their dresses. The men adjusted shiny suits, thrust out their chins and made conversation about the parking. And then we were on the beach, and it was huge. Wind and light chased up it in cold or muggy onslaughts and goose bumps raced over our skin. Over centuries, prevailing southwesterlies had dried sand, lifted it, dumped and sculpted it into dunes through which tracks trickled to the caravan sites where one of my sisters and her family holidayed in a static. I met them here sometimes – the kids would fall out of a car crammed with cricket bats and fishing nets and race into the sea. We rested in a slack. The wind caressed our skin and covered us in sand that stuck to our sun cream.

We continued and the beach narrowed, around an old man standing naked in the wind with his eyes closed who everyone pretended not to see, to a shingly peninsula – Y Mochras. I'd come here on a school trip and slept in an orange tent which collapsed on us when boys pulled the pegs out. 'Shell Island' was still a big campsite full of West Midlanders and I felt disoriented as if the child I'd been and adult I'd become were meeting. It was strange to recognise the windy fields and standpipe, and the gift shop I overlooked now, for the distant purple mountains I'd ignored. I felt a sense of time passing. The tents had changed – they were wobbling bouncy castles now, losing pegs to the wind. Kids ran amok, granddads hunkered with radios behind windbreaks, and young bare-chested Dads in baseball caps fiddled with car stereos or crabbed with their kids off the causeway. I looked in a bucket at the little green crabs. Their captor said "there's not much in it yet" and turned away, fiercely sweeping his net.

Llanbedr, to which cottage gardens had granted a genteel veneer, was full of English people too. We went to the pub for football results, pie, chips and pints, before dragging ourselves up, and on through the boat club, where the air was thick with smoke and the smell of musty wetsuits, and an instructor tipped frozen burgers onto a grill.

A sulphurous reek rose from the saltmarsh. Oystercatchers called. The sea was distant, the light weakening. We pitched our tent in the lea of a dyke and heard a noisy gang of kids and later, as we were drifting off, a child saying it was a stupid place to camp. We woke to a loud slosh. The sea was black and almost level with the top of the dyke. Rob checked the tide times on his phone and we stayed awake till it began its retreat.

A morning mist muted distant sound so our tent and jacket zips seemed loud. A farmer was coming towards us with his dogs and I became too nervous to speak Cymraeg as we'd been trespassing, but he didn't mind. "We did

wonder about the water levels," said Rob, "in case a sluice gate got opened."
"Well there is that, yes," he said, in the thoughtful manner of the Gwynedd
farming community. The tourist industry met the rest of Cymru at the coast,
but you could easily miss it.

The sea had left salt-reek and mud and mist that quietened our minds, and
revealed the small stone church at Llandanwg which seemed to belong to the
marsh and the mist and the sea. Drizzle washed our skin. We sat on our
rucksacks among heaps of kelp and sea spaghetti jumping with sand hoppers,
to boil noodles and eggs, alone on the beach, and I loved it like this. Harlech
Castle was the only building in sight, stern above the dunes, one of Edward
I's built to subjugate Cymru.

The sun burst through so fiercely we stopped at the entrance of a caravan
site, to lose the waterproofs. Rob's zips were jammed with sand. A boy on a
scooter circled the flowerbeds whilst gazing hopefully at a static. Rob
wobbled. When I looked at caravan sites I imagined the landscape without
them, but I liked them too, for the holidays we'd had. And their imperma-
nence, like wind turbines. If we took them away they'd leave only concrete
pads.

The leisure centre was next to the school where I'd given workshops. I
knew Harlech was a Cymraeg heartland so I ordered coffee in Cymraeg and
got served in English. We could see over the pool to a window where blue
plastic film tinted the clouds. The swimmers' voices and splashes were muted
and everything seemed cinematic. I heard off-screen, in a world I couldn't be
part of, the lifeguards and café girl banter in Cymraeg. She said that she'd cook
them some sausages. We could see the castle flags too and it struck me that
Edward had failed.

Morfa Harlech was formed by the southwesterly accretion of silt which
evolved into saltmarsh. Very far away, sea crimped the dunes. A black cow was
profiled on the hills like an advertisement for Spanish sherry. Vast empty barns
made it feel like the wild west. We turned upriver. Teenagers raced out of a
farmhouse, jumped into a car and put the stereo on. "Are we still on the coast
path?" we asked and they laughed self-consciously. "Errrrr not sure." "We
never walk anywhere. I think there might be a footpath sign up the lane?"

Down at Ynys an empty road stretched to the estuary. 'Next High Tide
10.30. No Jet Skis. By order of the Rt. Hon Lord Harlech' had been written
on a board, and we joked that Lord Harlech was the man tinkering under a
car bonnet but it wasn't really funny, that lordships still existed, that huge

estates really were still inherited. The incumbent Lord Harlech would be succeeded in 2016 by his son Jasset Ormsby-Gore who would auction off 400 family treasures in order to pay for restorations to the family seat at Talsarnau. Aristocracy was hard to reconcile with the Cymru I knew – but this was 2012, before I'd read any history.

Talsarnau lay beyond reclaimed fields full of yearling sheep and we reached it eventually. An elderly woman checked us into the campsite and met my Cymraeg with a dignified silence. She didn't speak it, and I was embarrassed. I had lived here for years but had been so busy. Only now was I unpicking what it meant to be English in Cymru. The prevalence of the English language unsettled me but the Cymraeg world eluded me.

We crossed Pont Briwet and peered at Gwaith Powdwr Nature Reserve from the top of bramble-choked steps, and a large striped spider transferred itself to my jacket. Mining explosives and arms for both World Wars had been manufactured here in sheds with lead floors. Now it was home to nightjar, newts and lesser horseshoe bats. But Gwaith Powdwr had been the main employer in Penrhyndeudraeth. Now teenagers lounged outside Spar.

Y Dderwen's kitchen was closed for a christening party, so we ordered pints instead of food. A tipsy old man played the piano while two young kids crashed the keys. The other guests had gone. The landlord was rushing plates to the sinks where two women in frocks washed them up whilst chatting in Cymraeg, so I tried to join in when the landlord brought us leftover sandwiches. "No, no, I don't want any money," he said in English. We bought another pint. He brought onion bhajis. Shaking our hands as we left, as if we too had been guests, he suddenly noticed my attempts, straightened his back and slapped his heart. "Dwi'n Gymro," he said quietly with tears in his eyes. "Rydwi'n falch" which could mean either 'I am pleased' or 'I am proud'. I was both. Acknowledgement! But there was reason for his caution. Speaking your native language in your native land isn't straightforward in Cymru. Two years earlier in that same pub, a different landlord, newly-arrived and English, had taken offence when locals ordered beer from his wife in Cymraeg, and had threatened them with an air rifle.

The teens were still outside Spar when we left town hand in hand. "You're in love!" they shouted in English. "Yes we are!" we shouted back, sending them into volleys of Cymraeg I'd no hope of ever understanding. The sun was setting as we crossed Pont Briwet. The water was deep and clear. Light silvered the pylons and the sky flushed a deep hot pink. The rail and road toll bridge was unsuitable for emergency vehicles. A replacement crossing would open in 2015 after an engineering operation hampered by storms and, (according to a train refreshment trolley operator I met at the time), by a poorly engineered rerouting of the river, which toppled one of the pylons. Pont Briwet was meant to have been left for pedestrians but the heavy piling rendered it unstable and it was destroyed, as lovely things are.

Monday morning. Rob was heading back for work, the only passenger to board the train at Llandecwyn. The two carriages were silhouetted by glittering sea and I felt bereft as I watched them pull away. I wanted to go with him. I walked to Portmeirion instead.

Sir Clough Williams-Ellis had designed this mock-Italianate village to demonstrate that new developments could enhance rather than spoil a landscape. I forgave him for being practically an aristocrat – because Clough had campaigned *against* pollution, industrialisation and urban sprawl, and *for* the creation of National Parks which he claimed were for 'the multitudes without solitudes'. He built Portmeirion outside the boundary to avoid National Park planning restrictions. Heras fencing was being erected for Festival No.6 in two weeks' time, which I'd bought tickets for with my last wages. Seeing the preparations excited me so much I considered camping out under the hydrangeas with a stash of cider. I was so excited I informed the ticket officer in Cymraeg that I'd lost the path, not realising I'd muddled colli (to lose) and codi (to raise), confusing him so much that he stammered and blushed and I felt like a muppet.

A few adult learners I knew could speak Cymraeg fluently. But most wouldn't speak it outside classes for fear of getting it wrong. I was somewhere in the middle, blundering about. It wasn't easy for anyone, least of all for the Cymry-Cymraeg (Welsh-speaking Welsh). My vague intention to speak Cymraeg on my walk was already in tatters.

Afon Glaslyn, seen from on high, was so stunning as it shivered across its green mountain-ringed valley, that I gasped. But what do you do with such beauty? Gaze and walk on. The Cob carried the road, coast path and Ffestiniog Railway to Porthmadog. I found myself among sidings and sheds with cracked glass at Boston Lodge where some twenty railwaymen sat on benches overlooking the sea, eating sandwiches and drinking from flasks in a scene straight from Ford Madox Brown. They wore caps and faded blue overalls, volunteers every last one. Some had lined faces and looked very old. Some had a dreamy gaze, others chewed their bread seriously, and none paid me any attention. I can't excuse the burning of coal, I will miss steam trains if they go. But if anyone can work out how to power them sustainably these railwaymen can.

William Madocks had intended The Cob to form part of a post-road to Dublin, but Thomas Telford beat him to it with a route via Caergybi. I stopped halfway across to eat. Birds poked about in the mudflats. A wheatear landed beside me. A train left Boston Lodge and grew bigger and louder till it passed in a billow of steam, chuntering roar and gleam of brass. A guard with thick black beard hung from the last carriage. His expression of surprise lingered with the echo of wheels and whistle. I was losing my grip on space and time.

Pen Llŷn oozed a gentle character all of its own, even leaving Porthmadog. Borth-y-Gest was quiet enough to hear the thunk of ball hitting the rotten branch three children were playing cricket with. A few people were gathered under striped café awnings, rowing boats rested on marsh grass and mud, and pink floats bobbed in the bay. Suddenly a car alarm ruptured the peace then stopped abruptly. In the after-shock, calm returned layer by layer.

But there was a melancholy to the softness even though the path twisted and turned above bewitching coves. Perhaps it was the strange warm white air which trapped the scent of marram grass and ragwort. The oystercatchers were fractious, squabbling over weedy heaps, and I felt fractious too. Cars were allowed on Traeth Graig Ddu. They had stripped the sand of vegetation, save for sea spurge imprisoned in a small sad roped-off square.

At Cricieth I was startled by the sight of a family digging sandcastles in front of the ruined castle. I'd taken a photo as a child of my family making castles at the same spot in similar weather. I didn't much like nostalgia, especially in my strange mood. It reminded me that everything must pass, including me. Nevertheless, we'd holidayed round so much of the Cymreig coast as kids it was inevitable. But living for the present is also hazardous if you care about the future. A few Scottish coach-party pensioners had stopped to watch a red-whiskered man in yellow waders dig at the water's edge. "Are they cockles?" called one of the women, as he rushed buckets up the beach to dump in his boot. "No!" he replied, running back to his pitchfork. "Winkles!" he shouted.

We'd come to Cricieth twice as kids. Gran had given us money for Cadwalader's ice cream she said was the best in the world. Cadwalader's was still here, noisy with chatter, music and kids, except for a woman sipping coffee in a pinstriped suit, reading very neatly beside a child staring unhappily at the floor. I felt strangely mopey myself. It was Rob's fault. Before setting out I'd been irritated I'd have to break my journey now and again for this and that. I'd wanted to do it all in one go, I loved solo walking. When Rob and I had got together, I'd told him I'd be heading off alone every year, but I hadn't anticipated how compatible a walking companion he'd be. Missing him was infuriating. Upstairs by the toilets a photograph showed stiff waitresses in mobcaps and aprons. Downstairs, the sulky black-haired girls played gangsta music too loud and wiped up melted ice cream in a huff. The pinstriped woman closed her book and left without looking at the miserable child in her wake. I was sad for the kid. But the tea and scones improved my mood.

I remembered there being swans on the sea. Mum still had a photo by her reading lamp of Dad with a big smile, large sideburns, and the swans in the background, and I got sad again thinking about him. Afon Dwyfor flowed quietly between driftwood banks that yielded underfoot. There were the swans! Drifting apart then together, absorbed in their own small worlds. They made it seem like the passing of time was OK – that there was continuity.

A cow pushed through gorse and sloshed through the bog, drinking with great happy slurps. It was gentle by the river with the smell of warm salt and seaweed and the Llŷn hills an undulating blue line just visible through yellow grasses. But there was nowhere to camp, so I made for the Caravan Club site at Llanystumdwy, where a man jumped from an awning with a frisson of triumph and propelled me to reception as if to prison. Mine was the only tent between two rows of touring caravans. The shower block was decked out with flowers, their scent mingling with a septic-tank stench.

One rainy afternoon, Gran said she and Grandpa had driven out of Cricieth and nearly knocked over an elderly gentleman with an umbrella stepping out of a gate. "Do you know who it was?" she'd said. "Lloyd George!" I'd never heard of him. David Lloyd George, Prime Minister for the Liberal Party during the First World War, was brought up in Llanystumdwy and had later moved back there. He lived at Tŷ Newydd, now owned by Literature Wales, where I'd be attending a writing course in a few weeks. The gate opened onto a quiet lane above which squirrels traversed the beeches with stealthy grace. I felt odd standing there, imagining Gran and Grandpa in a motor car, and a startled man with an umbrella.

The path accompanied the A497 for two miles. Spray-bejewelled birds-foot trefoil trembled in wheel-wake on the bank. A Volvo lorry honked, all monstrous wheels and fumes with yellow lamps around the cab like a fairground ride. I felt in the way. Quiet resumed at Porth Fechan. I boiled tea and four ringed plovers took flight. The drizzle stopped, I took down my hood and felt free. Crouching on the beach made me happy. I cooked noodles, eggs and onions and burned off the meths. The blue and yellow flame leapt over the stones. I loved this hillbilly liberty. I kicked the onion skins and eggshells into heaps of seaweed and sun-bleached plastic. But melancholy was still lurking despite my intrinsic contentment.

I was alone on Aber-erch save for one man and his dog in the distance and a boat pulling a water skier. The skier stood and fell, stood and fell. Engine-drone, instructor's voice and swell-smack rang clear against the lull and drift of shore-lap and bird call. The glittering sea was almost a meditation. I faltered, struggling with warm then cool air, putting down my rucksack to take off clothes then stopping to put them back on.

Until now, Pwllheli had only meant the end of the line to me, the place where I'd transferred from train to bus, on my way to teach in schools further north. I'd never seen Hafan Marina, where yachts like white coffins were moored between empty berths. Marinas were not the lure they had been in the nineties, and neither were people as rich. The economic downturn, increasing storms and dredging costs had forced up fees. Once there'd been waiting lists, but by 2018 half the berths would be empty. Now only two people were in sight – a man on a bench trying to eat a burger without the onions sliding out, the other whistling as he wiped the counter of his van, under big red letters spelling BARRY.

I'd been alone long enough to feel odd in public. The station café was a theatre, with spot-lit sausage rolls. Off-stage, the café girl smoked in the doorway, shouting in Cymraeg to her colleague frying eggs in the kitchen who couldn't hear a word. 'Beth?' (what?) she shouted back. A man in a long coat doffed his hat, said 'Diolch' in a deep voice and half-bowed as he left. Two rotund characters in hi-viz ate the bargain fry-ups. I had a sensation of not knowing what era I was in, let alone country.

Back on the path, a man wearing beanie and sloppy trainers asked where I was going with my rucksack. "Lots of up and down hills by Rhiw," he said. "I used to go fishing there. There's a big field going down to the sea. It's alright going down, but you try climbing up it with a sack of mackerel on your back."

A dog howled, then the quiet of the coast returned. It had settled round Llanbedrog and its beach huts, where the sand was cool and wet to my bare feet, flecked with black broken leaves, beechnuts and sharp twigs straight off the trees. I still felt slightly adrift. I paused outside Plas Glyn-y-Weddw.

The gothic mansion had been built to house Elizabeth Love-Jones's art collection. I hated grand old houses with fussy antiques and ticking clocks reminding me time was passing. I hated wealth acquired through inheritance or exploitation, but the gallery was run now by a charitable trust exhibiting work by Cymreig artists. I didn't look much at the art. I left my boots at the desk. The carpets were thick and soft. My socks were shabby and damp but I kept them on because my feet were worse. Lozenges of light fell onto the staircase and the air smelt of polish. I sat on the window-seat, feeling strange to be inside, with birdsong and wind filtered by the building. The best art perhaps, was outside.

And back outside, insect drones became confused with my breathing as I lay in the heather with no reason to get up. Perhaps this explained my gentle melancholy. I had been so busy at the eco-centre, work had occupied every waking hour and sometimes my dreams. I'd loved my job, my colleagues, the people I'd taught, but had also felt trapped. Now I felt free. Also a kind of exhaustion. I pulled myself up and heard a woman pretending to sing. She fell silent and blushed when I came upon her in sunhat and National Trust shirt. Her colleague smiled and carried on raking up heather clippings. Their Landrover was parked on the hill, its wheels a-straddle on the rocks, a coffee mug on the dashboard and flask on the seat. It reminded me of jobs I'd enjoyed – roguing wild oats, watering flowers, grading potatoes. What was my work now? I wasn't a writer yet, I hadn't written anything. I felt a little overwhelmed, a little inadequate.

Abersoch was crammed with shops selling boats, surf lessons, designer flip-flops and crew clothing. I don't own a phone but it was Mum's birthday, so I trekked round the headland past signs for Private Beaches, Private Roads, Private Gardens and Private Parking, then found a call box where I'd started, outside Spar. The glass was broken. The receiver dangled, smeared in something disgusting. I stared at it. Suddenly I was desperate to get out of Abersoch. I hurried over the golf course past dog-walkers trailing perfume and a man in checked shorts shaking his head in a bunker, until at Penrhyn Du, I collapsed on my rucksack, relieved to be back on the edge.

Dusk fell. A lighthouse swung a beam on Tudwal Fawr. The island was owned by celebrity survival expert Bear Grylls. He'd built a holiday home on it, and a slide into the sea for which he was undergoing a planning investigation by Gwynedd Council. Rabbits thumped the ground and the temperature dropped. Three curlews flew south, so I sent with them, birthday greetings to my Mum.

"Bore da" I said to the sheep, startling them and myself with the sound of my voice. The promontories were striking. The sky was blue. But the path left Porth Ceiriad for fields down which a river of slurry was running. I wanted a break from environmental problems, but they are not easy to escape. Generally, slurry is put back on the fields. But due to the increasing intensification of livestock farming more is produced than can be absorbed. Dealing with the excess is expensive for dairy farmers who often receive too little as it is for their milk, sometimes less than it costs to produce. When slurry gets in the water system, bacteria already present use it to multiply, deoxygenating the water, killing fish and invertebrates. Slurry also emits ammonia which travels on the wind.

I didn't want to think about it, but perhaps this was the cause of my uncertain mood. At the eco-centre we had countered problems with positivity. People seeking sustainable solutions sought us out. Now I was back in a world where people ignored the problems. Denied their existence. It seemed the percentage of solution-ready people was incredibly small. Nevertheless, it was easier to forget environmental collapse on the edge of Cymru than in the middle. Much of the coast is a continuous wildlife corridor, too salty and steep for agriculture. Even the border with England is largely upland with rough, rather than 'improved' pasture.

And now Ynys Enlli glided into view. Gulls and crows circled, choughs squawked, skylarks sang and goldfinches flitted about scabious surging in a sea of pink and gold grasses. A kestrel quivered, I watched it lift, hold, flutter, dive. And when I cooked pasta among crates and broken polystyrene on the beach, a glossy raven landed nearby with a blue sheen to its plumage and the muscular build of a bull.

Porth Neigwl's cliffs were eroding so quickly the path veered inland. I didn't mind at first. Scarlet pimpernel entwined wheat stalks which rustled like old paper. But a crow-scarer exploded right next to me, sending off a smaller explosion in my heart which made me jittery. Arable gave to pasture and a hundred heifers surrounded me, rolling their eyes, tossing their heads. I stepped to the right and they mirrored me like people trying to pass on the stairs. Eventually I walked purposefully forward setting them snorting and cantering around me in a circle of panic they maintained for the length of the field. But when I looked back they regarded me calmly as if nothing had happened.

The long improved grass fields were tiresome. Distant mountains taunted me. The coast path signs were camouflaged from a distance and set at confusing angles – one post had so many stapled around it I forgot which direction I'd come from. I cursed the farmer racing towards me on a quadbike. But he was young with rosy cheeks and the wind in his hair, three collies smiling over his shoulder. And he spoke in such melodic, careful English (clearly his second language) and wished me well so gently that he lifted my spirits. The farming community enchanted me. Its remoteness and continuity had preserved culture and language. I watched this young farmer bump his quad over the wind-fields like a Mongolian on horseback, as his own ancestors would have travelled, not many generations back.

On the brackened crag of Mynydd Rhiw, a line of pink and white linen flapped outside a row of stone cottages and I, exhilarated at last, wanted to stop and live in that bright light with that view and that washing. Crisp light and altitude make me feel as if I belong to the mountainous regions of this world, to places I've never been. The pillowcases billowed like prayer flags. Stone cottages were all about, built for the miners who'd extracted manganese deposits in the Industrial Age, industry that was hard to imagine now the hills belonged to ravens and salty-maned ponies, and to Ynys Enlli tugging at its moorings ahead.

I was tired but kept on to Aberdaron, whose huddle of inns and cafés were busy with holidaymakers. But local people had not been terribly outnumbered here, and appeared in control. They served me chips. I tore into them greedily and choked on vinegar vapour. Evening light filled the phone box like a lantern. I called Mum, then carried on to Porth Meudwy, from where boats to Enlli still depart. Old tractors cwtched up to lobster pots, and I was suddenly so tired I could barely drag myself up the creek to the campsite where the farmhouse door, slightly ajar, revealed a stout lad watching television with his feet up. "Drws! Drws!" he shouted over his shoulder, it being clearly not his job to answer it. It was his mother's. Sue. She said I looked exhausted.

"Come in now for a cup of tea," she said. I bent to unlace my boots but her eyebrows shot into her hair. "You will not take your boots off! We're not posh!"

I was stinking and filthy, she was clean and crisp in a floral blouse. We drank tea at the kitchen table while she chatted and I tried now and again to say something in Cymraeg, which reminded her that one of her regular campers had just now after several years, started to learn the language. Sue made me feel welcome. "One of our regulars, Mr Woods has lost his wife, he's only thirty-two but he's met someone else, the lovely Gloria," she said. A bowl of glazed china fruit sat on the windowsill. An orchid soaked in the sink and three giant bags of Yorkshire puddings defrosted on the draining board. Sue said when she'd been young one of her teachers had boxed her ears, and another, Sister Seraphina who'd been very tall like a giraffe had become a nun because she was too tall for ballet. "Last night," said Sue "three boys from Yorkshire came on motorbikes and wanted to go fishing in the dark. Lads!" she said, nodding towards the front room, and opened the dishwasher, releasing a cloud of fragrant steam. "What can you do with them?"

Swallows swooped in and out of the barn where I was waiting for the kettle to boil. Sue's husband William came to introduce himself and ask where I'd learned Cymraeg. "Mostly Aberystwyth," I began in Cymraeg. "Ah well," he interrupted in English "it's different in the south. You've got to stick to one or the other," which surprised me, because it wasn't so different.

I asked in English if I'd pass any shops. "Not till Nefyn," William said gravely. "The shops, schools and pubs, they've closed. The community has changed." William lowered his voice to add that it hadn't been helped by retired English couples coming in. "They are putting up the house prices," he said, and feeling instantly guilty, I mumbled something about not being able to afford any property either. "No, no!" said William alarmed, "it's alright when *young* people move in, because you create jobs and your children go to the schools. In Machynlleth you've got schools and pubs and shops still open, and new jobs. But here on Llŷn now, there are no jobs for the kids who've gone to university. There's only farming and the creamery. And the council," he added darkly, "but they look after themselves." Swallows zoomed over our heads. "When we go to the doctor's surgery now," said William "we don't know anyone in the waiting room. They keep to themselves you see. Nobody knows them until they get ill and when one of them dies, the other one goes back to family in England, and the body goes too." He shook his head. "There's not many English in the graveyards," he said regretfully.

Life was tough for farming communities. Many farms couldn't sustain the next generation and young families couldn't afford to buy or rent homes. But what he'd said startled me. Had William and Sue been so forthcoming and friendly, because I was learning Cymraeg or because I lived in Cymru, or because being hospitable was just second nature? It had never occurred to me that language wasn't necessarily the be-all and end-all, but it should have done. After all, Rob, for all his intelligence and creativity was no linguist. He just about remembered 'bonjour' and 'merci' from school, not necessarily in the right order. But he'd lived for years in the Machynlleth area, where his boys had gone through school. He'd run a cyber café and been a firefighter – useful things. People knew him. Whereas I'd gone straight to the eco-centre, which was something of a mystery to locals, though on reflection I'd taught so many of their kids I'd probably integrated better than I knew.

At the eco-centre, the education department in which I was one of six quali-fied teachers, had worked with students, teachers, tutors, lecturers, exam boards and curriculum officials throughout Cymru and in Machynlleth. But I'd been so conscious of how we eco-incomers were perceived as a whole, had heard so many tales of peoples' kids (now adults my age) who'd been bullied at school, had heard more than once among Cymraeg speakers that Free Tibet was all very well but what about Free Cymru, that I'd been completely oblivi-ous to the notion that some Cymry were positive about our presence. My surprise after talking to William was so substantial; only now did I fully appre-ciate the guilt I'd been carrying. Over subsequent years I would meet enough farmers to understand they had come to respect the eco-centre for its work in promoting the renewable energy they now depended on but had pilloried at first – most hadn't long been connected to the National Grid when the eco-centre was founded in the 1970s, and the idea of returning to the hydro-power they'd just ditched was understandably ridiculous. But I didn't know this as I drank tea in the barn, watching swallows feed their young in mid-flight. William had given me wings. Just perhaps it was OK to be English.

The smell of the sea was strong. Cliffs, sea, and birds dominated, but it was Ynys Enlli sliding in and out of view between headlands, the destination of pilgrims following in the footsteps of early Christians, that captured my imagi-nation. I saw it through harebells and yarrow, and across the dark creek at Porth Felen. The sun reached its mountain. Haloed in gold, radiant as stained glass and perfectly framed by the creek in which the sea seemed even now, to be the magical colour of night.

The hills were awash with light. They dazzled and danced, purple and gold with heather and gorse as I sped along in the wind. A line of sheep moved along a distant track but there were no people and I felt euphoric till I reached Porth Oer and its car park. The crowds weren't unpleasant; it was just that the wildness had gone. One middle-aged couple were picking sloes on the lane. "Are they ready?" I asked, and the woman jumped and looked guilty. "Well we don't know," she said. "We saw it on the TV, making gin, and thought we'd give it a go." They were from Abertawe – Lloyd, who spoke Cymraeg and Margaret, who did not. "But I can't understand the accent up here," Lloyd said. "And what I don't understand, when I went into the shop in Aberdaron," he sounded hurt, "the woman started speaking to me in Welsh. Well I said to her, 'how do you know I speak Welsh?'" The language issue was more complex than I'd appreciated. I sat on a rock and brooded.

I had found it useful, in other countries, to learn the language, but Cymru was different. A large number of Cymry particularly in the south, did not speak Cymraeg and while I'd met some for whom this was an embarrassment, I also remembered taxi drivers, council workers and teachers grumbling about Cymraeg being brought back into schools. They felt threatened by language legislation introduced by the new Llywodraeth Cymru, excluded from potential jobs and their own culture.

An 1847 government report which had criticised the use of Cymraeg in schools, had resulted in pupils found speaking it being punished – in some areas well into the twentieth century. Generations of Cymry subsequently felt ashamed of their own language. Many hadn't passed it on. Some believed their own Cymraeg wasn't as good as that taught in evening classes. Once, in the pub watching rugby, I'd babbled in tipsy Cymraeg to a farmer friend of Rob's who'd said "Your Welsh is better than mine. I'm just a country bumpkin, we don't speak properly", and I'd been really shocked, being a clumsy beginner with a grammar allergy. But he'd not been joking. He assumed my Cymraeg was more proper than his and it made him embarrassed and sad.

Though most of my eco-colleagues had not learned the language, they were respectful of it. I'd been unaware that Cymraeg was still oppressed. I'd heard the stories of weird English people who preferred not to hear Cymraeg spoken in Cymru, but had assumed other claims were exaggerated. I was yet to meet the girl moved to Tywyn from Leicester who'd tell me 'the Welsh are backward'. I was yet to read TripAdvisor reviews describing a friend's café as 'very nice but too Welsh'. Another friend was yet to tell me about the English-woman who turned up at the farm where she gardened to enquire about holiday accommodation because the others she'd seen were also 'too Welsh' and that the farmer had meekly shown her round and not even complained when she'd gone. 'Too Welsh'! In the middle of Cymru?

No wonder that after centuries of bullying from the English and even, now, from the Cymry di-Gymraeg (Non-Welsh-speaking Welsh), some Cymry-Cymraeg were reluctant to use their language. They were in my experience, humble, polite and easily embarrassed when learners made fools of themselves. Furthermore, it was hard to know who spoke what. There are as many fluent-in-Cymraeg English-accented young people as there are Cymreig-accented old folk who'd lost their Cymraeg. Communicating in English was usual till a common language could be established. But neither I nor Rob wished anyone to prioritise English on our behalf and the fact that anyone could be offended at hearing Cymraeg in Cymru was wretched. A middle-aged couple arrived and began to set up in front of me. I smiled and got a scowl in return. The woman used her shoe to bang in the windbreak poles and without a word her husband took the windbreak down, tweaked it, and put it back up to his liking. Still ignoring each other they settled into deckchairs and opened their books. Some people are beyond needing language at all.

The cliffs were black and lower now, with flat fields stretching to their edge. Land and water birds mingled. Wheatears and fulmars, linnets and gannets. Curlews and swallows shared beaches and fields, while pied wagtails, stonechats and rock pipits bounced over rocks. The wind was strong. At Penllech it hurled black sand across a backdrop of white sea, and blew my stove so fiercely I had to top up the burner. When the vegetables were finally soft, they were bitter with meths and I tipped them away.

I set up my tent among gorse. "Coo-eee – it's only us!" called an elderly couple, walking a small dog. The sun was setting in a thin gold wind. But I was tired and hungry. My euphoria had gone. I finished reading a book about a man who'd got home after a long trek to find his wife had left him, and actually burst into tears. Why? I was doing exactly what I loved – walking, camping, travelling. But I was tired. Physically tired from the weight of my rucksack. Emotionally tired in the post-job void that had suddenly opened and left me at sea. And although I was going home in the morning, to sign on, host visitors, and go to the festival, I missed Rob.

Two weeks later, the train back to Pwllheli was busy with senior citizens unwrapping foil-packed sandwiches. We'd had fun at Festival No.6. It had been a rare celebration of Cymreig and English culture, New Order meeting Brythoniaid Male Voice Choir. Jan Morris. Gruff Rhys. Harmony and respect between both nations that would sustain me – the arts it seemed, did it best. Now the seasons had moved on. Caravan-site hydrangeas were blowsy brown and the rosehips scarlet. But I was setting out less eagerly, resigned to missing Rob, questioning my journey. I'd not spoken Cymraeg at home and my enthusiasm for it had fizzled.

Men banged in fence posts around self-conscious rams – several ewes were already marked with blue paint from bars strapped around the rams' middles, indicating their impregnation. A tern crashed into the waves and an oyster-catcher called, replacing two weeks at home with something slower and quieter and I was glad, after all, to be back. This was what I had longed for, when I'd been so busy teaching. Bruised clouds leaked light that left little silver sickles on the water. Periwinkles crept slowly over rocks. Green and red jasper lay among sea junk and driftwood, and wrack and kelp bobbing at the surface, were shot through with amber light.

I walked east, towards mountains that glowered. A young couple pointed down from the cliffs, to several Atlantic grey seals and their pups in woolly white coats. In 1970 when the Conservation of Seals Act was introduced, the British seal population was estimated to be 70,000. By 2013 their numbers had swelled to over 111,000. Some lay still, while others craned their necks and tails. Some wobbled awkwardly down to the beach, but were fluid as oil in the sea.

In a rocky nook at Porth Dinllaen, a woman sang a sad and beautiful song while a man played a ukulele. Fishing boats tugged gently at their ropes and the lifeboat was a fiery orange, against the brown-purple mountains ahead. Lunchtime drinkers in hats and down jackets still lingered with empty glasses outside Tŷ Coch. I tried to keep the song in my head, but it slipped away somewhere near Nefyn.

I read an information board about how Nefyn had once been an important herring port. By the turn of the twentieth century, it said, steam trawlers had ousted sailing ships and stripped the seas, causing stocks to collapse that have still not recovered. The enormous schools of herring that once foraged around the coast have gone. The Atlantic grey seals' recovery after humans had finally agreed to stop persecuting them was a rare success story. Reminders of my old job kept popping up, like arcade-game crocodiles I couldn't hammer down. The environmental problems we had found solutions for at the eco-centre, now seemed enormous. I was haunted by the knowledge that despite its constitutional commitment, aspirational targets and baby steps, Cymru wasn't doing any better than anywhere else. Species are still becoming extinct in Cymru as rapidly as they are elsewhere in the UK and globally. The monitoring and protection of isolated habitats has not been enough.

The church at Nefyn was being converted into a maritime museum, and taunting me on the door was a picture of an African log-boat which possibly arrived in Liverpool on a ship carrying palm oil from the Niger Delta. Some of the world's most biodiverse forests, especially in Malaysia and Indonesia, are felled to make way for palm oil plantations – palm oil being an ingredient in 50 per cent of processed supermarket products from chocolate to shampoo. People were queuing on the street, for chips probably fried in palm oil, and that is what happens — mundane actions make us complicit. It is easy to feel innocent. To blame the governments, multi-nationals and supermarkets, whilst shoring them up with our demand for cheap products. Who doesn't love chips? I do.

Light was fading. I found a farm campsite where two women chatted in a garden. "Throw up your tent in the field" they said "and knock on that door." A very old man in a red jumper was already stood on the step. I greeted him in Cymraeg and then English and he looked at me carefully and pushed away my purse. "I don't want anything" was all he said. His face was very old and lined, his cheeks red, and his eyes merry, as if he understood the way of the world.

I boiled tea and eggs behind a drystone wall. It was the kind of weather that looked miserable from indoors but my eyes had adjusted to the dying heather and breaking bracken, transformed now by water vapour into subtly gleaming auburns and purples. The gentle rain was uplifting till I lost the waymarks. Only then did I notice my rucksack was heavy and that I was sweating inside my waterproofs. My feet were wet in my old cracked boots, as I trudged up and down the hedgerow and stared for a long time at a herd of ginger cows and distant pink cottage at the foot of a dark mountain. The scene was elegiac yet I was pathetic, getting lost on a coast path.

Eventually I slithered down to a rocky beach, wondering, with steely sea pressing towards a rock wall, whether there was any way off the far end. But a raggle-haired man, whistling as he poked at the strandline, must have come from somewhere, so I pressed on, my rucksack sliding around my waterproofs as I struggled on slimy rocks. A fresh breeze blew, a fishing boat chugged into view and two seals were out, only their heads visible. I sat on my rucksack. The seals and I watched each other, and I felt content.

The end of the beach was a muddle of slagheaps, jetties and pits over which the stricken mountains seemed to be falling. But among their wrecked rocks, a new tarmac path appeared. It led me to a gleaming café and suddenly I understood where I was. Nant Gwrtheyrn – the former quarry workers' village, which was now an adult-learners' language centre. Cymraeg!

The spinner of learners' books excited me, but the café girl was too busy setting up for a conference to chat, so I grinned stupidly out to sea with my coffee before ambushing the man setting out chairs in the heritage centre. No he said, unfortunately he didn't know who the people were in the black and white photos on the wall. One image stayed with me. Young people in long winter coats holding placards, sitting on the road in Aberystwyth having closed Trefechan Bridge to traffic – the first Welsh Language Society protest in 1963. My people. I felt proud. But they weren't my people. I was an outsider. I'd have blundered about on the edge, not understanding.

Nant Gwrtheyrn granite had been exported by boat to pave Liverpool and Manchester because the road, which smelt of wet tarmac and resin as I climbed it now, buzzing on caffeine, was too precipitous. At the top I met the coast path which had crept along the hilltops. Yr Eifl's summits swirled in cloud above me while below, prehistoric cairns mingled with industrial scars. Humanity felt present, yet fleeting as the clouds whose indigo shadows flashed across red and black cliffs. From the bwlch the view to the north was of hills shimmering beneath radiant blue Eryri leviathans that roared up nipple-cairned and tooth-topped, and Ynys Môn adrift in a green whipped-up sea, Mynydd Twr just a pimple. Directly below was Trefor and its tiny harbour. I shouted "Wow!" several times then sat down to eat, whereupon a lurcher appeared and stuck his muzzle into my jar of peanut butter. "Oh God, sorry!" shouted his Cymreig owners, switching to English.

A granite amalgam of quartz and porphyrite was still extracted from Yr Eifl for monuments, and until recently for Olympic curling stones. I hair-pinned down, around blasted holes and broken buildings where lumps of concrete dangled from rusted cable. A JCB lumbered uphill, the driver grinning wildly and I knew how he felt. Trefor's colourful doors and little bright boats were strange after the raw granite. The mountain had thrilled me. But the coast path walker heading south and relaxing on a bench, was nonchalant. The route had been mostly flat, he explained, except for Holyhead Mountain (Mynydd Twr) which was a killer. "What's it like the other way?" he said idly, licking lollipop drips from his arm. I pointed to Yr Eifl and he panicked.

It was Friday. I called Rob from a kiosk, arranged to meet him in Penygroes, and headed down traffic-free lanes the green of late summer, suffused in old gold light. They were empty except for an elderly man in tweed, clambering carefully over a gate who seemed annoyed at being seen, and a couple strolling hand-in-hand whose old-fashioned demeanour – of people at ease in their neighbourhood, wasn't diminished by facial piercings and thick black make-up. The teenagers gave me such careful directions I knew they didn't drive, and it took me precisely as long to reach Penygroes as they said.

Penygroes was snared by main roads and mountains, unreached by the evening sun. Girls screamed outside pebbledash houses, mechanics left the bus depot, people streamed in and out of the offy. A man with a clipboard spotted me sitting on my rucksack. "Do you have any need for Sky TV?" he said. I said I didn't even have electricity and felt like I'd let him down.

The stove hissed quietly as Rob cooked noodles in peanut butter beneath the yellow moon. We'd set up camp on the glacial drumlin at Dinas Dinlle and the warm night was like velvet till a helicopter on a training exercise ripped it up. Later, peace returned to the rippling black sea and we squeezed into my one-man tent laughing, barely able to crane our necks for enough leverage to wobble over, like Atlantic grey seals.

The air sparkled. Yr Eifl was extraordinarily distinct. People were already out walking dogs and sweeping the sky in micro-lites. "That's where we'll live," said Rob, indicating a wooden shack on the marsh, "if we win the lottery." The micro-lites were touching down or lifting off from Caernarfon Airport. Above our heads, hundreds of shimmering gossamer strands were sailing the breeze, miniature spiders seeking places to mature and mate. Crisp light made everything photogenic, even rusting radar equipment, and a man on a roof pouring fuel through a flashing steel funnel. At Y Foryd, the light picked out pinks in sea aster and sea purslane, bringing La Camargue to mind, though instead of flamingos, curlews stalked the brilliant blue pools.

Ynys Môn was close and clear across Y Fenai. The water hissed around shingle spits and left strand-lines of seaweed and sticks. Oystercatchers poked at waterlogged fields and sparrows chattered in rosehips sprouting from bulwarks. The remarkable light illuminated yellow atlas lichen and turnstones' orange legs, and put everyone in a holiday mood. Cyclists steamed past, adults strolled, children dashed. People in cars trained binoculars onto waders, and two men puffed tobacco smoke out of a van. A sightseeing boat, tannoy crackling, chugged behind a red fishing boat, a coffee-cup lid drifted along like a jellyfish, and even a group of white-faced teenagers were out throwing stones in the water. We rounded the headland, and there was Caernarfon Castle, jolly flags in its turrets.

The old tyrant Edward I had built it, colonised the town with English and banished the Cymry. We preferred the old salty slate quay, but were hungry and made for the cafés in the castle square. Tourists were buying handbags from market stalls and pulling café chairs under parasols. We wolfed down pie, chips and beans by a group of elderly sightseers chatting over doughnuts and coffee. The atmosphere was sun-soaked and English-speaking. I couldn't reconcile it with the Caernarfon I knew from work trips, just two streets away at the bus stops, where buses would be sulking and seagulls loitering on wheelie bins outside William Hill. Where tired passengers would be waiting with their shopping in carrier bags, chatting in Cymraeg, inhaling the exhaust of cars driving up the multi-storey car park and the fag smoke of overweight drivers who spoke Cymraeg so thickly I'd thought at first they were Russian. Tourism may be an important part of Cymru's economy but it can make Cymry invisible and their language inaudible.

The woman in the tourist information centre said they weren't tourists, they were parents because it was Freshers' Week in Bangor. We took the last room in town. An Irish blessing hung in the lobby and an Irish girl showed us our room with wicker chairs and a view over Morrisons. Later we went to the marina. Ynys Môn might have been on fire the sky was so brilliant, so smoky, so apocalyptic. But the parents had all gone for dinner. Only one couple leant over the railings to see the oars of a single boat sending orange ripples across blood-red water. We watched till it was over, then went shopping.

Morrisons was cold, the electric light harsh in comparison. In the toilets the atmosphere was tense, as if breath was being held. It was – two pairs of trainers were visible under the cubicle wall. Back in the fruit aisle a stricken teenager stood by the bananas, empty basket dangling from a limp hand, waiting, presumably, for his friends to finish bonking.

By morning the weather was drab and our mood less jubilant. We lost our way in a mess of main roads outside Bangor, and wound up on the A55.

Traffic ground past, a wall of noise. We pressed on behind the crash barrier
with branches whipping our faces, sliding on cans and a bin-bag of fetid
slime, till on reaching Britannia Bridge, we beat through scrub into a field
and felt free. Pylons sailed down it like ships. At the bottom, a fox and two
fat lambs were arranged as if to illustrate an Aesop's fable. The lambs
regarded us placidly while the fox maintained his gaze on them from just a
metre away. We got close enough to see his aquiline profile and hazel eyes,
his grace and poise and tension, and it seemed we could reach out and touch
him, till he shot us a dirty look and slunk into the trees, and the lambs
walked calmly away.

In Bangor we drank coffee in Debenhams. Outside the window, aerials
bristled on the BT offices, puddles glimmered dully on Marks and Spencer's
flat roof, and bus passengers ignored the park junkies pestering them for
money. It was an unromantic setting. We kissed, Rob left, and my heart grew
heavy as I watched his bus pull away.

Bangor felt gritty. I wanted to be rid of it, to be back on the coast. Kids
kicked a football and boats were moored in the mud where slate from
Penrhyn, the largest slate quarry in the world at the end of the nineteenth
century, had been exported. The path took an age to circumnavigate the
grounds of the mock castle built for George Hay Dawkins-Pennant who'd
inherited the estate and slate quarry from London-born Richard Pennant
who'd acquired it through marriage, having already made his fortune from
Jamaican sugar plantations worked by 600 slaves. The quarrymen were next
to be exploited. And in the Great Strike of 1900-1903, his descendant George
Sholto Gordon Douglas-Pennant had caused starvation by barring quarrymen
demanding better pay and conditions, from working. I didn't know any of this,
but muttered 'bastards' anyway, at the ostentatious gates.

The coast lifted my spirits. Y Fenai had widened but Ynys Môn and Ynys
Seiriol were clearly outlined, as if by ink. Twice a day the water is sucked
and funnelled by tides between Caernarfon and Liverpool, the constant
churning and oxygenation creating a nutrient-rich soup which at low tide
exposes 2,500 acres of mud and sand, where tens of thousands of water-
birds gather in winter. Now it was late September. Marsh samphire still
spiked muddy pools. Shells, shingle, and saltmarsh made a landscape of
sickles and stripes.

But heavy rain was due and everything seemed to portend it. A combine
harvester was out at the fag-end of a wet summer. The sky was dark. Sea

mayweed, pebbles and weed crusts had a saturated intensity. Stormlight flooded green saltmarsh and silvered the sea. I crouched on the stones to boil noodles. I fried pepper, onion, mushrooms and spinach in butter, then sprinkled the lot with sachets of Debenhams' salt and pepper. The mushroom bag caught alight and filmy fragments floated away.

There was a beauty in the tension, in the birds gathering in pools and marshy fields. Egrets stood alone in muddy dykes. Crows patrolled the pebble ridge and a flock of mallards came in to land. Water flowed between black banks, thistles swayed, fireweed and coltsfoot went to seed, brown sheep grazed. I put up my tent in a spinney then sat on the beach, surrounded by birds. There were so many, there was so much life, but I knew there should have been more. Four thousand curlews overwintered here – but since the 1990s, their population has crashed by 80 per cent. Global wildlife populations have declined by 60 per cent in just half a century. I remembered one of my nephews stroking the cartoons in my 'Extinct Boids' book. "I miss them," he'd said. I knew how he felt. Species were being lost to climate change, habitat loss, deforestation and pollution. The water cycle, carbon cycle and nitrogen cycle no longer properly functioned. Humans rather than natural forces were now the primary drivers of planetary change, globally, and here in Cymru. If everyone in the world lived like the average person in England and Cymru we'd need three planets' worth of resources. We have wrecked this planet to the extent it can no longer adequately regenerate. In recent years, only one country in the world has enjoyed good standards of healthcare, education and nutrition without exceeding the Earth's resources – Cuba in 2006, with other Latin American countries very close. But try telling people that (and I had) without them becoming uneasy. In 2008 I contacted the WWF to ask why they'd stopped including that particular graph in their Living Planet Report and they told me it was because too many people had accused them of promoting Communism. We fabulous, flawed humans had messed up. But how? My trip was inspiring me to find out more about Cymru. Now I realised, with the environmental problems I'd hoped to escape looming large at every turn, I also wanted to work out when and how we'd gone wrong. I would have to turn to history.

Meanwhile, hundreds of birds were pressed up the beach by high tide. Under a liquid black sky, they faced the sea in their groups – herring gulls, black-backed gulls and oystercatchers. Dotted among them were crows, egrets, curlews and small brown birds I couldn't identify. Something disturbed them and they rushed up in one magnificent wave, wings flashing bright against the inky sky like silver fish bellies in a bait ball.

It was hammering down as I left Gwynedd for a brief dash into Sir Conwy (I would walk around Ynys Môn when I returned). I stopped to smell a voluptuous wet rose. "Lovely weather," shouted two men unloading a truck in the rain. "There's a train to Conwy, why do you want to walk there?" I shouted back that I didn't mind the weather. "We think you're mental!" they yelled cheerfully, and I was cheerful too. It was the freshness of it, the freedom.

Low cloud obscured lamppost tops. I heard the wing-beat and honk of unseen geese above the rustling of my hood. Rain poured into my old boots and jacket. Brown sea heaved. But it was purifying, this washing away of colour and sound as if thoughts too, were being cleansed by the rain.

The coast path and cycle track were bolted to the A55, dependent on it like a blue-streak wrasse to a shark, and I was alone save for a cyclist whizzing past in a billow of poncho, with a cheerful "Good Morning!" Water gushed off rocky hillsides into drains. Below me, Monday-morning traffic was a fug of warped noise and spray-distorted headlamps. Concrete towers held the dripping road above Penmaenmawr seafront and the path to town and its cafes was flooded, so I swigged water from the public toilets and ate my last crust of bread. Beyond the skateboard ramps the sea slopped like soup. But I felt content. Rain defined the landscape at my feet. A pair of bloated milk cartons lay like small dead sheep in the weeds. Sometimes when I looked up, clouds parted to reveal quarried rock. A petrol station glowed a red and yellow unreachable invitation over the roads, diffused by lorry spray like a Japanese lantern. Tunnels swallowed the cars but the path clung to the cliffs. At Conwy I left it for beach. Wet sand coated my boots. My hood was useless so I took it down, felt released and heard the mewling of gulls.

The marina was forlorn. I went into a pub just being opened for the day. "Nice weather," said the man behind the bar, looking me up and down. "She's been swimming," he said to his wife, and I laughed but suddenly it wasn't really funny. My face was stiff and I found it hard to speak. I hung my useless waterproofs by the stove. Pools developed on the floor. Now I was inside, the rain felt wrong. My flesh was numb and my thighs, when I saw them in the toilets, were blue with clothes dye. The television forecaster warned of floods, gales, a month's worth of rain over the next twenty-four hours, and advised people not to travel. I got a train to Bangor and a bus home from there. But it was just rain. Nothing compared with what we were about to face.

I was still being offered teaching work and on a Friday at the end of October, went to Machynlleth Primary School to explain to the Head that I really had given it up. We spoke in Cymraeg (she being one of only two people I knew then, to indulge my efforts), and she said she'd continue to prioritise the pupils' wellbeing despite new government targets. I left feeling warm, and proud of having been involved at that lovely school, blessed, and free to move on. But on Monday one of those loved pupils was abducted from outside her home.

Machynlleth imploded and rallied. Over and again we scrutinised our memories. We joined search parties that were sometimes called off because we left footprints and tyre tracks where there'd been none for years. A police camp sprouted at the edge of town. Mountain rescue teams came, and people from Manchester, Liverpool and across Cymru came too, wanting to help. Nationality didn't matter. Journalists with long coats and floppy hair appeared in cafés trying to look discreet, and camera crews gathered at the bridge to film divers walking up and down the bank in the rain with rope tied round their waists. There were so many of us, we sometimes believed we'd find her. But in the hills our hope dispersed. Forests were thick with wind-broken trees, slate quarries stretched for miles underground, ditches creased empty fields. We found black bogs in the woods and valleys with hanging bramble floors. The landscape wept. The little girl's killer was arrested on an afternoon when the air was still and stern.

I left for Ynys Môn. There were pictures of her – April – smiling all over the bus. The passengers were silent. We all wore pink ribbons, and there were pink ribbons tied to fences and lampposts, and photos of April in houses and shop windows all the way to Bangor, as if, in some way, she lived on.

INTENSIFICATION

During the Second World War the Cymreig coast bristled with anti-tank guns and pillboxes, defences against invasion via Ireland. War industries sprang up across Cymru, like the arsenal at Pen-y-bont, and weapons were tested. Children from English cities were evacuated to Cymru. American and British troops trained in Cymru, and Jewish, Czechoslovakian, Polish and Dutch refugees were homed there. Hundreds of civilians died in bombing raids and 15,000 troops were killed in active service.

Europe slid into post-war economic decline. In 1945, the Labour Party (with several Cymreig MPs) replaced Winston Churchill's Conservative UK government. The Labour Party established a welfare state, the National Health Service and industrial estates. Wartime ammunitions factories now produced concrete and plastics. The war had contributed to a sense of united Britishness, and transport, utilities and industries were nationalised. Slums were demolished and social housing built, requiring migrant labourers from Poland, Ukraine, Ireland and Italy.

By 1951 the population of Cymru was just over 2.5 million (and 41 million in England). The UK Conservative Party regained power but with only five MPs Cymru had no effective voice in Westminster. Cheap textiles were imported contributing to a slump in the wool market. But agriculture had revived in the war and was protected by post-war subsidies, and an act giving tenant farmers security. Farms became larger, more mechanised and required less labour as oil became cheaper. Fertilisers were produced by makers of wartime weapons. Mixed farming declined as small farms were sold and amalgamated.

The economy shifted from manufacturing to services. Having been heavily industrial, Cymru suffered huge unemployment, which the Office of Minister for Welsh Affairs was established to address. After a series of by-elections in which Plaid Cymru threatened Labour seats, Cymraeg-medium schools were founded and electronic companies, the DVLA and Royal Mint, were installed in the south to create jobs. Caravan sites and the new National Parks attracted English holidaymakers, but unemployment remained substantial.

In 1964, Labour returned to power and established a Secretary of State for Wales and a Welsh Office with responsibility for health, tourism, primary and secondary education, childcare, water sanitation, industry and agriculture in

Cymru. But despite the oil industry at Aberdaugleddau and new nuclear power stations, unemployment was still greater than in England and resentment simmered, particularly in 1965 when Cwm Tryweryn was flooded to supply Liverpool with water. 'Cofiwch Tryweryn' (Remember Tryweryn) became a lasting symbol of resistance. Nationalism increased. The Welsh Language Society, formed in 1962, continued to defend and promote the language. In 1966 Gwynfor Evans became Plaid Cymru's first MP, and in 1967 the Welsh Language Act was passed allowing Cymraeg to be used in legal proceedings for the first time in more than 300 years.

Nevertheless, devolution was controversial. Influential Cymreig Labour politicians, including Jim Griffiths (first Secretary of State for Wales), and Aneurin Bevan (creator of the NHS), had been anti-devolution, believing that British working classes were stronger together, and their influence endured. In a referendum in 1979, devolution was rejected.

Many rail-lines closed, but air traffic and car ownership increased, spawning roads and out-of-town shopping centres. Commuting became common. Nuclear power and hydro-electricity had connected most homes to the National Grid, and people stayed home to watch television.

In 1974 Cymru's thirteen counties were re-organised into eight. Britain had been accepted into the European Economic Community (EEC) in 1973, and Cymru received European funding for agriculture, roads and cleaner seas, but industry suffered through competition with partner nations. Fishing waters were extended by the EEC Fisheries Act in 1976, but due to scarcity, herring fishing was banned between 1970 and 1981.

Meanwhile, following strikes, the Labour Party had been replaced by Margaret Thatcher's Conservative Government. By 1980 the coal industry was crippled, leading to strikes (mines had been closing as oil and gas use increased). By 1982, 170,000 jobs had been lost. Over time, post-industrial land was converted into nature reserves, factories became flats and offices, and chapels were converted or demolished, religious practise having dwindled. Farms and cottages became holiday homes, frequently attacked by nationalist groups because during the 1980s and 1990s, local buyers were being priced out of the market by English people buying second homes occupied just a few months a year.

Breakup of the British Empire in the 1950s and 1960s resulted in immigrants from commonwealth countries. Vietnamese and Somalian refugees arrived in Cymru. English settlers moving to rural areas outnumbered them. They were largely retired, or younger and fed up with environmental degradation. The latter lived low-impact lives, established environmental communities and businesses, and many of their children learned Cymraeg. Meanwhile, young Cymry left in search of work.

By 1986 unemployment was 4 per cent higher than the British average of 16 per cent. The Chernobyl nuclear disaster drenched upland Britain with rain containing high levels of caesium and iodine, and trade from 344 Cymreig sheep farms was restricted. (High caesium levels were reported till 2011.) The agricultural workforce had halved since the beginning of the century. Steelworks struggled to compete in a global economy. But the service industry (including tourism), had grown and a media industry was developing. Electronics companies expanded, with help from Japanese investment and immigration.

Globalisation and immigration had affected the language. In 1991 numbers able to speak Cymraeg had dropped to 19 percent, but in 1993, for the first time since the sixteenth-century Acts of Union, Cymraeg was granted legal status alongside English. In 1997 a second referendum was held and the population voted very narrowly for a devolved government. The National Assembly was launched in 1999 and took on most of the limited law-making powers of the Welsh Office and Secretary of State for Wales.

Numbers of Nature Reserves and Sites of Special Scientific Interest grew. European Conservation Directives led to the creation of Special Protected Areas and Special Areas of Conservation for threatened birds, fauna, flora, wetlands and fisheries. Some species were helped. As heavy industry declined rivers became cleaner, and stickleback, eel, trout, minnow, and salmon began to return. Heavy-metal tolerant plants, lichens, bryophytes and wildlife began to colonise abandoned slagheaps and coal tips. Goshawks moved into conifer plantations. Red kites made a spectacular recovery. The new open country of large farms and small woods benefitted buzzards, kites, sparrowhawks and owls, while close-grazed pasture and combine stubble was good for gulls, crows and starlings, choughs, rooks, jackdaws and pigeons. Gannets on Ynys Gwales increased in number. The Forestry Commission continued to plant large upland conifer plantations, but there was a slight improvement in their management for wildlife. Large new reservoirs destroyed wildlife, but shallow ones attracted birds. Numbers of polecats increased after gin traps were banned.

But on the whole biodiversity suffered. Herring gulls became rare on the coast. Aberdaugleddau's herring harvest had peaked in 1946 at 49,000 tons, then crashed. Fish stocks at sea didn't recover and numbers of sturgeon, skate and ray were among those in decline. Development had fragmented habitats. Much wildlife disappeared with mixed farms. Orchards and associated biodiversity had declined by 90 per cent and cultivated areas by 75 per cent over the century. Drainage, ploughing, herbicides and fertiliser use all had negative impacts, with DDT being particularly deadly. Otters and peregrine numbers crashed. Farm pond habitats were lost when piped water arrived. Myxamotosis dented the rabbit population and their predators. Strychnine was used to kill moles. Red squirrels were largely supplanted by greys. Hedgerow habitats of mammals, birds, insects, mosses, lichens and flowers were grubbed up to make larger fields for large machinery, and field margin habitats were obliterated by herbicides. Woodlarks disappeared and there was a general decline in numbers of bramblings, lapwings, golden plovers, yellow wagtails, stonechats, nightingales, wheatears, corncrakes, red-backed shrikes, tree sparrows, yellowhammers, whinchats, linnets, grey partridges, kestrels and barn owls.

Subsidies, better sheep shelters, winter feed, breeding and fertiliser-use on grass crops led to more sheep (but fewer beef cattle). Ninety-one per cent of wild 'unimproved' neutral grassland was lost from 1930 to 1990, replaced with 'improved' grassland consisting mainly of rye grass and clover. Between 1950 and 1999, the number of sheep rose from 3.8 to 11.6 million, with many habitats devastated by over-grazing. And in 1999, 2,700 acres of land and mudflat habitats, (some internationally protected), were redeveloped into Bae Caerdydd.

It was easy really, to see how we had arrived at environmental apocalypse. I was also learning that it was not unusual to have moved to Cymru – to have come from elsewhere.

SIR FÔN (YNYS MÔN)

When ice sheets thawed and sea levels rose, Ynys Môn became an island. Now the dunes, flats, slacks, mires, swards and Atlantic salt meadows harbour Baltic stonewort, nail fungus, and Welsh marsh orchid, while lime-loving plants grow in glacial deposits lying over the older mix of acidic and lime-rich rocks. Red squirrels survive, gannets thrive, and a third of the global population of roseate terns breed at Ynys Feurig.

I'd seen only anguish for days and was puzzled when a passer-by smiled. When I tried to respond, I realised my own face was rigid. A group of oystercatchers took flight, rising as one, piping their wild tune, and I stared – they touched something. But when I looked down into Y Fenai from Menai Bridge, my mind was hard. I could see that it was green and lovely but I saw it from a distance. I was wracked with irrational guilt, sure I should have been able to remember some useful detail in time to have saved young April. Guilt that I'd left the community too soon. I wanted to go back, but Rob was already on his way.

We were staying with friends in Niwbwrch and I was late, but each payphone was broken. I stared at another swinging receiver, waiting to feel angry, but I was empty. I knocked at the door of a house with an egg stall outside, confusing the owner who was expecting someone else. A van rolled up while I used his phone and he ran out in white socks pulled halfway up his shins to take delivery of a fridge.

I trudged on, numb. Confused by several waymarks stapled around a post wrapped in barbed wire, I floundered onto a cattle-run ankle-deep in slurry with light failing, my way blocked by five-barred gates between which, cows were stampeding. When they'd gone I scrambled to the road. A bus with bright windows passed and I wished I was on it. Rob was. He'd seen me, got off, and was waiting, the sky behind him deep pink. We held each other tightly.

Our friends Tim and Melissa were waiting. The kids were in pyjamas, too excited, because of visitors, for bed. It was strange to be with people who knew what had happened in Machynlleth but who couldn't know what it was like to be there. The kids chattered while we ate blackberry pie, and warmth, light and goodness washed over us. We drank it in a sip at a time.

The sky was soft and the landscape gentle but we were still raw, flinching at the sound of a helicopter, still regarding footprints with suspicion. Expansive dunes were crisscrossed by little paths and we followed them to marshy creeks, wandering from one to another. Eventually we came to a spit where thousands of tiny rose petal tellin shells were washed up in delicate drifts. Most of them were still hinged. And they looked like little pink ribbons. We sat for a long time among them and then, something shifted, we got up and walked on.

Suddenly people were spilling through Coed Niwbwrch wearing red and purple jackets that were vivid against the green forest. They were making for Ynys Llanddwyn, and we followed, all jammed together but separate. A black seal broke the surface then rolled back into the sea and everyone pointed and cried "Look!"

In contrast, Traeth Penrhos was empty. A small ridge of sand had accumulated behind every shell. We walked barefoot up Afon Cefni then waded through a dyke into Coed Niwbwrch – the Corsican pine plantation planted after the Second World War to provide timber and stabilise the dunes, now blamed for lowering the water table and destroying dune slacks and their plant communities. But parts of it were deep-rooted mixed woodland of native trees and alien exotics. The earth was soft and brown. The collusion of branches filtered the light. Breeze whispered. Golden leaves danced overhead and the air smelt of resin.

The blue night was beginning to pale and birdsong floated about the picnic bench. Melissa had sent us to Llyn Parc Mawr Community Woodland in search of red squirrels. Suddenly, one hurtled down a pine. Six or seven more crept stealthily to the feeders. Their eyes were black, their ears tufted. They were orange swirls and smoke wisps flying between boughs like feathers on the breeze. Their numbers on Ynys Môn had increased from forty in 1998 to 700 in 2013 after 3,000 greys were trapped and killed – reds succumb to squirrel pox that non-native greys spread. The reds watched us, their tails a question mark.

Tim bribed the kids out of bed and into the van with cheese croissants, and at the station the train that would take Rob home was already on the platform, so he rolled out with his rucksack and was gone. The kids grumbled. "Why do we have to go to the beach AGAIN Dad?" but when we got there, spilled into carefree worlds. The marram grass had unrolled in the mild humidity. Its leaves roll into spikes to reduce evaporation – I'd taught pupils this, but felt as if I'd never really observed unrolled marram grass before and for a few moments it surprised me. As if something very quiet and still had been happening while I'd been too busy to notice. Tim said that in the past it had been woven into mats, and that bread baked from Ynys Môn grains had supplied quarrymen on the mainland.

My friends had only been in Cymru a year, but Tim knew more local history than me, and the kids, being young, were already nearly fluent in Cymraeg. To my shame, Melissa, was almost as good. "It's a no-brainer," she said. "You move to a country, you learn the language." I would come to realise that part of my uneasiness about being English was because environmentalist-incomers were so disproportionately numerous in Machynlleth. Here there was no such baggage. I could see more clearly that my friends were more than integrators, they were contributors.

Barclodiad y Gawres, the Neolithic burial tomb on the headland with its dark stone passage to a central chamber, was soothing somehow. I felt like I'd have curled up in that stone womb, had I been on my own. I liked that we could walk, without fees or fuss, into the belly of time. When my friends went home, I walked on. April's death had given me new perspective. It didn't seem important anymore, that I was English. I didn't care now, about finishing my walk by Christmas. I would take my time. I was grateful to be here at all, and see the marram grass unroll.

The landscape was restorative. From the last dune, Rhosneigr was a pencil-drawn village on a greetings card, and Eryri and Pen Llŷn beyond were a deep smoking blue. Rocky islands were black in the chiffon sea and the sun was a lazy white. The warm air kept distant go-karts audible for miles, but thankfully, being Sunday, there were no fighter jets screaming out of RAF Valley. On training days they screamed all the way to Machynlleth leaving brain-shattering voids between the first, second, third jet. Having low-aviation-photographer friends gave me a morsel of comfort, I liked their enthusiasm. "At least Aled's happy," I'd think, as my nerves shredded. I appreciated the technology, but not the purpose, not the warfare. Not the noise. Not the heinous carbon dioxide emissions.

Like so many military bases, RAF Valley was born in the Second World War. During which, on 28th August 1941, gales had caused a Blackburn Botha torpedo bomber (sent to reconnoitre an area where a German submarine had been spotted attacking a Merchant Navy convoy) to crash into the sea. Villagers, airmen and soldiers had scrambled but failed to save three crew members clinging to the wreckage – as we had scrambled, and failed to save April. Two teenage holidaymakers had rescued the pilot then were saved when their dinghy capsized, by holidaymakers who'd roped themselves together. Eleven rescuers including a coastguard, a merchant seaman on leave, the village policeman, and an RAF driver, had died along with the crew. History was illuminating. At least now I understood why the air base, dislike it though I did, had been established. War was why.

I thought about Rob who'd be stepping off the bus, walking up the track, lighting the stove, and had the strange sensation that we were both in both places – I with him by the fire and he with me in the thistle-fields. It was a comforting thought. I was in a strange mood.

Instead of crossing by the bridge at Pont-rhyd-y-bont to continue round Ynys Gybi in the clockwise direction I'd intended, I daydreamed along the Cymyran Strait by a lane which high tides had mulched with seaweed and dead crabs. It led me to the embankment Lord Stanley had commissioned Thomas Telford to build, to carry his road to Caergybi, lying now on the sea like a steel rule on silk.

Across it in Penrhos Park, fidgety men sat in cars, leaned on bonnets, or walked about smoking, waiting for the boat to Ireland. They wanted to be on the move. I too, loved moving. Penrhos Estate had been requisitioned from the Stanleys for troops in the Second World War then fallen into ruin, and now was a Country Park. The chimneys of an aluminium plant built there in 1969 still speared the sky though the plant had stopped smelting in 2009, and would stop re-melting in 2013. The decommissioning of Yr Wylfa nuclear power station had ceased the abundant supply of cheap electricity which made the production of aluminium – one of the most energy intensively produced metals in the world, economically viable.

The park gates were locked at dusk, so I hid from the park keeper on a Napoleonic battery and watched birds squabbling around water fluming through the embankment till it was dark enough to pitch my tent. The temperature dropped. I put on two sets of thermals, ate cheese rolls and brushed my teeth, then watched the birds from my sleeping bag. A starling murmuration rose and fell. Black-backed gulls, herring gulls and oystercatchers cried and piped. A green light winked at the end of Caergybi Pier, which was lit up in sodium orange. It was very cold, but drawn to the ferry lights and their suggestion of journeying, I kept the tent unzipped for a long time.

I strode quickly round the headland. It was raining on the dog poo and beer cans littering the playing field of a council estate painted like a bathroom colour chart. I was heading for the writing course in Llanystumdwy, but had time for coffee in Caergybi. "We're not open yet!" said a woman wiping tables, so I chose a café with an OPEN sign on the door. "We're not open yet!" cried the woman wielding a mop. In the third, a man looked up from emptying coins into the till. "We're not open yet," he said, and I retreated, to the amusement of a man on the street. "It takes us a while to wake up," he said and sent me to Caffi Empire, which was full of steam, and workmen eating fried eggs and sausages, and women with carrier bags at their feet who looked up from their tea with friendly curiosity. The sound of scraping chairs mingled with the memory of nicotine and smells of grease and wet coats, and I was glad to be a stranger and part of it all. The radio played 'It's a Beautiful Day' and everyone laughed.

Two weeks later I was back. The reek of seaweed hit me as I stepped off the bus at Pont-rhyd-y-bont. Oystercatchers stood about boats pulled high up the bank. Scummy foam amassed around piles of limpet shells. Bog bubbled. The footpath had gone. A woman came out of a cottage and folded her arms. "It came up to the second bar last night," she said, nodding to the service pipes on the bridge. "Every four weeks there's an extra high tide. I don't know why they put the path there…" she shrugged. Behind the housing estate birds roamed in gangs over new watery territory. An egret watched me sink to my knees in marsh and I laughed at being soaked so soon. Worrying about getting wet was worse than actually being wet. I retreated onto quiet roads between muddy paddocks of mournful sheep and a few greylag geese.

It was the end of October. I'd attended the writing course then written my first magazine assignment – about the coast path. It had taken me this long to realise that landscape was what I wanted to write about. I was glad of the journey for its own sake, for its freedom. Perhaps it had purpose. I was a witness of Cymru's edge at a point in time, before it changed, and changed again. I would write about that.

Mermaids' purses and crab claws were strewn over silver sand. Three cormorants flew in formation, braked in mid-air and changed direction. It was so different to our green valley, speckled red and orange now, fragrant with wood-smoke and humus. I was already understanding that Cymru was so diverse, belonging here was easier than I'd realised. No-one could deny me these wide beaches, these wooded valleys, these gritty towns – but I was just passing through. One landscape welcomed me, then passed me onto the next, and I liked it this way. The swollen sea heaved, capricious and storm-lit, with a powerful smell. A shower smacked the wayside rosehips. I scrambled into my waterproofs but within moments it had passed and tarmac and weeds steamed. It was good to be back.

This coast reminded me of Brittany; the sporadic groupings of white houses at field edges, in creeks and on headlands, and the small grey oyster boat bobbing at Borthwen. The red campion, montbretia and rushes shaking in windy profusion. But I'd never even heard about this wild west part of Ynys Gybi, where cinematic light bathed the castellated cliffs, enhancing at every turn new textures and colours, rust-brown to pink with red folds. Two white dots – goats, watched from a high ledge. Greenery festooned rubescent rock. Stone walls crumbled in fields but it was the coast that bewitched me, vivid, wind-whipped and Polaroid, except among the shadows, where colours flickered like old cine film.

The cliffs were low and black and the sea whipped black and white and black and white around them. A starling cloud shot from below them. Waves pestered them. A cormorant perched on them and orange weed draped them, while boulders tumbled in arches and coves. At Trearddur, caravans squeezed into a creek, a windmill stood proud on the moor and light shimmered over the sea like silver gelatin. Starlings whistled – out of tune radios on the telegraph wire drooping over the empty road that swung briefly to the beach. It felt as if the white houses and bungalows were occupied by people hiding from the cold and peeping out, as if the bright light anticipated winter, and the world was poised between seasons. A dead fox was washed up on the beach. Turnstones poked at the strandline. The moors ahead were already inky dark.

On them footpaths were trodden into dark sodden peat and the cliffs were riven with creeks. Stormy light silhouetted a woman stroking her horses. Everywhere was a black and white photograph under red light in a darkroom. I pitched my tent and watched the clouds – stone angels and temples powered by a strong southwesterly, till the rosiness drained from them and lights came on in the scatter of cottages across the fuliginous moor. In the night, a helicopter. The temperature plummeted and hail lashed the canvas but I was kept warm by the sod. Each time I woke I looked out and saw a hint of moon sailing through orange cloud and half a sky of stars.

Like wiping soot from an oil painting, light gradually dissolved the night and bathed the sea but the moors held their darkness longer. A wheatear flew low, between russet bracken the texture of paint on canvas.

The lighthouse faced the sea, alert for turbulence like a steward watching the crowd at a football match, its soft white winks melting holes in the blue air. In the car park a man hunched over his steering wheel, craned bloodshot eyes to the horizon. He wound down his window. "Have you seen Ireland?" he asked. "Can you see Ireland from here?" I wasn't sure. "Jayzus you're braver than me," he said, on finding I'd slept in a tent. A pair of ankles on the dashboard uncrossed and a blonde woman surfaced, smiled and retreated. He was going to visit family in Limerick for the first time in twenty years, he said. "City of stabs they call it. Christ…" he scowled. "Mind you – it's all AK47s now." He laughed. "It's alright – I've got a helmet in the boot!" I descended the lighthouse steps and sat in a fissure. A pair of choughs flipped about like bale-wrap caught on a fence. Back on the clifftop the Irishman stared at the horizon. I waved but he didn't see.

Gerald, who I'd met on the writing course lived in Caergybi. He'd written about this stretch of coast and his cadence followed me down the track along which he'd said donkeys had carried provisions to the lighthouse, and around Mynydd Twr, where shattered quartzite rock roared up from rush-fringed pools. 'Interesting word, yacht' he'd said, but I couldn't remember why. I watched a ferry berth in Caergybi with a blast of its horn, and an effervescent cloud hurry in from the south. Below it, on the beach, a young man poked at rocks and wrote notes.

On the path was a memorial to the crew of a US Airforce B-24 Liberator Bomber which had used on-board radio transmitters to jam enemy communication. There'd been pillboxes at Tywyn, so I'd grown up knowing that the coast had been fortified in the Second World War, but I'd not known the extent of wartime activity. The bomber had been diverted when bad weather prevented it from landing in Buckinghamshire, but two of its engines failed whilst awaiting landing instructions. Ten of the crew parachuted out and the plane crashed into the sea. Soldiers from Tŷ Croes artillery range, RAF and American ground crews, police, and boats under HMS Bee, had searched for survivors but found only the pilot in a field, and the co-pilot in the water. The memorial was fashioned from a propeller blade salvaged in 1992.

In Caergybi, smashed beer bottles added sparkle to public shelters. The lifeboat house had served as air-raid shelter for the Dutch Navy in the Second World War. Dutch fishing trawlers, torpedo boats, auxiliary patrol boats and guard boats had fled to Britain when the Netherlands was occupied, and been sent here, to protect Môr Iwerddon. The Zeemanshop lifeboat had arrived with forty-six mostly Jewish refugees who stayed on after the war, and The Stuyvesant and Oranje Nassau had been used for accommodation. Now the lifeboat house was a museum, after a spell storing council lawnmowers.

The docked Stena Line ferry was huge, backdropping a group of allotments like a nasty hotel. Caergybi had been a transit hub between Britain and Ireland for centuries. The most recent terminal was built in 1996 to house the largest high-speed catamaran ferry in the world with a thirty-minute turnaround. The journey time has lengthened since 2008, due to the increasing price of oil – HSS Explorer cruises more efficiently now. I watched an old man shovel manure into a wheelbarrow, envious of his leeks and cabbages and black rich soil. In our wooded valley, leeks took two years to reach the size of spring onions. It felt very far from here, very different.

It seemed ferry passengers didn't often bother with Caergybi, where the streets were neglected and most of the pubs boarded up. A woman smoked a cigarette in a doorway. The Conservative Club's paint had flaked off. People stared at my rucksack and a woman crossed the street to tell me she'd seen me yesterday, walking through Trearddur. I followed two stout men over The Celtic Gateway. They had a Dublin-look about them – dark suits contrasting with the swirl of modern steel, a plastic bag dangling from a wrist. Another man asked if I was catching the boat. "No," I said, "are you?" "Christ no," he laughed. "I'm one of the local savages!"

Having walked already around the headland from Stanley Embankment, I took the bus to Y Fali with a woman who said she was just going to Tesco's with her bus pass. In *The Bank Manager and the Holy Grail* Byron Rogers had written, "Tesco is opening a supermarket there [Caergybi] later this year, but distractedly, like an empire that has just been reminded of a remote possession." Tesco jostled with the other out-of-town stores – KFC, Pets at Home, Morrisons, Argos, Iceland, Wilko. Small wonder the high street was shabby.

I had a vague arrangement to meet Rob, it being Friday, and was hovering at the bus stop when a big man rushed up and hugged me. Gerald from the writing course! He bundled me into the barbers, where I was given coffee, and he was wrapped in a yellow poncho. He chattered non-stop to my reflection but I couldn't hear a word above the dryers. "What?" I mouthed. "ISN'T THIS FUN?!" he bellowed. We found Rob down the road. He had missed his stop due to a cryptic crossword clue and was now puzzled further at being ambushed by a big man he'd never met jumping out of a small orange car. But Gerald's wife Gwyneth, defrosting an orange iceberg on the Aga, was unflustered by unexpected guests. "It's mystery soup," she announced. We ate it with bread and butter at the kitchen table with three adult red-haired children who spoke Cymraeg to Gwyneth and English to Gerald, which made me uncomfortable but didn't bother anyone else. I wanted to join in the Cymraeg but perhaps it would have been showing off. I didn't know anymore. Instead I asked Gerald to remind me what he'd written about yachts.

"Interesting word, yacht," he said. "The combination of *cht* is unique in English because it's from the Dutch 'jacht', to hunt. *Jachtsteppen* were used for chasing and intercepting slower ships but one given to Charles II was used for pleasure till it sank on the Skerries. There's a fascinating story of the aristocratic female passengers stepping ashore using the mast as a gangplank." That was it.

We made slow progress over sodden fields that dragged at our feet, strewn with dead crabs. The sea was a shining foil. Penrhos Park and the smelter chimneys at the aluminium works seemed very close across it. Finally we pitched up at Porth Penrhyn Mawr campsite, and were alone till dark, when the touring caravans arrived, and their occupants came out to greet each other. Fishing lights flashed on the rocks and someone set off fireworks on the beach. The night was still but we were woken by a brief rainstorm so violent we thought the canvas would burst. Pegs were torn from the ground and our boots in the porch filled with rain but it didn't matter because they were already soaked, and such things don't matter, when you're in love.

Next morning my mouth was cold and wet. I assumed the tent had leaked, but a large black slug had come in with the storm and settled under my nose.

Nervous birds with speckled young slipped in and out of the brash – game birds, harried and doomed. We had been diverted inland across the Mynachdy Estate which was closed in winter for pheasant, partridge and duck-shooting, and were hesitating among vast fields when a second-storey barn door opened and a woman emerged on the threshold, surprised to see us and blinking in the sun. "Are we still on the coast path?" we asked. "Yes. No. I don't know. Where's Jonty?" she said, turning round and bumping into the man behind who, confused by her change of direction also turned and bumped into the man behind him, who was shaky on his feet. Six or seven more rubicund men stumbled out of the door and down the steps, bits of straw protruding from beige woollen jumpers, save for the oldest, who wore tweed and brandished a stick. Last out was Jonty, younger and more sober. "Yes," he said tersely and ushered his charges away.

Even the squat 1970s assembly of old concrete buildings – Yr Wylfa nuclear power station, looked like a classical temple in this clear light, though we weren't pleased to see it. It would be decommissioned in 2015. During the Second World War, uranium, previously mined for luminous paint and medical applications was used for research into nuclear weapons — research which began at the mustard gas armaments factory in Rhyd-y-mwyn and led to the atomic bomb. Magnox reactors, of which this was the last one in Britain, were created to produce plutonium for the nuclear weapons industry, electricity being at first just a useful by-product.

But in 1957, MacMillan's Conservative government invested in nuclear power to reduce the bargaining power of the coalmining unions, despite knowing that reactors would be 57 per cent more expensive than coal-fired power stations. Eleven Magnox reactors were built in the UK, as well as one in Japan and one in North Korea. They had a low fuel burn-up and couldn't compete with pressurised-water reactors. By 1995, plutonium production for weapons had ceased in Britain. But the last consignment of Magnox fuel wouldn't leave Springfield's Nuclear Fuel Manufacturing plant in Preston till December 2011. Meanwhile, as the reactors aged the core degraded and couldn't be replaced.

In 1993 part of the refuelling equipment had fallen into the reactor core, resulting in more than twice the weekly limit of Sulphur 35 being released. In 2000, it had been temporarily shut down due to reactor core damage and weld failures, and in the same year, Yr Wylfa was found to have been discharging sodium hydrochloride into the Irish Sea at more than 20,000 times the legal concentration. But it was all ending now. Hundreds of jobs were being lost both here and at the aluminium plant which had consumed half its electricity. Decommissioning would employ people in ever-decreasing numbers till 2026, and in 2124, the reactor will be safe to dismantle.

Meanwhile, spent fuel rods will continue to be dispatched by train to Sellafield in Cumbria for reprocessing although Sellafield receives more than it can deal with. Nuclear waste, (which consists of technetium-99 with a half-life of 220,000 years, iodine-129 with a half-life of more than 15 million years, neptunium-237 with a half-life of 2 million years, and plutonium-239 with a half-life of 24,000 years) is usually stored at reactor sites, satisfactory deep geologic storage solutions for its disposal having yet to be found!

The coast path crossed Yr Wylfa's grounds but a security guard preoccupied with the rush of staff leaving the car park at the end of a shift, shooed us away. Eat your heart out Homer Simpson. By the year 2000 the British nuclear industry had made a loss of £37 million and the UK's Magnox power plants were being decommissioned at a cost of £12.6 billion. But the industry with evil beginnings, massive potential for accident and terrorist attack, and one heck of a toxic waste problem was ending. Like the chemical weapons manufacturers who'd post-war churned out polluting plastics, detergents and fertilisers instead, like the proliferation of military bases around the coast, nuclear power was another ugly legacy of the Second World War. Now we could embrace clean energy and the jobs that went with it. In. My. Dreams.

British Magnox reactors would be replaced by Advanced Gas-cooled reactors. Fuel would continue to be produced by Springfield in Preston, who supply more than 140 mainly light-water reactors in fifteen countries, all of which require uranium sourced from Canada, Australia, Kazakhstan, the US, South Africa, Namibia, Brazil, Niger or Russia. The International Atomic Energy Agency predict that there is enough high-grade uranium to supply the existing fleet for the next forty to fifty years, after which low-grade uranium mining will result in greater environmental devastation and greenhouse gas emissions. In 2017 it would be announced that Wylfa Newydd – an Advanced Boiling Water Reactor to be managed by the Japanese company Horizon Nuclear Power, would come online in the mid-2020s. I emailed Horizon. They told me that uranium would probably be freighted from its source (they weren't sure where that would be) through North America or North Europe to Preston to be converted into gas and enriched, then transported to Global Nuclear Fuel in North Carolina to be converted into ceramic pellets and made into fuel before being shipped to Wylfa Newydd. They ignored my question about how the waste would be stored. In 2019, Horizon would pull out.

We didn't know all this as we passed through, just enough to feel sick and impotent as we followed the cars full of nice people grateful for salaries so they could feed their kids and enjoy a Duff Beer at the end of the day. We left the road and sat in a field of stubble grazed by curious sheep, feeling angry. But Rob said it would be nice to stay in a bed and that's all the excuse we needed to forget about Yr Wylfa for a while.

We found a B&B right away at the edge of Cemaes. A bespectacled woman, Ellen, brandishing a trug and pruning saw, bustled to meet us. "I'm sorry about the state of me," she said. We were plastered in mud from the knees down. She chattered and polished all the way to our room before chivvying us straight back outside. "The table's a bit wobbly, I'll get Pat to look at it, sit here and he'll bring you the tray," she said. "You'll be wanting to use the cashpoint in the back of the shop but it's lottery night so there'll be queues and you'll have to go down the right-hand aisle." She paused as Pat arrived with tea and biscuits and said I had a nice smile. "It's his Irish descent," she explained. "He's off to Donegal next week, because his other name's Don. He'll be kissing the Blarney Stone and I'll have a bit of peace and quiet and be able to sort out the spare room." She poured the tea. "Look!" she said triumphantly, pointing: "The Isle of Man!" It looked like a pink sugar mouse on the horizon.

The steep harbour road reminded us of towns on the Elbe. We gobbled pie, chips and peas in The Stag next to a toddler eating beer mats, while a very small girl beat her Dad at pool, and then thrashed his mates.

Ellen brought scrambled eggs and said she was sorry we were stretched for time with Rob having to catch his bus. "You'll be pushing it," she warned, fetching an album to show us pictures of her family. Pat saw us off in his apron. "Before you go," he said "I have some things I'd like to tell you." We were late and fidgety but they were so kind. "The coast of Anglesey used to be joined to Japan," Pat was saying when Ellen interrupted. "You're holding them up now! Take care on the paths they're very slippy. Last year one of our guests, a Canadian woman slipped and fell over and broke her leg in the mud..." She followed us into the garden. "Her husband was with her but he didn't have a phone and had to go all the way down to the fishermen on the rocks. Well he was in a terrible state, he was white as a sheet. His wife had broken her leg and do you know who came to rescue her?" we waved goodbye. "Prince William!" shouted Ellen over the gate. "In a helicopter!"

Gulls soared all about and the rising sun cast the cliffs into shadow. They were craggy as sticks of rock sucked to lacerated points. Magpies flew into the light, iridescent blue in their plumage. We jogged along pausing for breath at a cluster of small wind turbines, some of the first in Cymru, which Rob had done monitoring for back in the early nineties. "I came up once a month to measure the wind," he said. "Once I got stuck in a bog." I laughed but was getting a stitch. Rhyd-y-Groes Wind Farm began operating in 1992, with the normal fuss. "We were trying to do something good and people treated us like we were doing something awful," Rob said quietly. It wasn't easy being green. The twenty-four turbines produced 7.2 MW of electricity, enough for 4,000 homes. In 2016 consent would be given to replace them with larger more efficient models with an output of 9.9 MW. With no toxic waste whatsoever.

I thought I glimpsed something big and black in the sea which perhaps had a white throat, but it rolled below the surface almost before I'd seen it, and we raced on, arriving in Amlwch with ten minutes to spare. I sat with the rucksacks while Rob shopped in Co-op. I watched him cross the road, checked shirt tucked into his muddy trousers, rangy and relaxed. He boarded the bus. I took my turn in Co-op and when I came out he had gone, leaving me bereft, our mad dash and laughter all vanished.

Amlwch looked shabby in the sunlight. People on the street had thin bleached hair, smokers' coughs and white faces. They spoke Cymraeg with a rich Ynys Môn accent I loved, or north-coast English with a Merseyside twang. I followed a woman in leopard-skin leggings, a Haribo bucket on each pushchair handle, passed kids screaming on a tyre-swing at the end of a pebbledash terrace, and picked up the path on a football pitch with sofas pulled under the goalposts.

A man was rolling pungent blue paint onto a boat, radio loud, in the harbour which two centuries ago, had been large enough to accommodate vessels collecting copper ore from the Mynydd Parys quarry inland. There'd been so many boats waiting, their hulls had become coated in copper discharged from the mine. The copper had repelled weed growth, creating a demand for copper plates. Toxic water still running from Mynydd Parys had been contained by a dam till it threatened to burst, and is now released straight into Môr Iwerddon where it is capable of damaging the kidneys, livers and nervous systems of most aquatic life.

A teenage couple whispered on a bench, families strolled up the hill and I left them all behind, save for a sweaty man with a day-pack, who hurried to catch me up. A big bowl of blue sky reached to the horizon in all directions and a gentle breeze stirred the heather. "I saw the weather this morning," he beamed "and just had to get out." He was proud of having driven from Manchester on a whim but I couldn't bring myself either to praise such an extravagant use of petrol or condemn it when he seemed so confident of my approval. There was an awkward pause before we parted. I wasn't usually so judgmental. I was twitchy because I no longer had a vehicle for dealing with environmental problems, beyond signing online petitions. Teaching about solutions had let me off the hook. It had been easy, teaching people looking for answers. They'd been receptive, grateful and keen. I wasn't sure I had the character to challenge the status quo uninvited, in cold blood. Out here, in the 'real world' as people called it, being an environmentalist (by which I mean someone striving to stop environmental collapse) was a problem. Environmentalism was encouraged at primary school, tolerated at secondary school, but then you'd better grow out of it or risk being ridiculed, patronised, challenged, or at best indulged for pursuing a kind of hobby. We environmentalists knew we were supposed to keep quiet in the real world. And I did – I don't like conflict.

Suddenly, on turning the top corner of Ynys Môn I was facing Mynyddoedd Eryri again, a pastel-brown tsunami of mountains. The change in direction brought a shift in the breeze and my mood. I felt tiny in these huge grasslands, exhilarated by sun, wind, and altitude. A dot became a German Shepherd loping towards and around me before returning to guard his spot above a couple of fishermen on rocks very far below. Wind combed the grasses and the coast stretched ahead in ochre folds. The fishermen had left footprints, but I felt as if no-one had ever been there. A buzzard flew across the sun casting an old familiar shadow on land which swooped and fell into the distance, yellow, green and brown, edged with wind-crippled hawthorns, and cows, just specks, grazing sea-hills ahead. I came upon them eventually – black short-horned cattle that hadn't seen me coming. One jumped so high with fright I saw a metre of sky beneath her hooves.

Eventually I turned onto a leafier lane where cars were parked on the verge outside a church, and I thought of my Dad and felt sad. He'd sung alto in a town church choir which had sometimes been invited to sing in small parish churches on sun-dappled evenings like this – lost, long-ago evenings now. I'd gone along sometimes, and been proud.

At Traeth Dulas the water was blue. As I stepped onto a footbridge a small mammal plopped into Afon Goch and I wanted it to be a water vole, but it was impossible. Water voles were sensitive, almost extinct, and Afon Goch, due to Mynydd Parys run-off, was one of the most acidic and metal-contaminated streams in the UK. Kids played in an old double-decker outside a pub on the far bank. I went in for tap water. So many families were eating Sunday roasts that I felt like a stranger at a party.

It was better to be alone on the green lane that took me back to the coast, where I felt again that the landscape was unpeopled, that no-one was there and no-one would come. I pitched near a lake in the grass. A half-moon was rising in lilac sky, bathing the sea in its light, while the sun blazed a trail like a commercial for throat-sweets. An hour after it had set, a strip of sky was still orange. Lights came on aboard an anchored tanker. A flock of ducks flew around the rain-lake and were joined by another that came in from the hills. They circled together, before landing.

At first light the ducks flew into a wet pink sky. A hare crossed the slope, and seeing me, crouched low and still lower into a divot. Moles had been busy. Sycamore leaves were still damp with night. Mushrooms had sprouted at the foot of a stile. An oak copse thinned to a clearing where a pink square of television light wobbled in a bungalow window. Pheasants spluttered and a stoat bounded from the nettles with a wren in its mouth, paused and seemed to dissolve into the background. An ethereal light bathed the wooded lane and the wind breathed an autumnal sigh.

There was a freshness to the sea, and I was alert to everything – mewling gulls and piping curlews, lurking ships on the horizon, the lone jogger on the beach who stopped to circle his arms, his song floating up to the clifftop. Rosehips rambling around the car park. Jackdaws scavenging at an overflowing bin. Although the heat had gone, bloated blackberries, pink campion, ragwort and honeysuckle clung onto summer. But it was over. A bird rattled a warning from within dying bracken. Someone had pinned a 'NO TO WINDFARMS' sign on a fence and someone else had crossed out 'NO' and written 'YES' with a thick black marker.

A man unlocking the lifeboat station flashed me a grin, proud of his work and the boat, with good reason. The rocks where cormorants were drying their wings offshore had wrecked The Royal Charter, drowning 450 passengers, in the Great Storm of 1859 – Moelfre's biggest, but not its only tragedy. On the day war was declared in September 1939, it was here that the wreck of submarine HMS Thetis was finally brought ashore after a three-month salvage operation to recover ninety-nine bodies. A diver also died of the bends. The submarine, its crew doubled by engineers and officers who wanted to see the technology, had sunk on its maiden voyage from Birkenhead.

Two men hammered on a roof. I was reading on a plaque that street lighting had been installed in remembrance of those who fell in the Second World War, when seeing me, a woman came to the door of the pub she was hoovering to offer me use of the toilets. She said there was a shop up the hill, so I went there for vending machine coffee. A girl was stacking the fridge with milk. "I like walking," she said, "but my boyfriend's at uni…" she broke off to slice ham for a customer and her sentence remained unfinished.

There was an end-of-season quiet to the weather. Car parks were empty and a tyre swung from a bare tree. Buddleia drooped, giving itself up to winter. At Benllech, I drank tea in a café overlooking the beach. A group of women on the next table were discussing scone recipes in Cymraeg, as far as I could work out – the last Cymraeg I would hear on my journey for a very long time. About which I minded. I'd not realised how fragile it was.

I liked the pause in weather, the grey respite. The tide was low enough to follow dog walkers around the headland to Traeth Goch among worm casts and gulls, where in 1947, Maurice Wilks, (who'd worked on gas-turbine aircraft in the war as Rover's chief engineer and then bought a farm) had drawn a Landrover in the sand for his brother Spencer, Rover's Managing Director. More than two million Land Rover Defenders would be made before production ceased in 2016 – and demand brought them back in 2020.

I lost most of the walkers to The Ship Inn at the end of the bay – I wanted to go with them, but was glad I couldn't afford to. Avoiding comfort made me alive, more observant. Suddenly a marsh harrier zoomed overhead, chocolate brown, her wings a valley. Just arrived – winter was coming. The ash trees were already bare, black buds on pewter-grey twigs. Urgent bird calls were tossed about by the wind and a skeleton leaf flapped in the grass. I digressed into woods finding autumn still ripe and riotous with coloured leaves and fungi, but just as quickly stepped back into wintry light. The cold sky was a dirty yellow. I was glad to be heading home.

I hurried past Llanddona, once known for the red-haired witches who'd been washed up with their husbands in the sixteenth century, in an oarless, rudderless boat. When I asked a friend from Llanddona about them, he'd shrugged. "Yes there was talk at school. If you had red hair, or an extra finger, they said you were a witch." I sped along and waited for my bus in Glanrafon where I saw and heard no-one, and an apple fell from a tree.

I returned for a single day, to complete my journey around Môn. I was only ever a bus ride or two from home, but it felt faraway. It felt like being on the road. Travelling was an attitude. In 2020, lockdown wouldn't bother me. I travelled at home. In Cymru every valley is different, and the people too. Here, they were silver-haired and rather genteel, clearing leaves and clipping hedges before winter set in.

A man crossed Traeth Penmon with a kayak, despite it being nearly November. A squall spattered the stones. Redpolls flew across the toll road from the scrub. The toll-booth attendant, talking Merseyside English into his phone, waved me into the abbey gardens where coins wobbled in Seiriol's well. The church (unlike the abbey) had survived the Reformation, so I went in, lit a candle for my Dad and listened to a blackbird outside. I sat so still in my effort to listen, in my attempt to be at one with sadness and joy and the moment, that the automatic light turned off and wouldn't come back on.

The coast was pale and wintry. Mynyddoedd Eryri reared up across gungrey Y Fenai, colossal clouds resting on the mountains like snow. Icy wind hurried me over the stony beach, where a lump of cliff had split asunder complete with rooted tree and murder of rooks. A man and puppy were approaching, the man's coat scarlet against the cold sky. The puppy tried to eat my boots. The man apologised and scooped it up.

There were disused quays on the beach and a puddled slipway at Llanfaes that had survived since the Second World War. I would discover it had been used for American Catalina flying boats which had been fitted with long-range fuel tanks and bomb-racks by 200 people on an estate behind the trees requisitioned from the Bulkeley family, whose manor was converted into offices, and whose grounds had sprouted workshops and hangars. The flying boats had escorted Merchant Navy convoys and bombed submarines. The level of decision-making and purpose that transformed Britain in the Second World War amazed me. That estates had been wrested from gentry! The climate crisis demanded equivalent radical action, which either our governments didn't yet understand or were too timid to address. They were afraid of causing offence, like the English in Cymru, or crashed about making things worse, also like the English in Cymru – or so it sometimes seemed in my apologetic state. I never imagined that a virus would trigger the next reforms. A mere rehearsal for climate chaos.

Learning about Cymru's history bolstered my inkling that the Second World War had contributed to a sense of Britishness that was to some people, more important than being English or Cymreig, muddying waters in which I sought clarity. I was also beginning to understand how we had arrived at such environmental catastrophe. The Second World War had fostered dependency on plastics, fertilisers, nuclear power, agricultural subsidies, and left a legacy of military bases. But it didn't explain everything – the copper pollution at Amlwch, for example. I had more to learn. I had to go back further still.

Biwmares Castle appeared, a bellicose monster, despite being unfinished. Hundreds of cars were parked outside and the pavement teemed with people paying homage to Edward I's colonisation, its grandeur particularly crass on this raw coast. I stayed on the beach instead, to eat my sandwiches by a ruined house with flapping tarps and gaping holes, on which someone had graffitied 'LET'S GET WRECKED ON CHEESE'.

The footpath turned inland to avoid large private properties, but the castle had irritated me so I stuck to the coast where my rebellion quickly turned to remorse as bladderwrack popped under my feet, and got worse when the bladderwrack gave to mussel beds. But the beach now was bristling with signs warning of burglar alarms and security cameras, so I floundered on till eventually thwarted by quicksand surrounding a private pier, I climbed into a garden, stalked with pounding heart between ornamental shrubs up a graceful drive, and escaped through wrought-iron gates, apprehended neither by dogs, alarms, nor posh people. But I felt like a groundling.

The pavement, ankle-deep in smashed orange leaves, acorns, hazelnuts and beech-mast led to Porthaethwy. I bought coffee in the Bulkeley Arms, where two elderly men, a Cymro in a jumper and an Irishman with combed hair and tweed jacket, had planted their elbows and pints on the table between them. My eyes adjusted to the dark. "A guinea apiece up in the windy night and I'm thinking back, you had to do it to get any salmon," the Irishman said. "I was oh, eighteen or nineteen then." "Salmon fishing," said the Cymro. "If I had a cine-camera, the things I've seen. We were slaying them, trapping them." "I tell you, take them to Barry's," said the Irishman. "They give you fifteen shilling and you wouldn't have to send them to Dublin."

"There was a cock pheasant there" the Irishman continued, after a pause. "They were lovely boids. He breeds 'em. He doesn't eat them now, 'cos you know he has about a hun'ert. I tell you now, on Tuesday morning, I was going for the papers in Tesco's. Coming back, I was going to the forest where the ducks are, and there were two cock pheasants on the grass. I tought they were lovely, sunbathing." "They were guarding the hens," said the Cymro. "This is how they were. They were fighting. Just kicking like that, just jumping up and down like that. Twenty minutes I was watching them. There were two or three learner drivers there in those driving-school cars. They had to stop three times or they'd have kilt 'em. So I tell you, it was sexual. They had sex there, somewhere close." There was a pause. "Well you see the goils now," said the Irishman. There was another pause, longer and prudish. But the silence was comfortable. The old men looked like an oil painting. They listened to each other, took turns to speak, paused between sentences. Outside the window, cars zipped back and forth, headlights on. A crowd of young men lounged at the bar, insulting each other and checking their phones.

My bus crossed Menai Bridge above the Belgian Promenade built in 1916 by refugees in gratitude for their accommodation. Two hundred and fourteen thousand Belgians had fled to Britain after the German invasion, and sixty-three had been welcomed to Porthaethwy by the Bishop of Bangor, The Royal Welsh Fusiliers, an enthusiastic crowd, the Belgian National Anthem and a guard of honour on the bridge. I would remember this in 2016, when Syrian refugees gave out roses on Aberystwyth seafront tied with notes saying 'Thank you for welcoming us' in Cymraeg and English, and in 2019, when Plaid Cymru would announce repeatedly that refugees were welcome in Cymru, which would make me very proud. I imagine a day when climate change refugees will be my neighbours. But this was 2012, and I still felt apologetic about migrating to Cymru myself. The bus slowed to a crawl and seemed to hold its breath as it passed between the parapets, an inch to spare on either side.

It was very cold in Bangor. I waited for my bus next to a rack of crisps in Subways. Two lads came in shouting. One bought a cup of tea and threw it in the gutter. The tea made an arc in the air. People with shopping trolleys waited for buses under sodium-orange lights. Skinny boys with baseball caps and puffer jackets smoked. Chubby long-haired girls in leggings chatted. Now and again a bus glided in and then out. An overweight man with shopping bags and florid face ran after one, dropping his phone without noticing. Quick as a flash one of the skinny boys grabbed it, pulled his cap down and collar up, and ran fast on big-soled trainers to return it just in time as the bus pulled away. How I loved all these people of Cymru.

DEPRESSION

At the outset of the First World War in which 40,000 Cymry were killed, Lloyd George was Chancellor of the Exchequer for the Liberal Party. He became Secretary of State for War, and by the war's end was Prime Minister. The Liberal Party had engineered huge social reforms, laid foundations for the welfare state and helped the church of Cymru gain independence from Canterbury. But fall-out from the war halted its momentum.

Lloyd George resigned in 1922 and the Conservative Party won the subsequent election. But the Labour Party was increasing in strength, particularly in mining constituencies where union membership gave a voice to beleaguered workers. Support for 'Home Rule' had declined with the Liberal Party, and Labour believed devolution would undermine the unity of the British working class. Plaid Cymru was founded in 1925 calling for an independent Cymru, but remained a fringe party till the 1960s.

Heavy industry and agriculture had been vital during the war, but had collapsed with the post-war economy. By 1925 Germany was exporting 'free coal' in reparation for war crimes, and an energy transition from coal to oil and then gas was underway. Coal prices crashed and strikes ensued. The slate industry collapsed when house-building slumped. The last lead mines closed, demand for steel declined and in 1929 the New York stock market crashed causing The Great Depression. By 1932 unemployment had risen to nearly 43 per cent in Cymru, and Cymru was one of the world's most depressed countries.

Following Lloyd George's taxation of the rich, the gentry, many of whom were English, declined in number and sold off surplus estates, many of which were in Cymru. Their tenants bought the land, often those whose families had farmed it for generations. Despite being cheap to buy the farms were expensive to run in a market flooded by cheap imports. Dairy cows, beef cattle, sheep, pigs and poultry all increased in number as milk and meat production required less labour than crops. Wool mills which had produced wartime uniforms, declined in the face of imported textiles. More herrings were landed at Aberdaugleddau in 1920 than in any other port in England or Cymru, but then the industry collapsed – an industrialised fishing fleet had reduced UK fish stocks by an average of 94 per cent over 118 years.

Five hundred thousand people left Cymru to seek work in England,

Australia, the US, and Canada, while others arrived. Caerdydd was a busy multicultural port. Italian cafés remained a popular alternative to pubs. But racist attacks continued and ship owners were accused of recruiting too many people from Arabic-speaking nations.

Immigration, emigration, English-language cinema and radio, and the continued reluctance to teach Cymraeg in schools (with numerous parents as a result, also unwilling to pass the language on), saw numbers of Cymraeg-speakers drop. Nevertheless language and culture were promoted by newly founded Urdd Gobaith Cymru (The Welsh League of Youth) and eisteddfo-dau. Male voice choirs were popular, and Cymraeg literature and poetry thrived. In 1936, three protestors (one of whom, Saunders Lewis, would be nominated for a Nobel Literature Prize) set fire to a shed at RAF Penrhos – a bombing school which had been imposed on Aber-erch despite great public protest. The protestors received prison sentences, and the bombing school was built anyway.

The landscape changed too. Car ownership increased between the wars and roads were improved. Airfields were built. The Forestry Commission was established in 1919 to produce timber. Land, homes and farms were subsequently bought or requisitioned, rhos (species-rich purple moor-grass pasture) was ploughed in, boggy moorland (habitat for lapwings, snipes, redshanks and curlews) was drained, and deciduous trees felled, to make way for millions of Sitka spruce. Bird populations fluctuated. The gentry's decline meant less persecution of raptors and mammals that predated on game. But pollution caused by mining and industry had stripped the rivers of fish.

Evolution of the political landscape interested me. I understood that Labour had become dominant in the twentieth century due to the beleaguered and consequently unionised industrial workers. But the Liberal Party had first planted the seeds of welfare reform. Seeds which flourished, unlike those the Liberal Party had scattered in hope of political independence. Many of them withered. But some lay dormant, to flower occasionally in subsequent decades, resulting in Devolution. Perhaps one day they will lead to full independence.

CONWY

Mantles of bilberry, heather, sheep's-fescue and blanket bog, conceal dark acid rocks. The mountains extend to the coast, where Y Gogarth is notable for its limestone pavement, and populations of grayling, brown argus, silver studded blue and belted beauty butterflies which depend on plants growing among the clints and grikes. Among the plants are spring cinquefoil, hoary rockrose, dark-red helleborine, three varieties of native whitebeam and wild cotoneaster, found nowhere else in Britain.

Holm oaks bent over the harbour wall, where yachts outnumbered fishing boats and a woman in national dress entreated visitors to enter 'Britain's Tiniest House.' I'd only seen the bleak marina, when I'd arrived on that day of heavy rain. Souvenirs were for sale on the quay – like Caernarfon, Conwy is a UNESCO World Heritage site on account of the walled town and castle Edward I had demolished a Cistercian Abbey to make way for. He'd also banished Cymry and settled Conwy with English merchants. But dragon flags fluttered in the turrets now, and money at least, was being won in independent shops on the medieval streets. Halfway across Afon Conwy, I turned back to see a boiling black cloud obscure Mynydd Conwy and creep towards the castle in ambush.

It crossed the river, and deluged Deganwy's pavement shelters and boats, and me, as I made for Y Gogarth. Cliffs soared above and fell away below the path, and over the bay Y Carneddau glowered like a bruise. A beam broke the cloud and swept the sea like a searchlight, narrowed to a pen and scribbled silver ink on the water then widened again, coming closer and larger till it caught me in its light. Rain slashed in streaming silver ribbons which brought unravelling cassette tapes to mind, then turned to hail that pelted my face. It was wild and lovely.

At the end of Y Gogarth the path joined Marine Drive and I was astonished by goats grazing the cliffs and wandering over the road. One shot me a malevolent look. They were Kashmir goats apparently, naturalised salty descendants of a flock Queen Victoria had given to Lord Mostyn who'd made a resort of Llandudno. A tourist pulled up his car, jumped out and photographed the goats. "You'd have to go to Greece to see that," he said, and sped off. Arabic-speaking families piled out of cars to snap each other in front of a crag, shrieking in delight at the wind, but there were more walkers and cyclists than toll-paying motorists, despite the weather.

Rob wasn't where we'd arranged to meet so I mooched down Llandudno Pier. Only one kiosk was open, selling sausage baps to no-one, gusts of tinny rock-and-roll whipped from its speakers. 'I am Zoltar, come with me to hear the rhythm of the ancients' boomed an automated fortune teller outside the amusement arcade, making me jump. Inside, machines for shoving in pennies or grabbing soft toys, Plants versus Zombies, Ice Balls, Angry Birds and Hello Kitty, whirred and flashed, clicked and clacked in a maelstrom of coin spills and jingles, but a middle-aged couple throwing balls into top hats were the only customers. 'I am the great gypsy, come and seek your fortune' said Zoltar as I left. At the end of the pier, two men were fishing off a new landing stage funded by Gwynt y Môr offshore windfarm so that The Waverley, the world's last sea-going paddle steamer, could dock once more in Llandudno.

I thought the First World War had happened overseas, I'd been naive. I'd not known there'd been submarines around the coast and that ships had been frequently mined. War had been omnipresent, even in Cymru. An airship towed to Llandudno Pier still airborne on April 26th 1918, must have been light relief for the gathering crowds (who were warned not to smoke). The Llangefni-based airship had been searching for a German submarine spotted near the Formby lightship when it suffered engine failure. An armed trawler picked up its mayday message and towed it to the end of the pier from where it was pulled ashore by a platoon of soldiers lodging in town. The pilot had been invited to rest at the Hydro Hotel, and allegedly lent a rather gaudy tie (for a man of his station) by the hotel manager.

The wind was bitter and the sky black, and there was still no sign of Rob by the Punch and Judy. Stormlight silver-plated the palm trees thrashing about on the traffic island like footage of Caribbean hurricanes. I called Rob from a phone box. He was running late but had booked us a room in the backpacker hostel so I checked in, aching from wind, and hugged the radiator. By the time he arrived I felt better. Lights were on now, in the seafront hotels and elderly people peered out of bay windows where glass and cutlery flashed. An elegant silver-haired couple smoked cigarettes on a lawn, their bodies bending like willows in the wind and diminishing light.

It was on the seafront here in 1915, that Lloyd George had been saluted by members of the North Wales Brigade of the Welsh Army Corps in a parade attended by thousands. Two years later, some of the soldiers were likely among those ordered to take Mametz Wood on the Somme, despite it being heavily defended by well-entrenched Germans. Over two days, 4,000 were killed or wounded. As Chancellor of the Exchequer Lloyd George was one of many authority figures who'd actively promoted military conscription. His popularity had waned when the war wasn't, as he and many others had claimed, over by Christmas, and when so very many were killed. After the war his Coalition Government collapsed following a scandal in which he was accused of selling honours. Womanising further tarnished his reputation. Yet Lloyd George had been a radical politician whose achievements in laying the foundations for a welfare state were substantial. He had introduced state pensions, the children's charter, National Health insurance, the vote for women, had protected tenants from exorbitant rent increases, improved employment insurance, introduced taxes on land and luxuries, and reduced the vetoing power of the House of Lords. Despite being for many, the man who won the war, he is not lionised in Cymru as Churchill is in England. I think it's because Cymru is small enough for its famous figures to be regarded as part of the family. I've encountered quiet shame regarding Lloyd George (a friend's great aunties once refused to serve him tea in the best china) but the pride I encounter is quiet too. There isn't much trumpet-blowing in Cymru. There is emotion and celebration — but that is different.

People bustled along under pavement shelters supported by decorous poles, a Christmas-card world of shop windows and sweets and hot chocolate and tinsel, of bright things glowing in a lustrous dark. But while we ate, the streets grew dark and became quiet, till on returning to the hostel, a crash of electric guitars drew us into The Cross Keys. We got enthusiastically drunk with a rock crowd, before sleeping squashed together in the top bunk.

A middle-aged French couple murmured over their cereal, but no-one else was up. We consumed so much watered-down orange juice, coffee, cornflakes and floppy white toast that our hangovers retreated under a pile of nasty plastic jam and butter containers.

On the seafront, juvenile herring gulls loitered in an empty paddling pool which I remembered — just one year earlier, I'd delivered a training day to teachers at a school up the road. At lunch, when searching for a pasty, I'd seen, for the first time, a council truck with 'Recycle More' on the side, which had depressed me for its brazen contradiction of my message. I had muttered away to myself. 'There's a reason why Recycle is at the bottom of that list *under*

Reduce and Reuse. But no, Reduce doesn't comply, does it, with the consumerist capitalist economy. It's not a desirable message for governments shored up by companies that want us to buy their stuff to promote. 'Recycle More' just means BUY MORE doesn't it? And by peddling this useless phrase you've created a society of nice people who think that buying endless new stuff made from finite resources and energy is FINE as long as we flipping RECYCLE it thereby using EVEN MORE ENERGY!' The teachers had understood. It seemed like a long time ago. It wasn't the well-intentioned council I'd been mad with, it was the capitalist economy that normalised conspicuous consumption. Recycling had become a mainstream idea in the 1970s yet was still being leapt on as if it was something new. I felt despair again, remembering. Because it allowed over-consumption to continue, recycling was one of few subjects that environmentalists were allowed, encouraged even, to promote. As if recycling would keep us quiet. As if recycling could solve climate change.

Light was bright on the sea. At Bae Penrhyn, windows shone and hedges were neatly clipped, though the estate was so quiet we softened our voices. Eventually we came across a man power-washing his drive, but he didn't look up.

Llandrillo-yn-Rhos was livelier, with boats and waves, and the sea pushing turnstones close to the prom. Italian immigrants had opened eateries across Cymru in the late nineteenth and early twentieth centuries, mostly in the industrial south, after a pioneer had sold ice cream in the Rhondda coalfields. The Fortes were latecomers when they opened a snack-shack here in 1956, which was now a busy restaurant packed with families, couples and bevies of girls. A chatter cloud engulfed us as we entered, and polite teenage staff in crisp black and white served us roast dinners and old-fashioned puddings at our table next to a cabinet full of strawberry tarts, meringues and chocolate éclairs, revolving on paper plates.

We were heading east along the north coast now, and the sun was dropping not over the sea we were used to, but behind shoulders of land. The sea heaved with a wave that didn't break but rolled along slapping the sea-wall with smatters of spray.

Decrepit public shelters harboured puddles and broken glass and Bae Colwyn's pier was boarded up and broken. Cormorants roosted at the end like graveside mourners. Piers had proliferated in the age of travelling Pierrots. The Victoria was built in 1900 with an opulent pavilion for nightly concerts and an audience of 2,500, which included steamship passengers from Liverpool. Piers had been elaborate landing stages rather than the curious carbuncles they seemed now. Wounded troops attended concerts here in the First World War. The Bijou Theatre was added in 1917. In 1922 the pavilion burned down and was rebuilt with council funding, but in 1933, the pavilion *and* Bijou Theatre were lost in separate fires. The pavilion was again rebuilt, this time to seat 750, with a grand dance floor and Art Deco lounge. But society changed. Pleasure steamers ceased to run. Victoria Pier's recent history involved discos, neglect and council corruption. The fretwork was twisted. Cormorants gave the last rites. It was boarded up, and even the boards were broken.

Along the seafront, men sat on tackle boxes fishing. One sat in his car, watching his rod. Two small boys were fishing too, and throwing stones and yelling at the sea, while the A55 rumbled behind a huge wall. But the seafront was wide enough for us to ignore the road. Concrete defences spilled along it for a mile like giant jack and five-stones, not unlike Japanese tsunami defences. Warnings of security guards and 'Unleashed Dogs' were fixed to miles of Heras fencing, while other signs promoted a watersports complex due to have opened six months previously of which there was no evidence. Everything was broken but its novelty to us made it thrilling. Road-stone hoppers were idle and small fairgrounds, where plastic bags of candyfloss swayed in the wind, had no customers. A ride attendant leaning against a booth, hands in pockets, stared out to sea from under his hood.

Behind us huge clouds piled up, and a rainbow shimmered over the offshore turbines of North Hoyle and Rhyl Flats, soon to be joined by Gwynt y Môr, one of the largest offshore wind farms in the world with 160 150m-high turbines producing 576 MW of electricity. The Crown Estate own the seabed, European companies largely own the turbines, but 400,000 Cymreig homes at least, will benefit from the electricity. Our knees throbbed from pounding the concrete.

Bryniau Clwyd, doused in orange water-light, marked the route south I'd take via Offa's Dyke Path after reaching Chester, and I felt excited at the sight of unknown hills, that would lead me to places equally unknown. The flat seafront was a conveyor belt, but no less intriguing – the density of Abergele's static caravans crammed behind security fences, and between housing estates, car parks, fields and rubble heaps, was a sight to behold.

The fairgrounds were mostly run by families who'd been travelling show-people for generations. They lived in caravans based loosely in large towns like Wrecsam, touring the coast in summer and towns in winter, following a tradition dating back to the Middle Ages when markets and fairs were granted by Royal Charter. Dragon flags flapped on Knightley's Famous Fun Park's twisters, top-spins and ghost trains, and rows of lights whizzed, but the season was over. A man brooded in the ticket booth. Two more flat-packed a ride into a lorry. And down on the hard grey beach, another two were boxing with fierce concentration.

The gathering dark, bitter wind, security fences, canned coin-spills and ghost-train woo-ha-has conjured up menace and thrill. We zoomed along as if we had a plan, wondering where we were and where we'd camp. At Kinmel Bay the concrete gave to dunes. In the First World War there'd been an army training ground here, and in 1919, when the war was over, 17,000 Canadian soldiers had awaited ships home in overcrowded bitterly cold conditions. Several ships had been cancelled or had taken US troops instead. Riots erupted on 4th March 1919. Allegedly, officers and sergeants' messes were broken into and shops looted due to profiteering shopkeepers. Twenty-three soldiers were injured, forty-one later court-martialled, and five were killed. They are buried in Bodelwyddan alongside eighty-five comrades who died of Spanish flu. Everyone knows now, that Spanish flu killed more people during the winter of 1918-1919 than the First World War had done. Learning about it pre-Covid, I was shocked. How quickly we forget.

Skinny kids and dads from the caravans, with shaved heads, black leather jackets and football shirts, walked staffies and bulldogs on the beach in the last of the light, striding quickly with hunched shoulders, grimacing at the icy wind. "Do you know where we are?" we asked one of the dads, causing him too, to look lost. He stared wildly about, before brightening. "There's Asda!" he said, pointing.

It was nearly dark. Rob thought we should walk into Y Rhyl and stay in a B&B, and I was delighted, being too skint for such good ideas. We paused to get the football scores on his phone. The sea had retreated and the sand was flat, scattered with razor shells. We roamed on it, delighting in the space and dark wind. The sodium-orange lights of Y Rhyl screamed ahead. Like disoriented turtles we headed towards them, but were turned off the beach by fences and signs saying 'DANGER GRIT BLASTING' where Afon Clwyd flows into the sea.

INDUSTRIALISATION

As the British Empire and its demand for resources expanded, Cymru became one of the first countries in the world to have most of its workforce employed in industry. The population of 587,000 in 1800 would increase to 2.5 million by 1921.

The iron industry, which had provided armaments for the Napoleonic Wars till they ended in 1815, became fundamental to the railway industry, while coal, (which had initially powered the iron industry) went on to fuel steam ships and trains. The biggest coalfield was in the south, but a smaller one lay in the north. Gwynedd slate quarries roofed industrial towns. Lead and silver mines boomed in Ceredigion, and there was a brief gold rush near Dolgellau in the late nineteenth century. The wool industry expanded in Y Drenewydd and Llanidloes and in Dyffryn Teifi, where labourers' clothing was made. Cornish tin powered the Llanelli tinplate industry which would collapse when the US introduced tariffs, and be replaced in the early twentieth century by a steel industry. South Cymru was particularly industrial with chemical, nickel, and tinplate works and coalmines served by busy docks. But the wooden shipbuilding industry declined with the switch from sail to steam.

Fishing was revolutionised by large steam-powered trawlers. Rural life changed rapidly too. As labourers left the land to seek a better living in mines and metalworks, agriculture struggled to feed a growing population and Britain became more dependent on imported food. Food prices had collapsed following the Napoleonic Wars. Corn Laws kept the price of grain artificially high, resulting in mill closures. Free trade gathered momentum and steam ships transported larger cargoes more quickly. American grain was imported in the 1870s. Ports boomed, but arable farms went bust, and droving dwindled when the railways started carrying livestock.

Acts of Enclosure (which had begun in the seventeenth century), often brought by landowners living in England, continued to result in woodland being felled, wetland being drained and common land being replaced by large sheep farms – and poor people continued to lose access to land on which they depended. New agricultural methods were adopted in fertile lowlying areas, particularly Sir Fynwy. Steam ploughs replaced horses, chemical fertilisers were introduced, and high-yield crops such as wheat replaced rye. Availability of manure increased with herd sizes and animals overwintered indoors. Goat farming declined after goats ate young trees in the first conifer plantations and because their hair was no longer wanted for rough wigs.

Urban industrial working conditions were particularly terrible, and the rapid population increase contributed to poverty, overcrowding, starvation and disease – tuberculosis was rife. There were multiple industrial accidents – such as at Senghenydd Colliery, where 439 men died in a gas explosion in 1913. But ordinary people attempting to address these horrors were hampered and oppressed by the elite. (And still are.)

Chartism, a movement for electoral and parliamentary reform, spread to Cymru from England. In Casnewydd in 1839, twenty-two Chartists were shot by police. The Rebecca Riots occurred in the 1830s in rural southwest Cymru, tollgates were destroyed and tithe payments to the Anglican Church protested against. Trade unions were founded in an attempt to address industrial grievances, and membership increased throughout the nineteenth century. In 1900, in one of the longest strikes in UK history, Bethesda slate quarrymen were locked out for being union members demanding better terms of employment. After three years troops were called in. Troops also shot protesting ironworkers and colliers at Tonypandy Colliery in 1910, and a year later shot two men dead in Llanelli when rail-workers and colliers joined strikes organised by Caerdydd dockers. Rights we take for granted today, were very hard won.

The industries were served by an improving transport network. Rivers were diverted and new ports constructed. Roads to Caergybi were built following the 1800 Act of Union which merged the parliaments of Ireland and Britain. Canals built to serve agriculture and industry were largely made redundant by the railway revolution.

Railways facilitated holidays for Cymry and English, first the rich and then the working class. Spa-towns evolved in Powys, and seaside resorts boomed. Darwinism, and the new study of geology, brought geologists to study Cymru's rocks and give Cymreig names – Cambrian, Ordovician and Silurian, to geological periods, while the work of Edward Lhuyd inspired botanists and naturalists. Communication improved and telegraph stations were built between Caergybi and Liverpool.

In 1832 property-owning middle-class men were allowed to vote, the landed gentry's power began to decline and the industrialists' to rise. Coal seams were sub-let to contractors, and agents who employed managers and engineers, leading to a growth in the middle-class. Some later capitalists were

English and Cymreig, liberals and nonconformists, who paid better wages than the earlier (usually English) industrialists. By 1884, 60 per cent of British men had the right to vote. The Liberal Party grew stronger and Tory MPs lost seats. By the end of the nineteenth century, industrialists were wealthy and powerful, and tenant farmers were beginning to buy farms once owned by the gentry.

By the latter half of the nineteenth century half the population lived in the industrial south where 30,000 Irish potato famine refugees had arrived, and tens of thousands of immigrants from England, Spain, China, Yemen, India, Somalia, Norway and the West Indies sought work. Tiger Bay in Caerdydd became multi-cultural. Italians opened cafés, Chinese sailors set up laundries, Jews sold goods throughout Cymru, English lead miners were recruited. But immigrants were not always welcomed. In 1911, with poor people in debt to Jewish shopkeepers, there were Anti-Jewish riots in the valleys, and Chinese sailors – outcompeting others by working for lower wages, were attacked. Immigration was matched by mass emigration and by the beginning of the twentieth century hundreds of thousands of slate, iron and tinplate-workers left to seek work in the US, Canada, England or Australia. In 1865 a Congregational Minister founded a Cymraeg-speaking nonconformist community in Patagonia.

Nonconformism dominated religion, and workplace prayers were common. Nonconformists (or dissenters) were protestant Christians such as Baptists, Independents and Methodists seeking separation from the Anglican Church with its tithes and English language. Nonconformism was more democratically organised, giving everyone, including women (who had a voice and leadership roles only achieved in the Anglican Church nearly 100 years later) the opportunity to debate religious, social and political issues. It was associated with Liberal politics, social ideals, education, democracy, Cymraeg, national identity and temperance. A flurry of chapel building accompanied religious revivals especially in the 1880s.

Many chapels ran their own schools and sustained Cymraeg-medium education, particularly in response to 'The Treachery of the Blue Books' – the 1847 British government report which attacked Cymreig morality and criticised the use of Cymraeg in schools. The report led to English-language schools being established where pupils caught speaking Cymraeg were forced to wear a piece of wood carved into the letters 'WN' (for 'Welsh Not') round their necks. The child wearing it at the end of the day was beaten. But in 1872,

Aberystwyth University College was founded, followed by universities in Caerdydd and Bangor – all funded by donations from thousands of Cymry.

Cymraeg was threatened by English-language education, immigration and emigration. The first language census in 1891 showed that nearly 55 percent of the population could speak Cymraeg fluently, after which numbers dropped, inspiring attempts to boost language and culture, particularly by Cymry in London. Modernised eisteddfodau were popular, and the first National Eisteddfod took place in Aberdâr in 1861. In 1907, the National Library of Wales was created in Aberystwyth, and the National Museum of Wales in Caerdydd. And in 1886, Cymru Fydd had been founded in support of Cymreig Home Rule.

The Conservative Party won the 1900 UK General Election, but in Cymru twenty-eight out of thirty-four seats were won by Liberals, with Scot Keir Hardie becoming the first Independent Labour Party MP, for Merthyr Tudful. The Conservative government was replaced by a Liberal one in 1905 followed by a Liberal landslide in 1906, which rid Cymru of Conservatives. Lloyd George for the Liberal Party became Chancellor of the Exchequer in 1908 and introduced The Coal Mines Regulation Act limiting miners' shifts to eight hours, the Old Age Pensions Act, the Children's Charter, and the National Insurance Act, and in 1911, the House of Commons passed a law that ended the rights of the House of Lords to block legislation. By 1912, six branches of the Independent Labour Party were active in the coalfields.

Industrial changes to landscape were profound. New habitats for insects, reptiles, and native and alien plants were created by chance on railway embankments, but unregulated industrialisation was terrible for biodiversity. Ecosystems were polluted. Rivers were stripped of fish. Ships accidentally imported alien species such as American cord-grass which was deliberately spread further by landowners wanting to increase coastal grazing, smothering plants such as glass-wort and sea-blite. Spoonbills and bitterns stopped breeding.

Stone walls and hedges crisscrossed the land as a result of enclosures, consolidating a grazing culture. By the end of the nineteenth century much mixed farming and droving had been replaced by sheep and cattle farming. Wildcats became extinct and blue stag beetles and goshawks disappeared as forests continued to be felled. Rhododendron escaped from large estates and began to compete with native vegetation. Merlins were captured for falconry. Predators of pheasant and other fashionable game were persecuted by keepers

— pine martens and hen harriers survived but only just. Great-crested grebes were hunted almost to extinction for their head plumes to decorate hats. Grey squirrels escaped from private estates where they'd been introduced as a novelty from America, and reds started declining due to pox. The first conifer plantations were developed in the 1890s on the Sychnant moorlands to provide timber. Meanwhile an epic decline in salmon stocks resulted in the use of traps such as putcher baskets being made illegal. Disease and over-exploitation also led to declines in other species, like oysters.

Habitat destruction has been happening for a long time. Small wonder that now, biodiversity loss is snowballing.

SIR DDINBYCH

*T*wo-thirds of the county is hill country, with snowfields on Mynyddoedd Berwynion
lasting longer than anywhere else in Cymru. Black grouse and red grouse breed
on the moors. Rare limestone woundwort grows near Rhuthun, a few freshwater pearl
mussels survive, and the rare black poplar grows in a layby on the Dinbych to Rhuthun
road. At Gronant the coastal dunes are home to natterjack toads, sand lizards, and the
only breeding little tern colony in Cymru.

Ground floors of semi-detached houses had been converted into Chinese
takeaways, funeral directors, unisex hair salons, and shops selling second-hand
domestic appliances. Pubs were boarded up. Police sirens wailed, traffic was
heavy. We asked a man hunched into his jacket if he knew where we could
find a B&B. "What, here?" he said, confused, but pointed out the Imperial
Hotel by the station. We'd assumed we were in the suburbs but this was Y Rhyl
town centre. The Imperial had no vacancies.

A tearoom stood out smartly in the grimy dark, with its shiny red paint.
But I recognised the name – I'd spent a summer working twelve-hour shifts
in a factory which supplied it, which, like other factories I'd worked in, had
taught me a lot about food waste. There'd been strawberry syrup floods. Ice-
cream catastrophes. Hoses, drains and industrial bins. My experience further
added credibility to reports claiming that we produce enough food to feed
everyone, were it not for inefficient manufacture, distribution and storage.
At the factory I was told by tannoy not to lean against a table for a few seconds
before the next avalanche of frozen cones hurtled down the conveyor belt
which I, stooped and contorted, packed into boxes for hours. At the factory
I had spent at least ten minutes of both half-hour breaks queuing to clock out,
scrub my hands, struggle out of and shortly after back into, overalls and
wellies. But at least I'd been allowed to banter with the cheerful men and
motherly women, unlike in one packing warehouse I'd worked at, where
talking had been forbidden. "Stop it!" the women at the factory had hissed
when I'd started stacking boxes. "That's men's work. We'll all have to do it if
they see you!" The factory was wonderful compared to degrading conditions
and poverty suffered by overseas labourers producing our high street brands.
We take our rights, so very hard won in the industrial age, for granted. Our
factories and smelters no longer belch smoke over Cymru and blacken its

rivers. We pollute foreign air and rivers now instead, whilst finding new ways to poison our own.

Y Rhyl crackled with energy. Its rotten police station was spiky with aerials, as we hurried past Argos, Phone Warehouse, Rhyl Language Centre, Domino's Pizza, William Hill, charity shops, pubs, KFC and Wilko, while Y Rhyl people zipped along in the cold, overweight and florid, or underweight and pale with dark rings beneath their eyes – women in heels, skinny jeans and bright lipstick and men in tracksuits, all speaking English in the rapid north-coast accent. A thirty-something man wearing shorts and thick coat buttoned batman style round his neck, cycled haphazardly down the road, while a companion on foot swigged from a 2-litre Coke bottle. "All you… All YOU… ex-army… YOU know they are LIARS…" he shouted. Litter blew round the streets. A crowd smoked outside Wetherspoon. Y Rhyl was exciting, but we were dead beat.

On the seafront, wind blew sand round an empty car park and arcade lights flickered. The black sea was crimped with white foam. We found a row of Victorian guest houses with names like Kensington and Westminster, and rang a bell at random. A tall quiet man answered the door, invited us into a boiled-brassica smelling hall, and showed us a chilly room where he plugged in the heater. It issued smells of burning dust. The bed was damp and lumpy with broken springs. We climbed in with a bag of groceries and squinted at Match of the Day flickering on an old portable TV, but couldn't keep awake.

From the bay window we saw blue sky and snow on Yr Wyddfa. "It's noice here, they dow a good breakfast," said the other guest (long-term, at a guess), a sixty-something man with a *Sunday Mirror* tucked under one arm and a basket of condiments dangling from a finger. He wore tight musty-smelling army fatigues and walked with a mince. "Oh the promenade used to be fun," he reminisced. "Yow should have been here in the oyties. The Sun Centre! And the caffs!" The memories made him sad. His eyes were rheumy. I said I remembered the Sun Centre.

In the eighteenth century, before Acts of Enclosure granted the construction of sea defences and drainage channels, Y Rhyl had been a fishing village. By the 1820s it had lodging houses and two hotels. By 1848 it was one of the first fourteen stations on the Chester to Caergybi Railway and had become a resort. Steamboat passengers crisscrossed between here and Liverpool and occasionally Biwmares, Porthaethwy and Bangor. Y Rhyl sprouted a pier and a lake, bathing machines and boarding houses, a church and nonconformist chapels, newsrooms, libraries, a billiard room and bowling green, for the miners, quarrymen, Lancashire factory workers and Liverpool dockers, arriving by charabanc, bus and train. Y Rhyl was as much a product of the Industrial Revolution as any manufacturing town.

The owner preparing our paperwork at the hall desk noticed us looking at pictures on the wall. "That's me" he said pointing to a black and white photograph of a man leading cattle through London. "I was a butcher in Earl's Hill." He pointed to an older, sepia photograph, of a man with a horse and cart. "That's my Dad" he said, "in Croydon." "What brought you here?" I asked. "Well," he said gently after a pause "it was just a place to come to." He seemed part of the building itself, quiet and dark and dignified.

We went back into town for groceries. It bristled with communications towers, gulls and second-hand furniture shops. A man unloaded a sofa. 'All your home elegance under one roof' said a sign above the rotting frame of a broken window. Despite not having been a nonconformist stronghold, Y Rhyl had acquired nineteen churches and chapels. They were boarded up or converted now – one was an Islamic Cultural Centre, another a pawnbrokers and internet café.

In August 2013, the Centre for Social Justice think tank reported that seven out of twenty towns in Britain with the biggest welfare dependency were seaside resorts – industrial-era towns which had grown when the railways arrived but died in the age of cheap flights. Y Rhyl and English towns like Margate and Clacton-on-Sea, were described as 'ghettos for the unemployed and benefits dependent'. With abundant empty holiday accommodation, rent was cheap and attracted transient tenants with low qualifications. Two-thirds of working age people in Y Rhyl were benefit-dependent. I knew people who were rude about Y Rhyl. It was almost fashionable, as if poverty was a joke.

Women with shopping bags and elderly men with hearing aids strolled about greeting each other, or trundled by on mobility-scooters. A bespectacled man in an anorak with a carrier bag round his wrist noticed me taking photographs. "It's be-yootiful isn't it?" he smiled revealing missing front teeth. "The architecture." He waved his walking stick at Queen's Market Hall. "It's bricks, all bricks. I know about bricks, I made them in Wrexham. You can see them all up the high street." He took us past Zoha Factory Seconds, McDonald's and Shoezone, and gestured to HSBC. "These cream ones are called buff. B U F F." "Where did they come from?" I asked. "Well the same place as the red ones", he said, surprised. "Anywhere there's a brickfield, different coloured clays, you know. From out of the ground. And this one..." he brandished his stick at a redbrick façade above WH Smiths where a row of anti-pigeon spikes unpeeled from the roof. "Be-yootiful," he said proudly. It was.

The palm trees were swaddled for winter. The arcades were closed, the flowerbeds bare, the paddling pools empty, the Sun Centre shabby — it would be demolished in 2016. Concrete was a bulwark against the capricious sea, but further development was banned due to risk of flooding. One day in the late nineteenth century, before the sea walls were built, a whale had been beached at the bottom of the high street. Now the sea was on its way back. I wished that the whales were too.

It was only four miles to Prestatyn, where Rob had a train to catch, it being Sunday. We hugged on the platform and little feathers squeezed out of his charity-shop jacket and into the air. The train arrived, he was gone and I felt lost. I didn't know what had happened to me. Much of my best travel had been on my own. Had meeting the man of my dreams made me less of a woman? I went back to the seafront and looked back at Y Rhyl. A white church tower pierced the crisp blue sky, complementing Yr Wyddfa's snowy peak.

NONCONFORMISTS

In 1707 the English and Scottish Parliaments combined to form Britain, by 1721 Britain had its first Prime Minister, and in 1746, Parliament stipulated that laws in England also applied to Cymru. The main parties were the Whigs and the Tories, formed by members of the gentry who had complete political control and bullied their constituents into voting for them, or bribed them with charitable donations and the funding of public projects.

Nascent industries in Cymru were usually run by English capitalists employing local workers. Ports and industrial towns expanded and ship-building boomed. By the latter half of the century, copper was mined at Mynydd Parys and copperworks established in the south and in Sir y Fflint. The slate industry began to prosper and lead and silver mines opened in the mid-west. Ironworks were established around Wrecsam and in the south, and coke furnaces introduced. Water still powered much of the industry, with water wheels a familiar landscape feature. Iron production expanded during the Seven Years War from 1756-1763 and the Napoleonic Wars of 1799-1815. But most industrial development was in the north-east – by the late eighteenth century Sir y Fflint had nineteen metalworks at Treffynnon, fourteen potteries at Bwcle, numerous lead and coal mines, and cotton mills at Treffynnon and Yr Wyddgrug.

Nevertheless, Cymru was still mostly rural, and miners and quarrymen still depended on the land, as their pay was low and irregular. Coastal farmers supplemented their income by fishing. Much food was exported by landlords for profit, but diet was bolstered by potatoes towards the end of the century, contributing to a population increase.

In the uplands, sheep- and cattle-rearing was dominant, but oats were also grown in the acidic soil. Farmers still took their flocks to the hills in the summer, to 'hafod' pastures where they lived in simple buildings and returned with them to lowlying pastures, 'hendre', in winter as they had for centuries. The lowland landscape was a mix of villages, small towns and manor estates owned by increasingly absent landowners who often fell into debt. Tenant farmers paid rent and grew corn, oats and barley, ground by wind and water mills. When the price of corn rose in the 1790s, arable farming increased, but was only well-established on the fertile soils of Sir Fynwy where clover and winter fodder such as turnips were introduced, resulting in a reduction of fallow land. Crop rotation was generally neglected and soils and yields were poor. Steer and bullocks were reared on Penrhyn Gŵyr and Sir Benfro, and dairy cattle on Dyffryn Tywi's lush pasture, but fresh meat wasn't generally available, though bacon sometimes was. Instead, horses, cattle (particularly Welsh Blacks), sheep and geese were walked by drovers to be fattened on English pastures and sold at large livestock markets such as Smithfield in London. By the end of the century, English breeds of cattle were introduced on the border but the growing demand for wool saw sheep displace them.

Wool continued to be a staple commodity. Y Bala specialised in knitted stockings and a wool industry developed in Sir Meirionnydd. Wool was spun at home, and woven in village weaving houses and fulling mills. Robust flannel was exported to clothe, among others, slaves in the West Indies and North America providing cottage producers with a more stable income than farming, and financial control of Cymru-made flannel shifted from Shrewsbury drapers to the Atlantic ports of Bristol and Liverpool. By the 1770s, Y Bermo was also exporting flannel, but even as late as the 1790s Shrewsbury drapers still employed 600 shearmen to raise nap on one side of the flannels purchased from the market at Y Trallwng every other Monday.

Gentry, clergy, and poor alike, were entertained by bullbaiting, cockfighting, drinking, dancing, gambling and football matches, and itinerant players and musicians. Men and women played harps, sang, or recited poetry at each other's homes to save fuel. Folk beliefs such as weather-lore, witchcraft, and tylwyth teg (fairies) co-existed with Christianity.

The Anglican Church was associated with the gentry and imposition of the English language, so church attendance was low unless enforced by landowners. Quakers were persecuted, resulting in the emigration of 2,000 families to Pennsylvania. Nonconformism, anticipated by a brief dalliance with Puritanism, evolved. By 1715 there were already some seventy nonconformist chapels in Cymru, mostly in the south. The Baptist community increased after the 1790s but was overtaken in popularity by Methodism which began within the Anglican Church. Energetic preachers proclaimed that Methodism was for everyone, and the first Sunday School in Cymru opened in Y Bala in 1789. Circulating Schools for Religious Salvation contributed to 75 per cent of the population being literate in Cymraeg by the end of the century.

About ninety percent of the population spoke Cymraeg, many people only spoke it, and as printing improved, Cymraeg publications increased. By the

end of the century English-language literature was also popular, but Cymry
in London influenced a cultural revival, among them Iolo Morganwg who
made eisteddfodau popular, adding fanciful touches like stone circles. From
the 1770s, artists and poets of the Romantic Movement inspired a trend for
tours of Cymru, particularly when the French Revolution and Napoleonic
Wars made European travel impossible.

Their visits were aided by more than 200 new roads financed by tolls,
(which would provoke the Rebecca Riots), resulting in an increase in horse-
drawn vehicles, while goods such as iron ore and wool were carried by pack
horse and ponies. By the 1790s canals were being built in the south. But most
communication across distance was still undertaken by watchmen on hills
using fires and flags.

Land enclosures by parliamentary act continued to change open ground
into enclosed areas. Three-quarters of Cymru, including coastal plateaus, bogs
and dunes, valley marshland, grazing land, hill and moorland had been
enclosed by 1800. A little was claimed by tenant farmers, cottagers, and squat-
ters including a few French prisoners of war, for grazing or building tai unnos
(houses that could be claimed if built in one day with smoke coming from the
chimney by night), but most was enclosed by the rich. By the end of the
century their enclosures were planned by surveyors, resulting in straight stone
walls running up mountains, unlike earlier smaller enclosures that followed
the lands' contours. Commoners lost their rights to growing, grazing, and
collecting turf for fuel. Riots ensued, poverty increased and poor weather and
harvests led to malnutrition and disease. Winter was particularly hard and
subsequently there appear to have been more ships deliberately wrecked in
winter months. Poaching was rife.

The division between rich and poor was huge. Some gentry were
descended from Anglo-Normans, others from Cymreig nobility. Some
improved their own wealth or prestige by entering office, commercial enterprises, smuggling or marriage. English nobles married into Cymreig estates.
Cymreig nobles became anglicised in London, neglecting properties, farms
and tenants. By the nineteenth century, twenty families owned at least 20,000
acres each. But an evolving group of industrialists, nonconformists, liberals,
doctors, lawyers, estate agents, government officials, craftsmen and freehold-
ers wished to challenge the political control of the gentry, and reform society.

The Napoleonic Wars left the coast bristling with forts built due to fear of
invasion by France. The British Admiralty had a base at Doc Benfro. In 1797

French troops landed in Abergwaun but were repelled. By this time the rising population, wartime inflation and poor harvests made worse by hoarding farmers and middlemen, had led to substantial poverty and an increase in corn riots. Many Cymry sought work in England. Poverty-induced emigration to the United States continued, and from 1788-1792, the first Cymry arrived in Australia. Meanwhile immigrants came to Cymru and were not always welcomed – English colliers were attacked in Sir Ddinbych.

The enclosures caused substantial habitat loss. Wetland and marsh disappeared as land was reclaimed and drained. Ancient oak woodlands were felled for shipbuilding and tanning. Some former forest species survived in spinneys, hedgerows, orchards, gardens, churchyards, and parks. Others hung on in the new mosaic of farms and scattered woodland but many woodland species, such as roe deer, specialist invertebrates, plants, and large-lobed lichens such as tree lungwort, remained only in undisturbed pockets. The gentry hunted for sport and employed gamekeepers to keep their estates free of predators such as wildcats, martens, polecats, stoats, weasels, buzzards and kites. Without predators, rabbits became a pest. Brown rats arrived by ship from Asia and black rats disappeared. Alien plants arrived accidentally in the ballast of ships.

Enclosures imposed by the rich are still visible – in the reclaimed land, the remarkably straight stone walls, the dominance of grazing, the deforested landscape. Those drystone walls I had thought so romantic, so Cymreig – I see them in a new light now.

SIR Y FFLINT

Aber Dyfrdwy where more than 130,000 birds including dunlin, knot, and snow bunting overwinter and Atlantic grey seals and harbour porpoise swim, was tidal as far as Chester before silting up. The county has relatively low rainfall, quick-draining limestone hills, and a multitude of ponds dug for mineral extraction, now populated by great crested newts.

Families spilled through the dunes, and photographed Y Parlwr Du lighthouse whose red and white tower inset with small windows, had been painted by Dulux for an advert a year previously. The paint was already flaking off, but age accounted for its tilt. Built in 1776 when Aber Dyfrdwy teemed with ships, it looked as if a paraffin flame might still wobble its glass, when estuary light is lost to the vagaries of night.

Ffynnongroyw had been a quiet place till a coal mine opened in the late nineteenth century and was quiet now, till I got to The Railway Inn. A wide-eyed woman flitted among the men watching football, passing pints. The barman dunked a teabag in a mug and forgot it, till I got his attention. The woman sat close and watched me drink as if she'd never seen tea. One of the men spiralled his finger in the air, smiled kindly, and shrugged.

The coast path continued down the A548, but I was fed up with traffic and wanted the sea. I stood on tiptoe to look over the concrete wall and was amazed that roosting below on the rocks despite the traffic's roar, were hundreds, thousands, of oystercatchers. Just here, incredible beauty, co-existing, surviving somehow, so close to our noise and fumes. I jumped up and down for more glimpses, but the wall was too slimy to climb.

By 1702, Lord Mostyn had built a colliery to fuel his lead mine and smelter which supplied East Ireland, when Mostyn was one of the best natural ports on the north coast. Now it was the only one still active. I tried to sneak through the security barriers but the guard turned me away and it wasn't long anyhow, before I was back on the estuary. It was vast and the tide was high. Fishermen perched on boulders sprayed with phone numbers and 'BAIT'. One fisherman wobbled towards me on a bicycle he steered with one hand whilst steadying a tackle-box with the other, his balance made even more perilous by swaying rods protruding at all angles like a crayfish.

I was anxious to find somewhere safe to camp but the coast was congested.

Finding camping spots never used to bother me much, and my anxiety seemed another indication of how my relationship with Rob had changed me – as if I was taking care of the two of us rather than just myself. Something large and extraordinary loomed ahead, its shape distorted by twilight. Eventually I saw it was a ship pulled right up the bank. Rust leached into huge murals sprayed on its flanks – a man in hard-hat and balaclava, three wise monkeys in dinner jackets. Two security guards patrolled behind a weed-choked fence, and fairy lights on top deck made pin-pricks of light that swayed in the breeze like strange rigging. The ship was curious and wonderful, but now it was dark.

I was saved by The Old Tavern, across the A548. A shanty-shop had been built against it, brightly lit by fluorescent tubes. The only things for sale were sacks of compost, boxes of eggs, and a fridge full of coke. The shop triggered half-memories of Zimbabwe and Russia, and I felt the thrill of the road. "I've done some camping in my time," said the woman behind the counter in a Yorkshire accent, and led me behind the pub where I put up my tent. After a moment or two she returned, made me take it down on account of the cold, and showed me to a touring caravan instead, moving horse saddles off the bunk to make room. The grass was already freezing.

The Old Tavern was huge, full of draughts. I found the bar between a dark ghostly dining room and an empty canteen with salt and pepper pots on plastic gingham cloths. A small huddle of men nodded and looked away except for the landlord, Mark, who got up to introduce himself. He seemed embarrassed, as if not used to strangers. I settled in with my book and a large glass of wine, and looked up now and again at the football, but had begun to lose sense of where I was in time and space. It felt more like Croatia than Cymru, with the stove crackling and the men half-watching, shy and courteous in an old-fashioned way. This was solo travelling as I remembered it, exciting and strange, a thin line between being anonymous and part of it all. The barwoman cooked me pie, chips and gravy, and then came over to quiz me.

"Where are you walking to?" she said. "Chester," I replied and the men grunted. "We had some people from Connah's Quay once," she remembered, "a father and son, but they were on bikes. No-one's ever walked here from Chester." She said the men were worried about me and asked if I was married. "I will be in March," I said and heard mutters. "What does your fiancé think of you out on your own?" she said, scandalised, "aren't you scared?" But on discovering I was from Shrewsbury she wobbled. "You'll have heard of my

nephew then," she said quietly. "Steve Jones. Soldier. Killed in Iraq." I thought
of my little nephews. Tragedy hovered above us. "I wouldn't do what you're
doing," she said. "I'd carry a gun."

At ten o'clock I closed my book and Mark stood up shyly. "We'd like you
to sleep in here, you can put your head down on the sofa," he said. They were
so kind. But having already moved everything once I declined and was very
warm under the horse blankets.

Frost crusted the grass, the ship blushed rosy with dawn, and birds on the
sandflats were beginning to squabble. The orange sky was etched with
telegraph wires like music staves. The frosted cattle pasture had been marsh
intersected with tidal rills before eighteenth-century embankments were
built.

A lad in a beanie hunkered on the rocks with a tripod and two collies, one
barking hysterically. I asked if I'd be ruining his photography and he said no it
didn't matter then added quickly "I've been waiting ages for a day like this",
so I stopped and we watched the red sun break clear of the horizon, while
the mad dog attacked the placid one. "She's a rescue dog," said the photogra-
pher, worriedly. Her barks were disturbing. I asked about the ship. "It was
supposed to be a disco boat," he said "but the council stopped it because you
can't get ambulances under the bridge. They just use it for market storage,
it's a right balls-up". The rescue dog tried to bite me, so we agreed the photograph was probably done.

Light scoured the sandflats but mist dissolved Cei Connah's towers and
chimneys. The Wirral glistened. The sky was large and the water sucked up
its light and shone it back. Water-birds guzzled the estuary soup, while
roaming finches fed on the wasteland teasels, thistles and fireweed. Sir y
Fflint's eighteenth-century industry haunted the twenty-first-century
recycling depots, auto-parts and repair set-ups, warehouses, cranes and
noise it had birthed – uncomplained about probably, by a community in
want of work.

Maes-glas once had a copper-works and wharf where forty ships traded
raw materials and finished goods. Ferries ran to Chester and Liverpool, till
being scuppered by silt. Now it was a muddy creek with moored wooden
flats used for gathering shrimp and cockles. Bright light hurt my eyes. A goose
flew west. The wasteland sparkled, still frosty in shadow, but leaky brown in
the sun. A tannoy crackled over a car park. "Would Kerry please come to

reception… would Kerry come to reception please." A seed-head lay on the path in precision iced geometry.

Water gushed from Milwr Tunnel, built to drain the Treffynon and Mynydd Helygain lead mines, while at Bettisfield and Bagillt, the Gadlys mine had been opened in 1704 by London Quakers Edward Wright and Associates, to smelt lead with sea coal and pit coal. The fishing quays had duly expanded to handle lead, copper, zinc, chemicals, and grain, but this port had silted up too. One or two industrious-looking fishing boats were moored at the mouth of a wide inlet. A car spares depot stood on the bank. I climbed the hillock and sat on a stone slab to boil tea. Whole cities, bridges and chimneys, were lost in a steamy horizon. Dog walkers greeted each other but seemed put out to see me. I liked it on the rock, in the sun, so I cooked pasta too. The flame flared fast and bright. "Nobody knows about this place," said an elderly man suspiciously. "But it's on the Wales Coast Path," I said and he relaxed, impressed to hear his patch was part of something bigger. "But you won't make it to Chester," said his wife. "It was on the news this morning. They've found body parts in the river," and I flinched.

The day had become very warm. In the dancing shade of a birch copse I was overtaken by a sprightly old couple with rucksacks. "Where are you walking to?" I asked, impressed. "Sainsbury's," they said, "we always come this way, through the trees." Y Fflint Castle rose from a pool-table lawn, stripped bare of other flora as most civic grass unfathomably is, in a completely unnecessary assault on biodiversity. November fifth, and council workers were building a bonfire from pallets in the moat. The battered castle was a skull with blackened sockets, the first built by Edward I in his subjugation of Cymru. Nothing remained of the town walls, but the town — the most symmetrical planned settlement of medieval Britain, survived, despite declining so much in the sixteenth century that it had no alehouse. It expanded again with the export of coal and lead.

The old Town Hall was a Ladbrokes. Blocks of flats like shoeboxes, peeped over the main street. A man stood outside Bargain Booze, and a lad dressed in black with wild hair swayed on the traffic island where he'd been shipwrecked, halfway between Subway and Tesco Express. A girl talked into her mobile outside the Polish grocers, traffic thundered, and a man on a bench raised a hand to cup his lighter.

Above the net curtains, 'Café Ritz' flashed an invitation and a wiry-haired woman stirring her tea, shot me a grin as I entered. Two women joined my table, the younger in a hoody, speaking quickly and monotonously. "I'd have got a screwdriver to it," she said. "Where did you get the paint from?" asked her companion. "£12.99 that paint cost me. All the sheets... and the carpet. I just stood there thinking 'what can I do'. I got a tea towel and scooped it all up with a mop." "What would have happened if you'd gone after them? Would the landlord have gone in like?" The young woman didn't answer. I heard change being counted and eggs being whisked. A group of labourers came in, one slamming the door in the face of the one behind, another with freshly-washed hair that floated about his head. "Shot like a pig I was," he said. "I'd been bending down all day, picking up litter." The wiry-haired woman waved as I left.

Paper, artificial silk and flannel were all made in Y Fflint but the dominant industries were lead and coal – Mynydd Helygain lead was smelted here even before the Romans arrived. By the seventeenth century, gunpowder had revolutionised the industry and by the eighteenth century, imported lead was smelted too. But as woodland disappeared, charcoal for smelting became scarce, and the coal that replaced it caused sulphurous emissions and acidic rain that destroyed crops. In 1728 following poor harvests, the London investors, many of them Quakers, shipped in corn, oats, barley and wheat for the miners. Extra men were recruited from Derbyshire (which had similar minerals and geology), but by mid-eighteenth century the accessible mines were exhausted, the deeper ones had drainage problems and returns were diminishing. A tax on lead, imposed when Afon Dyfrdwy was canalised, increased financial problems, and though light Chester cheese ships required heavy lead ballast, the industry struggled. By the nineteenth century, surviving lead mines were worked by national or international companies and Cornish miners were recruited for their experience in steam-powered pumps and crushers, inciting local resentment. Associated industries such as zinc, silver, calamine, lead-oxides, glassworks and soap-works sprang up, but after reaching a peak in the mid-nineteenth century, the lead industry all but ended.

Conditions in the coalmines on which the smelters and potteries depended were even worse. Children worked twelve-hour shifts operating ventilation doors or pumps. Colliers were crushed by rock falls, choked by firedamp or killed by explosions. Davy Lamps improved safety but miners had to pay for them – as well as a weekly fee to the pit doctor. Y Fflint colliers rioted when miners arrived from Brymbo and Northumbria. Colliers earned even less than the lead miners and worked twelve- rather than ten-hour shifts, a boast used to attract English investors. They lived in dirty, overcrowded, badly ventilated homes with straw beds and earth floors and survived on potatoes, oatmeal and milk. After 1825, coalfields with higher-grade coal in south Cymru expanded and the north-east coal trade slumped. Leaving an impoverished workforce even more destitute.

A couple with pale skin, thin hair and paunches hanging out of sloppy track-suits, stopped in front of me to check a lottery scratch card. Was it fanciful to say they were poor through being descendants of people Britain had forced to work in harrowing conditions to power its brutal colonial expansion? No. Colonialism had a lot to answer for. When I looked back from the castle, the tower blocks were bright in the sun. A slim woman jogged past in a fuchsia-pink tracksuit and matching lipstick. Dog walkers sped back and forth, as the sound of drills and traffic and the smell of old pizza, floated from Y Fflint on the breeze. The estuary glimmered. Starlings fluttered like gnats. The creeks had red banks, and smoke in the distance was silver.

At Oakenholt the path crossed the railway and ran along the A548 and I entered a noisy domain where the dual-carriageway din was immense, and dominated by a monster – E-ON's 1420 MW combined-cycle gas turbine, processing gas from fields in Liverpool Bay. The gas came in by Y Parlwr Du pipeline, built on the site of a coal-fired power station. Gas too, will one day be phased out. Meanwhile it is piped to the power station at Cei Connah where I eventually arrived, via the B5129.

My legs throbbed and my head ached from traffic, but still the coast path ran on hard ground beneath an arabesque of power-lines, past students loiter-ing outside college, till suddenly, it ducked between Capricorn Car Sales and Goftyn Church, and returned me to Aber Dyfrdwy, which was narrower now, more river than estuary. The Irish Coal Company had developed a port here, which had transformed Goftyn hamlet into the shipbuilding town of Cei Connah – allegedly named after an Irishman who'd owned The Old Quay House, currently closed for refurbishment – the incumbent landlord having recently appeared in court for attacking someone outside a kebab shop.

But Yvonne's Diner, operating from a portacabin, was open. A lad in a Liverpool cap looked up from his butty and grinned. A woman crushed a pile of cardboard boxes, another cleaned the hopper. Another, older, presumably Yvonne, squirted mayonnaise into a roll to which she added a slice of packet ham, sat down and opened a bag of crisps, before reading the *Daily Post* and then the *Daily Mail*. Grubby men bought Styrofoam take-outs, and I felt excited, remembering former colleagues. Part of me wanted to ask for a job.

I hated the continued exploitation of people and landscape by the rich and powerful who shielded themselves from, and denied their role in, the subsequent poverty and pollution. Nevertheless there was energy in the landscape and these dignified people who looked me in the eye because I was a stranger, instead of away because it was rude to stare. Nearing the border on this tough north coast, so different to the rural west, I had begun to think of people in terms of wealthy or working class, rather than English and Cymreig.

Afon Dyfrdwy was tidal all the way to Chester. Egrets perched on the banks. Boats were stacked with crates and buoys, a plastic box of rope and bits of canvas was lashed to a bike, two council trucks had pulled alongside so the drivers could chat over sandwiches, and two more men were fishing. "What are you catching?" I asked. "Nothing yet," said one. "Crabs probably," said the other "there's loads out there." "I got a heavy weight on the line but she's pulled right up. She's coming in fast," said the first.

To combat silt, 2,000 acres of Saltney Marsh had been reclaimed and the river canalised in the eighteenth century, but silt had won, and Liverpool became a bigger port than Chester. Now cows grazed the reclaimed land and more goldfinches than I'd ever seen flitted beneath the pylons. Fishermen lined the bank, a roller-skating woman chatted in Polish to a little girl furiously pedalling a training bike, and used cars were for sale where once ships had been built to navigate the Amazon and Nile.

I crossed Afon Dyfrdwy at Queensferry. Canalisation had straightened it. Black-headed gulls patrolled it. Poplar, sycamore or hawthorn boundaries divided stubble fields on one bank, while on the other, mechanical screeches reverberated from Airbus, where wings for the largest passenger jet in the world were shipped down Afon Dyfrdwy en route to Toulouse for assembly.

It was hot as summer. An old man with a black woolly hat was pushing his bike towards me, with a saw strapped to the back and the basket loaded with firewood. He looked like a Van Gogh drawing. I said hello, wasn't the weather lovely, and he said cheerfully, "I didn't know that" and tapped his hearing aid. The afternoon was gold and white, the river a lake of light. A flock of lapwings took off from a field, sun bright on their black and white plumage. Then a plane rose from Penarlâg, huge and silent like a surfacing river dolphin.

Eventually I came to a policeman eating a bag of crisps in a car. The river path was closed with blue and white tape. I turned up Ferry Road into Chester (Caer in Cymraeg) and entered England where gas pipes were being dug up in the road. From here, I would head south – down the border.

CIVIL WAR

James I succeeded Elizabeth I to the throne in 1603 and continued with her Irish 'plantations', settling Protestants from England, Scotland and Cymru into land confiscated from Irish Catholic inhabitants of Ulster. At this time, more Cymry lived in London than in any town in Cymru, the four largest of which were Wrecsam, Caerfyrddin, Aberhonddu and Hwlffordd with populations of 2,000 each.

The gentry formed five per cent of a population of 380,000. They began to develop estates using Acts of Enclosure, particularly in the south where they drained and reclaimed land, and poor people became tenants on land they'd thought of as theirs. There was a middleclass of craftsmen, shopkeepers and yeomen (people who held at least 80 acres), but half the population were in poverty that worsened over the century, as population increase outstripped economic growth. A storm surge in 1607 swept up Môr Hafren killing 2,000 people, demolishing villages and flooding 200 miles of reclaimed land. Famine struck from 1620-1623.

Coal was mined on the north and south coasts for blacksmiths, furnaces and the gentry, and some for export to Ireland and France. Copper, gold, zinc and silver were extracted, and smelted with charcoal from the forests. A lead and copper industry was established in Castell-nedd and Abertawe, and a few lead and silver mines opened in Ceredigion and Sir y Fflint. Iron was forged in Morgannwg and slate quarried in Caernarfon for local markets and export to Ireland. The mid-Cymru wool industry continued to be controlled by the Shrewsbury Drapers Company, where rough woollen flannel was sent to be finished. Towards the end of the century, flannel was exported to clothe slaves in the West Indies and North America.

Waterways were used more than roads for transport and for travel, and the coast was a busy interface. Pirates (numerous since at least the tenth century) such as Barti Ddu and Harri Morgan (one of Rob's ancestors according to an uncle), plundered the Caribbean seas.

In 1625 Charles I succeeded James I. In 1641, the Irish revolted against the settlers. Meanwhile the English Civil War was fought across Britain from 1642-1649 between Parliamentarians (Roundheads), who wanted the king's power to be limited, and the Royalists (Cavaliers) who didn't. Nonconformists, who'd been persecuted by Charles, supported Parliament. So did some influential figures like Thomas Myddelton, a Puritan MP for Sir Ddynbich. Charles, head of the Anglican Church, was supported by Anglicans, Catholics, the gentry and their bullied peasant tenants, and people to whom Charles had sold trading rights for goods like salt or soap. At first Cymru was largely Royalist.

From headquarters in Shrewsbury, Charles recruited support in north Cymru. His officers were English nobles but many of his foot soldiers were Cymry, and they died in battle at Edgehill, Tewkesbury, and Hereford. Parliament won Hwlffordd, Dinbych-y-pysgod, Caeriw, Caerfyrddin and Caerdydd, but Royalists won them back. Parliamentarians captured Wrecsam, Y Trallwng and Y Drenewydd. In the Battle of Trefaldwyn they killed 1,500 Royalists, putting most of Cymru under Parliamentary control. Parliamentarians captured Rhaglan, Rhuthun, Y Waun, Caernarfon, Biwmares, Rhuddlan, Y Fflint and Harlech. The Royalist army surrendered in 1646, and Charles fled to Scotland, where he was captured by Scottish Parliamentarians.

Parliament planned to disband the army but still owed wages to soldiers, and the public, worried about tax increases, became unsettled. A rebellion began in Penfro with some Parliamentarians defecting to Royalists, which Parliament sent Oliver Cromwell to quell – and the rebels surrendered. But Parliamentarians were divided as to what to do with Charles I – execute him or just limit his power. Eventually moderates were expelled and Charles I was executed in 1649. Cromwell ordered castles to be slighted so they could not be used in battle again.

Oliver Cromwell became head of the Commonwealth which replaced the monarchy, and Puritan head of the Protestant Church. Many Royalists emigrated to Canada, Ireland, Virginia and Barbados. In the 1650s thousands of Cromwell's protectorate troops settled in Ireland, creating large areas with a British Protestant identity. After his death in 1658 an uprising took place in Cheshire and North Cymru in favour of restoring the monarchy, and Protestant Charles II was proclaimed King at Wrecsam in 1660.

Nonconformism had evolved under Puritan Cromwell, and the first nonconformist chapel was built by Congregationalists in Sir Fynwy in 1639. In England in 1652, George Fox, believing it was possible to experience Christ without the intervention of the clergy, had founded the Quaker movement, which spread quickly in Cymru. But when the monarchy was restored, Quakers, Catholics and nonconformists were all persecuted. More than 3,000 Cymreig Quakers were jailed from 1650 to 1689. Thousands more, particularly from Sir Feirionnydd, Sir Drefaldwyn and Sir Benfro, emigrated to Pennsylvania, while Baptists fled to other parts of the United States.

Charles II was succeeded at his death by Catholic James II, and in what became known as the Glorious Revolution in 1688, William of Orange, a Dutch Protestant, was invited to replace him. James fled to France. William of Orange, (William III), ruled with his wife Mary II. In 1689 he granted religious freedom to Baptists and Independents but not to Quakers, Catholics, and non-Trinitarians who refused to swear allegiance to the Church of England due to the king's authority over it.

An increase in chapel building, literacy and availability of religious books followed. Cromwell had created schools in Cymru but pupils were taught in English. New schools developed alongside Baptist and Independent congregations, and the Welsh Trust was founded to tackle illiteracy. Their work was continued by the Society for the Promotion of Christian Knowledge which taught over 250,000 people to read and write using William Morgan's Bible in Cymraeg. Meanwhile culture was nurtured by two crown-endorsed local eisteddfodau, but the practise of employing professional bards died out.

The climate was mild. Before the Acts of Enclosure, farmers had kept cattle and goats in the uplands and grown cereals, root crops and hay, sometimes on hilltops. Hendre and hafod farming, and droving continued. Sheep were kept for their wool. Animals were killed in autumn so as not to require feeding in winter, and their meat salted. Pigeons provided fresh meat. Herring shoals were two miles wide and four miles long during spawning season, and the catch was exported to Bristol, Ireland, Chester and Liverpool, with Nefyn the herring capital. Eagles were reported on Yr Wyddfa. Spoonbills and bitterns bred, grey whales swam in the sea. Nevertheless, habitat loss and hunting continued, and wild boar probably disappeared during this time.

BORDER

*T*he concepts of England and Cymru were only just emerging in the eighth century when Offa ruled Mercia. Germanic-speaking peoples had been gradually settling in Britain since even before the Romans' departure and by 650 most of future England was under their control, and their Saxon ways and language absorbed. But Cymru was still fiercely defended by speakers of Celtic languages.

Battles between Anglo-Saxon Mercia and Cymreig dynasties were rife when Offa commissioned his dyke, apparently to demarcate the border. It was aggressively sited, with surveillance over Cymru, from which he snaffled the fertile plains of Môr Hafren and Aber Dyfrdwy. Offa's Dyke was the biggest engineering project in Europe at the time of its construction, consisting of an earth bank, probably stone-capped, with a ditch on the west and sometimes the east as well. Built partly due to supposed threat and perhaps partly to impress his contemporaries, (particularly the Franks who were similarly defining borders in Europe) it was possibly patrolled, with trade and transit controlled.

The modern administrative border still largely follows the geography of the north to south hills and doesn't wildly differ from the route of Offa's Dyke, though the north end of the border is just west of Chester on Aber Dyfrdwy, and the north end of the dyke seems to have been nearer Prestatyn. English border towns' pre-Saxon names are still used in Cymraeg, while several places on the English side of the border, never acquired a Saxon (English) name at all.

Remnants of the dyke are still visible more or less, for eighty-one miles. The long-distance trail – Offa's Dyke Path, runs along most of its length between Prestatyn and Cas-gwent, crisscrossing the border multiple times.

Sir y Fflint and Sir Ddinbych flashed by the train, grainy, like under-exposed film. Shadowy figures stood round a fire, horses drank from a flooded field, cars pulled up at a burger van, wind turbines turned over the sea. Oyster-catchers roosted on saltmarsh, and dark clouds with a purple patina hung over Bryniau Clwyd.

From the top of the first hill I heard a vehicle reversing down in Prestatyn. Already it was strange to be walking away from the coast. The air smelt rich and earthy and crackled with cackling jays. Bryony berries and travellers' joy crept over gorse, and damp harebells lingered. Eventually the sea was out of sight and suddenly there was less light.

I walked between fields that were ploughed, planted with beet, or grazed by horses and llamas. There were views of the sea again but it seemed far away. The air was damp, not brisk and salty, full of rain-threat and mildew. Apart from the distant drone of the A55 it was quiet. Winter was still waiting, a full month since I'd smelt it in Trearddur. Skeletal trees etched Dyffryn Clwyd, in which, three miles west, was the village-sized city of Llanelwy, with the smallest cathedral in England and Cymru, whose windows had been destroyed by Cromwell's soldiers during the Civil War. Their horses had drunk from the font. But it was better known for being where William Morgan – whose translation of the Bible had been fundamental in helping Cymraeg to flourish when under threat – had been Bishop. His work was quiet, passive. Nobody died, as far as I know, in the process. But his powerful literacy legacy still shines brightly. They do say the pen is mightier than the sword.

I startled ducks from a ditch, sent pheasants into a panic, and was accompanied for a while by a band of long-tailed tits. But the only people I met on these leaf-softened lanes where crushed crab apples were silent testament to traffic, were two ancient sparrow-like women, driving very slowly, who paused to look at the view then collapsed into giggles on seeing me. I loved that it was quiet, but maybe it was too quiet. As if we, in our urban habits, had forgotten the land. Bryniau Clwyd stretched ahead, red and lovely with breaking bracken.

I arrived in Bodfari too early to meet Sarah, who like Gerald, I'd met on the writing course and with whom I'd be staying two nights. I waited in the church, where twins were repairing the organ. "You're lucky we're here," said one, "it wouldn't normally be open. There's a list somewhere of open churches in the parish, always something interesting to see. All those rich dead people in the walls," he made a flourishing gesture. They said they had to take the back off. I sat in a pew for a while, till a loud bang and flash was followed by stunned silence, then "SHIT!" shouted in unison.

In the morning, Sarah and Charlie returned me to Bodfari. Collies ran alongside me on the other side of the fence, swirling in circles with flowing tails and not a single bark between them, then melted away. My path ahead was a strip of grass rising through the mist as if to another dimension.

The eleven hills of Bryniau Clwyd extend for twenty miles up Dyffryn Clwyd. After the glaciers' retreat, they had been colonised by trees which pollen samples indicate Mesolithic hunters partly cleared by burning, to attract grazing herbivores. Deforestation became so ingrained in human behaviour it is easy to assume the hills have always been treeless. They are mostly heath now, heather and bilberry being able to survive the impoverished, acidified soils, and are deliberately maintained this way – saplings removed.

I climbed Penycloddiau (the largest Iron Age fort in Cymru, and one of six on Bryniau Clwyd) and reached the sun. Dyffryn Clwyd below was still full of smoky blue mist. Across it, Mynyddoedd Eryri rose like thick paper, torn into breaking waves. The path dipped to skirt Coed Llangwyfan, a recovering conifer plantation from where bird chatter from the mixed woodland and understorey of moss and ferns was more plentiful than on the hills. As if they remembered what the hills had been like, and would be again, if left to their own devices.

Doomed sentinels protruded from brown heather – rowan saplings, soon to be uprooted by conservationists. A kestrel hovered. The thrilling ascents and descents made my heart pound. Deforestation allowed the hills' shapes to emerge like comfortable sofas. I slunk between cushions and scaled the head-rests. But much as I loved the unobstructed views (and vivid purple heather in summer), I struggled to understand the rationale for maintaining a particular habitat at the expense of a more biodiverse one.

The sky was magnificently blue and there was a party atmosphere among the crowd on Moel Famau, the tallest hill. It was like being on a ship. We looked down on Dyffryn Clwyd, still full of mist, while out west, Eryri's peaks sank and re-emerged from an ocean of dazzling white. A few children were among the adults, off school or home-schooled, and three men from Wigan asked me to take their picture. "We've come to the sunny south," said one, "visibility's been so bad these past few weeks in the Lakes." Even the council had driven up in a truck to collect litter, and a tractor was razing patches and stripes in the heather – to make space for black grouse to breed and feed. I was glad for the grouse and not particularly perturbed the hills now resembled pets shaved for complicated surgery, but the patches made me uneasy in the same way that bird-boxes do – indicators of habitat loss.

I wouldn't fully make sense of my feelings until reading about light-intervention approaches at places like Ennerdale in Cumbria and Knepp in Sussex, where numbers of breeding birds and rare species were bucking the national and global trend by rising instead of crashing. While I strode over treeless Bryniau Clwyd, at Knepp and Ennerdale, species thought to be representative of a certain habitat were proving when left to their own devices to prefer completely different ones. Huge numbers of purple emperor butterflies for example, so rare they'd been assumed to be an ancient woodland species, were breeding prolifically in thick willow scrub at Knepp. Scrub it transpires, is important. And mere conservation too conservative.

Human-controlled conservation has failed to stop biodiversity crashing. Not that devastated habitats don't need restoring – at Knepp for example, a canal was filled in and weirs were removed from the river. Now the Adur flows freely, trout have returned and wetlands have formed unaided, attracting water-birds, amphibians, marsh plants and riverine trees. But Knepp is not just a nature reserve. Knepp cattle, which forage freely to replicate the large herbivores that once roamed Britain, are slaughtered for meat – Knepp is also a farm.

Restoring biodiverse habitats requires freeing up and connecting large areas of land – some nature reserves are too small and isolated. And species whose life cycles have been permanently interrupted won't arrive without being reintroduced. (In 2020, reintroduced stork would breed at Knepp for the first time in England for 600 years.) But once the reintroduced species are established, and once a habitat has been restored, it seems both astonishing and simultaneously blindingly obvious that nature copes so much better when left alone. And yet here we are, pulling out saplings. In the autumn of 2020, seeking a footpath in diminishing light, Rob and I would stumble through a farm in Cwm Nantcol with mature trees, bush and scrub. Birds darted from ditches. Insect clouds lifted from flowering shrubs, and cattle contentedly bent their heads to fragrant herbs or stretched to sample the trees. It was like something we'd never experienced but which felt innately familiar. A Mesolithic safari. The past and the future.

I fell into step with two stout men and their portly black Labradors. "It took us two years to walk Offa's Dyke," said one. "We were always in the pubs, that's why," said his pal. Dyffryn Clwyd was finally revealed as the mist sizzled away — irregular fields on the foothills, and on the valley floor, large rectangular fields interspersed with estates and small medieval grey towns. Dinbych and Rhuthun.

During the Civil War in 1646, Rhuthun Castle, not long after being restored, fell to the Parliamentarians. Dinbych Castle was next. The Parliamentarians began their siege on 17th April but despite Charles I's surrender in Scotland, William Salesbury, Dinbych Castle's Royalist Captain, refused to submit – perhaps his particularly stubborn loyalty was because Charles had been given asylum there for two nights in 1645 after the Battle of Rowton Moor. Salesbury couldn't control Dinbych beyond the castle walls, but neither could the Parliamentarians get in – storming castles by force was rarely successful, even though by the end of the fifteenth century this one had been largely stripped of its timber and lead, and had neither weapons nor glass. The foot soldiers camped in the fields over summer and moved into town as winter approached while the cavalry set up nearby. But the siege was relatively courteous and eventually letters between Salesbury and Charles resulted in an honourable surrender on 6th October. Soon after the Restoration of the Monarchy, the castle was destroyed by order of Charles II.

I'd assumed castles were ruined by bombast and neglect. It turns out most were deliberately 'slighted' to prevent further use. The Civil War had marked the end of an era. Castles, testament to Cymru having been a battlefield for centuries, great medieval war-machines which had also controlled trade, law, and who lived in the towns inside their walls, were suddenly redundant. Their destruction must have felt very odd.

I had Moel Fenlli to myself and ate my sandwiches whilst watching ravens somersault into warm air rising off the edge of the hill. Two pairs flew level with me then flipped upside down, grunting like pigs. I'd been questioning the preservation of heather at the expense of forest, but the sheep fields that followed were spartan. With scant wire fences their nitrogen-enriched grass resembled a Microsoft screensaver, they were so biodiversity poor.

I didn't want to acknowledge farming as a cause of wildlife apocalypse. It was bad enough being an environmentalist – I knew better than to express uninvited opinion, especially here in Cymru. Farmers, who have managed the land for millennia, are largely – unless they have the vision, money, grit *and* luck to try something different – slaves to government policy and the market, and under enormous stress. Only for people like me to describe their fields as 'screensaver-green', dismissing their lives and livelihood. I didn't want to go there. Farmers and renewable energy champions had only recently become bedfellows, and despite stellar examples such as at Knepp and Cwm Nantcol, the concept of habitat restoration or 'rewilding' seemed to threaten that friendship afresh. The word 'rewilding' when misinterpreted, misunderstood, misrepresented or mis-managed, seemed alarming to farmers. A triple whammy. A reintroduction of lamb-killing predators perhaps. Reforestation so soon after the awful Forestry Commission land grabs maybe. And worst of all, the notion that farmers would have nothing to do. As if their work had no value. Rewilding doesn't have to mean any of that. But its advocates were largely young urbanites who parachuted insensitively into rural areas without knowledge of culture, history, or farming. Or language. The situation was similar in England. But in Cymru, being English made it so much worse. Not that Cymreig ecological experts weren't also calling for habitat restoration – I heard them on Radio Cymru. But they spoke more gently. I pushed the matter out of my mind but it didn't really go away, only festered there and nibbled at me.

Sarah and Charlie were waiting in Llandegla, and drove me to their home in Rhyd-y-mwyn, where we listened to the shipping forecast and put on down jackets to admire the campervan Charlie had refurbished. The night was dark. The metal was cold to touch. The sky was hard with stars.

By morning, Mynydd Rhiwabon was a palette of frosted peat under porcelain sky. Cold gave altitude extra thrill and I loved it and felt alive. Puddles had frozen, the boardwalk was icy and heather husks crystallised, though water still bubbled in flushes. Here too, strips had been mown into heather for black grouse. Sarah, who was walking with me, said she had seen the spring lek when rufous greyhens gather to watch scarlet-wattled blackcocks strut, leap and display their lyre-shaped tails. In winter they gather in flocks. We startled a few from the tussocks, and they flew like inland puffins, plump as humbugs.

Sarah (from the Wirral), and Charlie (from Liverpool), were testament to the relationship between Merseyside and north Cymru that began when thousands of Cymry worked on the docks, and continued when Merseyside evacuees came to Cymru in the Second World War. "A lot came back," said Sarah, "for holidays and that. We ended up in Rhyd-y-mwyn because Charlie was a sales rep for a quarry selling stone from Halkyn to Tarmac. But he came as a child too, to Nant Alyn campsite. He remembers going to the farmhouse to buy eggs. It meant a lot to him."

"Wales was our go-to destination too," Sarah said. "My Dad had a company car, the only car in the council estate, a little Mini, and we'd all get in and drive to Bala Lake or somewhere on the coast, and my Mum would pack a huge Tupperware box of pilchard sandwiches. When I'm in Liverpool I feel like a huge big giant with one foot on either side of the Mersey and when I come back here, I get that feeling, when I see the rolling hills like whales' backs, that I'm home. In Rhyd-y-mwyn most people I know have moved in. But when I first arrived, an old lady used to take me on walks and tell me about the village. She was Welsh, but she didn't speak it because she used to get punished for it at school and had to stand in the corner." A guilt bubble formed in my stomach.

We arrived at the road between Wrecsam and Llangollen where we met two cyclists but no other traffic. Bryniau Clwyd looked like crumpled paper bags stuck onto thin blue tissue. It is difficult taking on a new culture and language when your neighbours are incomers too. I'd not encountered Cymraeg on my journey, since the women eating scones at Benllech. But nor had I sought it at home, where I'd been writing my first magazine articles — in English.

"Just occasionally, I hear Welsh spoken in Mold market," Sarah said. "But we've got friends in Denbigh where even people from other parts of Wales are considered incomers." Each valley was different. "I'm not a flag-wavy person, I like to get away from labels," Sarah went on. "Having said that, culture and history, communicated through language, are so important. But there shouldn't be any aggression, just appreciation. Mind you," she added, "it's easy saying that being English. It's sad being in a pub for the rugby when the Welsh fans support anyone playing against England. But when you know your history you can't blame them."

I'd been a student in Aberystwyth when the sight of heartbroken Cymry traipsing silently home in red shirts with daffodils limp in their pockets, had left a poetic impression on me. I'd supported Cymru ever since — in the rugby. But football was less straightforward. I'd grown up with Shrewsbury Town, Rob with Scunthorpe United. Eng-er-land. But each international tournament had left us more uneasy till suddenly it dawned on us we'd become Cymru fans by osmosis and now it seemed obvious — Cymru supported us and we supported Cymru. But we still felt some affection for old England. Not so the Cymry.

Travel writers I admired made confident statements. The Russians were like this, the Chinese were like that. I find it difficult. The world isn't like that anymore. Stereotyping upsets people. Cymry are diverse. And yet, there is something. That quiet, fierce, private pride. Cymry celebrating a sporting victory are nothing like English people doing the same. You'll maybe get one or two idiots. But a Cymreig crowd will not on the whole be provocative, or gloating, or even triumphant. They will be humble. Grateful. Privately overwhelmed. Yes, they will be singing. But perhaps with their eyes closed, joy being so close to suffering. But it is when Cymru lose that the difference is most pronounced. Cymru supporters support. They do not criticise. They do not become aggressive. They are proud of the effort, for getting this far. "Well done boys" they say. "Let's go home now."

And yes, it is also true that for the most part, Cymry like England to lose. In 1862, George Borrow wrote in *Wild Wales*, "All conquered people are suspicious of their conquerors. The English have forgotten that they have conquered the Welsh, but some ages will elapse before the Welsh forget that the English have conquered them." I was in London watching a match with a Zambian friend who laughed when I told him Cymry supported anyone but England. "Of course! There must be apology before forgiveness can be granted!" he chuckled. To my knowledge, England has never apologised for historical crimes against Cymru. (Meanwhile I know England fans of a certain age who still enjoy seeing France lose, which has, presumably, something to with Napoleon.)

The road dropped to Creigiau Eglwyseg, limestone crags which reminded me of the Dolomites, and we skittered over scree on steep slopes. A flock of fieldfares burst out of the trees. Sarah left for Llangollen and I continued alone along the escarpment. A stoat flashed across my path with prey in its mouth. A group of silver-haired ramblers stood around a bench eating sandwiches, but I met no-one else. The colours were soft and lovely, the trees full of berries for the extra blackbirds, thrushes and fieldfares newly arrived from Scandinavia, and making a noisy fuss.

ANGLICANISM

In 1509, Harri Tudur's son became King of England, Henry VIII. The population of London was 75,000, and in 1536 the population of Cymru had increased to about 278,000. England was still 95 percent rural and Cymru even more so.

At the start of Henry's reign the country was Catholic. Pilgrims travelled to sacred sites like Tyddewi, Penrhys and Ynys Enlli, stopping at holy wells and churches en route. When the Pope refused to acknowledge Henry VIII's divorce, the schism resulted in Catholicism being stymied and Henry becoming Head of the Church of England in 1535 – not from Protestant zeal but because he did not recognise the Pope's authority. To further reduce papal power he had monasteries destroyed in what was called the 'Reformation'. Land formerly owned by monastic orders was sold to the gentry. Pilgrimages ceased. Some Catholics were persecuted. Fearing a Catholic invasion of his new Protestant kingdom, Henry confiscated land in Ireland and settled it with English.

In 1536 and 1542 Henry VIII passed Acts of Union which bound Cymru and England as a single state. Partible inheritance was annulled, so estates were now inherited entirely by the eldest son, concentrating power in the hands of the few. Norman Marcher lordships were abolished and the Marcher lords' power reduced. The seven Marcher lordships and six counties of Cymru were each given a court and Justice of Peace. Cymru could now send twenty-seven MPs to Parliament and had some degree of influence in London. But English Law applied to Cymru and Cymreig laws which had survived Edward I's Common Law were abolished. English became the official language of the courts of law.

A significant number of gentry moved to London, where some gained important positions, and Cymraeg began to be confined to the lower and working classes. Meanwhile in England, the first translation of the Bible into English was published in 1539 and church services were held in English rather than Latin.

In 1547, Protestant Edward VI became King of England and Cymru, but was succeeded in 1553 by Catholic Mary I who restored papal power and burned Protestant heretics at the stake. In 1558, Mary was replaced by Elizabeth I who restored the Anglican Church – and persecuted Catholics. Some

Cymry fled to Rome but most conformed to Protestantism. Puritanism began as a religious trend within the Anglican Church and developed in Caerdydd, Abertawe, Wrecsam and Hwlffordd. Elizabeth I ordered the Bible to be translated into Cymraeg so that it be understood in Cymru. William Morgan's 1588 translation was the only book most people had access too, via the church. He created a high standard of written Cymraeg and inspired a writing renaissance, with Cymraeg dictionaries, grammars and scriptural translations appearing. Meanwhile poetry was changing, and the practice of households employing their own bards declined.

A new class of landlords began to rule. Some were proud of their heritage of Cymreig princes and nobles, others neglected their roots, others were Anglo-Norman lords. They comprised just 5 per cent of the population. About half the population were subsistence farmers who had enough food when the harvest was good, but suffered when it wasn't. Fifteen per cent were yeomen, merchants, and craftsmen who lived in stone houses in lowland villages. Thirty per cent lived in hovels without windows or chimneys. Their suffering increased in the 1590s when the plague (which had never completely disappeared), returned together with outbreaks of typhus and smallpox.

Travelling wasn't easy. Signposts were scant and guides essential. Roads were scarce and rough, but more were built after the first Highways Act of 1555. Cattle farming increased, and drovers walked livestock to London or the Midlands. Hafod and hendre farming began to decline. But families still kept pigs and geese, and mixed farming was practised even in fertile valleys and coastal plains where corn was grown for market – much of Cymru was fed by grain grown in Sir Benfro and Ynys Môn.

Although outnumbered by goats in the uplands, sheep were central to the agricultural economy. The centre of the wool industry shifted from south to mid- and north Cymru, with the market controlled by the Shrewsbury Drapers Company due to an Act by Elizabeth I. Mining also grew in importance, largely under estate management. The output of coal increased to supply smelting furnaces and domestic fuel, and demand for minerals outstripped the capacity of road and river to deliver them.

Land reclamation continued with the draining of marsh and mudflats. Though there were still well-wooded areas in the early part of the century, deforestation too, continued as the gentry acquired land and sold timber. Remaining woodland was managed by coppicing and pollarding. Sweet chestnut was introduced for fencing, sycamore for furniture and kitchenware, beech for tool handles and the beech-mast on which pigs were fed.

Henry VIII revived the hunting of fallow deer on the gentry's estates, but red deer and possibly cranes disappeared and the last wolf in Cymru was allegedly killed. Although fish were plentiful, over-fishing was already a concern, with the Bishop of Tyddewi pointing out that fishermen who took too many herrings in times of plenty were affecting their ability to breed. But nobody listened.

WRECSAM

B *eyond the urban conurbation and industrial belt, a few hay meadows and areas of unimproved pasture remain in isolated pockets. Orchids and butterflies populate disused sand and gravel quarries, while bats live in old limestone workings, and specialised plants thrive on lead-spoil heaps. Over 2,000 ponds — some post-glacial kettle holes, farm ponds or former marl pits for mines and quarries, sustain great crested newts and silver diving beetles.*

I bought a vending-machine coffee from the Anglo Welsh Canal Hire headquarters and drank it in a septic-tank stink, while a woman in yellow rubber gloves swabbed a hire-boat deck. There was no-one else.

Pontcysyllte Aqueduct was so tall it was impossible to see all of it at once. Wintry light made it spectral. Crossing gave me the strange sensation that my feet might not be heavy enough to stop me sailing from the towpath into the vale or toppling into the canal. The colossal stone piers were very far below me, straddling Afon Dyfrdwy. A mere lip of iron split water from sky. I could see Y Waun Aqueduct downriver, like a design on a willow-patterned tea plate in a fruit-pastille forest sugared with mist. No boats crossed, but leaves floated by at walking pace.

Wood smoke from a moored narrowboat hovered over the water and a line of light lapped the revetments. Offa's Dyke Path left for the fields, but I kept to the quiet canal, drawn to the water which was dark as an antique mirror with a dusty film, and the brick tunnels with holes of light, while reflected red, orange and yellow trees made other tunnels. I liked this quiet, autumnal world which was soft underfoot.

At Y Waun a train stacked with spruce logs destined for chipboard backed into a siding, which seemed neither the most noble nor efficient use of such a fragrant virgin resource. The Kronospan factory had been associated with several incidents of air and water pollution, and in 2003 fuel-oil pollutants had triggered a red alert. Complaints from residents about dust, formaldehyde and fires (five in 2012 alone) were ongoing. It dominated the skyline, all pipes and tanks and tubes and smoke, more Willy Wonka than the chocolate factory next door, which had been built in the sixties to create jobs when the coal mines collapsed. As kids we'd wound the car windows down to smell the chocolate — laced perhaps with formaldehyde.

Starlings whistled in lime trees. Molehills crossed the medieval green. It seems that the Myddeltons who acquired the castle in 1595, had developed Y Waun. Pig iron was forged, coal mined in small collieries, and slate, granite, china-stone, lime and cloth were produced in Glyn Ceiriog. Now shop windows lit November like a lantern – chicken kievs in the butcher's, sticky buns in the bakers, squashes, dirty carrots and melons outside the greengrocers. Horse chestnut leaves cushioned the pavement and pansies flowered at the pelican crossing.

Outside The Hand, staff on a fag break huddled under the fire escape. I was too early to meet Rob and my old friend Grebo, but went in and sat by the coal fire in the lobby. Silver wallpaper and piped music belied the building's age till the staircase creaked, and I asked the woman at reception how old it was. "1610," she said between phone calls, "so there's lots we can't do. We can't even put in a lift. I'll get my husband, he loves the history." Paul sat on the sofa and said different parts were built at different times. "The Myddeltons used it as a town house for their guests, but they sold nearly all of Chirk. Technically the oldest bit is by the bar. But the *really* old part" he leaned forward, "the oldest bit, *I* think, the old motte there's talk of that no-one can find, is down in the cellar."

"Chirk's been a battleground for centuries," he went on. "It was the only place in Wales not to have to pay taxes to the king, because it's on the English side of the castle and the dyke. But the locals are Welsh through and through. Well I had union flags up for the Queen's birthday or something like that, I got some stick. But it's not simple. If you go five miles in either way it's a different accent. There were three coal pits see, but a lot of miners came from the Potteries or Yorkshire and people from here went there. I've been here since I was four. My father was a Stoke man, his father came to work in the mines so we came too."

Identity is not straightforward, especially on the border. And because Cymru is a nation state of the UK, working out how Cymreig you are is complicated (though I have friends who maintain it is a matter of the heart). But there is no Cymreig passport, and if the rules for representing Cymru in football are anything to go by I wouldn't qualify for one anyway. Henry VIII on the other hand, whose Dad was Harri Tudur, could have played football for Cymru. Which seems unfair, being as I support full independence and he annexed Cymru to England – albeit with little apparent resistance at the time, from the Cymry themselves. I suppose he'd have been captain, staying calm while others lost their heads.

After a pint it was dark and the grocers were bringing in their vegetables. A postman left Spar with the mail sacks. Two Asian mothers pushed buggies up the street, and the butcher cashed up under the sign saying 'HALF WELSH LAMB', which seemed appropriate.

Grebo and I had been friends as teenagers in Shropshire, and students in Aberystwyth. He was a land surveyor now, living at Weston Rhyn one mile inside England. He said his mains water came from Severn Trent but as the wastewater ran into Cymru, it was treated by Welsh Water. His wife Tracy, a Fine Art lecturer, grew up in London, from where a relative had just visited and asked why there was Cymraeg first on the road signs, what with it being a dead language. "We were livid!" said Tracy with passion. "I mean I've got Welsh students who struggle sometimes, to find the word they want in English. The Welsh language is such an intrinsic part of their culture and it's the language of their *work*. Mind you," she laughed, "I do get irritated now and again when some of the office staff grumble in Welsh. BUT!" she added fiercely, "I *absolutely* defend their right to do so!"

Over fish pie and wine, Grebo said "I love Wales and Welsh people. But I remember going to Caernarfon with my parents in the eighties when sometimes it was just rude. I'd be queuing in a shop with my Dad and they'd serve everyone that came in behind, before they'd serve us. But then that was the time of all the fires and painting letterboxes green so you can understand it, maybe they thought we had a second home. I'm proud of Shropshire. But I'm not English. English to me is London and the southeast. I feel more Welsh than English, but obviously I'm not, so really I guess I'm Marches."

Marches! I hadn't thought of that. Marches was the name given to Norman-won territories on the border and across south Cymru. The concept intrigued me. Did all border people feel the same? "No," Grebo said. "English border people say they're Marches, but the Welsh say they're Welsh, because they've got a more defined cultural identity." It seemed that over the centuries, aggressive Norman colonisation had mellowed into a kind of get-out clause for people like me and Grebo, who just weren't that comfortable being English.

Grebo made us big mugs of tea and Marmite on toast like when we'd been hungover students, then dropped us off and turned back to his car with a raised arm and pivoting skip I'd forgotten. In a few years, Covid would remind us the border is less dormant than it appears – not surprisingly, considering its history. We peered down at Afon Ceiriog, tumbling darkly under a bridge on which a plaque commemorated the 1165 Battle of the Berwynion, when

Henry II, attempting to conquer Cymru, had been ambushed by Owain Gwynedd. Henry had been forced back to Shrewsbury where he mutilated the twenty-two hostages he'd captured – including two of Owain Gwynedd's sons. And the dyke! It surprised me. I'd not appreciated how much still survived as a real landmark – a low earth bank riddled with badger setts, that still formed the border here.

Y Waun castle was visible in wooded hills behind us. Cromwell had spared its destruction, perhaps because Thomas Myddelton had been a Parliamentarian General. Myddelton had turned Royalist later, but there it was anyhow, an oppressive rectangle that displayed its original aggression in a way romantic ruins do not. The National Trust acquired it in 1981 but the Myddeltons remained resident in part of it till 2004, when Guy Myddelton told BBC Wales "We are moving to a smaller house so we had to be brave and leave some things behind. Some of the paintings are enormous and we just can't fit them in." The definition of bravery has changed perhaps, over time.

Scrubby hawthorns clawed stony ground, the Cheshire Plain was swathed in blue haze. In Racecourse Wood, condensing water coursed down cedars, beech roots wrestled the dyke and tall trees reached for the light. At Trefonen the dyke ran so prominently across a large field that we stopped. Ancient oaks on the top enhanced its magnitude and I was suddenly awed it was still here, after more than a thousand years, that any of it had survived agriculture, construction, trees and badgers. Yet still it marched on, across fields with indefinite edges.

From Moelydd there were views to Eryri, which seemed a long way from this Marches landscape of woods and rolling hills. The landscape looked and smelt like Shropshire – my home county. The springy turf and views felt familiar. My Dad would have loved this view, the trig point, finding it on the map, the sun on his face, and I wished he could have been there. We descended. "We're glad to see you out enjoying the sun," said an old man in scarlet woolly hat outside his cottage, and suddenly everything was unfamiliar. This quarrying country at the far edge of Shropshire with Cymraeg place names – Trefonen, Nantmawr, Cefn Lane, felt neither Shropshire nor Cymru, nor even Marches, but slightly surreal, as if we'd fallen into a fairy-tale.

Presently, we crossed back into Cymru. On Bryn Llanymynech, conifers gave to broadleaf. The sun slid down a porcelain sky to a golf-course soundtrack of metal hitting balls. The limestone escarpment was part of the same ridge I'd met outcropping on Ynys Môn, Y Gogarth, and Eglwyseg. Here, twelve different types of limestone had been extracted from quarries both sides of the border, that were rivals till a tunnel united them. Crows croaked in the overhangs and in summer, butterflies fluttered around 300 species of plants. Now traveller's joy framed pink sky, and the flood plain below, where the Hoffman Kiln chimney protruded through trees, was smoky with rising cold.

We got the football results in The Dolphin. The pub's name had been contracted from 'Godolphin' – the seventeenth-century owner. But in the sixteenth century, when beer casks had been buried under holly bushes before a fair, it was known as The Hollybush Inn. It was dark when we came out, and below freezing. There were no buses, so we hitched.

REVOLT

Both population and economy were in decline following fourteenth-century plagues. Only villages with marketable commodities survived, and development was hampered by ongoing conflict with England. In 1400, Richard II died, presumed murdered by his cousin who seized the throne and became Henry IV, and Cymreig gentry to whom Richard had given powerful positions to keep Marcher lords in check, were left with uncertain loyalties. In 1402, Henry IV passed laws forbidding Cymry to own land in the Marches, bear arms, live in fortified towns, assemble, or hold office.

Owain Glyndŵr was born in Glyndyfrdwy. A Cymreig prince by inheritance who'd married into a Marcher family, he had spent time in England and served in Richard II's army. But when Henry refused to mediate fairly against Glyndŵr's neighbour Grey of Rhuthun (who'd stolen some of Glyndŵr's land), Glyndŵr took Grey to court, and when his case failed, he revolted. He attacked English castles and settlements, fought battles, and was crowned Prince of Cymru in Machynlleth in 1404. But eventually, Henry's power was too great, Glyndŵr's support waned and he disappeared, after which many of the gentry who'd supported him began to cooperate with English authorities. Massive economic devastation followed the upheaval.

In 1413, Henry IV's son became Henry V. Born in Trefynwy he recruited large numbers of Cymreig archers to fight in the Hundred Years War in France (which would end in 1453, in defeat). When Henry V died in 1422 his son was placed under the authority of his mother, Catherine de Valois, till old enough to be crowned Henry VI in 1429. Two years later Catherine married Owain ap Maredudd (Owain Tudur) from Ynys Môn, and had two sons.

The War of the Roses broke out between the rival Royal Houses of Lancaster and York in 1453. Substantial intermarriage between Cymreig and English nobility meant that English aristocrats with both Yorkist and Lancastrian allegiances had acquired land in Cymru. Lancastrians were descendants or supporters of Edward III's second son John Duke of Lancaster (who'd been usurped to the throne by Henry IV eighty years earlier) while the Yorkists supported his fifth son Edward of Langley. Most of Cymru was Lancastrian while the Marches were Yorkist. Battles were fought across England and Cymru. Power swung between Yorkists and Lancastrians. Eventually in 1485, Lancastrian Harri Tudur, (Catherine de Valois and Owain Tudor's grandson who'd been living in exile in Brittany), landed in Sir Benfro with an army of French and Breton soldiers, where they joined a Cymreig army and marched to Leicester to kill Richard III in the Battle of Bosworth, ending the War of the Roses. Harri became Henry VII.

The bards saw Harri Tudur as the fulfilment of an ancient prophecy – a British hero who'd driven the Saxons from Cymru and reclaimed the sovereignty of Britain. But though he was sympathetic to Cymru during his reign, he did little beyond abolishing the system of free and unfree peasants in the north. Nevertheless, many Cymreig nobles flocked to London, gained important positions in court, became anglicised and adopted English names.

The peasant system was replaced by labourers, tenant farmers, and yeomen. But land was still shared among landowner's sons, creating small farms which often sank into poverty. In the southern Marches, the Norman feudal system collapsed, and landowners rented vast tracts of land to farmers.

It was decades after Glyndŵr's revolt and a century after the Black Death before the economy began to slowly recover. Large areas of land had been neglected, and forestry in the hills had begun to regenerate. Arable farming had been largely replaced by labour-saving livestock, particularly hardy upland cattle. Drovers walked livestock to England. Meanwhile, sheep's wool was spun and woven into flannel for domestic use, or sold in border-town markets and at the annual Bartholomew Fair in London. Finished friezes, (course woollen cloth with a nap on one side) were made to clothe working men. The quality of wool depended on breed and was particularly good in the southeast. Meanwhile, blast furnaces were established on riverbanks using water to power mechanical bellows which increased the temperature and output of iron production.

By the end of the century the population had risen again to 1300 levels, but the climate was deteriorating. Summers were warm but winters were cold and stormy. With food shortages and inadequate housing, disease was rife.

POWYS

*W*ind farms, sheep farming and forestry plantations dominate the uplands of the largest and most sparsely populated county. Reservoirs supply English cities and settlements in mid- and south-Cymru. Grassland supports dwindling populations of dunlin and golden plover, and ffridd sustains whinchat, ring ouzel, red kite, and cuckoo, while goshawk, requiring woodland edge and large habitats, are increasing in number. A few ancient oaks remain on the Hafren plain.

I took a train through blue dark to Gobowen. A suggestion of streets hunkered in bitter cold air. I waited with school kids and a man reading a newspaper, for the Oswestry bus, an old double-decker with ceiling props and carpeted walls, dark, save for raised seats at the back where the cool kids sat, spot-lit actors.

The sun rose like a ripe peach over England. But until recently, low-rise red-brick Oswestry (Croesoswallt in Cymraeg), the only English town with a team in the Welsh Premier League (having merged with Llansantffraid Football Club to form The New Saints), had a Cymraeg chapel and Cymreig Tourist Information Centre. And it had been in Cymru on 22nd October 1400 when Owain Glyndŵr attacked, having already ransacked Rhuthun, Dinbych, Rhuddlan, Y Fflint, Penarlâg and Holt. From here he moved south towards Y Trallwng, as I was doing, with somewhat less ferocity. Before the Llanymynech bus I had time for coffee, which I bought from a man in a pink café, who perhaps had an Indian accent and was puzzled by my rucksack. "Are you going to climb a mountain?" he asked.

I'd spent my whole life crisscrossing over the border but had never really observed it. "It's right down the middle of the high street," said the woman in Llanymynech Post Office. "That big old derelict building down there was The Lion. The border ran right through it — you couldn't drink in the Welsh bar on a Sunday but you could on the English side." What nationality were Llanymynech people, I wondered, expecting a vague response. "Well I'm English and Jane's Welsh," she said without pause, indicating her colleague unloading newspapers in the back. "A few speak it now, but less," she added, lowering her voice. "The little Welsh primary school down the road — when the kids leave, they have to choose whether to go to secondary school in Wales or England and they get split up." Cymraeg was spoken on the border! It was easy to miss. And I, no Glyndŵr, was too chicken even to try. I still felt it was important to pin my allegiance to Cymru, to support its language and culture. But I was discovering Cymru was not an easily defined concept. It was a diversity of landscapes and customs and peoples, not all of whom seemed much to care whether I supported them or not. I wasn't sure how I felt about this, but it took the pressure off.

Swans hissed on Trefaldwyn Canal. This was their domain, now that limestone was no longer burned in canalside kilns with coal from Y Waun and Oswestry, in order to improve crops. Bridges, locks and ruined redbrick buildings, remembered the mills and dairies, and fields nourished with the lime that fertilisers replaced. The crops went when cheap imported grain caused farms to go bust. Another abandoned landscape. A heron lifted into the air. I opened a gate, flushing complaining ducks and moorhens from the rushes.

The rain began at Four Crosses. A farmer herding her cows across muddy fields, said it would rain for two days and that was it, they'd be in for winter now, the ground was too wet. I put on my £3 cycling cape and in half an hour the wind had torn it to ribbons. Offa's Dyke was a visible mound on the Hafren floodplain. Nests of driftwood had collected against it. Drab fields squelched underfoot. The cows had gone but the rain kept the cowpats fresh.

I ate a slice of Mum's lemon sponge under an ash, and watched a buzzard glide from the crown. Mizzle freshened my face and the silence was bliss as I let my eyes run over Bryniau Breidden, where yellow excavators were scratching out road-stone on the summits. An appetite, fresh air and sandwiches are rich treasures.

In Y Trallwng, the air was thick with fumes. Landrovers and tractors crawled up the High Street and a lorry swung over the pavement to make the sharp bend at the crossroads. I sat in the grounds of Powis Castle which Edward I had allowed Gruffydd ap Gwenwynwyn to build in return for supporting his conquest of Cymru. By the fifteenth century the castle had passed by marriage into the Charlton Estate. It was Edward Charlton, fifth Lord of Powis, who just about kept Glyndŵr at bay in 1400. In 1406, in his new charter for Y Trallwng, Charlton recorded the need to preserve the town as a centre of English influence and exclude the 'foreign Welsh' from its government.

I didn't know of Charlton's arrogance as I sat there, but noticed the usual exclusivity – ponds on graceful lawns, aesthetically-positioned trees. There were fallow deer apparently in the woods, which, having first been brought to Britain by the Romans, were re-introduced in the Middle Ages as venison and sport for the gentry.

There is not much deer-stalking left in Cymru, but pheasant-shoots are increasing. I would stumble upon one in 2019, when visiting a church in Mynyddoedd Berwynion. The sound of gunshot had shocked me out from within its thick stone walls, and I'd dashed out to see the field which had been grazed by sheep minutes earlier, full of people with guns. Some of the pheasants, flushed straight overhead from a wooded hillside were killed outright. Others tried to drag their broken bodies to cover. When it was over the people lowered their guns, waited for orders, climbed into open-sided vehicles and were driven away, while the sheep were returned to the field. I found it harrowing. The way the pheasants had died, and how the people had stood dumbly awaiting commands, without imagination, spirit or purpose. For this, raptors were illegally poisoned for predating on pheasants bred in such unnatural density they were disease-prone and often unable to walk properly. But I thought I understood why the rich did it. Not because they were innately evil. I thought it was probably something they'd done with their Dads.

My Dad had taken me to the football. Some of my friends deride football, seeing only overpaid celebrities where I also see working-class achievement, racism where I also see black empowerment, and tribalism where I also see community. They are blind to the magic of a beautiful pass and I don't mind, because part of the reason I love football, is because I love my Dad. It's non-negotiable.

But I wasn't thinking about pheasant shooting or fathers or football as I sat on a fallen great oak. I was thinking that the landscaped estate made me feel like a groundling, even though Powis Castle was now owned by the National Trust which didn't completely hide the exploitative history of their properties. I didn't envy the elite. The Happy Planet Index routinely shows that people with enough money for shelter, healthcare, food and education but not enough for luxuries, are the most content. Costa Ricans topped the table in 2016. In my job at the eco-centre, we had asked hundreds probably thousands, of adults, teenagers and kids, what made life worth living for them. Topping each of their lists were friends, family and love, usually followed by sunshine, animals and music. Our point was that you don't have to do without the things you value most to live sustainably. But neither are these things expensive. The rich could keep on rattling about in enormous homes that made them paranoid about working class thieves and socialist taxes as far as I was concerned. I didn't hate the rich (some are lovely) – if anything I felt sorry for them. I just hated that their wealth was and still is dependent on keeping the 'working class' in economic and intellectual poverty. I sulked till the fallow deer slipped out of the woods, furtive, lovely, and silhouetted, like cave art, by the lake.

The platform sparkled with grit and frost – at last it was winter. Dickensian passengers traipsed with bowed heads over the footbridge to the industrial estate where I'd worked at the dessert factory and the packing warehouse where I'd not been allowed to talk or sit down, or use the toilet without asking permission. I was glad to be going in the opposite direction.

The canal was almost frozen over. I heard the sound of beaks – ducks nibbling at the ice to keep it back. The freezing fog was white and thin but tangible as if I was pushing it before me. I was excited. It had been years since we'd had cold like this. I'd even wondered if my nieces and nephews would ever see snow. But climate change is not a simple, general, gentle warming – more an unpredictable catalogue of increasingly catastrophic storms and weather events.

Holly trees crackled with avian techno. A black cat crouched, with eyes on the coots the ice had made accessible. Hoarfrost prickled hedgerows and rosehips and swans swayed like moored meringues with their heads tucked under their wings. The A548 traffic ground through slushy grit. I crossed and looked back at the strange wall of noise and flickering orange lights. A car and lorry had broken down. But it was quiet in the fields, where the drivers couldn't see me, and where sheep were brown against frost. They hurried away, keeping to the hedge. Sky suffocated the hills. This was the excitement – the frost and the half-light. Being unseen.

The air was thick as a walk-in freezer. Fog curled around me as I climbed. Cefn Digoll was rough and steep, patched with conifer plantations and transmitter masts. I saw nearby things – fences, sheep, conifers, the summit. A quad-bike struggling up the track and the farmer turning in his seat to toss out a bale without cutting the engine, a brown hare race across frost. I was hot from climbing but my hands were numb in my gloves. I cherished and explored the rare cold, the icy stabs when I inhaled, the storm of noise in my hat when I turned my head. The whiteness.

It was on this hill in 1485, that Harri Tudur, having marched across

Cymru with an army of mercenaries, had met Rhys ap Thomas's army from the south, and soldiers, supplies, oxen and cattle from the north. En route to Cefn Digoll he'd apparently stayed one night at Dafydd Llwyd the bard's home near Machynlleth. Bards are still esteemed in Cymru but back then they were the spin-doctors. The influencers. Dafydd is credited with composing the marching poem Pawb at Dewi. '...Pawb doed pob dydd i'n rhoi yn rhydd, At bab y ffydd aed pawb â'i ffon. Dyma'r amser y daw'r ymswrn.' ('May everyone come forth every day to set us free, May everyone bring his spear to the pope. This is the time when conflict shall come.') Four thousand strong, his army sang, marched, and defeated Richard III in Leicestershire, who had twice as many men. But all I knew as I stood there in 2012, was that two years earlier, Richard had been exhumed from a car park in Leicester.

There were no views, just white layers. The hint of a distant hill materialised, ice-white on fog-white, fleeting but brilliant, an angel wing. Harri Tudur was crowned Henry VII, reclaiming the throne for the Lancastrians and founding the Tudor Dynasty. In the wake of Edward's colonisation, Henry IV's oppression and Glyndŵr's failed revolt, he fulfilled bardic dreams for a British (rather than Anglo-Saxon or Norman) king and was referred to as 'Mab Darogan' (son of prophesy). Yet he was of royal birth, mixed descent, and had grown up abroad. He appointed Cymreig sheriffs, bailiffs, justices of peace, bards and musicians to his court, and wealthy Cymry prospered – many settled in boroughs in the Marches. But he did not repeal Henry IV's punitive laws and did little for ordinary people. The bards were disappointed. So was I.

On the B438, a frozen cobweb on a footpath sign trembling in traffic vibrations, appeared luminous it was such a pure white. An elderly couple were advancing along the verge, bent over their sticks, the woman with a hat like an acorn cup. They stopped and looked up when they reached me, merry eyes in faces like wrinkled old apples. "Just come to look at the trees in the frost," said the old man. "It is so beautiful," said his wife, "we wouldn't want to live in a town." Their accents were richly rural and indefinable, neither English nor Cymreig, the kind you hear on crackling radio archives. I wanted to freeze them in time and space. But they smiled, bent and continued as if the heavy traffic wasn't there. As if they existed in another dimension.

Blackbirds pecked apples hanging onto a garden tree. Geese honked overhead in formation. I ate a sandwich cold enough to hurt my teeth, and drank from a bottle of ice crystals, under an ancient oak. Ice had defined cobwebs all over the bark. These fields had seen the largest battle of the Civil War in 1644. The slaughtered were audibly silent. I ate an apple, left plenty for the birds and tossed them the core. On the B4386 I met a bus bound for Shrewsbury and boarded, planning to come back the following day.

But my Dad had other ideas. He was worried about the weather and glad to have me home, as was Mum. "You're not walking today," he announced, with a mischievous air. "I've decided. You're spending the day with us." Parkinson's Disease had shaken his confidence as well as his body and mind, and it had been a long time since I'd seen him this pleased with himself. I looped my arm through his, and with Mum on the other side, we shuffled to town – Shrewsbury. A frontier town.

I'd grown up in Shrewsbury where women speaking Cymraeg in Marks and Spencer were viewed with suspicion. From where the EBF (English Border Front) – marginalised skinny boys in baseball caps, went to pick fights in Oswestry and Y Trallwng. And where till 1996, Shrewsbury Town had competed in the Welsh Cup.

In the seventh century, the kingdom of Powys stretched deep into what is now the English Midlands. Shrewsbury (Amwythig in Cymraeg) possibly developed round Pengwern, which was either a district of or capital of Powys, when the concepts of England and Cymru were evolving. In 656, Pengwern was captured by Anglo-Saxon Oswy of Northumbria, and was later absorbed into the expanding kingdom of Mercia – so when Offa built his dyke, Pengwern was on the English side. The exact location of Pengwern the old capital of Powys is unknown. But a small riverside district of Shrewsbury, (with sheltered accommodation and a boat club) is called Pengwern (deriving from either 'hill of alders' or 'Hafren headwaters').

In 1071, Roger de Montgomery was bequeathed land by William the Conqueror to establish Anglo-Norman authority on the border. He built a sandstone castle here in 'Scrobbesbyrig' (Old English for fortified place in the scrub) whose gardens to me, are a peaceful place to wait for a train. The castle was later rebuilt and refortified by Edward I to strengthen his stranglehold of Cymru.

My hometown is affluent, Tory-voting, and English. But its wealth was built on Cymreig wool – Shrewsbury merchants controlled the price they paid Cymry for rough flannel, which was finished in Shrewsbury by hundreds of shearmen and drapers. By the fifteenth century the drapers had achieved independent guild status and grown rich. The flannel producers of mid-Cymru had not. But we weren't taught Cymreig history at school. We weren't taught Shropshire history. Or British history. Cymraeg had not been a language option even though only a few kids spent summers in France and *everyone* else went to caravan sites in Cymru. Shrewsbury has a Welsh Bridge and an English Bridge but it took moving to Cymru for me to appreciate their significance.

I still watch Shrewsbury Town a few times a season though not as often as some Machynlleth-born Cymraeg-speaking friends of mine. Dad took us to an organ recital in the church where he'd sung in the choir before becoming ill, and the gallery sparkled with Christmas trees. Then he treated us to lunch in the new Wetherspoon, which was noisy and brash, and busy with shoppers and students. "Is it alright?" he said, uncertain again. It was more than alright, we said. It was brilliant.

Several Saturdays after Christmas I came back to Trefaldwyn with Rob. I'd been busy writing. Judging by the numerous offers of help we'd received, we should also perhaps have been wedding planning, and had possibly underestimated the importance of bunting.

Our bus stopped outside the town hall where a man unloaded tables from a van. "You don't sound Welsh," he said. Nor did he. "Montgomery born and bred," he said proudly. "I'm Welsh alright. We don't speak it. What gets me is when these retired English come in and go round as if we should all be speaking it. Welsh hasn't been spoken here since that castle was built!" he said, pointing. The retired English were always in the wrong, putting up house prices, changing the political spectrum, not learning Cymraeg. Learning Cymraeg. But who could blame them for loving Cymru? They just needed a better induction package. We all did.

Trefaldwyn had thrived after Henry III had encouraged Shrewsbury burgesses to settle, and it still smelt affluent. From large muddy fields in which the dyke was prominent, it looked snug and smug at the foot of the castle. We were still following in Glyndŵr's footsteps. In 1401, it was reported that the whole of north Cymru had defected to him and that his army was attacking English towns. By 1403 the revolt was national. Civilian rule was breaking down, taxes could not be collected, and local government was handed over to military commanders at Faesyfed, Aberhonddu and here at Trefaldwyn, where a garrison of 120 repelled Glyndŵr in 1403. But the town walls had been ruined in the fight, causing a temporary decline in

Trefaldwyn's wealth. The soldiers stayed till 1408 by which time Glyndŵr's support had waned and large parts of Cymru had succumbed once again to English rule. It wasn't until Covid that I would appreciate the strangeness of upheaval. Even so it was hard to imagine Machynlleth under attack and garrisoned with soldiers – though we did get a Community Police Officer.

The dyke seemed huge and startling coming upon it from below, despite ambush by hawthorn and badgers. A farmer threw salt-cakes to sheep from his quadbike, and the hills were spread out in a smoke-blue and brown panorama. There were snow crusts on the ground but it felt like spring. A buzzard flew into the woods, its wingspan defined by dark space, and the sight of its glide between trees stirred something primeval within me. The air was richly silent, save for an infrequent whisper of timeless wind. We were off with the dyke. It rode high, sheltering sheep and secretive birds in bracken caves. A yellowhammer darted through larch. It was an elemental landscape and in its remoteness still felt like frontier country, a place of border skirmishes, where guerrillas might swiftly appear then melt again into the hills. We looked back and saw a hawthorn hedge silhouetted like calligraphy across a band of blue sky.

Churchtown was a church, that was it. A plastic sheet covered the altar and a sign on the door said that three types of bat were resident so 'The church is not as clean as we'd like'. Beyond it were ancient oaks, more prolific on the border than elsewhere in Britain. We ran our hands over these colossal, cobwebby living museums, some more than 500 years old. The dyke was impressive too, but aggressive. At Hergan Hill it was built at a right-angle to maximise surveillance of Cymru. But for all its bellicose swagger, it must have contributed to an evolving sense of Cymru as a nation and to the preservation of its language and culture. Perhaps without the dyke there would be no Cymru. Take note, ye builders of walls.

Rob had booked us a room in Clun. We took quiet lanes between old hedges to reach it, with heights and blue distances still playing on our minds. We watched the FA Cup in the White Horse, and ate in the fifteenth-century Sun Inn which had a cruck construction, exposed oak beams, wattle and daub and an open fire, though our room in the stable block was so comfortably renovated all sense of antiquity had gone.

Across the valley hundreds of mole hills were apparently moving about – free-range hens, it turned out, of a modest enterprise, unlike the monsters to come. In Powys alone, ninety-nine applications for intensive poultry sheds would be made between 2011 and 2018, for a combined total of 3 million birds. Animal-welfare concerns notwithstanding, the risk of pollution from air-borne ammonia and manure run-off into watercourses is substantial. The fact that we would apparently post-Brexit, be importing US-chlorinated chicken presented an opportunity for struggling farmers. There were better ways. But how to talk about such things without people getting upset? I was fed up of conflict. I had assumed that Glyndŵr and Harri Tudur would become my heroes on reading more about them. But their histories were full of combat, slaughter and devastation. I preferred William Morgan's passive power. Festival No.6's harmony.

Passerines sang and a woodpecker drummed. Spring had begun in the valleys but it was winter still, on the hills, and cloud swaddled the sun. Cars and Land Rovers were parked along a lane, among whining dogs and men with guns. "Hello," we said conversationally "what are you up to?" There was a long pause before someone replied. "Shooting." The men watched us walk out of sight. We felt threatened, they probably did too. We were outsiders with opinions about shooting and chicken farms, but it was a typical farm hunt as far as we could tell. Farmers are allowed to pursue foxes that have been harrying sheep – fox predation on lambs can cause a lot of damage to an income of £10,000 and with all their predators or killers (wolves, bears, lynx, golden eagle) now extinct in Cymru, there are four times as many foxes as there were in the Mesolithic Age.

Cloud made everything murky. Scraggy dogs watched from a farmyard piled with junk. A man vanished into a shed, a Laurie Lee character clad in sacks tied up with string. The hill-fields were full of crows and muddy sheep. Mossy trees came at us out of the gloom, as if we were snorkelling in a silty river. We caught up with the dyke on Llanfair Hill, looming like an iceberg at sea. The cloud grew colder, whiter, thicker. My wrists froze where my gloves and sleeves didn't meet. A murmuration flashed towards us then over the dyke which was lumpy but continuous like the keel of an upturned boat. Ravens possessed fence posts like sentries. An abandoned plough lay wrecked, as if on a cold ocean bed. Cows passed like ships, the trig point was a buoy and the dyke rose from the ground like a bone. Suddenly, we dropped to a stream where red trumpet fungus and moss were vivid after the white.

The dyke was lower, more field division than frontier. Trefyclawdd was at the foot of a steep wet slope. Rob slipped first, and trying to stop, executed a vigorous roll, becoming so mud-plastered I stumbled from laughing and flumed downhill with water gushing up my jacket and filling my waterproof trousers. We caught the train home, drowsy, happy, the sun through the window, warm on our faces. Spring, we thought. But it wasn't.

Euphoria and a hint of the surreal hit me on the platform. Family and friends were in the carriages, shouting and cheering. Sun flickered through steam and sulphurous smoke which put our eco-friends in a naughty mood. I clutched Fair Trade roses from the Co-op feeling suddenly shy, till my nieces picked up my dress. At Abergynolwyn, I took my Dad's arm. Rob and I made our vows, his boys presented the rings, and a nephew ran off with the flowers.

We honeymooned hiking another of the pilgrim routes to Santiago in Spain, only vaguely wondering why we couldn't get any football results. It wasn't till reading a paper on the homebound ferry we realised how much snow had blanketed Britain – the matches had all been postponed. Ponies and sheep had perished in Eryri. A family near Wrecsam had been able to step over their washing line the snow was so deep, and been forced to burn their furniture for warmth.

When we returned to Trefyclawdd in April, the only passengers on the early train, it really was spring. A misty moon hung over half-timbered buildings that were typical of border towns regaining prosperity after the economic collapse that followed the Black Death and Glyndŵr's revolt. Wind-chimes peeled quietly in a garden. Rooks began croaking. When Spar opened its doors and lights came on in the bakers and butchers, it was light enough – just, to leave town. A homebound cat emerged from the woods and a tawny owl hooted. A buzzard took off and we heard its wings. A roe deer nibbling the ground, looked up and danced away. Wooded hills rose out of the night and here we were, back in Cymru, following the dyke.

The lambs were already old enough to hang out in small groups. Some were piled in lazy heaps like teenagers outside Spar. Remembering the goats we'd seen in Spain, I said "Wouldn't it be lovely if these sheep had bells?" Rob thought it would be better if they all had electric guitars. Villagers on the Camino had been eager to chat, whether we understood Spanish or not, and with shock I realised I'd had more conversations in Spanish than Cymraeg over the years, despite having had no Spanish lessons or ever living there. It was a grim revelation – to fully realise the extent of how Cymraeg has been cowed.

But to my shame, it made me sulk. I thought it wasn't my fault my Cymraeg was clumsy if no-one would let me practise, and I gave it up, for a while.

Down across the Lugg in the village of Pilleth, Bryn Glas was identifiable for its white church and the Wellingtonia marking the graves of those who'd died in one of Glyndŵr's battles. His opponent, Edmund Mortimer of Herefordshire who owned swathes of land in Cymru and the Marches, had represented Henry IV with an army of 2,000 men. Henry had already been vanquished by Glyndŵr's guerrilla tactics in Mynyddoedd Cambria, and most Cymry including the clergy, now recognised Glyndŵr's authority. On seeing Pilleth Church ablaze Mortimer had crossed a marsh, and advanced towards some 600 men he saw on the ridge, whereupon the rest of them swarmed over the summit. Mortimer was captured and many of his archers (Sir Faesyfed and West Herefordshire conscripts) switched sides. Henry refused to pay Mortimer's ransom, and Mortimer allied with Glyndŵr and married his daughter Catrin. 'Go Glyndŵr!' I thought, then remembered the 800 men beneath the Wellingtonia. Conflict was never cool.

The hilltop hiding the sheer drop to Afon Lugg, now and again revealed glimpses of hanging mixed woodland. By contrast, the summits were divided by post-and-wire fences into large bare fields where only stunted gorse survived onslaughts of wind and sheep. The wind had wrecked a rusty barn. It looked like an abandoned whaling station, while nearby lay a wooden wagon wheel, like one I'd seen neglected in Mongolia. I stopped to hunt for my pen, and when I looked up Rob was tiny, dwarfed by rolling grassland that was also like Mongolia. I loved these high empty hills. But repeated glimpses of hanging forest reminded me of what had been lost.

Down in the valley, goldfinches flew under a field maple. But we climbed again, and Rob's jacket, the colour of Mongolian prayer-flags, matched patches of sky. Lambs were bleating, hundreds and hundreds of them as if the sheep meat industry was booming. Yet sales of fresh and frozen lamb had plummeted by 35 percent between 1995 and 2011, and in 2015, farm-gate prices would be particularly low, with farmers losing as much as £25 per lamb. Exports to the EU, and the British Muslim community (who despite making up only 5 per cent of the population consumed a fifth of all British sheep meat) kept the industry afloat.

As if that wasn't bad enough, farmers were also learning of their livestock's impacts on biodiversity and climate change. That nitrogen-enriched 'improved' grass, when inefficiently managed, emits nitrogen oxide which is

300 times more powerful a greenhouse gas than carbon dioxide. That feed supplements of grain and soya are usually grown in plantations for which tropical rainforest has been felled. That it takes a lot more energy, water and land to produce a kilo of meat than it does to produce a kilo of beans, so that with our increasing population, even organically farmed livestock has a big impact. (Though at least on the few farms where free-ranging cattle browse a range of herbs and grasses, like at Cwm Nantcol and Knepp, the cattle produce less flatulence (thus less methane), biodiversity increases, animal health improves, human health benefits (natural grass-fed meat and dairy being rich in omega-3), and there is less water loss and erosion – natural grassland having long-reaching root systems which store carbon and alleviate flooding.)

Veganism isn't a pre-requisite of a climate-friendly diet, but vastly reducing the quantity of meat and dairy we eat is. The eco-centre where I'd worked were among those who had crunched the numbers, and shown that eliminating meat wasn't necessary, in a report called Zero Carbon Britain. But the message was not being heard then in 2013, or in the chaos of subsequent years during which some (not all) rewilding advocates would call for huge quantities of grazing land to be abandoned, some (not all) vegans would call for a total halt to meat and dairy production, and a few foolish politicians would propose Britain stop farming altogether and import all its food. Provoking some (not all) farmers, already humiliated by the subsidy-dependency which had made their dignified profession inglorious, to the verge of meltdown. (Subsidies which were only necessary because the market is flooded by food kept cheap by the damagingly low price of oil which underpins the production of intensively-farmed and processed food.) Farmers were food producers. The most important people in the world. They deserved gratitude, sympathy and support, not stress. While I didn't know anything about these large border farms, I knew sheep on smaller farms further west that were selectively bred from flocks owned by great-grandfathers who'd bought farms from the gentry early in the twentieth century. Livestock was part of the family. Farms were the fabric of the rural community I called home.

Brexit would bring an opportunity to rethink the subsidy regime. Farmers would cling to the Welsh Lamb brand officially recognised by the EU, which had purchased 92 per cent of the 40 per cent of lamb exported from Cymru, and there would be talk of new markets – perhaps Japan, which would make me despair. Why weren't the meat-eaters of Cymru buying it? If those who wished to eat meat and dairy ate substantially less of it but made sure it was local, we could reduce pressure on land, climate change, biodiversity and farmers. I knew this. But I was afraid to share this information now I no longer taught endless groups of eager people wanting solutions. I was back in the world of bargains and BOGOFs. Where people wanted big cheap supermarkets to skulk around in for special offers. Where I'd even met a livestock farmer I knew buying cheap meat. (To be fair it was evening, and the butcher who'd fought for a local abattoir to support local farmers was closed.) Hey, none of us are perfect. In 2017-18 the average UK family spent just over ten per cent of their income on food whereas in 1957 it had been thirty-three per cent. We want food cheaper than it costs to produce. But it wasn't just fear of upsetting shoppers that kept me quiet. It was fear of getting muddled and inadvertently upsetting farmers. They were so Cymreig. I was so English. The frolicking lambs had pink light in their ears, and I loved them.

A rising field obscured England and then we descended. At Burfa, a big group of women in pink and orange fleeces emerged from parked cars, consulted maps and fell into step behind us until one realised, to hoots of laughter, they were going the wrong way.

"Oh what are you barking at now?" The quavering voice at the foot of Herrock Hill, belonged to a tall willowy man in threadbare shirt and braces with a thatch of white hair cut in short-back-and-sides. This was the southeast corner of Powys, once the old county of Sir Faesyfed. The farmer looked, dressed and sounded different to farmers we knew in old Sir Drefaldwyn in west Powys who were shorter, stouter, darker, scruffier, and spoke to their dogs in Cymraeg. I romanticised farmers like I did Mongolian herdsman and Portuguese cork-cutters. To me they were elusive and poetic. Endangered.

The dyke reappeared, topped with a line of low gorse. We seemed never to notice its absence and were always surprised by its return as if it had slipped off for a sneaky fag. Rob hurried ahead with his camera, then turned round and his smile changed to a look of horror. Behind me, a tsunami of black cloud with a hole around the sun was boiling over the sky like ink in water, about to swallow the world. We ran. Lightning pulsed and daylight vanished. Hail-lashed golfers jumped into buggies. We charged downhill to Kington, where the sun re-emerged, wet and fierce.

Kington, in Herefordshire, has been in England for over a thousand years but lies west of the dyke. A woman saw us peer at the closed museum. "It's very rural here," she said. "Kington is a grey-haired town. When I moved here I used to, and still do, use a kind of shampoo that makes grey hair silver, rather than yellow. I thought I might not be able to buy it in such a small place, but I needn't have worried, there are shelves-full of the stuff. Oh there are plenty of things to keep us old ones occupied, University of the Third Age and societies for this and that. But there's nothing for the young people. They just sit on the backs of benches and put their feet on the seats."

Bell peals and cherry blossom swirled about the elderly congregation making for church as we left Kington. The old ladies were dressed like the Queen Elizabeth in pastel coats, smelling of honeysuckle cream. Rob said they had honeysuckle hair too.

A sparrow was trying and failing to fly away with a large white feather as we passed Hergest Court, which in the fifteenth century had been home to Black Vaughan, who'd fought for both Lancastrians and Yorkists and had been decapitated in battle. Whereupon – allegedly, his bloodhound had raced off with his head. The ghosts of Black Vaughan and his dog had remained at large, harbingers of death that left locals too scared to go out till the ghosts were caught, shrunk to the size of a fly, stuffed in a snuff box and placed under a stone slab. Now Hergest Court had gardens open to visitors.

Drovers had crossed Hergest Ridge, which was broad and long like a gym horse, with luminous, magic lantern-like views. On the summit was the Whet Stone, which had been deposited by a glacier and apparently used as an exchange stone during the Black Death, where people had left goods for others to collect. On reading this I struggled to imagine the trauma and charity of the plague-fearing people who'd used it. Little did I know that in 2020, a friend and I would have our own exchange stone on the wild garlic path, where she would leave plants and I'd leave dandelion honey, and it would seem completely normal.

The drovers had lodged in Llanfair Llythynwg, where now we drank tea in the Royal Oak's pink wingback chairs on which a smell of dogs had settled. Two farmers at the bar went home for dinner and were replaced by a couple from Portsmouth. "We had family from here," said the man, "farriers. They moved to Canning Town in London in the 1860s. But my father was a Marine, that's how he came to be in Portsmouth." "Farriers is still a good business," said the barman, "there's plenty of horses about, £60 a shoe it costs." "Yes," said the woman, "I suppose it's countrified here".

The lanes held pockets of warmth but the sun had gone. At Llannewydd, a mother and daughter eating lunch in the graveyard beckoned us over. Lucy was walking the dyke from south to north. Her mother, along for the weekend, was angry it wasn't like the Pennine Way. "There's no shuttles. We've got to get taxis to take stuff between Bed and Breakfasts, there's no other way," she glared at our rucksacks. Lucy smiled. We made excuses and followed four cheerful Canadians into the church, with whom we shared our biscuits in the pews around a plug-in heater. One made tea in the vestry, but it was milky and weird. "I might have used peppermint teabags by mistake," he said. It was fun.

Nevertheless, Rob's imminent departure made me gloomy. Hatterall Ridge looked ominous, Afon Gwy metallic. A man drinking from a can threw logs into it, one by one. In Y Gelli we had time for a pint before Rob's bus and I missed him even while he sat next to me. The Canadian walkers came in, but were tired and looked at us blankly.

I shuffled morosely around one of the two Norman castles, whose alcoves were stuffed with damp books, and was glancing through the *Hertz Survival Guide for Travelling Businessmen*, when the chip shop closed. I went to one of the pubs instead, where the chips cost £3.95 and were served standing up in a coffee cup there were so few of them. A teenager came in while I was trying to eke them out, and asked what the soup was. "Vegetable," said the bar girl. "What, still?" said the teenager, tossing her hair and stalking out as four teenage boys arrived and got given a huge (free) bowl of leftover roast potatoes. They tucked in, conversing loudly about malt whisky, Anne Boleyn and what they wanted to do to certain girls, till one said they were being obscene and should apologise to 'that woman'. His friends jeered and called him a knob.

It pleased me to think no-one inside the farmhouses knew that 'that woman' was passing. Even the pheasants didn't startle. The soft evening felt like a secret, and my mood was already lifting. Dusky Hatterall Ridge vanished into mist rising suddenly from the ground, which revealed as it did, dozens of Welsh Blacks, sheep and ponies, so I hopped back over the stile to set up my tent. A bullock had sensed me. He sniffed the air and rubbed his head against the fence. The birds were still singing.

Dawn sparkled the grass and haloed the sheep at the foot of Hatterall Ridge. My Mars Bar was so cold it was hard to chew. The wrapper rustled loudly and I heard a bleat at my feet. A lamb was cwtched under the hedge, radiant in gold light.

The ridge formed the border between Herefordshire in England, and in

Cymru, Bannau Brycheiniog National Park in Powys and Sir Fynwy. There were snow pockets on the top. The Herefordshire valleys lay in dewy folds. The trail was exhilarating, high and steady as if I was walking along a diplodocus from its head to the end of its tail. Sometimes enough sun broke through to bathe the heather with russet light, as I left Powys for Sir Fynwy.

PLAGUE

In 1301 Edward I made his sixteen-year-old son the first ever English Prince of Wales, ending hopes of a Cymreig Principality and beginning a tradition that endures to this day. In 1307, Edward I died and his son became Edward II. In constant conflict with the Anglo-Norman barons, Edward II reduced the size of their Marcher lordships to diminish their power, and divided the Principality of Cymru (the part not included in the Marches) into six counties. Some passed to Anglo-Norman lords. They fought over Casnewydd, Caerdydd and Caerffili, while Cymry attacked their castles at Y Trallwng and Y Waun. In the famine of 1314-15, Llywelyn Bren led a rebellion in the south-east but was hung, drawn and quartered in Caerdydd.

The climate was deteriorating. Winters were very cold and most summers wet or warm and stormy. Harvests were poor, particularly between 1315 and 1318 when huge quantities of rain fell. Trefynwy suffered three decades of flooding. Storms battered the coast. Sand dunes rolled across fields and began to bury settlements like Niwbwrch, Cynffig and Cydweli. A sandbar grew across Y Tywi, preventing ships reaching Caerfyrddin, and rivers suffered from silting. The soil was eroded and exhausted. Crops failed, famine spread, and cattle were diseased. People kept on as they could. Herring fisheries thrived, ships were built and by 1327 Caerfyrddin was the staple port, importing goods like French wine.

In 1325 Edward II, having failed to secure Anglo-Norman territories in France sent his French wife Isabella and Lord Mortimer to negotiate with the French King. Instead they fell in love and returned to overthrow Edward and Anglo-Norman lords in south Cymru. Edward and Isabella's son became Edward III in 1326. The Hundred Years War began in France a year later, in which large numbers of Cymry would fight either for Edward III or his son The Black Prince. Cymreig archers helped win major battles, but some, like Owain Lawgoch, fought for the French. Meanwhile, Anglo-Norman unrest continued throughout Cymru.

The black rat arrived in British ports. Its fleas spread the plague (or Black Death) which reached Cymru in 1349 killing two-thirds of the impoverished population, reducing it to 100,000. The population of Aberteifi fell from 104 to seven. A third of land was uncultivated, fields became mass graves, and landowners' incomes fell – so they increased taxes.

By 1350, water-powered fulling mills enabled wool manufacturing to become one of the main rural economies. Most cottages had a spinning wheel, and carders, spinners, weavers, and fullers produced garments and goods for local use. The monks at Tyndyrn, Margam and Castell-nedd in the southeast developed the industry on a larger scale and Edward III, recognising its international value, encouraged Flemish weavers to set up in England and Cymru, which suited the Flemings seeking refuge from war with France.

In 1361, a drought was followed by the return of The Black Death. In 1362, Edward III became the first King to use English in parliament though French was still the dominant legal language and remained so till the seventeenth century. Anglo-Norman ruling classes began to neglect their French origins in favour of an English identity. The Black Prince died in 1377 so Edward III's grandson, Richard II, became king.

Catholic Christianity was the state religion and by now thirteen Cistercian monasteries had been established in Cymru by the Normans. In 1395 John Wycliffe was condemned by the Catholic Church and his followers persecuted, for translating the Bible from Latin into English. Cymraeg manuscripts like the White Book of Rhydderch and Red Book of Hergest were produced. Dafydd ap Gwilym was the premier bard – many gentry employed household bards to praise their greatness.

Storms continued and the plague kept returning. Deaths among the poor created a demand for labourers while deaths among the wealthy caused complex land divisions. Many adopted English law, bequeathing their entire property to the eldest son, resulting in extensive landed estates. The gentry established heronries as game for falconers, introduced coarse fish for sport, and fallow deer for hunting.

The landscape was a mosaic of enclosed fields and individual holdings, large fields, common land, woodland, and villages. Bogs were burned annually to stop malaria spreading. Woodland was coppiced for spindles, fence posts and firewood, and tannin for use in the leather industry. But plague-induced population collapse meant the land was worked less and some woodland began to recover. Warrens fell into disuse and rabbits dispersed.

In 1399 Richard II, who had links with many Cymreig gentry, exiled his cousin Henry Bolingbroke and took control of the House of Lancaster. Bolingbroke marched to Cymru, and confronted Richard who was returning from Ireland. Bolingbroke dethroned Richard at Castell Y Fflint and became Henry IV in 1399 – the first King of England to swear allegiance in English.

SIR FYNWY

*T*waite shad, salmon, trout and native crayfish swim and crawl in mineral-rich
*Afon Gwy, which flows from rolling uplands to the lowlying south, where land
has been reclaimed by the sea. Once a wilderness of coastal swampy forests and saltings,
Morfa Gwent (which extends west to Caerdydd) after 2,000 years of drainage, cultivation and grazing is now home to lapwing and yellow wagtail. Notable plants in the
reens include celery-leaved buttercup, spiked water milfoil and lesser water-parsnip.*

The Herefordshire hills lined up like silver whales, and distant lakes shone
like new coins. Mountain ponies turned their backs to the wind, the sound of
which was everywhere. The clouds were low but fast, revealing shreds of blue
sky. Skylarks chattered and whistled in the heather. When the wind paused,
the sun shone and a lark would rise singing, then drop when the wind
returned. Some tumbled through the air fighting or amorously wheeling. I
startled a red grouse. It chuckled into the air and was gone, leaving an impression of scarlet wattle and glossy plumage.

Crowds of chattering hikers were ascending from Pandy as I dropped off
the ridge, which, being an early bird, I'd had all to myself. Celandines glossed
the hedge-banks. A farmer in ochre coat and soft peaked hat waved from a
chuntering machine more lawnmower than tractor. I crossed the railway track
and stopped to pee, just as a train passed.

Pandy (meaning fulling mill) had no shop and both pubs were closed, but
the landlady of one was catering for men digging up the road and made me a
packed lunch for £5. She said it was funny on Mondays. "You know it was
supposed to snow today?" one of the labourers said. I dried my tent on a hedge,
put the crisps in my sandwiches, and drifted off in the heat.

Sir Fynwy was new to me. A woman hand-sawing a fallen tree into
firewood, far away down an undulating field while trying to keep her child
in sight, looked like a Gainsborough. The Hunters Moon in Llangatwg-
Lingoed had a glossy look too. It had been trading since the thirteenth
century – but it was closed, being funny on Mondays, so I went to the church
next door to make tea. In it, a fifteenth-century mural of red and ochre blobs
apparently depicted St George slaying a dragon. One theory holds it was
painted in celebration of victory over Glyndŵr. The dyke ran right through
the village. Border tensions would have been high. Such strife was hard to

imagine as I boiled the kettle in the vestry. Mice had pooed on the sugar and teabag containers and a hand-written note explained that the tea was 'Funded by the Monmouthshire Economic Development Board but must be made at own risk'.

The sun slid over improved fields where the loam was already rich and fertile compared to the thin-soiled acidic hill-pasture I was used to in the north-west. A young couple waved happily down from the biggest tractor I'd ever seen. A herd of young heifers followed close at my heels and their breath was warm on my neck, while an old man collecting sticks from the side of an empty road regarded me shyly from under a scarlet hat.

Llantilio Castle was unusual in that fragments of lime-wash plaster remained, and its moat, clattering with dragonflies, was full. Hubert de Burgh – an Anglo-Norman lord from Norfolk had built it. After his death, all three of his castles were acquired by the Crown and became centres of estate management and revenue collection. A dragon flag fluttered at the cottage next door, where an elderly man chopped firewood. Later, on reading about Norman dominion, I remembered the flag and was glad. A cyclist panted to the top of the hill, and waited for his son in a summery cloud of thrips.

The light was syrupy gold and the air still warm when I put up my tent in an improved field among frisky lambs. I looked back at Hatterall Ridge. It was blue and the sky above it was blue and the sun was dropping behind a smoke-blue cloud from which gold beams radiated. Snow my arse.

Next morning I heard the 'peewit' call, and watched lapwing tumbling above a waterlogged field. But this was cider country and soon there were orchards behind the hedges. Cider apple cultivation had improved after the Norman Conquest, but was industrialised now and the orchards had scant biodiversity and very few apple varieties compared to the 2,000 grown in Victorian Britain. I crossed a Bulmers orchard where young standards stood in neat rows, the ground vegetation-bereft.

Two council workers with clipboards welcomed me to Trefynwy, which was helpful, as I'd not really known where I was. A humming man in a suit overtook me on Mynwy Bridge. I would learn that in the thirteenth and fourteenth centuries, even as this bridge was being built, Trefynwy was badly flooded. In 1349 it had rained every day between Easter and Christmas and Monnow Street had been abandoned as earth houses collapsed, leaving a thick layer of brown silt still exposed by modern excavations. The Black Death arrived the same year, having spread west from the Gobi Desert where it had reappeared after being dormant for centuries. During construction work in 2015 a stone hearth would be discovered in the silt underneath Commerce House. Fragments of a fourteenth-century jug in the form of a medieval woman were found too. The woman wears a brooch, carries a small pot, and has a key and purse hanging from her belt. Some people had enjoyed stability and professions, crafts and possessions before being hit by disaster. The gap between rich and poor had been huge – Cymru still accommodates both.

In 2002, twenty families were evacuated from Trefynwy due to heavy flooding, and a flooding scheme was developed on an outlying estate. Contemporary flooding has been attributed partly to the clearance by local authorities in the 1990s of timber blockages from tributaries to Afon Gwy which had taken centuries to form. Climate change, soil erosion and impermeable surfaces were also to blame.

Thirty years of flooding is not difficult to imagine as we teeter on the brink of climate chaos. After all, we clamour for dredging (which is only temporarily effective) and flood-barriers (which push the problem somewhere else), but fiercely resist natural solutions – afforestation, rivers being allowed to flow their own course, the reintroduction of beavers whose dams, like the timber blockages, regulate the flow and filter out pollutants (while the shallow pools they create increase biodiversity by up to four times). Bigger and more general solutions to climate change are dismissed outright. We might hate change, but it's coming anyway, and so are the beavers.

In the fourteenth century the land was already deforested and beavers already extinct. Perhaps otherwise the flooding might not have been so bad. As I read about Trefynwy's history, I wondered how we'd cope today with thirty years of flooding topped off with a pandemic. I didn't realise quite how close I'd get to finding out.

When I returned a few weeks later, the sky was black and wind was whipping the magnolias. Traffic and pedestrians bustled past Specsavers, Superdrug, Greggs, The British Heart Foundation and WH Smiths, but there was a honeyed feeling to Trefynwy and its mellow stone buildings, despite all the chain stores. A queue of posh school kids in blazers spilled out of the bakery advertising hot baguettes for £1.20 but I had so little money I didn't dare buy one. I had food, but knowing I couldn't afford one made me feel left out. I was getting regular magazine work now, but one commission a month didn't amount to much of a salary. Sixth-formers in suits jostled each other in the subway and two men with clipboards counted vehicles as I left town.

In Coed Beaulieu, cherry blossom whirled, a gust of wind blew all the salad out of my sandwich, and the rain began.

But the wind was exciting and the wooded ridge overlooking Afon Gwy was ripe with birdsong. Blossom whirled over lady's smock. Bluebells fell away in drifts. I knelt to smell them and got a whiff of humus too, before the weight of my rucksack toppled me forward to land face down and laughing, wetter, muddier, fresher. Trees were in bud or new leaf – lime, hazel, chestnut. Ferns were unrolling. I threaded a bluebell through my zip and put a cherry blossom sprig in my hair. But the rain was persistent, the strong wind consistent and my old raincoat leaked. Sticks blew off trees and wood anemones suffered. A man approaching with walking poles nodded grimly, his chin set at the weather, his poncho red against green.

The rain reached my skin and numbed my flesh. I fell into a trance and forgot what season it was as light failed. Occasional glimpses of Dyffryn Gwy were brown and cloud-swirled. Trunks poured with water that collected in moss and my eyebrows stopped working. I came to a cottage where a man in red shirt like a fairy-tale woodcutter was watching veils of rain from his porch. I asked if I was still on Offa's Dyke Path and saw him blurred, shaking his head with grave sorrow, as if I'd failed a magical quest. I found the path again eventually, beneath a floating mulch of old twigs.

Wind shrieked, trees thrashed, and cloud swirled at frightening speed around Devil's Pulpit, the craggy limestone pillar jutting into the valley, where I stood transfixed and haunted, as if all the border's torment was raging about me. Unseen below, Tyndyrn Abbey stood roofless and ruined. Built from red sandstone in the thirteenth and fourteenth centuries, the abbey had replaced a stone church which itself had replaced wooden structures built by monks from northern France. It was the first of fifteen Cistercian monasteries built in Cymru, and one of very few to have survived the Edwardian wars – perhaps because Edward II had stayed there in 1326. Despite it being almost impossible to attract new recruits following the Black Death, for 400 years (till being dissolved by Henry VIII), trade through Tyndyrn had dominated the local economy. The monks, apparently, had believed they were in danger of being seduced away from their work when like now, the pulpit couldn't be seen from the abbey, meaning that the devil was in it.

The path dropped into fields at the edge of Cas-gwent, the rain ceased, and the wind dropped to a stiff breeze that dried my clothes. The sky became luminous. The last of the dyke dwindled away on Beachley Peninsula, and before me Môr Hafren was wide and grand and shifting, a diminutive Mississippi, muddy and monstrous with a yacht sailing up it – just a tiny white triangle. I had reached the south end of the border. I pitched my tent.

I'd grown accustomed to the intimate Norman Marcher landscape of checkerboard hills and irregular fields, wooded copses, villages and timber-framed towns. The Marches had swept across southern Cymru in a reverse L, but the coast had its own character, and I suddenly craved its space and salty abrasion. The footbridge over Afon Gwy brought me back to the coast path which began, finished, or in my case continued, on the bank.

Cas-gwent had been noted in the Middle Ages for its exports of timber and bark and import of wine, and the smell of wine lingered now around the bistros. Fairy lights hung between lampposts and one of the trees had been yarn-bombed. The houses petered out, replaced by retail and industrial units, where buddleia crept through spiked fences, and a henna-haired cyclist emerged from a subway with shopping bags on each handlebar. Hafren Bridge crouched beneath an escort of pylons and cables, and through fireweed and brambles I saw men hammering at the hub of an offshore turbine – the First World War national shipyard had been based here, cementing Cas-gwent's industrial kudos.

The landscape opened out. Now pylons and ditches crossed large fields of legumes, corn and cows. The tops of small masts poked above a bank, and rushing up it, I saw before me gulls roosting, oil drums bobbing, and a red-sailed yacht nose into Môr Hafren. I was back on the coast. I felt joy and a kind of relief.

Brown estuary stole into me. Entire trees were washed up on its banks. Pale waves heaved. The second bridge ahead was newer and flatter – lorries crossed it on a cushion of air. Traffic and planes droned, but the wind in the rushes was louder. The land's flatness enhanced the orthogonal yacht masts and pylons spiking a huge sky with bridges and cables etched across it like technical drawings. A hen harrier skimmed the reeds. A reed bunting swayed on a stalk. Warm breeze carried scents of grass and salt and traffic.

At Blackrock a passer-by approached an old fisherman, and both men dashed to the rod. "That looks like a little eel to me," said the passer-by. "You here often?" "Fifteen year ago I had a heart attack," said the old man. "They let me go, and five years now, I'm a fisherman. Arhh it's them old mullet. Ahh. He's had his dinner and he's gone home." Light shone through the orange canvas of his chair.

A Welsh Water van waited outside the four-storey pump-house. Labourers who'd dug the railway tunnel under Môr Hafren had lived here in homes built from the excavated stone and shale, which evolved into the settlement of Sudbrook where cars were parked outside colourful terraces. A man ferried tools from his van. Another hammered bricks into a small front yard, radio loud. The labourers had spent four years trying to breach an underground river hit just before the tunnel's completion, before giving up and building the pump-house instead. Knowing that should the pump fail, the track would flood in twenty minutes, gives my train journeys extra frisson. But even the pump house was dwarfed by the Second Hafren Crossing, carrying the M4 overhead and casting a thin blue shadow on the water.

Out on the mudflats which high tide swamped with up to fourteen metres of water, courting goosanders entwined their necks. A woman with a small dog asked where I was headed. "Did you see Blackrock just there where you've passed now?" she said eagerly. "It's important to me, a special place. My uncle was a lave net fishermen." Blackrock's lave net fishermen knitted Y-shaped nets from strips of willow and walked out as the tide ebbed, to the reefs. They numbered only eight, and were restricted to a collective catch of fifteen salmon per season. But salmon and sewin stocks were in such a critical condition that in 2017, fisheries would reach an unprecedented low with twenty-one out of twenty-three salmon rivers giving cause for grave concern. She was disappointed I'd missed them, as was I. They might be out there by now, she thought. Fish stocks were so low, in 2020 even Blackrock fishermen would be denied a license unless they agreed to release their catch. They refused. I wish I'd seen them, I wish they were still able to fish, in the old way. I wished we'd not stripped the rivers of salmon. I wished we didn't destroy lovely things. "Stay safe!" she called after me. I walked barefoot on beaches of glistening mud. Môr Hafren was still more than two miles wide.

COLONISATION

Two centuries after William had conquered, society was militaristic and unrest endemic. In England, tension simmered between the Anglo-Norman barons and King John, while Anglo-Normans were still meeting fierce resistance in Cymru.

In 1205, Llywelyn ap Iorwerth of Gwynedd married King John's daughter Joan and expanded his territory by seizing north Ceredigion and Powys Wenwynwn, provoking John into sending an army to Gwynedd, and Joan into making the peace. King John fought battles in Normandy. Llywelyn ab Iorwerth led Cymreig princes to capture the Norman castles of Caerfyrddin, Cydweli, Llansteffan, Cilgerran and Aberteifi. He then allied with French and Anglo-Norman barons and captured Shrewsbury, one of the factors that forced King John to sign Magna Carta which granted more power to the barons, and weakened the Crown, and established that everybody, including the king, was meant to be subject to the law. When King John reneged on the agreement, the Barons War began. Anglo-Norman barons offered the English throne to Louis of France who became unofficial King of England till John's death, after which the barons recognised Joan's brother as Henry III.

Meanwhile in 1216 in Aberdyfi, Cymreig rulers recognised Llywelyn ab Iorwerth as overlord and Prince of Cymru, as did Henry III, the Pope, and Cymreig nobles in 1218. But in 1227, Henry III encroached on Llywelyn's lands by making Hubert de Burgh Lord of Trefaldwyn. Llywelyn captured Hubert then hung William de Braose after finding him in bed with Joan. Llywelyn married four of his daughters to Marcher Lords and fought battles in south Cymru, burning Aberhonddu and destroying Castell-nedd. Henry offered land in Cymru to Anglo-Irish knights in exchange for their help in subduing Llywelyn. But in 1234, Llewelyn formed an alliance with Richard Marshal (Earl of Pembroke) and seized Shrewsbury again, forcing Henry to sign 'The Peace of Middle' which allowed Llywelyn to continue ruling Powys Wenwynwn and made Cymreig lordships of Powys Fadog and Deheubarth. In 1240, Llywelyn ab Iorwerth, (who became known as Llywelyn Fawr – the Great), died after uniting most of Cymru through a mixture of politics and power. He'd had one illegitimate son, Gruffudd, and one legitimate son, Dafydd, who inherited the Principality and title Prince of Cymru.

But in 1241 Henry III invaded Cymru, took Gruffudd hostage and forced

Dafydd to yield all territory except Gwynedd. In 1246, Dafydd died without an heir and Gruffudd fell to his death trying to escape from the Tower of London, some inheritance passed to his sons, whose power Henry tried to dissolve. But one of them, Llywelyn ap Gruffudd, inherited most of Gwynedd.

Henry III forced Llywelyn ap Gruffudd to share land with his brother Owain, and took some for himself. In 1255 Llywelyn imprisoned his own brothers Dafydd and Owain for plotting against him, and took back the land given to Owain. In 1257, he defeated an Anglo-Norman army, by 1258, he'd declared himself Prince of Cymru and in 1263 had led forces into the Marches. In 1264, during the second baronial revolt, Henry III and his son Edward were captured by Simon de Montfort, an Anglo-Norman baron who'd allied with Llywelyn ap Gruffudd. In 1267, Henry III signed the Treaty of Montgomery allowing Llywelyn to retain a string of lordships in the south and recognising him as Prince of Cymru. In return, Llywelyn accepted that he was a vassal of Henry, King of England. But then Henry granted Gilbert de Clare castles at Y Fenni and Aberhonddu and in revenge, Llywelyn attacked north Morgannwg and seized Senghennydd.

Society was predominantly rural. Cymreig society was divided into two broad classes – the 'free' and the 'unfree'. The free were nobles who lived in fortified manors or timber castles and allotted land to the unfree in return for food and labour. Farmers owned or leased land, lived in dispersed settlements and pastured animals from their hafod and hendre dwellings. Meanwhile, Anglo-Norman lords who had been granted land by English royalty, lived in stone or timber manors in the Marches. They also had 'unfree' labourers to work their manor estates, which were divided into open fields, villages (where the unfree lived), moor and meadow pasture, and woodland where lords hunted deer.

Anglo-Normans had installed Catholic monasteries and abbeys across Cymru. The Cistercians were by now making an important contribution to the economy by employing people to farm, fish, mill and mine, sometimes paying rent to landowners, and owning large flocks of sheep whose fleeces were a major source of income. They would also become copyists of Cymreig manuscripts, and employ bards. English and French (and Latin, a Roman legacy) penetrated Cymru throughout the century, but Cymraeg poetry and prose was also written, and in 1250, the oldest surviving book in Cymru, the Black Book of Caerfyrddin was made.

In 1272 Henry III died and his son Edward I was crowned – the first English king to be fluent in English. Angered by Llywelyn ap Gruffudd's plans to marry Simon de Montfort's daughter Eleanor, he captured her in 1275. One of Llywelyn's brothers Dafydd and Gwenwynwyn of Powys defected to England. Llywelyn refused to meet Edward in London without the King of France as a go-between, so Edward sent an army to Gwynedd. They confiscated Ynys Môn's harvest which supplied much of the north, starving Llywelyn's army and forcing him to submit and yield some land to Dafydd and some to Edward I. Eleanor de Montfort was freed and Llywelyn retained the title Prince of Cymru and ruled over much of west Gwynedd. But Edward I now conquered Cymru. By 1277, to stymie Llywelyn, he undertook the most ambitious medieval building project in Europe by fortifying castles at Trefaldwyn, Caerfyrddin and Aberteifi, and commissioning new ones at Aberystwyth, Llanfair ym Muallt, Y Fflint and Rhuddlan.

Llywelyn still had support in some Cymreig lords, for whom English colonisation had not brought equality. Dafydd became disillusioned and attacked Penarlâg Castle in 1282, triggering a revolt Llywelyn didn't join, Eleanor having just died giving birth to their daughter Gwenllian. Edward I attacked Cymru with the biggest army seen since the 1066 invasion, which was eventually too powerful. In 1282, Llywelyn ap Gruffudd was tracked down and killed by Edward's men at Cilmeri. Dafydd continued to fight against Edward and assumed the title Prince of Cymru but was betrayed by one of his men and hung, drawn and quartered in Shrewsbury for high treason. In 1283 Edward built even more castles and walled towns at Y Trallwng, Caernarfon, Conwy, Cricieth, Harlech, Caerwys and Biwmares, and filled them with Anglo-Norman settlers. In a twelve-year period of castle building, in order to conquer Cymru, he'd spent more than ten times his annual income.

But he still wasn't done. In 1284, Edward I created the Statute of Rhuddlan, which disbanded the Principality of Gwynedd to create the counties of Ynys Môn, Meirionnydd and Caernarfon, which he staffed with sheriffs to collect taxes and administer justice using English Common Law, largely replacing The Laws of Hywel, supposedly established in the tenth century. He created new Marcher lordships for Anglo-Norman lords at Dinbych, Bromfield and Iâl, Y Waun and Rhuthun. Only Powys Wenwynwn (having supported Edward) retained the power of a Marcher lordship. A few more rebellions were crushed. Llywelyn's daughter Gwenllian and Dafydd's daughter Gwladus were sent to nunneries. Dafydd's sons spent their lives in prison. Of Llywelyn's other brothers, only Rhodri survived, and lived out his days in Surrey.

Cymru was colonised. Political independence had ended. The church was ruled by Canterbury. The Llywelyns campaign for a united Cymru led by a Cymreig Prince had been supported by the Cistercians, bards and some nobility, but not by those who objected to their supremacy. By the end of the thirteenth century a Principality had been created, but the princes would be sons of English Kings.

Meanwhile, intermarriage between Anglo-Normans and Cymreig nobility had become increasingly common, and confusion over identity and allegiance more pronounced, stirred up by the old bully Edward. In 1297 more than 5,000 Cymry fought alongside Edward I in Flanders, and in 1298 Cymreig archers helped him and the Anglo-Normans defeat William Wallace at the Battle of Falkirk. Through a combination of Anglo-Norman control and Edward's colonisation, Cymru had eighty towns by the end of the thirteenth century. They had become central to the growing economy even though townspeople only accounted for about 10 percent of the population. Edward's walled towns were built for English settlers. Bastions of colonisation, Cymry were locked out. In a long history of subjugation, this period was particularly hideous. This was at the root of why I felt uneasy about being English. This was why Cymry liked England to lose every match.

It is said that Henry III killed Cymru's last wild boar — in the Forest of Dean, across Afon Gwy in England, in 1260.

CASNEWYDD

The European eel swims in Afon Wysg. Smooth palmate newts live in lakes and ponds, many of which are manmade, and the canal, no longer navigable, sustains grass snakes and prickly sedge. Brownfield sites support the small ranunculus moth which feeds on prickly lettuce. The coast forms part of Morfa Gwent, reclaimed land with flower-rich meadows, and reens populated by rootless duckweed, the world's smallest flowering plant.

Even the water seemed to be fighting itself. A thirteenth-century boat packed with iron ore had been found in the mud a few miles inland at Magwyr, recalling a time when the coast teemed with craft. Although the Crown had claimed rights to tidal rivers, Magna Carta had given people free access to Môr Hafren. They had caught salmon, lamprey, eels and shad with nets, spears and basket traps. Multiple basket weirs made from Forest of Dean timber had extended from the banks, obstructing river traffic so often they were removed in the sixteenth century.

The weather was soporific. My hips and feet ached. I felt beaten. By yesterday's storm. By the weight of my pack. Often, I sat on it, and nearly fell asleep on the path at Allteuryn, where the land had been reclaimed by Benedictine monks. A few medieval field-strips survived, allocated to villagers and divided by low banks to demarcate crops in summer but allow cattle to graze the whole open field in winter. The back fen was undrained common land, grazed only in summer.

At the Nature Reserve I wanted to lie down on the boardwalk. I was lured across fields instead, to a pink wall on which large letters spelled 'The Waterloo Inn'. The landlord and one customer were smoking in the porch, surprised to see me, having forgotten their advert to the coast path. "Everyone in Wales should walk it," exclaimed the landlord, "like a rite of passage!" The customer heartily agreed, before adding that he'd do it on a donkey. Half a cider went straight to my head. I phoned Rob from the bar, met him on the path with a backdrop of wind turbines and ran into his embrace. We ate back at the pub, which had filled up with Friday-night drinkers. Two tipsy women entreated us to camp in their garden but we walked a little way on, and set up in a field of buttercups. I crashed out in Rob's arms before he could undress, my face in his warm checked shirt.

A moorhen was marooned on a tiny patch of wetland left apparently accidentally in a gap between Heras fencing at the port. The port too was a relic – the last of multiple docks in Casnewydd that had served the coal valleys. Heaps of bottles, boulders, and bricks awaited transport and rubbish blew around an incinerator. A red boat docked. The Transporter Bridge was closed, its gondola an empty bird cage, so we walked on past 'Friar the Van' and a dead rat in the gutter. The air stank of gas and rubbish.

But across Afon Wysg, everything was lively. Bunting fluttered outside Newport Auctions, a dragon-flag flapped over Autofix, and crowds trooped round an open-air market where sunlight flooded the canopies and dazzled the puddles. We shook rain off plastic chairs and bought rolls and Styrofoam cups of coffee, watching the market. Generators hummed. Women in hijabs flicked deftly through the clothes rail and men bought sacks of potatoes. A plump man in a green silk suit mused among the vegetables while another with fez and shiny waistcoat walked briskly between stalls, hands clasped comfortably behind him like a puffin. I recognised the red-haired Country Meat man from other markets in other towns. His Black-Country drone floated over the stalls. "Ladies and gents I can do you pork steaks… fresh pork steaks, two for £3." The smell of doughnuts filled the air and traffic whizzed past the fence.

The old dock accommodated newer developments – the City Fishing Centre, a dead seagull and a KFC cup on the bank. A powerboat moored at a jetty bodged from pallets and planks, wheelie bins outside Fanny's Rest Stop. And a housing estate where a woman in purple dressing gown put out her rubbish and a learner driver tried to reverse. The estate gave to a retail park of enormous warehouses – Lidl, Smyths Toy Superstore, Next Clearance and Argos. Two little boys pushed through the hedge outside Bargain Warehouse, plastic rifles over their shoulders. A middle-aged couple passed with shopping bags. "You've got to prime it, undercoat it…" said the man. White poplars lined the main road, cyclists threaded through traffic, a man wheelied his quadbike and rabbits scampered over the verge. It was an exciting, peopled landscape, but grimy with traffic as if like the moorhen, the people had also been accidentally hemmed in. An unhappy man positioned yellow sacks of potatoes along the road, and a sign saying '£4.99', then sat on the step of his van with his head in his hands.

Romans based at Caerleon had begun the land reclamation of Morfa Gwent to graze their cavalry horses, but after their withdrawal it reverted to saltmarsh till Normans rebuilt the seawall. In the Middle Ages, more reens were dug and dispersed hamlets and moated farmsteads built. Rushes whispered. Gulls hovered over a landfill site and a heron sailed over the grass. A white van passed slowly with a farmer at the wheel and two collies in pursuit while in the distance, a man shovelled muck into the trailer of a tractor painted with a giant dragon, and his little boy leapt about with a spade. We caught the smell of fresh water.

Môr Hafren was wide and brown. A farmer was staring at it from under his baseball cap, in a quadbike on top of the embankment. "I can remember when these docks here were ever so busy with coal coming in all the time and tugs bringing in the big ships," he said. "Now it's all containerised shipping. I can't understand how the economy works anymore. They're electrifying the railway now, this one you can see between Swansea and London. There's groups of men in hi-viz jackets standing around, doing nothing. I never see them do anything. None of them. Just standing around in groups. How does it work? Can you tell me?" We couldn't. The railway plans were a broken election promise – electrification would only reach Caerdydd.

Silver pools shaped like countries and continents had been left by the tide and a single white narcissus flowered. Swans trailed though duckweed, swallows swooped. There was a quietness to the Levels I appreciated. The Norman Marches had kicked across South Cymru, and though Llywelyn ab Iorwerth had attacked Castell Caerffili, even his authority had not stretched this far south, and Edward's conquest had left Marcher lordships unchanged and unchallenged. It would have been relatively quiet even in that war-torn period.

I was hobbling with what appeared to be a groin strain, like a footballer. We sat on our rucksacks to watch lapwings display and later rested on a concrete embankment among bladderwrack, beer cans and fag butts to watch Môr Hafren. Ripples in its wash made a loud whooshing sound.

The barman in the Lighthouse Inn made us coffee. We sat on patched window seats listening to him reminiscing with a group of old men from the caravan site. Each time one spoke the others guffawed. "We were jiving in the middle of the Millennium Stadium. Absolutely battered. Hundred different beers, sixty different ciders…" said one, and everyone snorted. "You ended up in Ebbw Vale on the train, I ended up in Cwm Carn," said another, to more hoots. "Cracking day," said the barman, "anyone who expects to come back half-tidy is well wrong." Everyone howled.

The tide had begun its retreat, leaving little muddy shelves on the shore. It was hard to tell what was sky, mud or water.

FEUDALISM

In 1066, William Duke of Normandy conquered England and was crowned William I in the chaos following King Harold Godwinson's battles against Harold Hardrada of Norway, and his own brother Tostig. Cymru too had been weakened by internal conflict following the death in 1063 of Gruffudd ap Llywelyn. Bleddyn ap Cynfyn who ruled Powys with his brother Rhiwallon formed an alliance with the Anglo-Saxon kingdom of Mercia in attempt to fight off the Normans, whose partial conquest of Cymru was gradual.

The Normans practised a feudalist system in which the king gave land to those who fought for him. William I recognised Rhys ap Tewdwr as ruler of Deheubarth and Iestyn ap Gwrgant as leader of Morgannwg, but placed Norman lords in Shrewsbury, Chester and Hereford to stamp authority on the border region, which became known as the Marches. Marcher Norman lords built castles, granted manors to their followers and were subjects of the English king but not to English law. They ran their lordships like independent kingdoms and continued to do so till Henry VIII's Act of Union.

William II succeeded his father in 1087 and Norman lords continued to attack Cymru. Morgannwg fell to Robert Fitzhamon, Rhys ap Tewdwr was killed, Brycheiniog seized, and the Norman lords of Shrewsbury powered southwest and built a castle at Penfro. In 1094, Gruffudd ap Cynan of Gwynedd allied with Cadwgan ap Bleddyn of Powys and drove the Normans out, initiating a general revolt crushed a year later by William II's forces. Gruffudd and Cadwgan fled to Ireland. Meanwhile the lords of Chester and Shrewsbury were beaten on the banks of Y Fenai by an alliance of Cymry and Scandinavian Vikings led by Magnus Barefoot. By 1100 the Normans were expelled from Gwynedd and most of Powys. Gruffudd ap Cynan returned to become ruler of Gwynedd, and Cadwgan ap Bleddyn ruled Powys, while Gruffudd ap Rhys ap Tewdwr attempted control of Deheubarth. Henry I succeeded William II and in 1105 organised a colony of Flemings, many of them dyers and weavers displaced by floods, or descendants of William I's allies who'd helped conquer England, to settle in south Dyfed. Stephen succeeded Henry I. Owain Gwynedd annexed Ceredigion to Gwynedd and became the first Cymreig ruler to use the title Princeps Wallensium (Prince of the Cymry). Legend claims his sister Gwenllian led an army to fight the Normans of Cydweli in 1136 but was killed.

In 1154, Henry II became king and received oaths of allegiance from Rhys ap Gruffudd of Deheubarth and Owain Gwynedd. In 1156, Henry's help was sought by Madog ap Maredudd of Powys to vanquish Owain Gwynedd – who reappeared in 1165 to defeat Henry's army in the Battle of the Berwynion. Fighting among the princes of Cymru, between them and Norman barons, and among the Norman barons continued. In 1189, Richard I became King of England and in 1199 he named his nephew Arthur as successor, from whom Richard's brother John seized the throne.

By the end of the twelfth century, Cymreig leaders had retained control throughout north and central Cymru, though Powys had been divided into two kingdoms – Powys Fadog and Powys Wenwynwyn, and Deheubarth and Gwynedd were fractious. Normans controlled the Marches along the border and most of South Cymru, and had settled it with Anglo-Norman lords. Their lordships included a Flemish colony and a few 'Englishries', but residents were largely Cymry. Both Cymreig and Norman lords recognised the authority of the English Crown.

The Normans – themselves descended from and named after Nordic Vikings who'd colonised northern France two centuries earlier, spoke French, which became the language of court and aristocracy. They colonised their conquered lands with English-, Flemish- and French-speaking followers, but Cymraeg thrived nonetheless. Cymraeg literature was recorded on parchment. Poetry was highly esteemed, and the first recorded ceremony resembling an eisteddfod was held in Aberteifi in 1176. In 1191, Gerallt Gymro (Gerald of Wales) a Cymreig-Norman archdeacon, royal clerk and historian, wrote *Itinerarium Cambriae* (Journey Through Cymru), the first known travel book of Cymru.

Faithful to the pope who had blessed their attack on Britain, the Normans promoted Roman Catholicism. They broke up existing clasau and founded dozens of monasteries and priories. In 1120, Dewi Sant (Saint David) was canonised by Rome. But in the same year, the dioceses of Cymru were incorporated into the Archdiocese of Canterbury. The Cistercians however, were evolving a Cymreig identity, their asceticism not dissimilar to that practised by earlier Cymreig Christians. By 1200, all the major Cymreig rulers had Cistercian monasteries. Meanwhile Catholic Christianity was spreading across the globe and being fiercely resisted by Islam. The ensuing Crusades were recruited for throughout Christian countries – including Cymru.

Normans controlled all aspects of life from religion to finance. Their invasion coincided with a time of European economic growth and a mild climate. Norman towns grew around stone churches, monasteries, and castles, with weekly markets and annual fairs. By the eleventh century the economy in England had become one of the richest in Europe with one hundred market towns. By comparison, Cymru's only sizeable town was Caerleon, a Roman legacy. Normans lived in manors on estates which included forests, fisheries and fields cultivated by tenants who lived in mud and wattle cabins in return for produce. Cymreig rulers also began to build castles, keep mounted knights, install monastic orders, and build using stone instead of timber.

The Marches were a patchwork of villages, woods, and fields divided by hedgerows, ditches and fences. The population grew. Woodland was cleared for agriculture and its regrowth was grazed by goats. Fish traps were built on intertidal zones. Oats supplemented the diet of herbs, vegetables, milk, cheese and butter, and though hafod and hendre farming continued it began to decline. The Cistercians opened mines, built ships and roads, farmed sheep on a large scale and the wool trade expanded. Sheep, (kept for milk and wool rather than meat) became more economically important than cattle. The Normans reintroduced rabbits (which it seems the Romans brought first) for food, and kept them in sand dunes or specially built earth warrens. Meanwhile Gerallt Gymro claimed Afon Teifi was the last haunt of the beaver in Britain.

CAERDYDD

Large forestry plantations are being restored to broad-leafed woodland. The most westerly natural beech woods in Britain harbour birds-nest orchid, toothwort and yellow birds-nest, while hawfinch, marsh and willow tits feed on the mast. To create the freshwater lagoon of Bae Caerdydd, rivers were impounded to flood mudflats and saltmarsh. Roots of coppiced willow and alder established to compensate displaced wildlife, provide a nursery for fry of ten species of coarse fish. Opportunistic birds have taken advantage of the new wetlands, but those displaced have fared poorly.

Afon Rhymni's mud banks glistened. Upriver were former coal and iron communities, but the water was no longer imperilled by mining waste. Grayling and brown trout had returned – but were declining afresh. Gulls swirled overhead. A moorhen swam. Strange blossom drifted over the hillside blowing gracefully through the air, landing in the river like thistledown and petals, to be borne out to sea. The hillside was a landfill site and the petals were plastic bags.

Ponies grazed the verge. It was burnt and littered with smashed bike lights and the wind played a broken fence post like a flute. The path ducked round a gypsy and traveller site. 'Ond heno pwy yr ei hynt? Nid oes namyn deufaen du, A dyrnaid o laswawr lwch, Ac arogl mwg lle bu' wrote Eifion Wyn, in Y Sipsiwn, (The Gipsy) in 1927. ('And who tonight can say where he is?, He has left behind on the green, Two blackened stones and some bluish dust, And a smell of smoke where he's been.')

Cymru's travelling community consists of some 25,000 fairground people, 15,000 New Age Travellers and approximately 2,000 gypsies. Gypsies – Romanis in England and lowlying southern Cymru, and Kaule in much of north upland Cymru which they negotiated by foot or donkey cart – differ only in the route they took to Britain in about the fifteenth century, having probably originated in northwest India centuries earlier. But they were no longer nomadic. 'Here then is the Gypsies' main problem' wrote Henwood in 1974. 'The law is against them at every turn: they are not allowed to camp on the roadside, so that they are faced with the impossible situation of travelling along roads on which they are literally forbidden to stop.' They were no longer free. Their culture had been crushed.

To add salt to the wound, the Rover Way site was built on a former landfill dump and was now at risk of contamination and coastal erosion. Over the wall we saw tightly-packed crates, trailers, bungalows and statics, shouting boys, barking dogs, and puppies yapping in stacked cages. Two kid goats jumped the wall. We shooed one back but the other refused, and stuck to Rob's heels with such adoration in her brown eyes I felt almost uncomfortable. When the path reached the road we tied her up with a bit of rope and were trying to figure out who to call when a van screeched to a halt and two lads in baseball caps jumped out. "There she is! Who tied her up?" they cried angrily. We crept away while they cuddled her. Five minutes later we met an overweight lad in baggy joggers who asked if we'd seen a goat. "Thank God!" he said when we told him, collapsing to his knees.

I also collapsed, or threw myself down at any rate, onto the verge of an industrial estate. It was nice among the daisies. Cars pulled up and people jumped out and ran past us to Greggs. Otherwise the road was empty, being Saturday, and the people returned upset, because Greggs, like the warehouses, was closed. My boots were fissured and split and my feet blistered from being permanently wet. My groin strain ached. It seemed a long way to the city centre. Rob had booked us a room in the suburbs, but I had to rest on a garden wall.

"We should never have let you book this room for two, it's just a broom cupboard!" said the receptionist and gave us £10 back. But I thought it was so luxurious with its shower and soft white bed I got emotional. "I owe you so much," I told Rob, and he welled up and said he owed me so much too. We watched Wigan win the FA Cup, and I felt better.

Rob had bought tickets for Clwb Ifor Bach from where John Peel had featured gigs we remembered. The club was named after Ifor ap Meurig whose tale is recorded by Gerallt Gymro in *Journey Through Cymru*. In 1158, Fitz Robert (a Norman), killed Morgan ap Owain (Lord of Caerleon and Gwynllŵg), captured Caerdydd Castle, and tried to take land which belonged to Ifor, (one of Morgan ap Owain's tenants). Whereupon Ifor scaled the castle walls, kidnapped Fitz Robert, his wife and son, and kept them in Coed Senghenydd till his land (and a bit extra for the trouble) were returned.

The club was exciting – small, dark and crowded, with stone walls and sticky floors. The first band was loud and electric. Then Sweet Baboo's Stephen Black swivelled his eyes around the room in a cabaret all of their own. "I've got a motor home, and a long stretch of straight road. Why don't we up sticks and go" he sang, and filled with the nomadic spirit which is socially acceptable for middleclass hikers and camper-vanners though not apparently, for gypsies, we drank and danced, and stuck to the floor and my groin strain vanished.

My face was covered in a rash and my hair was a hedge. I told Rob I looked mad and he said not to worry he was used to it. A big drunk group of lads were eating breakfast in the dining room and a few girls hovering at the door in night-before make-up and sequinned tops, giggled and retreated.

Caerdydd Castle was founded by William I and used as mint and administrative centre. By 1074 Caradog ap Gruffudd had apparently seized Gwent from Maredudd ap Owain with the help of Norman allies, possibly on condition he became a vassal of the Crown. Caradog was killed in 1081 by Rhys ap Tewdwr who on winning Morgannwg, agreed to pay William I an annual sum of £40, probably with coins minted at the castle. Fitzhamon assumed control of the Caerdydd lordship after Rhys ap Tewdwr's death, and passed it to his son-in-law Fitz Robert, who kept it till it was acquired through marriage by King John's daughter Isabel in 1183. It then passed to the de Clares in 1214, the Despensers in 1314, the Beauchamps in 1399, the Nevilles in 1445, and the Crown in 1483. History reveals oppression and strife and who and how diverse, those who came to live in Cymru have been for quite some time.

Gerallt Gymro for example, has also been known by his Latin name Giraldus Cambrensis, his French name Gerald de Barri, and his English name Gerald of Wales. He wrote *Journey Through Cymru* after accompanying the Archbishop of Canterbury on his horseback tour to recruit archers to fight Moslems in the Holy Land. Gerallt recounted that Gruffudd ap Rhys ap Tewdwr could apparently make the birds sing on request, and that Henry I, on hearing the claim, had said "I am not the slightest bit surprised. It is we who hold the power, and so we are free to commit acts of violence and injustice against these people, and yet we know full well that it is they who are the rightful heirs to the land." My outrage at this Norman pomp was tempered slightly by reading how eagerly, according to Gerallt, Cymry had joined the Crusades. "We saw a great number of men who wanted to take the Cross come running towards the castle where the Archbishop was, leaving their cloaks behind in the hands of the wives and friends who had tried to hold them back." History confirmed but also challenged my naïve impression of evil English oppressors and innocent Cymry. It was a whole lot more complex. People, whatever their nationality, behave either badly or well.

The more I learned the more complexity I found. Aggressors I'd assumed were English had seen themselves as Normans – even Edward I, the tyrant who'd colonised Cymru, was the first king to be fluent in English. Those I'd assumed Cymry had maybe identified themselves as Marcher or British – and this, before I'd even discovered the Saxons, Vikings, Romans and Celtic-speaking immigrants, who were neither 'English' nor 'Cymreig'. Loyalties had been as divided or unfixed in Cymru as elsewhere (and still are if you look at our bickering political parties). Soldiers were loyal to whoever paid them, the gentry and the ambitious to whoever bestowed land and favours on them. The poor had no choice but to support landowners who controlled them. And like everywhere else, Cymreig and English gentry had intermarried in order for either the groom, or bride's family, to gain land and titles. Largely, it had been less a case of the English subjugating Cymry, than the rich subjugating the poor. It had happened in England too. It happens everywhere still. Plus ça change.

We left via apartment blocks and terraces, and crossed a playing field behind a thin brown boy with a scarred face, burdened by the sack on his shoulders, struggling behind a tall empty-handed man in a tunic who scowled as we passed, and whose face was scarred too.

Over a thousand new apartments (many still unoccupied) were built on derelict land after the coal industry collapsed, and Afon Taf and Afon Elái were impounded to make Bae Caerdydd. Beneath it the old riverbeds were still full of heavy metals from the mines. In front of the Senedd a roundabout span, chairs akimbo, a gold carousel piped music and little girls on pink bikes whizzed round in the drizzle. We passed bits of old docks like black wrecks. Great-crested grebes dived between boats and a freshwater coot mingled with saltwater turnstones. Y Bae was a landscape all its own, fresh and salt, fanciful, functional, relic and resort. Drought-tolerant plants grew in the sand. A cormorant topped each rotting post. "Help me steer it will yer!" cried the small girl up front of a pedalo. Boys whizzed past on skateboards. "Skate parks two minutes away," said one, "it's not even that…"

Cranes, warehouses and floodlights were just visible in the surviving port. But of Tiger Bay – once the busiest port in the world where Cymru's oldest multi-ethnic community of sailors and workers from over fifty countries had lived, only broken lock gates survived, holding back a stagnant canal. Thousands of wading birds had been displaced too. Despite provision of alternative habitats, common redshanks were found to have a lower body weight than before and their winter survival rate declined. We circled the bay, with swifts skimming the tin-can-grey water like fighter jets, while out at sea, mizzle shrouded Ynys Echni and obscured the Somerset coast.

Yachts queued at the locks. Freshwater accumulating in Y Bae was released at low tide through five sluice gates. We looked down through the grilles at it, cappuccino-coloured, boiling, and powering out to sea.

SAXONS AND VIKINGS

In the seventh century, before the notions of Scotland, Cymru and England existed, Germanic-speaking peoples known as Angles, Jutes, and Saxons, continued to gradually colonise the land that would become known as England. These 'Anglo-Saxons' pressed west and north, but were resisted, as were Norwegian and Danish Vikings, by resident Celtic-speaking peoples in the land that would become Cymru. Fighting was rife between all perpetrators.

The Pope had already sent Augustine to convert the pagan Anglo-Saxons in England to Christianity, at the very end of the sixth century. Meanwhile Cymru had retained the Christianity bestowed on Britain by the Romans which had been refreshed by missionaries travelling between Cymru, Cornwall, Brittany and Ireland in the fifth and sixth centuries.

In Oswestry in 642, soldiers from Pengwern in Powys, allied with Penda of Mercia (which roughly covered the English west-midlands), and killed Oswald of Northumbria, who was trying to expand his kingdom. In 655, Oswald's brother Oswy killed Penda, and went onto capture and destroy Pengwern. East Powys was merged into Mercia. By now, most of future England was under Anglo-Saxon control. In 655, Cadwaladr of Gwynedd became King of Britain (the area not under Saxon control), till dying of the plague in 682. Over the next hundred years, conquered Britons in future England gradually absorbed Saxon culture and language.

At the beginning of the eighth century, Rhodri Molwynog of Gwynedd led a string of attacks on Mercia which Aethelbad subsequently built Wat's Dyke to defend. By the latter half of the eighth century, when Offa ruled and ruthlessly expanded Mercia, battles on the border with Cymreig dynasties were rife. Offa built his dyke, separating Celtic-speaking Britons in emerging Cymru from his powerful Anglo-Saxon kingdom.

Cymry and newly converted Anglo-Saxons found common ground in fighting the pagan Norwegian and Danish Vikings who began raiding the British coast. Throughout the ninth century the Vikings travelled the coast of Cymru attacking rich monasteries and the royal court of Aberffraw, developing coastal trading bases and cutting Cymru off from Ireland and Western Europe. The Vikings established large settlements and kingdoms elsewhere in Britain, but made comparatively little ingress into Cymru beyond the trading posts on the north coast (connecting Chester to Dublin) and south coast (connecting Bristol to Dublin). Many of the place names they used evolved into English place names, such as Anglesey (Ynys Môn) and Fishguard (Abergwaun). Swansea (Abertawe), from Sveinnsey, meaning Sveinn's Island, is believed to have been an unusually large Viking trading post.

Rhodri Molwynog won a battle against the Vikings on Ynys Môn in 856 after which he was known as Rhodri Mawr (Rhodri the Great), but was killed by Mercian 'English' in 877. At the end of the ninth century, Alfred the Great became King of Wessex – the only English kingdom powerful enough to survive Viking onslaught, and tried to unite and rule England. Hyfaidd of Dyfed and Eliseg of Brycheiniog allied with Alfred against Anarawd of Gwynedd (who had defeated Mercians in Conwy in 881) on condition they accepted Alfred as overlord, thus beginning a tradition of accepting English authority. In the 890s Anarawd and his brothers strengthened Cymreig resistance against Viking attacks by also allying with and submitting to Alfred. In 899, Alfred died and was succeeded by his son Edward. England as a nation was gaining strength but the Vikings were far from beaten. In 902, they raided Cymru from bases in Ireland and Brittany, killing Anarawd, before settling the area of northern France which became known as Normandy.

In 924, Alfred's grandson Athelstan became the first monarch known as King of all England, and Cymreig rulers – Hywel of Deheubarth, Owain of Gwent and Glywysing, Idwal Foel of Gwynedd, (and the King of Strathclyde)- recognised him as overlord. But Athelstan was succeeded by his brother Edmund to whom Idwal Foel refused to swear allegiance. Fighting between Cymreig dynasties and Saxons and Vikings continued, and also between Cymreig dynasties (and between Anglo-Saxon kingdoms). New kingdoms emerged. Hywel of Deheubarth annexed Powys and Gwynedd, and became King of nearly all Cymru. He became known as Hywel Dda (Hywel the Good), for allegedly overseeing the first written laws in Cymru, adapted from existing laws. Territorial battles continued. Iago and Ieuaf of Gwynedd fought Hywel Dda's sons and then each other – in 969, Iago captured Ieuaf who died in captivity, and Ieuaf's son Hywel captured his Uncle Iago. From 986-999 Hywel Dda's grandson Maredudd ap Owain united most of Cymru.

Meanwhile the Vikings had resumed their assaults, and by 961 had attacked religious settlements in Caergybi, Tywyn, Clynnog Fawr and Tyddewi. In 987, they seized 2,000 men from Ynys Môn and sold them as slaves. In 989 Maredudd ap Owain paid a tax to keep them at bay but four years later they ravaged Ynys Môn again. They plundered Tyddewi in Sir Penfro four times from 980-1000, and killed Bishop Morgenau in 999. From 1013-1016, Cnut of Denmark and Norway attacked Aethelred, and was crowned King Cnut of England.

In these bloodthirsty, power-hungry times allegiance was not straightforward. Perhaps it never has been. Gruffydd ap Llywelyn of Powys and Gwynedd defeated Leofric of Mercia at Rhyd-y-Groes, but in 1055 allied with Aelfgar of Mercia and defeated a Norman-French Anglo-Saxon coalition in Hereford and Gloucester. Meanwhile Gruffydd captured Deheubarth, and from 1057-1063 was king of all present-day Cymru, the only time this has ever been achieved by a Cymreig ruler. He was recognised by Edward the Confessor of England as the only King of Cymru. He won some respite from the Vikings during his reign. But in 1062 Harold II attacked Gruffydd ap Llwywelyn's court, destroyed his fleet of ships, and killed him in Eryri.

It was during this period, particularly after the construction of Offa's Dyke, that the concepts of separate nations arose. As the Celtic-speaking Britons in Cymru, southern Scotland and southwest England became isolated from each other, the Cymraeg, Cornish, Breton and Cumbric languages evolved (as did English). Cymreig monks wrote Cymru's history, and an official bard was attached to each court. Cymry adopted the Saxons' wooden buildings and their system of dividing land to define boundaries for summer and winter grazing. Hywel's Laws show that women were responsible for cheese and milk production, and taking livestock and children to the uplands. The laws also refer to the high value of beaver skins in comparison to those of marten, wolf, fox and otter. Meanwhile forest continued to be cleared, burned and grazed, stripping the soil of its fertility and encouraging the growth of heather, which thrived on the impoverished soil.

Y FRO MORGANNWG

The soils are rich, the topography gentle. Guelder rose and wild privet enrich the hedges. Field maple, spindle, spurge laurel and wayfaring trees survive in the woods while three kinds of whitebeam grow on limestone hills in the north. Adonis blue butterfly, great green bush-cricket, slender ground-hopper and screech beetle are among the invertebrates, while offshore, honeycomb-worm reefs harbour spiny dogfish, ling, native oysters and thornback ray.

Little waves broke in brown foam on the pebbles. A yacht tacked towards the wan sun and pigeons flocked over the pier where people sat on benches and peered from pavilion windows. There were new flats, pretty balconies, gardens and bistros. Up on the clifftop boulevarde, carers walked arm-in-arm with frail elderly charges or pushed them along in wheelchairs. After Caerdydd, Penarth seemed strangely sedate.

A large boat materialised between Ynys Echni (part of Caerdydd), and Steep Holm (part of Somerset) as if it too was an island. Holm was Old Norse for 'island in the estuary' – both had been used by Vikings. According to the Anglo-Saxon Chronicle, in 914, a Viking fleet from Brittany led by Oter and Hroald arrived on Steep Holm and used it as a base from which they raided south Cymru and captured Cyfeilog, the Bishop of Llandaf, for whom they received a £40 ransom from Saxon King Edward of England.

Ynys Echni (Flat Holm in English), had been known as Bradanreolice to the Anglo-Saxons. Reolice derived from Old Irish for churchyard, perhaps in reference to one established by Sant Cadoc. Gytha Thorkelsdottir (a Danish noble related to King Cnut and mother to Harold Godwinson), found refuge there en route to France at the outbreak of the Norman Conquest. Now the island is the domain of wild leek and slow worms with larger than usual blue markings.

Knapweed and hemp agrimony were reclaiming the nineteenth-century gun battery at Trwyn Larnog, refortified for the Second World War. Chiffchaffs called around the concrete arena, as if war was over, though the more history I read the more I understood it never would be. Humans have always been fighting – other nations, our own nations, neighbours and brothers. Bloody battles between Cymru and England still resonate. Cymru evolved as a nation both despite and because of them. Lessons are learned and forgotten and peace comes in lulls between carnage. A man in camouflage trod stealthily through the ruins with binoculars. I asked what he was looking at, and he said "spring migrants" very crossly, then ignored us.

On the lane a cheerier man poked the hedge with his stick. "Checking on the sloes," he said, "what's up?" We said were going to Y Barri. "I'm a Cardiff man. Cardiff born, Cardiff bred…" ('Strong in the arm and thick in the 'ead' – I thought I knew the ending, being a Shropshire lass.) "…and when I'm gone I'll be Cardiff dead," he finished, quoting a Frank Hennessey song apparently. Mention of Machynlleth doused his humour. "I've done the Cambrian March up past there. Up Cadair Idris and on that ridge, sleeping in ditches – an army thing. Conscription." He shuddered. "I was only eighteen." Old men knew. Veterans cherished peace.

Rob said Sully felt like the kind of place where rich footballers lived, and The Captain's Wife crowd looked wealthy enough, the men in jackets and the women in lipstick and scarves. "Anyone for drinks guys?" said a waist-coated man in a plummy voice to his chums, and I winced, then remembered a friend of mine from nearby with the same accent, and kicked myself for being judgmental.

The weather had turned fresh and squally. Stormy light bounced off wet sand and the yellow anorak of a woman striding out with a stick. We dog-legged to Craig Bendrick to see the dinosaur footprints I'd read about. Rough rock was red or egg-box-grey and the top layers had worked loose and wobbled. Some was like spilt cement. The three-toed prints, the only known footprints of an upper-Triassic theropod in Britain, were next to the slipway, full of water that caught the light. There were no interpretation displays because in 2005 someone had hacked a few out and tried to sell them online, and it was better this way. A trail of prints headed into the sea, as if the dinosaur, not long evolved from its crocodile-like ancestors, had just gone in for a dip. It had in fact walked across a shallow floodplain created by rivers bursting their banks after heavy rainfall in an arid terrestrial climate 220 *million* years ago. It boggled the mind how much Cymru had changed – and would do again. It was hard to make sense of the scene. A man sat smoking on a rock across the bay and we caught the smell of cannabis.

Squalls drenched us at the edge of Y Barri as we followed a girl with long black hair who was talking into her phone. "It's been lovely to speak to you," she said politely, "but I'll love you and leave you now, speak to you again soon…, yes, love you, bye… bye, bye…" She turned off her phone and screamed "TWAT!!"

Light through blue canvas cast a strange colour on our sleeping bags and skin. When we unzipped the tent we found ourselves surrounded by dog walkers pretending not to see us. It didn't take long to circuit Ynys Barri. Back on the mainland the kebab and pizza takeaways and tattoo shops were boarded up, and gulls picked at rubbish spilling out of black bags. Everything was closed except Wetherspoon, so that's where we ate fried breakfasts among a few old men nursing pints and memories in half-dark at separate tables. When we came out, the rubbish had been swept from the streets and the sky was bright.

But it was Monday. Rob withdrew the last of his money, kept enough for his fare, gave me £10 and I watched his train pull away. When I was walking everything was so new, an hour felt like two, and each day was a long adventure. But for Rob at work, time passed at the usual speed and he was surprised how much I missed him. "I'm always with you," he'd say earnestly. And later, when the walk was over, I did find it difficult to work out which parts he'd not been there for.

I missed him for hours. But I loved solo walking too, when ideas and memories came unbidden. Better to have them now than retire at sixty-five and be suddenly overwhelmed with regrets. At other times there were no thoughts at all, and I'd walk for hours with only roast potatoes on my mind.

The cliff was eroding. In 2011, 34,000 tons of it had collapsed leaving caravans dangling. Dampness had morphed my cracked boots into rigid new shapes that no longer fitted, and my feet were bleeding and swollen. I sat down to air them. A British Airways plane coming to land at Y Rhws filled the sky, preceding the sound of its engine, huge and weirdly silent, a kind of beautiful, if you didn't know.

If you didn't know that a person on a return flight from Caerdydd to Malaga was responsible for the emission of about 0.6 tons of carbon dioxide, and that a person on a return flight from Caerdydd to Sydney was responsible for about 6.2 tons of carbon dioxide. If you didn't know that a global sustainable fair share of emissions for *everything* (transport, food, heating and the rest) is about two tons per person per year. My frequent-flyer friends didn't want to know. They recycled religiously, as if that made up for it. But who was I to talk? We'd given up flying years ago. Hated shopping. Seldom ate meat. Lived off-grid in a tiny space that took a morsel of wood to heat. But had then gone and chartered a coal-powered steam train for our wedding.

"On a day like this, for walking, it's lovely isn't it?" said a lady with three pugs, and it was. The yellow cliffs were like old city walls with window-boxes of montbretia and samphire. I picked at a fallen chunk and it split easily into shards. Blackbirds and rooks chattered in cotoneaster, and holes in the hedge gave ivy-framed vignettes of silver sea and a yacht with black sails.

A man on the clifftop caravan site was clipping box into spheres, his grey hair cut in a fringe as straight as his teeth. I told him he had a great view. "You're right," he said, nodding to his static. "What you've got, you see, what these people don't realise, is that these now inside, they've got everything. They're like bungalows. I mean how much would it cost you for a view like that? And you've got Butlin's just over there," he nodded to the Devon coast, "that's all lit up at night. And you've got all the ships coming up, all kinds of boats. It's interesting even when the cloud's down. I'd stay here all year if I could."

Gulls and swans floated in pools on the saltmarsh. Scarlet pimpernel grew by the sandy path and a rabbit scampered across it. I was serenely happy, till a power station – Aberddawan B, loomed into view, gobbling the headland, and I remembered, once again, that I cared. About the planet. About Cymru, and all its human and wilder residents. Built to burn coal, Aberddawan released carbon pulled out of the atmosphere by plants over millions of years. Low-grade coal which required a chemical catalyst to ignite and produced more sulphur dioxide and carbon monoxide than more volatile coal. Aberddawan was responsible for some of the highest nitrous oxide emissions in Europe. Nitrous oxide (in addition to acidifying air and water and being 300 times more potent a greenhouse gas than carbon dioxide) causes respiratory diseases, but Aberddawan was allowed to survive due to an EU exemption for burning local fuel and employing 600 people. At first most of its coal had come from Tower Colliery at Hirwaun. More recently it came from the Ffos-y-frân land reclamation scheme, opencast mines in Cwm Nedd, and Cwmgwrach Colliery. But now 30 per cent was from Russia, rendering the EU exemption no longer applicable. Friends of mine had taken part in a protest at Ffos-y-frân in 2009, when I'd been teaching about sustainability instead. I felt my impotence. Where would Cymru be if its citizens hadn't burned down toll gates, raised a red flag on Comin Hirwaun, marched on Westgate Hotel, set fire to Penyberth bombing school, closed Trefechan

Bridge to traffic? Worse off. I was proud of Cymru's rich history of protest against injustices, and proud too, of my friends.

Two women and a frisky dog passed. "Any lunch in your bag? She's a food monster!" warned the one with sunglasses. "Remember — don't talk to strangers!" I continued round Aberddawan. Teasels and valerian sprang from cracks in the sea wall. Behind the security fence were coal hills fractured by vehicle tracks, an incinerator converting pulverised fuel-ash into fly-ash and high-carbon ash (some of which was sold to Generation Aggregates for use in construction) and stained concrete buildings barbed-wire-wrapped and flood-lit among chimneys and shacks. A man sat at a desk in a porta-cabin. A lorry drove through a washer. But there was little visible activity and the site reeked of abandon. RWE nPower had invested £230m to reduce emissions, installed a steam-turbine retrofit, and was developing a pilot carbon capture plant as yet (like all the others), unsuccessful. In 2016, the EU would take the UK to court — Aberddawan would be found to have been emitting double the legal amount of nitrous oxide for seven years, and ordered to pay costs.

But it wouldn't die quietly. In 2017, Aberddawan would be awarded a £10 million state subsidy to produce electricity for one more year, and would remain operational, running reduced hours to comply with emissions laws till finally closing in December 2019. About which I felt delight, huge relief and a kind of bereavement. So much of what I had learnt about Cymru's politics, community, and poetry (not to mention its steam trains) had been coal-fired. But the great black power was scarred, injured, dangerous, and best left in peace.

Waves smacked the concrete and the wind was loud and mad. A dog-poo bag was tied to the fence, a Costa cup span on the path, dandelions grew in a crack. I climbed the wall and saw a raft of oystercatchers afloat on wild grey waves. I heard rocks rolling in the sea and the hum of machinery, before finally, I was rid of Aberddawan.

I'd assumed the coast between Caerdydd and Abertawe would be densely populated. Instead I was kicking up dust. It was Viking territory. Artefacts discovered here bore witness to those who'd used the trading route between Bristol and Ireland. An Irish ninth-to-tenth century pseudo-penannular copper-alloy brooch. A hybrid Saxon-Viking-style ninth-to-eleventh century pommel. Vikings had made no impact on agriculture and not strayed far inland. But at the trading posts (particularly Abertawe), they had exchanged wheat, woollens, horses, tin, copper, silver and slaves — slavery being an

ancient habit. Slaves snatched from Europe probably accounted for a quarter
of the Scandinavian population. Men were taken for felling trees, rowing and
shipbuilding, and women for chores and sex – it was difficult apparently, for
the non-elite to find brides in a polygamous society. It was all very well now
to say Vikings made little permanent impact in Cymru, but it must have felt
significant at the time.

I bowled along between wind-raked hedges and fields thick with thistles
or beet, or flushed green with thrashing wheat, around islands of whiplashed
chestnuts. The stones were dark on the beaches. The cliffs were yellow, and
then the stones on the beaches were blue. I could see Trwyn yr As lighthouse
ahead and a low-slung coaster, but Devon was lost to mist. I saw grey houses
at Llanilltud Fawr, which had grown around the sixth-century clas and Christian college founded by Illtud, where more than 2,000 students had trained.
Being inland had given it some protection from Vikings, who on one occasion
had been allegedly lured to ambush by dancing girls and wine. But eventually
they succeeded in sacking the college in 987, as China would destroy Tibetan
monasteries, nigh on a thousand years later.

The cliffs were built of golden bricks, the beach plateau raked by Zen
monks. The blue lias cliffs had been formed from millions of sea creatures
compacted into limestone, separated by softer layers of mudstone or shale
which eroded more quickly, leaving the limestone unsupported. The cliffs at
Cwm Colhuw had collapsed on the beach like bombed churches, revealing
rock the colour of insulation foam. Windsurfers raced and young people in
down jackets and beanies, strode alone or hand in hand, with camper van-
sized white dogs. Gulls wheeled. Rock pipits hid. At Bae Tresilian I found two
ammonite fossils – white sugar spirals on smoother blue stone. Wind ravaged
the gorse. Yellow lichen encrusted the stone walls. The coast was a glorious
Rembrandt of gold cliffs, dark sky and sea. Sycamores hurled their sticks, and
at Atlantic College, a student stood alone on the slipway in a billow of hair.

I was aching, but the coast was wild and wonderful so I stumbled along,
and the rock slabs below were cracked into blocks as if left by Portuguese
calcateiros on a lunch break, and beyond the lighthouse, boulders were strewn
on the shore platforms like counters on a board game. Choughs somersaulted
into the sky and were buffeted back. Eventually I put up my tent in Cwm yr
As where the cliffs were yellow tufa. A year or two later, storms would expose
bones of Cistercian monks in them.

Being physically exhausted makes everything super-real. The light was

extraordinary. The patch of grass was luxurious. I sandwiched a cheese rind
between my last two flapjacks and it tasted amazing. An orange-squash sky
quenched the sun. Foam flew up the valley, the wind drove back the stream
in small plumes of spray, and crows and gulls were borne swiftly past, their
wings and feet tucked in. I felt part of it all, a little wild. Draughts shrieked
through my tent and the canvas caved in then ballooned. I built a shelter with
my rucksack and wore all my clothes and waterproofs but the wind still found
its way in. A lamb bleated outside but I didn't have the energy to extricate
myself, nor even remove my torch which had rolled under my sleeping bag
and was a lump in my back all night.

In the morning the air was so still a single feather fell without drifting. Skylarks
sang. Three flew low, with light on their wings. A kestrel hung almost motion-
less, and gulls and crows hovered too, as if waiting. The sky ahead was black.
I ignored it.

   The rough-grazed platcau was riven by wooded valleys. Cwm Bach had
dense flowering gorse that looked like gold leaf on an altar. Cwm Mawr had
a strong smell of fox. Birds scolded me in another, and a stoat flashed across
the path. Between the valleys, sea prowled over vast beaches. From Trwyn y
Witch I looked back to the swirling phalanx of cliffs, feeling deeply content,
then climbed the headland, and birdsong swelling from the patch of scrub and
conifers below was so loud, it was almost visible.

   It was only seven-thirty, but vehicles were rolling into Dwnrhefn car park
to stop alongside the black-windowed coach, four-by-fours, and lorries that
were already there. Burly security guards stood about with radios, but no-
one was eating the breakfast laid on under an awning, or drinking the
good-smelling coffee. A shack was ridiculously draped with fishing nets and
floats. "What's going on?" I asked one of the security guards. "They're filming
an advert," he said, bored. I remembered the farmer gazing over Môr Hafren,
wondering how the economy worked, and knew exactly how he felt.

   The path cruised upfolds and downfolds. Down by the brown sea, a man
was play-fighting his boxers with bare tattooed arms, but other dog-walkers
were hunched into coats. It started to rain. The woman unloading newspapers
in Aberogwr Post Office General Stores made me a mug of tea because she
was having one, and I drank it on a chair by the nut spinner. People came in
for papers. She went to turn on the boiled eggs in the café next door. "You're
in charge!" she said. When she came back she said she'd walked South West

Way with a friend. "We were drunk when we said we'd do it, on New Year's Eve. God it was cold, camping in January. But we had a hoot." Did she still go camping? "God no," she said "Never again!"

Sheep wandered over the road and lambs tucked in under the gorse. I heard the fart of tyres on the cattle grid, saw rain fall into Afon Ogwr and heard Canada geese honk. The rain got heavier. I rested in The Pelican in Her Piety's smoking shelter. Rain dripped into a full ashtray. I could see a woman inside, mopping the floor. Traffic sloshed past. The woman came out for a smoke. "It's going to get worse" she said, morbidly.

I crossed Afon Ewenny above its confluence with Afon Ogwr. Horses grazed and swans swam in a waterlogged field with Ogwr Castle a backdrop, as if it had been built for romance, rather than to subjugate the locals.

THE SAINTS

As the Romans gradually withdrew from Britain at the beginning of the fifth century, Celtic-speaking British peoples established kingdoms. Irish marauders plundered the west coast, taking slaves from areas that would become Cymru and Cornwall, and members of the Irish Déisi dynasty settled in future Sir Benfro and Gwynedd. Pictish raiders came from north Britain, and Germanic-speaking Angles and Saxons began to settle what would become England.

Gwrtheyrn (Vortigern) ruled over much of southern Britain from 420-450 and fought off the Pictish invasions. Possibly he adopted the Roman method of using one invader against another and may have invited Britons – notably Cunedda from the Firth of Forth, to settle in future north Cymru to help repel Irish invaders. He encouraged Saxons to settle in exchange for fighting the Picts, and allegedly, before fleeing to Nant Gwrtheyrn, he also allowed Saxons to bring weapons to a banquet with which they killed 300 Brittonic chieftains in an event known as the 'Treachery of the Long Knives'.

In 470, Cunedda's grandson Cadwallon defeated and expelled the Irish from Ynys Môn. By the end of the century Saxons had established kingdoms in future England but had made little advance into Cymru where, by the sixth century, there were Celtic-speaking kingdoms of various sizes. Silures had territory in the southeast. Powys, (from the Latin pagus, meaning hinterland) may have been Cornovii territory. Cunedda's descendants were said to rule Gwynedd. Irish Déisi allegedly won Brycheiniog and Dyfed, and joined resident Demetae.

In 536, dust from either a meteorite, or Central American volcano clouded most of Europe. Temperatures and rain fell, summers were cold, and the Bubonic Plague spread from Asia to Britain. By 550, pagan 'Anglo-Saxons', dominated most of future England.

Britons had been pagan before the Romans had introduced Christianity. The Romans had left settlements at Caerfyrddin and Caerwent (which became known as Gwent) that were still occupied in the fifth century, and had appointed bishops to English cities, but there were no cities in Cymru (or Scotland). Christianity had dwindled following their retreat, though possibly survived in southeast Cymru. In 428, Pope Celestine sent Bishops Germanus and Lucas to Britain to replace Pelegian heresy (the probably British belief which extolled the goodness of human nature) with the Catholic belief that goodness was attained by the grace of God. Germanus evangelised in southeast Cymru and died on Ynys Enlli. His disciples included Dyfrig, who founded a monastery at Hereford. Dyfrig's successor Illtud apparently reached Glywysing by sea and founded the college at Llanilltud Fawr. Illtud introduced monasticism, (believed to be influenced by the Egyptian Coptic Christian tradition of poverty, chastity and obedience), and the idea that the best path to holiness was to live in community dedicated to learning as well as prayer. His college, attended by nobles and monks alike, may have been the training place for almost all the early leaders of Irish, Breton, Cornish and Cymreig monasticism.

Christians travelled between Cymru, Ireland, Brittany, Cornwall, the Isle of Man and parts of Scotland. From at least the mid-sixth century, missionaries from Ireland and Brittany revitalised dispersed pockets of Christianity in Cymru. Their settlements were surrounded by a llan (enclosure) – often an oval ditch and bank around a consecrated burial ground, some of which evolved into churches. Others were clasau, founded and populated by celibates living as a farming community. Missionaries left them to establish more clasau or llanau. Llandaf was the hub of about sixty churches, and Bede reported that Bangor-Is-Coed (Bangor meaning wattle fence, referring to the enclosure) as having 2,000 monks who supported themselves with manual labour. In future Cymru, monks were revered more than bishops in distant cities.

The monks and missionaries were often referred to as saints (preceding the later Catholic tradition of canonisation). According to Rhygyfarch (writing in the eleventh century) Dewi Sant was a student at Sant Illtud's in the 520s, who established several llanau and clasau. Dewi apparently promoted abstinence, vegetarianism, and hard physical labour. Among his dozens of contemporaries were Teilo, Padarn, Beuno, Cadog and Deiniol who set up their own llanau and clasau. Fewer llanau were dedicated to typically Catholic saints like Peter or Mary. Sometimes the saints left the clasau to seek wild solitary places to feel closer to God. But their peaceful message was not always welcome.

In 597, Pope Gregory I gave Augustine authority over all the Christians of Britain, and sent him to evangelise the pagan Anglo-Saxons. Augustine reprimanded Christians in Cymru for not converting their pagan neighbours. They in turn, allegedly rejected Augustine for not standing up to greet them. But Augustine was welcomed by King Aethelbert in future England, which he succeeded in converting to Christianity gradually, allowing for example, the ritual sacrifice of cows and pigs in the grounds of new churches. He chose Canterbury as the seat of the Archbishopric to the disappointment of Tyddewi clerics, where Christianity had been established far longer.

Sea routes were travelled by traders and migrants, as well as missionaries. Irish were the most frequent settlers, leaving stones with Ogham (Old Irish script) inscriptions in south Cymru. Malefactors pushed out to sea in rudderless boats also turned up, while conflict with Anglo-Saxons and Irish raiders provoked migration to Brittany.

Cymreig heroic poetry, probably dating from the sixth century became the basis of one of the oldest European literary traditions. Bards – itinerants like minstrels and harpists, were a privileged class who wandered from chieftain to chieftain, employed by elite families who they praised in verse. A Brittonic language continued to be spoken in southwest England, Cymru and southern Scotland from which Cymraeg and Cornish would emerge. Goidelic was used in northern Scotland where it had been introduced by Irish settlers in previous centuries. Celtic-speaking peoples called themselves Combrogi, or Cymry, meaning comrades, and the word Cymru came to define the land where the Cymry lived. But Germanic settlers called the land Wales, which seems to have meant the land of the Latin-speakers – possibly because Latin, another Roman legacy, was still used for legal purposes and appeared on inscribed graves. (A more popular interpretation claims that 'Wales' meant land of the foreigners). The Germanic people called the people who lived in 'Wales' 'Welsh'. The English language also began to evolve.

Hafod and hendre farming was described in the sixth century by Gildas, who wrote that Cymru had 'mountains particularly suitable for the alternating pasturage of animals'. Despite the hills being already mostly deforested, upland peat from this era contains fragments of pollen from most woodland trees. Ash and elm were the first to completely disappear from the hills, followed by pine and lime. Lynx probably became extinct at this time.

PEN-Y-BONT AR OGWR

*S*pecies-rich hedgerows and a few small ancient woodlands survive. Dormice have moved into Island Farm from where prisoners of war escaped in 1945. Some coastal marsh is used for grazing, and sea-kale grows in the shingle. Water voles just about cling on. Pwll Cynffig, the largest freshwater lake in South Cymru, sustains migrating birds, brown-banded carder bees, hairy dragonflies, medicinal leech, fen orchids, and an important population of marsh fritillary and small blue butterflies.

Two girls were letting a horse graze the verge in the rain. "Keep away from the back legs!" snapped one, as I climbed the stile, though I was going nowhere near.

Merthyr Mawr's thatched cottages around the village green were luminous, and the air smelt of rain-soaked trees. Field maple trunks had split and cracked like a bread crust. A strawberry tree grew among red oak, sweet chestnut and lime. A tractor reversed round the corner but there was no-one else.

Merthyr Mawr had grown around the estate of a nineteenth-century mansion which accounted for the horsiness and thatch. But 'Merthyr' derives from martyr, and probably dates to the fifth or sixth centuries when Christianity was newly arrived and not wholly embraced. One local saint, Dyfodwg – who was either a chieftain or Breton monk and disciple of Illtud, allegedly had his tongue cut out to stop him preaching the gospel. Paganism is revered by gentle people now. But presumably the early Christian men and women who brought messages of peace, felt that as rape, slavery and war were rife, paganism had failed. They couldn't have known that the same atrocities would be committed in the name of Christianity over subsequent centuries. That everything is open to corruption. I thought them brave activists pitching up in their wooden boats. It was their penchant for wild and lonely places I liked, and their gentleness. For me, they were right up there with William Morgan and Gruff Rhys.

Sant Teilo's Church was built in Victorian times on the site of a medieval church which appears, like most of them, to have been constructed on the site of a fifth- or sixth-century llan. The graveyard was a rampant wet jungle under that dark wet sky. Bluebells tangled the grass, and birds sang in the rain falling onto cellophane-wrapped flowers. Behind the church was a lean-to sheltering stones found when the church was rebuilt or graves dug. The stones

looked awkward bunched together, like people waiting at a bus stop. The Paulinus Stone, dating to the fifth or sixth century, bore a damaged Latin inscription
– PAVLI FILI M (the stone of Paulinus, the son of M), and an emblem resembling a Greek omega, or incomplete cross. The top was rounded like an
old-fashioned lollipop. A dust of green lichen enhanced the incisions – deep
and crisp as if only just chiselled.

The car park was all puddles. Between the thirteenth and fifteenth centuries
when great storms mauled the coast, sand had swamped Candleston Castle.
Now the dunes harboured orchids, wild pansy and invertebrates like dune
tiger beetles and cuckoo bees. None were visible. The damp grey sand was
thick and ankle-turning and the paths unclear. A miserable humiliated-looking
crocodile of youths on community service trooped by with litter-pickers. I
felt sorry for them but when I smiled they looked even more humiliated – as
if I was laughing at their umbrella hats. I followed Afon Ogwr along a tideline
of weed and belly-up crabs where vetch and sea spurge grew among drift-
sticks. Signs informed me that sea buckthorn planted to prevent erosion was
now threatening native plants and being removed, and that turf was being
stripped to preserve dune habitats. Dunes are excellent sea defences, better
than concrete at buffering waves, but they need to wander at will. Nevertheless, the signs made me uneasy, testament to our constant meddling. But the
sand had wandered anyway. It had over-run the car park, swamping litter bins
and a fence.

A long residential street led to Porthcawl. A newsagent smoking in her
doorway stared as if she couldn't believe her eyes and only then did I realise
how wet I was. Now the pebbledash, shabby charity shops, dirty nets,
boarded-up windows, wheelie bins, and an empty playground conspired to
look morbid. A subway popped me back onto the seafront. I made for a pub
and my rucksack got jammed in the revolving door. It was brash and bright
inside, and the drinkers stared as I dripped on the shiny floor. They didn't
serve food anyway. I went to the pub next door and sat in the dark at the back,
suddenly in need of it. In need of a break. I took off my boots, hung up my
jacket and draped my wet socks, threadbare and crusty with pus on the rungs
of the chair. I sat cross-legged to warm my feet under my thighs and cradled
coffee for an hour before ordering food. A small frosted glass in the toilet
door reflected the front bay windows. Ben Harper songs softly caressed me.
I chewed my chips slowly. My cheeks began to radiate heat. I wanted to stay

but had no more money. The bar girl, whose frown I'd misinterpreted as one
of disapproval for loitering, filled my water bottle with concern.

The rain was torrential. The sea looked like soup. My waterproofs were
hopeless, though at least the hood stopped water pouring down my neck. The
noise of rain hitting it was hypnotic and a clamminess built up round my head.
A golf course disappeared to my right, Pink Bay was a blurry brown. These
dunes harboured a plethora of invertebrates and orchids but I only saw
hundreds of banded and garden snails slithering over the boardwalk to reclaim
the marram. Rain fell into Pwll Cynffig and flumed down the car park. The
M4 was an awful dirty wall of noise and spray.

I hadn't realised the coast path circumnavigated the steelworks and was
upset to be heading inland. I'd not planned going home till next day but had
changed my mind. I stopped to pee in a subway, releasing rain from my jacket
that gushed down my legs. Farm tracks were fast brown streams. A wet grey
serenity existed between railway and roads, full of affluent houses and farms
with campsites, but I kept on.

The path joined a B-Road where I would discover the Pumpeius Stone had
once stood on the site of an early monastery, inscribed with the Latinised
name 'Pumpeius Carantoris'. 'Pampes' was also discernible in Ogham on its
corners, suggesting a transition era when Irish raiders had become welcome
fellow Christians. On the outskirts of Y Pîl, I met the A48 and entered Castell-
nedd, feeling wretched.

THE ROMANS

British Celtic-speaking peoples had been trading with the Roman Empire for hundreds of years when Caesar rocked up in 54 BC with 800 vessels, and withdrew taking hostages with him. When Claudius arrived in 43, with soldiers, engineers, and accountants, it was clear the Romans were staying, at least for a while. They began settling future England.

They found Britain (deriving from the Latin 'Britannia'), populated by distinct peoples of broadly similar cultures living in dispersed fortified farmsteads. Some adopted Roman culture more readily than others. In future Cymru, the Deceangli dynasty in the northeast, the Ordovices in the northwest, the Demetae in the southwest, the Silures in the southeast and the Cornovii in the centre and along the future border, all resisted Roman occupation. The Deceangli raided parts of future England, but the Romans counter-attacked and conquered Afon Dyfrdwy. From 47-89 the Romans attacked Cymru and the future border thirteen times and divided British tribes by building fortresses on it. In 52 the Silures managed to defeat a Roman legion but their leader Caratacus (who'd united Silurian and Ordovician resistance after being driven from Essex) was captured two years later. By the mid-50s a 20-hectare fortress was built on Afon Wysg. The Demetae gave in – as a reward, fewer forts were erected to subdue them and their capital Moridunim (Caerfyrddin) was built.

In 60, the Romans attacked Ynys Môn, where the druids – the native Britons' spiritual leaders, were based. The Romans slaughtered the druids and destroyed their sacred oak groves. In 77, Frontinius (governor of Britain) allied with the Silures, who became Romanised with a capital at Caerwent which had baths, a basilica, houses, central heating, murals and mosaics. The fort of Deva (Chester) was built by the 70s. By the 80s the Ordovices had been defeated by the governor Agricola, and the whole of Cymru was under Roman control. But only the Silures and Demetae fully accepted Roman ways of self-government, taxes, and trade, and only the Ordovices (evidenced by the lack of coins, buildings and trade), fully resisted them.

According to Roman historian Tacitus, it was common practise across the Empire to reward higher grades of citizenship to those loyal to Roman culture, and the defeated British upper classes accepted positions in the army which allowed them to keep their status.

As soon as conquest was achieved, soldier numbers were reduced and some forts abandoned. Those still in use were like small towns. They relied on supplies that came by coast, river and straight roads a day's march apart. Settlements developed around them and at crossroads and fords, with multi-cultural populations around the bigger forts. Roads were furnished with bridges and milestones, and surfaced with gravel. Copper, lead, zinc, iron and silver were extracted by slaves for use across the Roman Empire. Farmers were taxed a percentage of their crop to provide food for the army, and garrisons had huge ovens to dry corn for storage. With increased demand and a stable warm climate, arable fields expanded, and crops like cabbage, aspara-gus, celery, beet, carrots, apples, plums, cherries, medlars and vines were introduced. So too probably, were brown hares, and white sheep, which the Romans bred with local black sheep to produce mountain sheep, whose wool was collected for clothing.

Despite obliterating the druids' power, Romans tolerated worship of native gods, and shrines of both pagan British and Roman gods were erected before Christianity arrived. By 310 Christianity was spreading through Britain and Gaul, by 320 there were bishops in London, York and Lincoln, and by 380 Christianity was the official religion of the Roman Empire, public displays of paganism were banned and Christian worship using Latin – (the Empire's official language), became widespread.

At the height of Roman occupation, the population of Britain was 3-5 million. Living conditions had improved for the élite, with central heating, plumbing, medicine and literacy. Some were rich foreigners, others locals made wealthy from trade, land or politics. But Roman occupation of Cymru was mainly military except for in places like Elái, Llanilltud and Caerwent in the southeast, where the élite lived in villas and corn was grown. Most people still had subsistence settlements, and in remote areas, Iron Age forts and roundhouses remained occupied by British speakers of Celtic languages.

But conflict between Romans was endemic. Rival governors fought each other. Emperors were murdered. To restrict their power, Britain was divided into provinces of which Cymru was probably one. In the year 260 the whole Empire was split into three rival factions with Britain, Spain, France and Germany forming the Gallic Empire. Southern Britain was being invaded by tribes from Ireland, Picts from Scotland, and Saxons from the continent. A stone wall was built round Caerwent, and ports in the southeast were forti-fied. By the end of the third century the economy was in decline as attacks on

Roman territory increased, trade was disrupted and less money circulated. Repairs to towns, roads and mines were neglected, literature disappeared and the British population dropped to 2 million. By 300, Germanic mercenaries were serving the Roman army in Britain, and Scandinavian settlers, and Saxons, Angles and Jutes – refugees of war, plague and famine, arrived.

The climate had deteriorated. Summers became wet. In 383 General Magnus Maximus of Britain, hoping to usurp the Emperor, led a Romano-British army to Gaul, taking soldiers from Cymru with him, possibly organising a population movement from southeast Scotland to northeast Cymru, and transferring authority to local rulers. By 390 there were no Roman troops in Cymru (and by 407 none in Britain). The Romans had left cities at Caerleon, Caernarfon and on the future border at Chester, a town at Caerfyrddin, and forts at Caerdydd and Caergybi. But Roman collapse had less impact in Cymru than in England where Latin language and Roman culture had been assimilated. In Cymru, Brittany, Cornwall and Scotland, the Brittonic language remained dominant with just a smattering of Latin terms. And Pen Llŷn and Sir Benfro had been largely outside Roman influence. Wolf, wild boar, wildcat, and deer still roamed.

CASTELL-NEDD PORT TALBOT

A quarter of Cymru's lowland hay meadow survives in the borough, harbouring crested dog's tail, rough hawkbit and green-winged orchid. Disused canals accommodate aquatic plants and invertebrates, and post-industrial land is regenerating. Bryn Tip has golden ringed dragonflies and dark green fritillary butterflies, while Glyncorrwg Colliery has been turned into fishponds. Salmon have returned to the rivers, though numbers are decreasing again, while bittern occasionally visit Cors Crymlyn, the most extensive area of lowland fen in Cymru.

"I wish I was home!" I shouted, and flagged down a bus. My fingers were so numb I gave my purse to the driver and blue dye ran onto his hands. When I got off at Port Talbot Parkway he gave back my fare and told me to get myself a cup of tea. I could barely speak or smile from surprise and cold so gave him a numb stiff wave.

I guessed I wouldn't get all the way home, but a train was due in half an hour for Caerfyrddin, which was in the right direction. But the cold steely waiting room was claimed by four white-faced dead-eyed lads drinking Stella talking about violence to women. One stared me down with such malice I was actually frightened, and left. The hotel bar's bright lights made me squint. Drunk men in office shirts looked me up and down. "Is it raining?" said one. The others roared with laughter. Water dripped from my hair into my tepid tea.

The train rolled in quietly. I could hardly believe it was for me, this purring purple dream that was so quiet, so warm, so comfortable. My teeth wouldn't stop chattering. When the guard arrived I asked for a single to Caerfyrddin but he ignored me. "Do you want a cup of tea?" he said. "I saw you on the platform." He went off and returned with piping hot tea and a paper bag full of fruitcake and shortbread. "I dunno," he said "you just look a bit cold." I saw my terrible reflection in the window. He went to investigate connections and returned to confirm I'd miss the last bus, asked what I'd do, and fidgeted when I told him I'd camp. "Don't take this the wrong way" he said carefully, not looking at me, "but you can stay at my place if you need to." He would tell the next guard to let me travel back to Swansea if I wanted, and wrote his name and number in big letters on the paper bag. MARTIN. "I dunno," he said, shaking his head. "I must be getting soft in my old age." I got off at Caerfyrddin and when I turned back, he was framed by light, like a saint, in the doorway. "You are a wonderful person!" I shouted.

There were fields by the station but the river looked ready to burst and it was too dark to head out of town. Black trees whipped over the churchyard, it would do, but I had money saved from the train, was buoyed my Martin's kindness, and went to try my luck in a pub. "Any chance I could sleep on the floor for £10?" I asked and heard how daft it sounded. "Er, no," said the lad behind the bar. He didn't have the authority to say yes, he said. The punters were young and tipsy, excited that the storm had brought them a benighted stranger. "Stay and have a drink!" they said but I declined, feeling foolish but cheered by the banter. We humans were alright.

Heading back to the church the long way, looking for civic grass, a wine bar caught my eye, about to close. I repeated the same cheeky question and immediately regretted it. I was OK now, warm enough. "No," said the lad cashing up, "I don't own the place" and I was already off when he called me back. "No! I mean yes! You can't stay here, but I'll sort you out!" Glenn was Irish and made me a cup of tea. "I'm walking through Ireland soon," he said, "from north to south." He lifted my rucksack and looked worried. "To be honest I usually cycle," he said, and went to make some calls, I assumed to ask a girlfriend if she'd mind me sleeping on the couch, but I was wrong.

"I've booked you a room in the Boar's Head," he announced and I was so shocked he had to tell me twice. I started stammering. "It's just on the corner," he explained, but I felt awful. I was so used to rain it hadn't occurred to me not to walk in it, but I'd been an idiot. You can get hypothermia even in mild temperatures, from being wet for a prolonged period. I'd become a nuisance. A blagger. A fraud. I could have gone back to Martin's. I could have camped in the churchyard. I tried to dissuade Glenn, but he was resolved so I hugged him.

My room was clean and warm and white. I spread the stinking contents of my rucksack on the radiators and ran a bath. My naked body was shocking. There were worms of black grime in all the creases of my skin. The vein running up my right thigh was swollen and blue, my bum was covered in a rash, and my toenails, blisters and cuts were ingrained with sock fluff – one blister had engulfed a toe and dislodged the nail. I left a tidemark around the bath and tried to wipe it off but the tissue just stuck to the grime. I flicked on the TV. There were flood warnings across the whole of south Cymru. I turned it off and lay in the big white bed with pillows under my knees, awash with guilt and gratitude, while wind and rain lashed the window.

I'd been stupid but people had been kind. It wasn't nationality that defined them, but benevolence. It is how we behave that matters. The day marked a turning point in my journey. As if having been broken and humbled, I had earned my right to walk with a carefree heart. I stopped fretting about being English, about conflict, and about environmental apocalypse – at least for a while.

A few weeks later I was back in Port Talbot, on a treeless street opposite the British Legion, which you might say, was a Roman legacy. Two veterans long returned from campaigning were smoking on the doorstep under a filthy union jack, and hacking up phlegm. A woman with a shopping trolley joined me. "I have to take the bus because I keep falling over," she said. The bus was busy. A man put his dog on his lap. "You don't want to walk this bit," he said. "You'll just end up round by yer, on the road all this way. Then it takes you through these houses," he nodded to the estates and lowered his voice. "Undesirable areas. What *I* like to do, is get lost in that woodland," he pointed to seething hills. "It's lovely in there." Inquisitive passengers chimed in with advice, but I managed to alight where I wanted – where I'd stopped.

Running parallel to the M4, the A48 was built on the Roman road that had connected the forts of Isca (Caerleon) with Nidum (Nedd) and Coelbren (Powys). I didn't know this as I tramped along, or that the original road was assumed to have taken a more easterly route around Cynffig, or that some of the Roman milestones were now displayed in Margam Museum, among them a 1.5-metre high sandstone pillar dating to the rule of Emperor Maximus from 309-313, which had in the sixth century been turned upside down and used as a memorial.

The road ran between the coastal industrial plain and wooded hills fringing the coalfield. Through a belt of white poplars and Japanese knotweed, I could see the M4 and the steelworks – blue units, chimneys, pylons, the reservoir supplying the rolling mills. Costa cups swivelled at my feet and Kronenburg cans cluttered the verge.

As well as the fort at Nidum, there'd been nearby, a Roman marching camp at Melin-cwrt, a fortlet at Hirfynydd which helped control Sarn Helen (the major north-south road) and a camp at Blaen Cwm Bach. Another stone found in Port Talbot was inscribed on one side with the letters IMP C M A

GORDIANVS AVG – an abbreviation of 'Imperator Caesar Marcus Antonius Gordianus Augustus'. Gordian III began his rule in 238 at the age of thirteen and was murdered six years later by his own soldiers. The other side of the stone referred to Licianus, an Emperor who'd ruled jointly with Constantine from 308-324, till the latter had ordered his public execution by hanging in Thessalonica. That the milestone had been updated bears witness to the extent of road building and renovation in the third and fourth centuries. That the emperors had both been murdered is testament to the violence and corruption during Roman rule. Take note ye builders of empires.

The steelworks were steaming saucepans. Brown and yellow brick houses crowded around them beneath a smoking skyline, while across the M4 and A48, bigger houses climbed the wooded hills. In the 1960s Port Talbot steel-works was one of the largest in Europe and it was still the biggest in Britain, despite falling demand and competition from China. In 2017 Tata would announce a £30-million investment to upgrade the works and produce advanced forms of steel for electric cars. I watched one yellow and six white plumes of smoke puff out of a bank of chimneys while a car belched exhaust over smutty dandelions existing somehow, among Red Bull cans and a box of broken eggs in the verge. A flame flared from a chimney. I turned off the old Roman road into the 'undesirable area'.

The only undesirables I saw were a mother and two toddlers knocking on a door, and a pair of mechanics under a car. Rain had spotted the grime coating parked cars in drives and on the streets, which were probably washed regularly if the neat small-windowed-semis and tidy gardens with straight-edged lawns, dahlias, dewy roses and plastic privet balls were anything to go by. It was the air that was dirty. It smelt of oil. The path joined the cycle route. Muddy desire paths ran up the bank to playing fields and a huge skulking tank. The steelworks were rusty old ships sailing a sea of triangular rooftops. The yellow smoke turned nasty orange.

The estate gave to older terraced houses backed with alleys. Street, alley, street, alley. Wind turbines touched clouds on hills to the north. I suspected they had been largely unobjected to. Wind-farm protestors tended to be privi-leged, their homes (or second homes) sited where their large polluting cars ('you just can't survive in the countryside without them') were not coated with industrial grime. I saw a fence running along the hilltops and imagined being up there. A drawn-out metallic crash drowned the sparrow chatter, and the path spat me onto the dual-carriageway where I faced full on, the hissing steel-producing monster bound with rusting brown pipes, spewing steam and smoke like a fabulous dragon.

Across Afon Afan, cranes moved coal at the port where the coking-coal to make steel was imported. I watched a man fishing down on the flats, his orange jacket reflected by the river which had wound its way through green misty hills and the saltmarsh. I was guilty of finding poetry in degraded industrial landscapes. I admired the dignity, humour and frankness of 'working-class' people who'd today not been around to distract me from seeing the pollution they endured. I watched the man dig for bait. The scene seemed to encapsulate the complexity of the world we steel-gobblers defiantly pollute as if it was our right, as if it was inevitable. Even while we mourn the planet's destruction, yearn for its solace and lament the lack of fish. In 2020 Sweden would announce the first ever zero-carbon steel plant, giving me hope.

I ate a hard-boiled egg in the dunes where the black rubbly spit met the beach. The egg smell mingled with the estuary smell. A woman at the door of a new seafront apartment was chatting to a man with a dog. "The big wind's worse by yer…" she said. I heard cutlery being sorted through an open window. A man cycled down the prom with trousers tucked into his socks and an elderly couple bent over the railings, trying to coax a small dog off the beach. Chatter and a smell of doughnuts wafted out of a glassy ice cream parlour as I passed, and children played in the sand. "Mermaids aren't even real anyway," said one, huffily.

I was staying with friends and running late as I crossed Afon Nedd on the A48. Techno thumped past. A disposable nappy rotted on the pavement, while on the banks below, cranes shifted scrap-metal. Upriver among misty hills, were the houses of Castell-nedd – the town which had developed round the Roman fort of Nidum, built to control the natives and attract settlers during the first Roman advance into Cymru.

IRON

A sword discovered in Cwm Rhondda dating to 600 BC, represents the beginning of the Iron Age in the land that would become Cymru. It was the heyday of Celtic-language speakers throughout Europe, and they came to populate Britain through a process of gradual settlement. While they didn't genetically change the physical and racial mix of the people already resident, they dominated the culture.

They excavated iron ore from opencast pits and made it into ingots for trading, or weapons and tools – agriculture and armed conflict consequently became more efficient. They used metal pins and brooches to fasten clothes woven from wool spun on spindles. Trade with Europe and the Roman Empire increased. Britain exported grain, cattle, gold, silver, iron, hides, slaves and dogs, and imported ivory, chains, necklaces, amber and glass. Iron ploughs requiring eight oxen and long fields replaced pointed sticks drawn by two oxen. Crop rotation was practised. Spelt, flax, barley, beans, peas, emmer wheat, rye, oats, turnips, carrots and parsnips were grown, but storing grain was difficult, so cattle, sheep, pigs and goats were also farmed. As the population increased, woodland was cleared. Bear possibly became extinct.

Organised pagan societies of extended families ruled by kings, queens or chieftains began to form – the Ordovices, Silures, Demetae and Deceangli. Warriors threw spears from horse-drawn chariots, then dismounted to fight with swords. The ruling class, whose wealth was related to numbers of cattle owned, had riches, jewellery and weapons. The dynasties shared language, religion and cultural expression, but were often at war with each other. Priests from across Britain and Gaul (modern France, Belgium and parts of Germany) received education from druids at Ynys Môn.

By 500 BC the climate was wet and a few degrees cooler than in the Bronze Age, so forts and agriculture developed on hills rather than mountains. The cooling climate and increasing population affected productivity and as food became scarce, resources were defended. A greater density of hillforts were built in future Cymru than anywhere else in Britain, with 200 along the coast. Although England and Cymru didn't exist, the twenty-two built on what would become the border were the largest at more than a hectare, while in the west they were defended farms, rarely more than an acre. The forts were surrounded by ramparts faced with stone and topped with a timber palisade.

Inside the ramparts, people lived in turf and timber-roofed round huts with wicker walls on stone foundations. In the northwest, stone instead of timber was used, and modified over centuries. In the southeast, hillforts were replaced by lowland settlements. But hillforts were rarely attacked before the Roman invasion, and were perhaps more symbols of prestige, places of refuge, food storage or social gathering, than defence. By 200 BC the climate was improving again. By 120 BC the population of Britain was about one million, and Romans were taking territories in Gaul.

ABERTAWE

The coalfield extends from Mynyddoedd Duon foothills to Abertawe, while Penrhyn Gŵyr is lowlying. Saltmarsh dominates its north coast, while the south coast is underpinned by Carboniferous limestone with cliffs, coves and caves that sustain black tar lichen, orange and yellow crust lichens, and acorn barnacles. Clifftop plants include spring cinquefoil, squinancywort, nit-grass, and wild asparagus. Rock pools harbour common coralline seaweed, sea lettuce, sponges, prawns and rare cushion starfish, while offshore, red seaweeds and grass kelp, sea squirts and sponges survive, along with twelve of eighteen British sea spiders.

A urine-stinking subway gave brief relief from the awful roads and flyovers on which vehicles raced by, their humans unseen. Sewage reeked. Detergent stank. I was aching and late, but by chance my friend Stu drove past and slowed up to yell that he'd meet me at Sainsbury's. Traffic roared like a migraine. The towpath was fenced off so I kept on, funnelled between Shell garages, traffic islands, warehouses, road-signs, multi-storey car parks, bus shelters, car parks, shipping containers, wind turbines, fences, floodlights, RAC flags, dragon flags, barns, McDonalds, Park and Ride, Aldi, Mercedes Benz, Atlantic Carwash, pebbledash houses, Velocity Health and Leisure, blue apartments, advertisement hoardings, the university, new developments, palm trees, birch trees and Sainsbury's, where I arrived at the same time as Stu.

We had met in our youth, stacking shelves at Wilko's. Now he was a family man baking a quiche in a kitchen, using huge shiny scales his partner Fran had inherited from her Dad, John the Rust. "I remember weighing out slug pellets on them," Fran said "and screws. So old-fashioned it was, the ironmongers, but I can still remember it, I can still smell it, the paraffin and window putty. Old ladies would come in to buy one nut or bolt and they'd stay for hours chatting. Dad had an accountant, she was bent double she was so old, she had a little room at the back of the counter and if anyone paid with a note – well, it was a big deal. You put it in a pot and it shot away in a tube, and she'd put the change in and send it back."

I was joggling little Flynn on my knee. "I took my Dad to McDonald's when it opened," said Fran. "It was the first one in Swansea, and I was only thirteen so of course I thought it was brilliant, not now I don't but I did then. Well he hated it. A bunfight he said it was. He said you had to queue for so long and they just threw the food at you." Flynn and I whizzed Thomas the Tank engine around in the salad spinner. "You just can't imagine what it will be like in another forty years," said Fran "when I think about online shopping and Tesco's deliveries now." With family in Aberdâr, Abertawe, and all over Gŵyr, Fran was properly Cymreig, but she brushed the concept aside. "As long as people are kind," she said "that's what matters." She was right, and I'd known it all along, but it had taken me longer than it should have to consciously reach the same conclusion.

Fran was so kind she gave me £5 for ice cream. I protested. "Resistance is futile," said Stu. He was dropping me off at the docks. His accent had become so Abertawe I asked if he'd gone proper native. "I'm a mun-ger-al," he said, stretching the vowels. "I've spent most of my adult life paying taxes in Wales, I've got Welsh bloodline, and I live here so I feel embedded in the Welsh nation. Am I Welsh? Nooooooooo. I'm British, a European. I love Wales with every heartbeat. I don't much care who wins the rugby. But I do care, deeply, when Westminster treats Wales unfairly." I agreed. Except I did care who won the rugby.

Grimy flats pestered older buildings the Second World War bombs had missed, while the new glassy Dragon Hotel soared. I'd been accommodated there when presenting at a conference two years earlier but the sight of it surprised me, as if its gloss had nothing to do with me, as if public-speaking had never been part of my life. I preferred scribbling quietly at the edge. I preferred the dingy shopping arcades where gloomy lads with wild hair slouched on piercing salon steps, and burly men in tracksuits with shaved heads and sky-blue eyes sat outside cafés, descendants perhaps, of Norwegian sailors. One of them gave me a grin. A white-faced woman was throwing punches and screaming at a scrawny man. "Swansea's finest," chuckled a woman at my shoulder. People passed with trolleys or sticks and shuffles and limps, and elderly women with dyed red hair wore sparkly earrings and shoes.

The marina boasted new bistros and apartments with glass balconies. The streets smelt of fags and bacon. Only the old dock walls and street names recalled what had gone – Fishermen's Way, Fishmarket Quay, Slipway Road. In 1850 4,000 Abertawe oysters a day had been sold in London and Liverpool, but by 1920, stocks were overfished, the bay polluted, and the oysters infected by flagellate protozoan, which ended the trade. But 40,000 oysters would be released in 2013, and their larvae carried by the tide to recolonise derelict beds. I clung onto these small hopeful stories. I sat among shining shells watching little waves lap the shore, till a man slithered out of the shrubs at the back of the beach in skimpy trunks, writhing his hips. "Does my body look alright?" he asked. I said I had to go.

Abertawe merged into Mwmbwls. The traffic, jammed up behind rattling palms, made way for an ambulance with a bin lorry in its wake. I spent Fran's money on lemon scoops and an espresso. The sea sparkled like broken glass. Beneath it was The Strombus which, having gone aground near the lighthouse, was the only place on Gŵyr where Devonshire cup coral and large conger eels, ocean triggerfish, spike barnacle, rosy feather star and candy-striped flatworm lived. On learning this I scuttled our defunct gas hob in the garden pond – the newts approve.

It was half term. An old lady with a black scarf wrapped round her wrinkled face like a Sicilian widow had closed her eyes to the car park full of metal, and the kids crawling over the playground, but otherwise a holiday spirit pervaded. Even jackdaws seemed excited, and I was buoyant to see Gŵyr stretching ahead. It felt like summer. "I'm looking for Lundy Island," said an elderly Cymro, who wore tweed and carried a knapsack, shading his eyes. But a slight blue haze had settled on the horizon. It was all double denim, blue sky and blue sea, set off by fragrant gorse with so many flowers its needles were barely visible. Men photographed it with huge cameras.

At Langland, people in big hats were reading newspapers outside the council beach huts. I'm glad I didn't know that the biggest apartment block there, all turrets and opulence overlooking the bay, had been built as a retreat for the Crawshays, the ironmasters of Merthyr Tudful – it would have ruined my mood. Back in the Iron Age, family members working at home had mixed iron ore with charcoal, fired it, drained off the slag, then heated the metal and hammered it into ingots or tools. But in the Industrial Age, William Crawshay had lowered wages at his ironworks so much his employees couldn't pay shopkeepers and had their property seized. Some were imprisoned. Their iron and coal-worker colleagues marched on Aberdâr demanding compensation and the captives' release, and raised a sheet soaked in blood on Comin Hirwaun. But troops shot into the crowd killing some two dozen people. Twenty-three year old miner Dic Penderyn (Richard Lewis) was hung at

Caerdydd Gaol. Lewis Lewis was exiled to Australia. Crawshay, the real crook, got off scot-free.

The coast path was riotous with flowers. "Little Pippa loves young women," said a lady of her silky-eared spaniel. "I think it's because of the girls in the rescue centre." Little Pippa bounded straight past me. The woman squinted, readjusting my age.

At Bae Caswell my heart leapt to see the 1960s concrete block of flats which I'd loved at the age of eleven when we'd stayed in the chalet park, and I'd thought they looked like America. Alongside was a mansion whose owner (made rich after founding a budget supermarket) had recently been in trouble with the council for landing his helicopter in the car park. People and beach-tents thronged the brown sand and pools shimmered in extraordinary rocks I'd forgotten. But I remembered the kiosk selling fishing nets and buckets, the happy-children screams, and the rinsing sound of the sea. I remembered a Mars Bar which had cost 13p and I'd had all to myself. I remembered cuddling my little brother. Wanting to live in one of those flats.

I'd forgotten the wooded headland of bluebells and shade-sustained ramsons — holidays had been all about the beach. Gŵyr's woodland had been cleared for agriculture even before the Iron Age. But now, ferns and trees swamped the banks and ditches of this Iron Age promontory fort which gave 'Caswell Bay' its name — Caswell derived from the Cymraeg 'Cas-wellt', meaning 'straw fort'.

A remarkable 50 percent of Penrhyn Gŵyr had escaped Acts of Enclosure, and commoners' grazing rights dated back to at least the Iron Age. Cows roamed the plateau, above caves where rhinoceros, elephant, bear, wolf and reindeer skeletons pre-dating the last Ice Age had been found. Pottery, hearths and artefacts had been discovered too, indicating the caves had been occupied from the Iron Age to early Middle Ages. And at Southgate, excavations of a promontory fort had yielded animal bones, shells, sling-stones, blue-green glass, a spindle whorl and a bowl dating to the late first century, when the Iron Age had overlapped with Roman occupation. I found it difficult to associate these artefacts, when I read about them, with my memory of the cliffs.

Not so, commoners' grazing rights. The orange cows browsing garden hedges at Southgate and chewing the cud in the car park, the calves on the headland, and the horse whose foliage-adorned head suddenly protruded through the gorse like a living Mari Lwyd, were especially vivid. Gŵyr people, like their Iron Age predecessors, still had rights to graze livestock, cut bracken bedding, feed pigs in the woodland, gather firewood, dig peat, fish, or take gravel. A cow rubbed her back on a hawthorn and it showered her in petals.

A silver pill meandered through saltmarsh onto Three Cliffs Bay. The tide was low, and the beach a single golden wonder of sand. Skylark and turnstone calls floated like music. Ferns uncurled in woods colonising mature dunes giving to nubile dunes which gave to dried mud, peppered with cockle and razor shells. It was gone six but still hot. People shimmered, dwarfed by the cliffs. There were bird prints at the sea's edge and bird calls in the air. Sunlight bathed the cliffs to their tapering tips and sprinkled little eddies of sand onto my tent. Summer stirred the marram grass, distilled kids' voices and the faraway bark of their dogs, and sent a black beetle struggling across the sand. Gradually the sand became pinker, the sky a little darker, the bird calls closer, the sea paler, the air chillier, and the sun dropped into the dunes. I leaned out. Two people were swimming, just tiny dots.

I wanted to live on this beach but I packed up and left. I didn't know what else to do. Two men were painting the toilet doors blue in the car park, but I had the coast to myself. Sant Illtud's church awash with sea light. Pungent woods full of blackbirds and ramsons like stars. Open hillsides with views of Rhosili, hanging in blue salty air. I stopped often to sit and gaze without realising I'd done so, my senses dominated by wobbling walls of fragrant gorse throbbing with insects, swallowing the sun.

There were people at Port Einon. A young Mum read a book in a buttercup glade while her new-born slept in a pram, and the beach was packed. The sand, created by Ice Age glaciers, was now slowly disappearing from the beach, possibly due to dredging in Môr Hafren, and the only sandbar to have once enclosed a saltmarsh had vanished, revealing footprints of deer and wild boar chased by a Mesolithic hunting party. The people gathered around car parks and cafés, finding reassurance in doing the same as each other. Friends of mine too (of any gender), didn't like walking or going out alone. Some were scared, most just got lonely, whereas I was right in my comfort zone. I observed more, thought more, met people better – or avoided them if I wanted. Carrying just what I needed. Not knowing much where I was. I only felt uneasy when missing Rob. Occasionally I'd become convinced some accident had befallen him – that perhaps he'd slipped in the stream and banged his head on a rock.

I lost myself to limestone cliffs rolling down the coast on which bird's foot trefoil, horseshoe vetch, Portland spurge, thrift, and yellow whitlow-grass –

a relic of the Arctic tundra that had followed the Ice Age, grew. Beneath were the bone caves, scoured out by waves when sea levels were eight metres higher than today, before they dropped to levels much lower than now, when the cliffs were far from the coast. Now sea smashed Paviland's arthritic fist again, and meadow pipits and wheatears sauntered over its summit. I crouched at the edge, peering down to frightening rocks piercing the foam. Somewhere below was the cave where Paviland Man had been found in 1823, dusted in red ochre and draped with jewellery made from bone, antlers and mammoth ivory, the oldest known ceremonial burial of a modern human (homo-sapien) anywhere in Western Europe. The sea had been a long way from here when he'd lived, 28,000 years ago, in a climate of cool summers and harsh winters, when Môr Hafren was a shallow river, and the ice just an hour's walk away.

They were incredible, these cliffs with piecrust overhangs, cliffs which flounced into green skirts and foam petticoats, gull-hung cliffs, striated and lichen-mottled, plummeting or ceding to gentler gorse slopes. A kestrel lifted vertically, held itself still, then slid down the air as if it was something solid. At Mewslade, the cliffs rose like curtains that were too long and gathered at the base, and I met the wind from the north. Water was rushing quietly towards Pen Pyrod. I came upon the coastguard hut, stepping up from the path almost against its window. Inside, folders, pens and binoculars were neatly arranged on a desk and two elderly gentlemen in crisp white shirts peered out to sea. Jumpers with epaulettes hung on their chairs. One sprang up and opened the cabin door. "National Coast Watch operates where the coastguard no longer does," he said proudly. Warmth from a small stove, and a smell of coffee wafted out, the flagpole halyard clanged, and a donation box rattled on the door.

Crowds of people were streaming along the peninsula between Pen Pyrod and Rhosili. Waves rushed up Traeth Llangennydd ahead, under a long hill of lowland heath, home apparently to the rare black bog ant, which is what the people on the beach resembled from here. The sun lit a distant strip of sand far away up the coast, and I thought I'd be walking there soon.

The pub where I'd arranged to meet Rob was crammed, and the car park glittered with metal. The pub was too dark. I felt blitzed as if I'd been walking alone for more than just three days. We left for the wind and drifts of tellin shells, and heart-urchins brittle as frost, my sunburnt legs warm in my trousers. But it was cooler now, so we put on more clothes and watched fishermen spread down the beach to meet the incoming tide. The sun was a silver liquid. We put up our tent in a dune slack, avoiding the pansies. I drifted into sleep and then opened my eyes. Rob was watching me, and smiling.

Two lads walked up the beach with a fish. "What have you got?" I asked. "Sea bass," they said, "Another. We're sick of them we've had so many." But they looked sublimely happy. "We've camped out for days, we're going feral" they grinned. All the happiest people I knew had gone a bit feral. I think it has something to do with escaping the shackles of stuff. I am happiest with a rucksack. Even the tiny caravan in which we live tidily, appears sometimes too full of frippery – I seem to be always cleaning the spice-jars.

Nine thousand years ago, when the sea was twelve miles across the Hafren Plain, Burry Holm had been used as a seasonal camp by Mesolithic versions of these two lads, and the men with rods and a freckled boy with thin white legs, who were picking their way over the rocks.

Plastic fishing junk had been used to decorate the trees by a static caravan belonging to a stout man in a Strongbow rugby shirt who escorted us to the site shop, where we joined a long queue of elderly men chatting so cheerfully they'd clearly come too early on purpose. Strongbow showed us the coffee machine and inquired on our behalf about pies. We ate them outside, greeted by every passing customer, all of them proudly Abertawe and proud too, that strangers had found their favourite spot. "I'm from Shrewsbury," I told one man. "Well that's not so bad" he said. "My son's wife was born on the west of the Severn, the 'right' side, as I call it," and I laughed. I had made peace with myself for being English. England and Cymru had been bound together since the formation of the first super-continents a billion years ago. I guess we had to put up with each other, one way or another.

One very elderly man, leaning carefully on his stick, advised us to look out for the stream at Llanmadog. "I'd not been able to cross it for a long time, because the banks you see, are steep," he said, slowly. "I never thought I'd cross that stream again. But now they've put stepping stones in," he paused. "Oh, it's beautiful. They let the water flow and all the little fishes pass." Another man asked if we'd been accepted yet, in Machynlleth. "I heard it takes twenty-five years up there," he said, wonderingly. It took about twenty-five seconds down here.

But it wasn't the first time I'd heard southerners say this, revealing the emotional tension between those who can and can't speak Cymraeg. Yet this man had taken on an awed distant look, as if asking for news of Inuit fur-traders rather than fellow countrymen. Cymru was a patchwork of diverse communities. Nevertheless, traditions and language had been largely sustained by the continuity and remoteness of the upland farming community which was largely in the north, though the idea made lowlanders prickly, as if accused of not being Cymreig enough. The disunity was thankfully not much in evidence when it came to international sporting events. An outsider might not discern it.

Although the old man's question was gentle, I felt loyal to Machynlleth and the northwest. Suddenly I understood that Cymreig rural society was shy. That people were unwilling to speak out of turn, were unhurried and thought-ful in a way I appreciated. I'd noticed it often when teaching at the eco-centre. Once I'd given the same lecture twice in a week to geography students from Liverpool and Bangor. The English group had participated enthusiastically, shouting out, applauding spontaneously. The Cymreig group had been serious, and queued up at the end to ask questions privately. Why had I not taken this into account when blundering about, imposing my clumsy Cymraeg on people? And it wasn't true anyway, that strangers were unwelcome. My uneasiness at being English had obscured me seeing how very welcome I *had* been made. More guilt bubbles dissolved. My journey was alka-seltzer.

We nearly trod on two green and brown speckled eggs in a hollow on the path. I looked about, and sure enough a lapwing was feigning injury to distract us. It was late for lapwing eggs – this would be a second clutch, to replace eggs already lost. I took off my boots. The path advanced up Trwyn Whitford to a rusting lighthouse then trickled back between trees under which grass was cool, and mud warm to my feet. Ahead was the saltmarsh that spread along north Gŵyr coast. And then, in a reclaimed bay, we came upon the very old man's stepping-stones. They were concrete cubes with holes in, and we stepped on them carefully, and saw the water and the little fishes pass.

My feet noticed smooth roots protruding from the earth path, but my eyes noticed only the marsh. I strayed onto it and sank to my knees in warm black mud which dried in little crusts. Its horizon was soft. A flock of starlings murmured over it like gnats. Purple crabs and brown wrack were scattered on it, wooden stakes marked a cockle-pickers' route over it, and silver channels wriggled through it. Foals roamed with wind-ruffled manes. They looked so wilful they could have been from another era, and I felt almost scared. Heat dissolved the boundaries between sky, sea and marsh. I was sorry when we left it for trees, but soon a warm wind stirred buttercups at the woods' edge and the marsh was back – enchanting and omnipresent, a strange brushed expanse. Sun flickered across it. The sea was a distant blue stripe. A heron took flight, but an egret remained in position.

Our eyes were parched by the sun, and our minds by the marsh. In Llanrhidian we drank cold cider. My face was scorched, but my feet felt tingly and massaged. An old dog sniffed our boots. It felt wrong to be inside, like when my Dad drew the curtains to watch cricket and sunbeams pierced the gloom to light dust motes. Outside, the hedgerow fizzed with flowers. The marsh was peppered with signs warning of land mines. This marsh, my marsh had been violated, used as a firing range for explosives and mustard gas in the Second World War, when anthrax biological warfare shells had apparently been tested on sheep, and unwanted munitions were buried off Trwyn Whitford. And yet it was lovely still.

Cockles have been harvested at Crofty since at least Roman times. In the 1970s, a change in river channel caused a decline, but oystercatchers were blamed, and nearly 10,000 shot. Cockles are still raked by hand at low tide, mostly for export to France and Spain, Cymry it seems, having lost their taste for shellfish.

Bus shelters shimmered on the long straight road to Pen-clawdd. The traffic was intrusive. The marsh fought back with a weedy stench. We looked at it over the seawall where pallets and cans had been tossed, at yellow iris growing among flattened reeds and the small blurs of creeping curlews. The Royal Oak wobbled in the distance. When we reached it, the two men at the bar were even more surprised to see us than the woman behind it. She ushered us swiftly to the dining area and turned up the music to full. The menu was written on a piece of cardboard propped against the beer pumps. 'Special £5 chicken curry' was the only thing on it. The bar woman yelled 'Habib!' and Habib too, seemed astonished. The curry was fiery, the cider ice-cold. We looked out at the marsh and at Swansea City posters on the wall and laughed, because Shakespeare's Sister was screaming too loudly for conversation.

Pen-clawdd had been a busy seaport serving coalmines and metal-works. It still had a few small shops, including CKs, founded by Caswell's helicopter millionaire, where boxes cluttered the aisles and the newspapers were upside down. We camped on a small promontory. The dry earth was patterned with hoof prints of ponies and sheep but it was hard to imagine the high tides that had forced them here – the sea was a distant stripe. Three boys arrived and took turns jumping off the hummock. Wild ponies galloped in the distance. We waited for the sun to set, but it disappeared without ceremony behind a cloud bank.

We said it was like Africa, being able to see so far across a brown plain. The ponies could have been wildebeest. But it was also perhaps, how the landscape had been here, when large herbivores had grazed tundra and forest clearings.

BRONZE

Between 2,500-2,000 BC when the climate was mild, small groups of people arrived from mainland Europe in boats, bringing animals, metals, swords, pots and jewellery. Most were Beaker people who may have originated from the Iberian Peninsula. They replaced more than 90 percent of the resident gene pool with one that remains dominant in Cymru today, and integrated with the resident Neolithic peoples with no evidence of conflict. Little is known about how they lived and nothing of their language and population size.

They took over monuments begun by Neolithic people, including Stone-henge which they worked on for centuries. In about 2,200 BC, they excavated eighty 4-ton bluestones from the Preselau and carried them either across land on axe-trading routes or part way by boat, to Stonehenge. (Recent evidence suggests they were at first erected near the Preselau, and transported to Stone-henge much later.) Feast-bone analysis shows that every year some 4,000 people from across Britain travelled to Stonehenge with cattle and pigs to celebrate winter solstice. About 900 stone circles were erected across Britain, possibly used for astronomical observations at seasonal festivals.

Beaker people lived in clans led by chiefs, in huts spread across fields of spelt, rye, oats and barley. Domesticated horses pulled carts. Beaker people prepared food on a central hearth, invented the loom, wove and dyed wool and plant fibres, and crafted bone spatulas, faience beads and leather.

Metal was introduced into Cymru as early as 2400 BC. Copper was mined by digging trenches and passages only big enough for children, which followed copper veins underground. Fires were lit against rock to weaken it. By 2100 BC, there were copper mines in Ynys Môn, Y Gogarth and Cwm Ystwyth. Copper axes, daggers, and trinkets were made and exchanged. Between 2150 and 2000 BC, tin discovered in Cornwall and Devon was mixed with copper to make bronze. Bronze axe heads, made by pouring molten metal into moulds, at first resembled stone axes and were used alongside stone and flint for a thousand years before eventually replacing it. By 2100 BC spearheads, knives and arrow tips were also being made, and gold was in circulation. A gold lunula (a moon-shaped necklace similar to those from Ireland, Brittany, Cornwall, and Scotland) was found in Llanllyfni.

Beaker people buried their dead in individual graves in round barrows made from earth in the lowlands, or stone cairns in the uplands – which often contained cists. The body was usually contracted and buried with a decorated ceramic beaker. After about 1900 BC, goods such as flint arrows, tools and copper knives were included in the graves – a gold cape, amber necklace and bronze knife were found with a woman buried 1900-1600 BC near Afon Dyfrdwy.

By the middle of the Bronze Age, huge sites like Stonehenge were abandoned in favour of smaller ceremonial sites, usually by water. Eventually megalithic building projects ceased altogether, and the passages of communal tombs were blocked.

It's not known when speakers of Celtic languages arrived to join and integrate with the Beaker folk. Gradually, people spread into the uplands and forest was cleared for timber, cereals and grazing. They founded settlements surrounded by fields in which they used ploughs, hoes and spades, and developed an agricultural economy. The population increased. Copper mining expanded and craftsmanship improved. Britain exported tin, copper, gold, hides, cloth, hunting dogs and slaves, and imported beans, peas, and spelt.

From 2,800 to 1,400 BC, the climate was warm and dry. Plants flourished. Bear and wolf lived in the woods. Oak, elm, lime and alder grew. Then the climate grew cooler and wetter and upland settlements were abandoned. Alder carr or grassland grew on the deforested hills, supplanted eventually in places by heather. Some deforested soils eroded and washed downhill to form flood meadows. By 1200 BC, many uplands had become blanket bog. From 1000-800 BC, the climate deteriorated to a mini Ice Age. Bad harvests led to disease. Buried hordes of coins, metal, and weapons suggest conflict, despite economic conditions having improved. The rising population, deteriorating climate and competition for land made society unstable. People began to construct forts on hills or coastal headlands. The earliest in Cymru was built at Dinorben in 1000 BC.

The areas of Britain that would eventually become Scotland, England and Cymru became segregated according to landscape, climate and building materials. Scotland and Cymru were higher, colder, stonier and wetter. In milder lowlying England, intensive farming developed and the wildwood was completely cleared for grazing and timber. Meanwhile as the climate deteriorated in the uplands, unpredictable harvests increased dependence on livestock, and cairns appeared on former arable land. Bear, wild boar, and wolf struggled as forests decreased. Auroch, the giant ancestors of domestic cattle, became extinct, and it's possible that red deer, moose, and walrus also disappeared at this time.

SIR GÂR (GAERFYRDDIN)

*C*omplex hedgerow networks contain a variety of woody shrubs and trees, with elm thriving in places. There are more dunes here than in nearly all the other counties combined. Estuaries dominate, with extensive areas of intertidal mudflats, and sandflats of bivalves and cockles. Bae Llwchwr sustains nearly half the British population of overwintering common scoter. Significant areas of grazing marsh survive. Golden plover over-winter at Gwendraeth and Pentywyn, and marshpea, frogbit, and tubular water drop-wort grow in base-rich ditches.

Intriguing little paths trickled onto mudflats. A twelve-mile stretch of post-industrial wasteland had been transformed into the Llanelli Millennium Coastal Park, which was busy with joggers and tubby men in lycra on bikes.

"I grew up with Llanelli steelworks," said a bald pink man going to meet his grandchildren, "but there's no work there now." Llanelli had been one of the largest tinplating centres in the world before tin was ousted by steel, and now only a few steel-works remained, mostly supplying the automobile industry. He said he liked the coastal park. "And the kids do too, and the wife. I've got a campervan now. We went trout fishing on Saturday morning. Caught nothing, but we made a cup of tea. We took it to Pembrey Forest for the Steam Fair and slept in it there by the trees." Desire paths trickled under pylons. There were brown geese in the water and construction works on the bank.

Rob was going home so we headed into Llanelli and sat on our rucksacks like hobos to eat pastries in Lidl car park, before dashing past chapels, eighties hair salons, and a banner on an old warehouse saying 'Wedding dance nerves? It should be fun!' which made us laugh, remembering the circle that had formed around us then tactfully dissolved at our wedding, when we'd started moshing. We arrived at the station with three minutes to spare and once again, in a flash, Rob was gone.

Pebbledash gave to brick. A woman in a Cymru rugby shirt smoking outside a pub, pointed my way down a street full of bin bags. Among bottle tops and cola gums on the pavement, a grimy pink love-heart said 'Kiss Me'. North Dock was resplendent in sea holly and yellow-horned poppies. Somewhat deflated, I bought coffee in a restaurant which had been converted from the old hydraulic accumulator tower. Families were eating Sunday dinners at tables

laid with white cloths, but I sat alone on the sofa and took off my boots. The
transition between Rob's company and sudden departures took adjusting to.
My socks had stuck to yesterday's mud and my blisters. I peeled them off and
soothed my feet on the cold slate floor.

I cheered up quickly enough. The coastal park was a modern promenade
where people had fun. Cyclists cruised, some in lycra, others wobbly with
fishing rods. Kids pedalled furiously or rattled on skateboards and scooters.
A heron took off from a fishing pond, Royal fern grew in copses, ox-eye daisies
bobbed. Hummocks had been sculpted to resemble Bronze Age barrows —
Beaker people had lived just a short way inland at Parc Howard, and been
followed or joined by the Celtic-language speaking Demetae dynasty who had
imported Cornish tin and copper to make bronze, establishing a trading
relationship which spawned an industrial-age metropolis, which had produced
a post-industrial coastal leisure park landscaped into humps that remembered
the Bronze Age. A lad stared at his phone, stubbed out his fag, then picked up
a rod and net. A goldfinch charm scattered.

At Porth Tywyn a squat lighthouse guarded the harbour once fed by a
chaotic system of canals and wagons. It was full of bright leisure boats now.
Everything dazzled and danced. An ice cream bell tinkled but I'd blown my
cash on the coffee, so I left for the vast empty dunes that were hot and still
like the desert.

I sat and gazed at brackish pools burning white on brown marsh. The
Rhosili hills beyond were brown as dust. It was quiet enough to hear a crow
beat its wings. Grasshoppers droned and skylarks sang high overhead. I could
hear the bike creaking before it came into view. An elderly man got off it with
difficulty and joined me on the bench. He said his name was Enrico Planes. "I
prefer the harbour how it used to be," Enrico Planes said. "I remember a day
when you could drop a line in from here and pull out bass or mackerel or
flatfish." He said he had four children, eleven grandchildren, and two great-
grandchildren. "They all tell me, 'be careful on that bike!'", he grinned. His
teeth were perfectly white. His face was dark and wrinkled and his brown
eyes mischievous. "My father was Spanish," he said. "He worked on the boats.
He met my mother, she was Welsh, when he came into St Dogmaels." He said
he should be getting home, and told me to remember him. "When I meet
girls like you I wish I was thirty years younger," he said, flashing me a Spanish
smile, as he creaked slowly away.

Due to flood damage the coast path was diverted around Coed Pen-bre, one of the Forestry Commission's first plantations. I stole into its nursery wood, Coed Pen y Bedd. In the car park, a middle-aged couple sat stiffly outside a campervan trying to ignore their noisy generator. In the woods were six houses, some of Lloyd George's 'Homes for Heroes'. A woman was washing dishes in one of them. Light flashed on a soapy plate.

The conifers had a broadleaf belt. I sat in a cloud of whistles, chirrups and warbles, watching the trees for two hours without seeing a single song-bird, while on sunlit fields between the two woods, pigeons and jackdaws swooped, Canada geese honked, and a shelduck slipped out of a pond. Cows roamed closer as light faded, and formed a nonchalant queue. One by one they pushed their way through a broken fence, slithered into the ditch and snorted up the opposite bank. Utterly content, I zipped up my tent and the birdsong sounded still closer, as if the birds were hovering just above the canvas.

I dangled my dirty feet over a wooden bridge, feeling like Huck Finn and ate a sandwich. In the water, minnows snatched bites from floating debris and large shore crabs squirted clouds of sperm. The brown canal had once been part of the network that had conveyed coal and anthracite from the Gwendraeth collieries to Porth Tywyn and Cydweli, from where coasters took it to Lacharn, Caerfyrddin, Sanclêr and Llansteffan. From deep within the reeds, a Cetti's warbler exploded into song.

The whole Sir Gâr coast was new to me. The air sparkled, it felt like abroad. Birds poked about a reflective striped landscape of mudflats, water and saltmarsh. Oystercatchers and egrets stalked the reeds, curlews were further out. Gulls were audible but invisible at the distant confluence of Afon Gwendraeth, Afon Tywi and Afon Tâf, just a thread of gold sand and white surf. Their calls carried on warm cushions of air. A man trained binoculars onto the mud. "There's nothing to look at," he teased when I told him I'd left mine at home. Silt and reduced demand for Cydweli tin had made Kymer's Dock redundant, save for black-headed gulls darting about a floating flip-flop. An egret stabbed for a fish. The air was heavy with heat. A man leaning over the railings in a white shirt and Panama hat was silhouetted by hot blue sky. Swallows skimmed the river, curlew chicks wobbled at its edge, a preening swan scattered white feathers onto glistening mud banks, and still those muted calls drifted in from that distant, glittering line.

I fell into step with a large-bellied man who came out of a pebbledash semi, and enthused about the quay. He said, "I never go down there to be honest. I have heard they had to change the gravel paths because the boy racers churned them up," and I was startled he didn't love it. What did he do? "There's no library here anymore," he said, "due to the council and their infinite wisdom. But there's the rugby. We got promoted last season. The aim was just to stay up but we finished sixth and we're delighted." He pointed out the club and we parted at the crossroads where a tired woman sat on a wall, shopping bags by her side. I crossed Afon Gwendraeth and followed it back to the coast.

The seabird chorus was filtered by rampant hedgerows and the air was hot and wet as an old laundrette. I sweltered up a steep farm track where ash trees met overhead. Cydweli had grown round a Benedictine Priory, though a small hoard of Bronze Age axes bore witness to even earlier settlement. Looking back from here, it appeared to have been built of little cardboard boxes, while Llansaint on the hilltop ahead resembled a Portuguese village on the Camino – it was the white church that did it. There was even a pub next to the church, but unlike in Portugal, it was closed. Just one woman was out, quietly wiping her window sill. A car drew up and a middle-aged couple unpacked groceries. The slam of their boot was intrusive. On leaving I startled a dog which alerted another and then another, into a chain reaction of barking, and that was like Portugal too.

The sea was white from this high plateau of improved grass and cowpats, where nettles were thick round a muckheap. The farming family who'd introduced the large fields couldn't have known they would eventually be so nitrogen-enriched and sown with such species-poor grass, that only rye grass and clover, nettle and dock, would remain. The hot heavy cows flicked their tails.

Not far away, in 2011, a metal detectorist discovered a Bronze Age hoard which had been buried in a small pit between 1000 and 800 BC. It's not known why Bronze and Iron Age people buried collections of weapons and tools – as religious offerings perhaps, or for safe keeping. Some hoards included swords, spears, axes, and ingots of raw metal for smelting, in good condition or deliberately broken. The 2011 hoard contained thirteen bronze items – a bracelet, a fragment of spearhead, an axe, and a collection of raw materials and casting by-products. The largest Bronze Age hoard found in Britain comprised 6,500 objects.

A sandpiper whistled past as I sat among cockle shells on the shore of Afon Tywi. Glanyfferi had been a cockle-picking village too, before hundreds of commercial pickers and tractors stripped the beach. In 1993, fights between gangs from Gŵyr, Liverpool, Aber Dyfrdwy and Glasgow had broken out, after which the beds were belatedly licensed.

A whiskery old dog followed me up an alley. "You're the third walker to go all the way round Wales," his owner announced. "There must have been more than that by now," I suggested, but he said definitely not, he'd have seen them. I bought chips and mushy peas in The Ferry Cabin, where young mums joggled babies, and two well-to-do men paused their conversation about cross-ing Asia by train to give a fellow traveller a nod. I'd crossed Asia by train too. But my attention was caught by a tiny lady in a brown cardigan with an apple-pie face, who sat hunched and alone, holding her cutlery high above her plate, sprinkling salt and vinegar with little raised fists.

My A4 pdf maps seemed to suggest Caerfyrddin was only five miles away, so I decided to dash for the bus home. It was a long five miles. I checked the maps and found I'd missed one out – it was ten, but now I was committed and broke into a sweaty jog. A herd of cows trotted behind me, trying to suck salt from my shirt, their breath hot on my neck. At last I reached the A484 where auto-parts warehouses conspired with McDonald's, and a cyclist zooming out of the station threw himself off his bike to avoid crashing into pedestrians. I jogged right onto the bus and pushed my rotten boots under the seat. They stank, but the windows were open. All the way home I watched fields being mown in golden light, and as dusk fell saw a fire somewhere near Aberaeron, figures just glimpsed, that looked ancient and pagan.

"If you like walking, you should climb Dragon Mountain at Crymych." The girl with half-shaved scarlet hair looked directly into my eyes as if delivering a message. "Thanks," I said. She said she was an art student and I said I'd been one too. "How's your course?" I said. "Art is bigger than the confines of the course," she said moodily and walked away. I was back at Caerfyrddin bus station. The passengers were mostly old ladies with shopping trolleys and grandchildren in pushchairs, chattering in English or Cymraeg. I'd not heard Cymraeg on my journey since Benllech. The realisation made me uneasy. Where was the language of Cymru? There were old ladies in the café too. One of the staff found a gold necklace on the floor and carried it like a duckling to each customer in turn. "Is it yours?" he asked in English. "Is it yours?" No-one claimed it. Gold jewellery was first made in Britain in the Bronze Age. In 2015 here in Caerfyrddin, on Llysonnen Road, three Bronze Age barrows would be excavated on a building site – classic circular ditches around a mound, one with satellite pits, two of which contained bodies interred in urns.

Summer had matured into something fat and ripe. The lanes were green, Afon Tywi was lazy. Three teenagers lolled in a playing field, hedge-banks wobbled with flowers. A fledgling robin gripped a twig, and a squeaking brood of fluffy blue tits flurried between trees in short awkward flights. But the air pulsed with biting insects, and the humidity was claustrophobic, making me impatient for the estuary. The road there was so empty it was several minutes after hearing sirens before I stepped onto the verge to let two police cars pass. Further along, a lad turned a 'Stop' sign to 'Go' without looking up from his book, a road-sweeper shuffled towards me, the driver waved, and that was it for the traffic.

The air was fresh and Llansteffan pretty on the spit between Afon Tywi and Afon Tâf. It felt part Dylan Thomas, part Postman Pat. "Help yourself to the apples love, no-one eats fruit in this village," said the shopkeeper, and an elderly lady in a pink cardigan, sat perched on a stool at the counter, nodded to confirm the awful truth. I ordered coffee and drank it in a cloud of furniture polish whilst admiring the antimacassars. A cat walked across the counter. The doorbell rang as customers came and went. Eventually I dragged myself up and away, and was accosted on leaving Llansteffan by an aggrieved rambler.

"It's a disgrace they wouldn't bring the path closer to the coast," he said. Three estuaries meeting in one bay had challenged the planners. "You'll see," he grumbled. But I had never seen anything as magnificent as the view from Wharley Point. A shawl of white sand stitched with wind-ruffled marram. Silver estuaries dissolving into sparkles. The tiny single-carriage train pulling into Glanyfferi, and beyond, Aber Gwendraeth, Penrhyn Gŵyr, and bottle-green Coed Pen-bre. I shouted "Wow!" and then said it again several times, in different voices.

A large shirtless man puffing up from the beach with a bucket, stopped to catch his breath. "Rock samphire, not marsh samphire," he said, showing me the golden stems. He was upset the cockles were too small to collect. "The bailiffs are on the beach making sure no-one picks 'em," he said, and I was glad they were. But I had detached myself from environmental angst and was possessed instead by the moment. The view ahead was phenomenal too – a shifting world of rivulets, mudflats and whale-shaped beaches with silver edges. Water shimmered like fish scales in green bobbled marsh, stippled by dunes at the edge. Light flashed on the sea, and cloud shadows raced. I looked back again at Afon Gwendraeth and Afon Tywi – one mingled great white, swirly whole. I couldn't remember having ever seen anything so spectacular. Helpless, I said "Wow" again, out loud and in my head and laughed, remembering the grumpy rambler.

True the path struck inland then, up Afon Tâf. I wandered sublimely through this world of irregular fields, buzzing bees, meadowsweet and birds, where swallows fished for thrips in green hedged lanes, and tractors baled hay in the distance. Ducks wobbled out of a gate and a farmer in red rugby shirt faded to pink, asked where I was headed. "Nice weather, best of luck to you," he said. A rolling cloud of pollen puffed from the trees and light was holy gold on an oak. Happy children sounds spilled from a garden with balloons on the gate in this storybook world. Even as fields filigreed by pylons grew larger with improved grass that hid cowpats in various stages of liquefaction, when I sat to rest under an oak and stuck out my bleeding feet, skylarks sang overhead. I heard rumbling tractors, and they were part of it all.

I'd met farmers on my journey but not many. Not compared to in the old travel books I was reading, that were full of reapers, sowers and herdsmen. Farms now were scant on labourers and though I'd not known it any other way (save for the golden summer I'd worked with a small team roguing wild oats out of Shropshire wheat), I missed them.

The path kissed Sanclêr's edge and played hide and seek with the A477 before ducking into meadows on the banks of Afon Tâf. They were buzzing with insects, rich in flowering grasses and cuckoo-spit, and rose-gold with Yorkshire fog. Ponies dipped their heads to drink among ragged robin. The last was a dream field, seething with flowers, a million miles from screensaver-green nitrogen-enriched rye grass. I unrolled my mat on a wind-flattened patch, surrounded by tall flowing grasses, buttercup, sorrel, rattle, great burnet, and sprays of white, mauve, pink and yellow flowers I couldn't name. We have lost 97 percent of our flower-rich hay meadows. This was a memory of something I didn't actually remember. (I would discover that the meadow's name was Whitehill Down and that later that summer, 176 species would be counted in it.) I watched the pink sky turn lilac and a waxing half-moon sail across it and heard distant bird-calls and tractors, and closer to, the sound of cars muffled by hedge, and the insects, thousands of insects, droning, and felt like crying, it was so lost and lovely.

A bee buzzed an inch from my head. A pink glimmer kissed Afon Tâf and the meadow was heavy with dew. Grasses and buttercups slapped my legs and coated my boots with seeds. Ragged robin and redshank grew, iris speared gaps in the boardwalk, and a single orchid rose purple and proud from its cushion of green. The path dipped into woods which showered me with birdsong like a handful of coins, and I rounded the headland to Lacharn.

From the path I peered down at the large yellow house where Dylan Thomas had lived and the garden across which, so I'd read, his wife Caitlin had swum on high tides to fetch in the washing, and ate a few wild strawberries that grew in the top of his wall. Thomas had only lived in Lacharn for four years, but the cafés and pubs around the square bore his name. The woman in Spar filled up my water bottles but warned me the water was awful and brown. "We use the hot tap when the tide's high," she said.

Pentywyn's six miles of sand was military land so the path took the A4066. I followed a council truck cutting the verges, slicing flowers and birdsong to an understorey of dried roots and crushed litter. The coast when I reached it, was stifling. Slews of sparkles silvered the sea but Pentywyn was drowning in mist. My face dripped with sweat and I cast a weak shadow over thrush-smashed snail shells on the path. White waves swilled around black rocks. I reached Sir Benfro and took a bus home.

FARMING

About 5000 BC, new people began to arrive in southeast Britain from the continent. They slowly spread north and west, possibly bringing diseases that decimated the nomadic hunter-gatherers round the coast. Survivors absorbed the new culture. The immigrants brought stone axes for quarrying, and fashioned flint arrowheads for hunting with elm and yew bows. They quarried stone at the edges of Eryri and spotted dolerite from the Preselau to make axes traded as far away as Antrim in Ireland and the Salisbury Plain. Polished stone axes from Paviland and Ystym Llwynarth have also been found.

Agriculture had been practised in Europe (where it had arrived from Asia) for a thousand years by the time Neolithic people brought it to Britain. They foraged and hunted, but also moved livestock from pasture to pasture and grew crops. Across millennia, they felled and burned trees growing on fertile land where they planted emmer wheat, barley and corn they'd brought with them, and grazed the domesticated cows, pigs and sheep they'd also brought. (Harvest mice and seeds of dead-nettle, charlock, poppies, dock and plantain apparently arrived accidentally, in grain, animal hides or fleeces.) People made clay pots to cook and store food. They span plant fibres and sheep's wool into yarns, and wove them into cloth. By about 3000 BC, organised farming had replaced the hunter-gatherer society.

Food was plentiful enough for the population to expand and people to spend time building cromlechi (megalithic burial chambers) where they gathered for rituals, fires, and feasts. At the start of the Neolithic Age, corpses were stripped of flesh and the bones buried together, suggesting society may have been egalitarian. Goods like pottery and flint were included in graves.

Earth and wood were also used, but cromlechi were built from stone where it was plentiful. Along the coast, massive capstones were placed on pillars and covered with earth. Various designs evolved. By 3,800 BC, there were passage tombs and sealed stone chambers on headlands south of Bae Ceredigion, on Ynys Môn, in Scotland and Northern Ireland, and portal tombs in sheltered valleys. Barclodiad y Gawres was built in about 3200 BC, and decorated with chevrons and lozenges similar to those found in Ireland. At least 400 cromlechi were built across Bae Ceredigion and southwest England – part of a burial culture which was probably shared with Ireland, Brittany and Spain. The construction of defended enclosures and evidence of battles fought along what would become the border between England and Cymru, began at least 3000 BC.

Waves of settlers continued to arrive from continental Europe. From about 4000-3500 BC the climate was warm and damp, and winters mild. But by 3500 BC, it was deteriorating and soil became waterlogged. Alder replaced oak as swamps developed in thick forests. Peat began to accumulate in the uplands as a result of deforestation followed by wet, cool conditions. Seasons were less reliable and the climate stormy. Crops failed, leading to food shortages and violent conflict, and the population collapsed to a pre-agricultural level. From 3200-3000 BC, the weather was particularly cold. Warfare began. Archers attacked enclosures and earthworks became defensive.

Britain grew colder earlier than the rest of Europe, and a ritual landscape developed of single standing stones, stone circles, stone rows, or pairs of standing stones and henges (circular earthworks with internal settings of timber or stone) which continued to be modified over the next 1,500 years. They were apparently gathering places possibly oriented for viewing the sun, moon and stars. A complex of earth and timber enclosures built at Hindwell in Powys from 3800-2500 BC, included a palisaded enclosure. At 34 hectares it is the largest of its kind known in Britain, and required thousands of tons of gravel and earth, and multiple oak posts. In 3100 BC, work on Stonehenge began.

Towards the late Neolithic, there appears to have been a shift from the communal to the cult of the individual, with round barrows built for the burial of single, intact bodies.

SIR BENFRO

S ir Benfro Coast National Park includes glacial meltwater valleys, and islands where sea-birds breed. The Preselau rise in the north, harbouring flushes of western butterwort. Kelp forests and seaweed meadows sustain sponges, sea squirts, anemones, starfish and sea urchins. Yellow-wort, blue fleabane, and wild basil survive in Afon Cleddau's sinuous waterways flowing into Dyfrffordd Aberdaugleddau, which divides the peninsula almost in two. Rare lichens and breeding Barbastelle bats live in North Sir Benfro Woodlands, though woodland is scarce.

I was the only passenger on the rickety bus with carpeted walls and seats that prickled my legs. It spluttered up hills belching black noise and smoke, and sweat poured into my eyes. I got off with a headache. So much for sustainable public transport. Just replacing petrol cars with electric ones won't solve our transport problems – there are still manufacturing impacts, particularly regarding batteries for a start. But if Cymru was served by efficient electric buses – would anyone be prepared to ditch their cars and use them? Food becomes scarce, conflicts increase, and populations and societal structures collapse when the climate deteriorates. It happens again and again. It will happen to us, because of these small reluctances.

When I was ten we'd swum at Amroth whilst on holiday in Saundersfoot and got stomach bugs from sewage, but now Clean Beach flags flopped above elderly people on benches, eating ice creams. I pulled a scarf over my head and bounced up the wooded headland in new boots. The editor of the magazine I wrote for, had sent me two pairs to review.

I remembered a kiosk selling orange dinghies and red buckets glowing like lanterns, that was no longer beside the stream flowing to Wiseman's Bridge – the beach where after storms, fossilised animal bones, antlers, nuts and Neolithic flints have been found in blue clay, and where too, my Dad had coaxed big crabs from the rock pools. In Saundersfoot, from where anthracite was once exported, I almost remembered the gaudy flowers and red harbour rails, and I definitely remembered a lone pine clinging to a cliff, which had brought to mind places I'd heard of like Canada. And I remembered too, that in Canada, aged nineteen, I'd photographed a lone pine on a beach that had reminded me of somewhere – here.

The parched hills were raucous with grasshoppers and rustled with thistles and scabious. Dinbych-y-pysgod, from where baby Harri Tudur had been protected before being taken to refuge in Brittany, was a hazy postcard of turrets and boats. As king, Harri had financed maintenance of the town walls and harbour which attracted well-heeled tourists for centuries to come. The kiss of Tudor wealth still lingered around the bistros and pizzeria, the pastel-hued buildings, and old town walls. An elderly lady sat on a rock, her pink skirt floating, face tilted to the sun. Her eyes were closed and a smile played on her lips, till sensing me nearby her eyelids fluttered with irritation. I dumped my rucksack and walked into the sea. Tiny spry glittered as I floated – weightless. Careless.

A sweaty lad drinking lager from a can, with a T-shirt slung over a shoulder was heading my way. "Watch out for the horseflies," he said, "they're horrible!" The wind played strange and beautiful music through a fence. I bounced on. My boots were comfortable though perhaps I'd laced them too tightly. Bays were dishes of light. Car-boot slams and drinking chatter wafted from the Euro Park campsite. At Lydstep, foam creamed up the slipway where a man smoking a fag in a tractor, waited for a boat. "Hot now mind, innit?" he said. Thistly pink clifftops dropped to sandy coves washed clean by green rolling waves. Scarlet pimpernel grew beside the path, brown butterflies billowed from under my feet and a cockchafer landed on my arm. But a tanned man, clutching an empty water bottle and striding quickly, wasn't happy. "The streams are drying up," he said morosely, and loped on. The sea roared into blowholes like thunder, a fearful, primitive noise. Hissing lines of foam repeated the line of the land, and fulmars and curlews glided.

The warm evening was fragrant with honeysuckle as I rounded Priest's Nose into Bae Maenorbŷr, where King's Quoit cromlech stood next to the path, five thousand years after two uprights and a huge capstone had been heaved into place. Neolithic monuments, though distributed across Sir Benfro, are particularly dense in two bands – from the Preselau to Tyddewi, and between Dinbych-y-pysgod and Bae Angle. People had raised these stones, covered them with earth, and buried their loved ones within, but I found the scenes hard to imagine.

I camped on orange sand by a storm bank of pink and blue pebbles, below red cliffs shot through with purple. A young arguing couple headed for the promontory from which dog walkers and fishermen were returning. Maenorbŷr's white church tower turned mauve. Darkness fell, the young couple came back separately. Silence floated above the gentle sea till the air

began to rumble and boom. High velocity missiles were being tested further
west, perhaps at Castellmartin – there were so many military sites it was difficult to tell. Orange flares blossomed in the sky, casting a motorway of fiery
light on the sea.

The morning was bright, and I was sublimely content – save for niggling
worries that perhaps Rob had been stung to death by the wasps nesting on
the veranda.

A peregrine perched on a fence-post ahead, grey wings folded, chest
barred, beak blue, talons yellow. I watched it through binoculars. I stepped
closer, and the gap in the gorse enlarged to reveal its mate on an adjacent post.
They swooped over the sea, fanned tails a sign-off. Then I watched linnets in
a burnet rose. Everything was beautiful. Lichen-mottled red sandstone cliffs.
Clifftop pines framing emerald sea and white sand. But hot. Thrift was desic-
cated, thistly grass dry and short, ponies drowsy. Butterflies wobbled. The
noon light was dry and choughs were struggling. They paced the wiry grass
looking for food to feed their squalling young. One, red beak agape, strolled
alongside me with crimson feet. I told myself it was just summer, that it had
nothing to do with climate change.

De Aberllydan was packed and the sand so white it hurt to look at. Discon-
certing missile booms and smoke from Castellmartin still crackled and fizzed,
but no-one seemed bothered. I cooled off in the sea, wrapped a scarf round
my head, lay down and was instantly too hot. A mother and daughter sat
behind me. The daughter said "that's a good idea, putting a scarf on your head"
in a strong Abertawe accent. Their little dog ran between us, and they chatted
towards me in an inviting way. I liked them but was too hot to be sociable. I
heard them lose a sausage roll in the sand. "We're causing chaos Mum!" said
the daughter.

Despite the blast and smoke, I forgot the path crossing the firing range
would be closed. The guard turned me onto the diversion with unreciprocated
cheeriness. I am a shade-loving creature. Never at my best in a heatwave, I
was suddenly at my worst. I wanted the coastal plateau – Sant Gofan's chapel
wedged in a fissure of limestone cliff, and especially I wanted the breeze.
Gunpowder hung in low clouds, and bangs ripped the air as I marched up the
hot road, finally admitting that despite being my size, despite my test-run, my
new boots were too small to accommodate my heat-swollen feet. I had blisters

on my soles. I rested in a bus shelter, but the shade was hot and even swallows swooping in to their nests failed to lighten my mood.

I didn't want to go inland around Castellmartin firing range with its signs that said DON'T PICK UP ANY MILITARY MATERIAL IT MIGHT EXPLODE AND KILL YOU. Where horseflies swarmed out of tall flowering grasses. I unrolled my sleeves and wrapped my sarong round my legs but the horseflies still attacked my face. I put on sunglasses to stop them biting my eyes but the glasses steamed up and slid down my nose in the sweat pouring out of my hat. My blisters began to burst and flood my boots with hot pus. I swore at the nature sign. I knew Castellmartin's grassland was species-rich, that military activity had perversely preserved the coastal ecology from other development. But it was an isolated pocket. A token gesture, a mere consequence. "So eco-friendly you are," I shouted. "You're an effing military base!" I was livid at the detour, the heat, the tight boots, the flies, the military.

The military are responsible for a significant amount of carbon dioxide emissions but have been omitted from carbon accounting due to an exemption negotiated by the US in 1997 at the Kyoto Protocol. In 2014, the Conservative UK Government would allocate £25 billion to the Ministry of Defence but only £1.5 billion to the Department for Energy and Climate Change which says all you need to know about its priorities. I'd read about the escalation of genocide after non-intervention and wasn't naïve enough to think if we de-militarised everyone else would too. But I didn't want it. Better technology just meant we could kill each other more efficiently. It had been so since at least the Neolithic Age. Where do we draw the line? There is no line.

Castellmartin, established in 1939 was now one of NATO's largest army training and firing ranges. I didn't want it and I didn't want it in Cymru, imposed here by the UK Government. If ever there was an argument for complete independence (and there were plenty in my opinion – for a start Cymreig MPs make up only 6 percent of UK parliament so lack influence), this was it. This – the proliferation of military sites across Cymru. The huge amounts of money they swallow and heinous amounts of greenhouse gases they emit. That Cymru had no choice but be complicit in whatever activity they resulted in. A dog fox ran across the field, followed moments later by a vixen. She watched me and barked – guarding cubs. At last I reached the camps where bored youths lolled in sentry boxes under limp flags. "What are you even doing?" I raged (to myself). I stormed down the road, passing a red-haired soldier daring to jog in the heat, daring to greet me. His smile died on his lips.

I am blessed with a positive spirit. If something upsets me, I address it and move on. There was nothing I could do about the military. So I was furious for three miles, but on reaching Freshwater West my anger vanished. The beach was how I remembered – full of surfers, with campervans parked up the slip road. Light was painting the bay in blue, pink, black and green stripes. Waves lulled. The night was deliciously warm. My tent door flapped gently in the whisper of starlit breeze. My sleeping bag was so soft.

The soles of my feet were like bubble-wrap. One blister covered my whole heel and my foot hurt as much to raise as put pressure on. I was heading inland again, this time around Dyfrffordd Aberdaugleddau, in horrible heat.

"Prince William came here!" A braying voice broke the rich silence in Old Point House, where I was sucking ice cubes, with my feet on the cool stone floor. A family of holidaymakers had arrived – Posh Dad came preceded by loud pronouncements. Posh Mum murmured something about cutlery. "He sat right here!" said Posh Dad to the teenage boys, his son presumably, and an Asian friend from boarding school I assumed, without evidence. "A splendid locals' pub!" Posh Dad swept his eyes over me and my rucksack in dismissal, though maybe it was me dismissing him, judging the rich again. At least he was trying to be sociable, and spending in a rural community, unlike me who had nothing to spend and nothing to say.

I wondered how people got rich – not the budget-store helicopter-million-aires, but holidaymakers like this, who reeked of inherited privilege. I would learn that an elite class had existed in the Bronze Age, and perhaps even earlier, in the late Neolithic, when there had been a shift from the communal to the cult of the individual. When round barrows had been built for the burial of single, intact bodies, rather than a community of bones. When agriculture had begun. I guess the rich had all been self-made traders at first. Protecting their interests. This then, the root of my prejudice.

Even from inside, the sparkling sea hurt to look at. The boats barely moved. Two men took beer outside and their voices drifted in. "Where's the harm in it?" said one, "they're wanting to know where I'm getting the red mullet from now". An elderly man came to lean on his stick in the porch. "Hello there!" whinnied Posh Dad. "Are you local?" The old man closed his eyes.

At Angle village shop I couldn't find my purse, assumed I'd left it in the pub, then found it in a never-used pocket. I bought bread and ate it in the church porch. The bread was dry and hard to swallow. An elderly lady arrived looking for *her* purse, scurried off and returned to tell me she'd found it in the pub. "I was putting up leaflets there about the fête," she said, fanning her face with them. "It's the heat. It's muddling us. I'll come back to sweep the aisles when it's cooler."

A cyclist bearing an umbrella for shade said there was a fire at Castellmartin, and I wondered whether the soldiers had lit it to kill the horseflies, and what had happened to the foxes. Smoke was settling on the water and stinging my eyes. It was too hot. Water-birds shimmered. Potatoes shrivelled at field edges. A giant bush cricket lay squashed in the road, in front of Angle Refinery. Wind turbines and radio-masts rose from a jungle of chimneys and tanks and a whiff of tar mingled with the smoke.

Oil refineries have been operating in Dyfrffordd Aberdaugleddau since the 1950s. Oil and liquefied natural gas are distributed by road, rail and sea to the Midlands and Manchester. Oil that was formed 66-252 million years ago when plankton and algae sank and were buried with their embodied carbon, at the bottom of ancient seas. Oil that when burned, releases carbon removed from the atmosphere over millions of years. The oil is transformed into petroleum (still our main source of transport fuel), pesticides, fertilisers, pharmaceuticals and plastics.

Gas was created when buried plant and animal matter, decomposed under intense heat and pressure. It burns with fewer particulates than oil, but is still carbon, its release and use as a fuel still devastating in terms of climate change. In its short industrial history, (the modern oil age only began in 1850) oil and gas have been responsible for about two thirds of global greenhouse gas emissions. Oil and gas companies have funded, advanced and financed climate denial. In 2019, the UK oil and gas industry would claim that the best way to tackle greenhouse gas emissions was to continue production at maximum levels of 1.1 million barrels a day, thereby reducing the need to import fossil fuels. Balderdash.

The Zero Carbon Britain report shows we can reduce energy demand by 60 percent through increased efficiency alone – with insulation, public transport, electrification, reduced meat and dairy consumption, and less flying. And that our subsequently reduced demand could be met with renewables. No fossil fuels. No nuclear. Nothing not yet invented. By adapting our agricultural systems and creating and nurturing natural carbon sinks like forests and bogs, we could balance out non-avoidable emissions from activities such as cement production and methane from livestock, to achieve net zero-carbon emissions. With knowledge and technology we already have. Yet every year, this pipeline still carried 9 million tons of crude oil sixty miles to the Llandarcy Refinery. The weather was too hot for despair. Heat was driving nails in my head.

People sizzled on beaches or cowered inside, and the waterway was empty. But the reason Rhoscrowdder was empty, was because Texaco had bought its residents houses in 1994 after a blast injured twenty-six people, caused the village to be evacuated, and made the medieval Church of Sant Decumanus unstable. In 2005, lightning had set a crude oil storage tank ablaze, and in 2011 four people were killed and a fifth seriously injured when a tank exploded. Renewables didn't do that.

The only people I encountered were a middle-aged couple sipping drinks under parasols in a disused car park, watching the boats. Their car-boot was crammed with cool boxes which played on my mind for hours as I trudged beneath reeking rigs and gantries, and over farmland where cows barely moved, butterflies rippled from ditches and a film of dust covered the vetch and scarlet pimpernel. The birds were silent, the shade full of blowsy flies and little black thunder beetles. I slept in a cove for an hour.

But the lane was still horribly hot. Chestnut horses kicked up dust that gave them veiled silhouettes. The lane led to Brownslate Farm where, like a desert oasis, a couple were pruning roses in the shade. "We're delighted to see you," said the woman, "do you need somewhere to camp?" I thought they must be a mirage, but put up my tent on the lawn. "We're ever so pleased to meet you," said Jane, inviting me in for apple juice. I took off my boots and stepped into the hall. The carpet was so soft and pink I wanted to lie on it. I held the cold glass and felt the cold juice travel all the way down my oesophagus. Jane said she liked having people to talk to. "We farm organically," she said, "and we get a good price for our beef. To keep our organic status we have to produce all our own feed on the farm, and it's often a challenge. But this year we're alright. We haven't got the hay in this early since 1976!" Harry smiled sleepily. Orange light flooded the brown Arts and Crafts patterned wallpaper. "On the radio they've been telling people to stay indoors and drink lots of liquids," said Jane. Her merry chatter floated as I tried to keep my eyes open. "I married the boy next door," she was smiling at Harry, "he's eighty now." Harry and I had planted our bare feet on the stone floor. The coolth crept up our legs. My mind swam. Harry looked like Farmer Hoggett from the kid's film *Babe*. I remembered Farmer Hoggett singing to the pig; 'If I were to, make a day for you, I'd sing you a morning, golden and new…'. I was hallucinating, I thought Harry actually *was* singing, and about to dance, slow then faster and faster before leaping into the air in a slow-motion spin of gold dust. "We have never really got over the pylons coming," I heard Jane say. "No," said Harry, his eyes closed and a smile on his lips.

By Neyland I was frazzled. The traffic, tarmac, and piles of bin bags heaped under trees, the second-hand shop with dirty nets, and the large winged insect dying on the pavement distressed me. But I had crossed the rivers now, and was bearing west, back to the coast. Tetchiness gave to somnambulance. A cloud passed over the sun and it took me seconds to process what had happened. The cloud moved on. A gassy stink hung around the refineries, but there were dragonflies, and speckled butterflies, red admirals, and a clouded yellow, fluttering out of the ditches, and blackberries that were juicy and warm.

I lingered too long by the fridges in Aberdaugleddau Spar. The contrasting heat outside made me queasy and I had to recover on the marina with a pint of orange juice and lemonade. International cruise passengers docked here now, but the husband of Nelson's mistress had invited seven Quaker families from Martha's Vineyard and Nantucket to establish a whaling fleet here in 1790. The whales were saved only because Aberdaugleddau was chosen for the Royal Navy dockyard instead (before it was moved to Doc Penfro). I'd been largely ignorant of Cymru's contribution to the industry that processed whales (3 million in the twentieth century alone) into lamp-oil and margarine. I had barely considered that palm-oil atrocities had a precedent. Now the customhouse, built to store whale oil, was a museum.

The marina was like all the others, full of lazy yachts. It was hard to imagine the fifty-five steam trawlers and 200 sailing smacks that had made it their base within weeks of the railway arriving. By 1914 Aberdaugleddau had a herring and mackerel market, smoke-houses, twice-daily fish-trains to London, and fleets that fished in Spanish, Irish, and Moroccan waters. By 1990 the fish had gone. The majority of fishing in Cymru now is small-scale, using pots, hooks and lines, with 90 percent of boats less than ten metres long operating less than six miles from the shore. Crustaceans such as edible crab, spider crab, lobster, scallop and common whelk dominate the catch. Meanwhile, our governments allow European trawlers and enormous multinational companies to further strip British waters, even in Marine Protected Areas. But we rarely blame ourselves for the disappearance of the fleets and of the fish. We say it is Europe's fault.

Clouds appeared and trapped the heat, making it closer, wetter, more insidious. Flies buzzed around dog turds but I lay on the red sand anyway. I was fractious. Seeds fell into my hand from wayside plants. But at Sandy Haven the air was cooler and the coast not far off. "We have a farm just a mile away," said the man who strolled over to where I sat waiting. He said it would take half an hour for the stepping stones to emerge. "We often come down for barbecues," he said, and went back to put a kettle on his camping stove. Laughter and cooking smells drifted over. The heat had broken me a little. Emotions came unbidden. The man and his wife were younger than my parents, and the young couple with them younger than me and Rob. My Dad could no longer really enjoy an evening like this, and I felt suddenly jealous of the family and hated the passing of time. But it was passing while I sat there, the tide receding as I watched, revealing weed on shining sand. Some boats were already resting on their keels. I heard wood pigeons, and kids playing and watched a single white feather float down from an empty sky. By eight forty-five the stepping stones were clear. Time had moved on. Barbecue Dad waved and I waved back, feeling happy then, for his family and my own, for times gone and yet to come.

I walked faster in the fresh evening air, while the sun set over yellow wheat. A family crossed the fields, the children's excited voices lifting on cooling air, reminding me of childhood holidays. A lilac field of phacelia seemed to herald the dusk and then, finally, I was back on the coast. A fat moon shone a path on the sea. I put up my tent and heard the laughter of people drinking on a small boat moored in the bay, and the splashes of tipsy night swimmers.

A cool morning breeze restored my customary bounce and set halyards clanking at Dale, where a windsurfer carried his board across gobbets of tar. Here, in 1996, the *Sea Empress* had grounded offshore, spilling 72,000 tons of crude oil which had killed thousands of birds and devastated communities of seaweed, invertebrates and shellfish. Renewables don't do that.

Penrhyn St Ann was red, from the red sandstone that underpinned it. The ploughed sprawling fields were red, and down on Bae Watwick, a family rushed pots and plates between bright tents pitched on red sand. When I looked back, the cliffs were a brilliant claret. Solitude and sun had affected me— the beauty of the coast was disorienting and shocking. I had only a vague idea where I was, recognising places where I'd camped or been hungry on previous occasions, and I was glad to drift. Flowers teemed with ladybirds and bees. Wheat billowed. Eventually the vegetated plateau became wider and wilder. The cliffs were red, the islands black, the sea blue and Marloes ahead, a vast orange bay ringed by red faulted cliffs. It was almost too beautiful – I didn't know what to do about it.

Rising tide had stranded sunbathing teenagers. They didn't care, but an overweight middle-aged couple stood dumbly perplexed in the water. They'd have to wait. At San Ffraid the tide was almost at its peak, squeezing families awkwardly together. A few kids were having diving lessons and a dog was refusing to swim – the water was cold. But I did, emerging just in time to snatch my rucksack before it was swamped, aware of the awkward silence, that no-one had wanted to save it in front of strangers. The families moved to the grass and lit disposable barbecues and the smell of hot food drove me crazy.

I had the brackened plateau to myself, save for perished shrews on the path, and dung beetles creeping across it. The cliffs were extraordinarily folded. I stopped several times and saw in a kind of reverie, the sea through whispering grasses and ships anchored out in the bay. A blue gauze materialised, fractured by shimmering light. I heard the flap of a cormorant's wings and became infused with an inner tranquillity. In that moment, I had clarity and balance, the landscape within and without. At one with time and space. It was a rare and precious experience, and I tried to retain the feeling, but could only keep hold of its memory.

Aber-bach was just one headland south of Aberllydan where I'd lodged as a student teacher, but its bunting and holidaymakers eating ice cream seemed curious, to me. I felt removed from the scene. A stranger. Solitude became me. At Aberllydan I sat on the beach to watch the sunset as I'd done every night sixteen years earlier with a menthol cigarette, and felt strange recalling the person I'd been. Then, I'd gone back to my lodgings where Tegwen my octogenarian landlady would tell me she'd enjoyed a smoke and an orange in the bath, when she'd been young. I wasn't so young anymore either, but that was OK.

I camped on the only dry patch of sand, in front of the pubs. It was littered with beer cans and disposable barbecues and smelt of piss. A rat darted into the overflow. After dark, lights came on in the oil tankers. Shrieking teenagers threw handfuls of wet sand at my tent, drove a car down the slipway and did handbrake turns on the beach. But at five in the morning it was the herring gulls that woke me. The sea crept calmly in a shroud of mist to within a metre of my tent and then slowly retreated. I caught the bus home.

When I returned, the heat had broken and rain had brought out the smell of the grasses. A teenager wobbled passed on a unicycle, his Dad trotting along-side, shouting encouragement. I had a stack of sandwiches, four boiled eggs, pasta, flapjack, dried apricots and exactly the right money for the bus home in three days. I wore the other pair of new boots and had a new waterproof. Its hood muffled the sea and blinkered my vision. I was glad to be back. The coast had got under my skin.

When I dumped my rucksack on Traeth Druidston, a harvestman crawled off and then back on. We'd come here as kids too – a waterfall still shivered down the cliffs. But it was empty, as was Nolton Haven, despite its pub and car park, and being August. Everyone was at Traeth Niwgwl. Parents pointed huge cameras at children in wetsuits learning to surf. A kite-sail followed me up the beach and the storm bank rolled noisily under my feet. On my teaching practice at Roch School just inland, I'd organised a litter-pick here with a man from the council. Though it had appeared clean, this storm bank had yielded several bin-bags of rubbish – mostly bits of plastic net and a few diver's glow sticks.

The headlands were empty for miles. It was just me and the red-tailed bumble bees, grasshoppers, painted ladies, and wet cobwebs dazzling on gorse and heather. But at Solfach, where flowers tumbled over garden walls and leisure boats filled up the harbour, wealthy holidaymakers thronged – the women in dresses or Breton tops, the men all curiously clad in maroon or mustard-coloured trousers. In the nineteenth century, Solfach had been an industrial ship-building place but wealth was a strange geography. The working-class poverty so tangible still in Amlwch, Y Fflint and Port Talbot had vanished on the sparsely populated coast, particularly in Sir Benfro which was dominated by the rich, who bought cottages built by and for the poor. I was pleased they were here instead of jet-setting, that their kids could afford wetsuits and surf lessons and enjoyed going wild on the coast. But I didn't like that local people had been priced out of the housing market. And the divide unsettled me – the rich in Sir Benfro. The poor in Sir Ddinbych.

I put up my tent on Penmaen Dewi and watched islets skulk like black boats. When I unpacked my rucksack, the harvestman climbed out, wobbled

over the grass like a drunk, then stopped and tried to return, but I shooed
him away.

A fishing boat wore a herring-gull halo. Supertankers were lit up like Christmas. I heard different sounds at each bend of the path — meadow pipits and
skylarks, swell slapping rock, the munching of mountain ponies, and parents
and kids from the campsites, up early to look at the sea. I ate my last egg on
Porthclais harbour wall. Rock pipits hopped. Swelling green water lifted a
raft of weed. The coast was a meditation. I dissolved.

I wasn't even much aware of my feet touching the ground now I had comfy
boots. I made myself notice heather brushing my ankles, gorse prickling my
knees, and gulls flock on shelves of rock. A stonechat and linnets chattering
as if to each other on grass stalks protruding from the same heather clump. A
swallow-skimmed pond like a blue chip of sky. I liked noticing and not noticing. I heard seals moan, and saw them slip away like oil.

It took me a while to notice that the towering headland with an escort of
islets was Ynys Dewi and not the other side of the bay. The Sound between it
and the mainland, was a cauldron of reefs and rips. A harbour porpoise disappeared as a boat passed too fast. A surfacing seal retreated, only just avoiding
a collision with another. A gannet plummeted. I advanced with an escort of
wheatears, and seal laments rose from the caves. Suddenly there were people
on the path, smelling of shampoo and laundry powder. Porth Mawr was
packed – at least a hundred kids were learning to surf. But only two families
had made it to the beach over the headland, where I swam. The cliffs were
crisply defined and Ynys Dewi was huge and brilliant. Land looked different
from the water, like being in a snow globe, as if I could see the earth's curve.

The coast became a chaotic rockscape dominated by carns – Carn Llidi,
Pen Beri, Pencaer and Garn Fawr. It felt very old. It was hard to imagine the
people who had built Arthur's Quoit. The 6,000-year-old Neolithic
chambered tomb from which the capstone had fallen, was still supported by
a single orthostat. People had been and gone and been and gone. Plants and
animals too (though too many had gone for good). In their absence now were
butterflies, linnets and stonechats. An occasional harebell in a matrix of
heather and gorse. Quartz sparkling against black earth. There was a faint
aroma of garlic too, that I couldn't place. White spray smashed the islets and
breeze fanned the sea like a feather. The knobbed cairns rose above inaccessible
coves and the sea was enormous and shining.

Then the cliffs were higher, foam flew, the garlic aroma wafted around the periphery of my senses and the coastal strip was a wild corridor, humanity insignificant. I was insignificant. It was OK. The unbidden memories and thoughts that accompanied my walk had helped me grow comfortable with the passing of time.

Aber Pwll was crammed with families in wetsuits. There'd been a kind of holiness in the emptiness, and now the magic had gone. The world was no less beautiful for having people in it – it was just that we wrecked everything. The further I delved into history, the more I understood that our destruction and dominion in Cymru as elsewhere – of each other and of wildlife, was so endemic, so ingrained, that hope of behaviour change was naïve. I still felt that it was my privilege (and good manners) as a citizen of Cymru to support its culture and language. But there could be no culture, language, or community, anywhere, without a functioning eco-system. It was also our duty and privilege to support Cymru's eco-systems – its non-human inhabitants, its air and land and water. I didn't want to give up on humanity, but it was tempting to imagine a Cymru – and a world, without people.

Abereiddi, with its black sand and black caves in black cliffs was busy too. After the collapse of its slate industry, fishermen had blasted a hole in the quarry wall to let the sea in and make a harbour. Now the harbour was a lagoon. Kids were jumping into it from the top of crumpled green cliffs. Further along, an old man leant on a stick, awaiting his wife who was looking out to sea. They were local people, with Cymreig accents, dressed in old brown clothes. "Can you see?" she asked. "Is that something moving or is it a rock?" We watched for a while and agreed it was a rock. "The weather is better now," she said. "It was no good for us old people, before. It was too hot you see."

Light shone through kelp that lifted and fell with the swell. I didn't know how to appreciate it. The red translucent kelp made me want to cry. It was all so beautiful. But I was tired and there was no dry sand above the high-tide mark. I continued with familiar fatigue – I never knew when to stop walking. I set up on the same promontory where I'd camped once with Rob, and discovered my tub of pasta had opened and doused my sleeping bag in garlic oil. The sun warmed me still. Insects jumped into the tent. The sea was blue chiffon. The springy turf was comfortable, the garlic smell not unpleasant. I heard footsteps approach and pass, and an indignant child say "Someone's put a tent there!" and his Dad reply "I don't blame them, I would too." "Would you?" said the child in a different tone, a whole world unfolding in his head.

I stood on Porthgain slipway inhaling the scent of sulphurous mud, looking at the cliff I'd descended. It was mantled with brick arches, hoppers, and windows, a gothic city of industrial ghosts. First Abereiddi slate, then bricks made from slate-waste, then granite, had been exported from here. The crumbling brick-scape was attractive to the middle classes now – as it was to me. The limekilns were stacked with lobster pots, the Sloop Inn was strung with coloured lights, quarry-workers' cottages were converted into art galleries, and shacks were festooned with floats. A man with a white beard climbed into his boat and grinned as he started the engine, sending jackdaws squawking and sparrows into flight from the scrub. The machine-shop was a gourmet chippy. A man in yellow wellies came out to hose down the yard, and said I'd picked a nice spot for breakfast. I ate my last sandwich scrutinised by a gull. The man put down water for dogs and swept the yard, the bus rattled into the bay, and took me away.

"In or out?" said a woman with hair in rollers and a blue checked overall. "Mug or cup?" she pushed a mop around the floor. Granules gathered moisture round the rim of a Nescafe tin. I was between buses in Aberteifi, between two worlds, home and journey.

And then I was back in Porthgain, where dead thrift announced summer's end and thistles and short yellow wheat shook in a grey wind. When the rain eased, a blue butterfly flew into the open. The road kissed the coast at Trefin, where abandoned millstones looked like gravestones, though I didn't know then, about William Williams' poem. 'Nid yw'r Felin heno'n malu yn Nhrefin ym min y mor...' ('The mill is not grinding tonight in Trefin at the edge of the sea...'.) The mill had ground wheat to make bread, and barley to feed winter livestock, for 500 years till 1918 when it closed due to cheaper grain imports.

I didn't know then, that it was in the Neolithic Age when people first grew grains which they too had ground or boiled, and baked into bread on flat stones. I'd not granted them such sophistication. But the more I learned, the more it seemed that wisdom wasn't accumulative, that our own society wasn't any wiser or more sophisticated, and anyway, it too would pass.

Neolithic people had built Carreg Samson, a chunky rock lintel supported by three uprights – a toffee slab balanced on fingertips. The stones had been lowered into an 8-metre-deep pit, propped up with boulders and roped in position, and the pit filled with clay and stones. A 1968 excavation had revealed four additional stone holes, suggesting it had been a passage grave. The covering earth mound was long gone and the stones stood, not inappropriately, in a field of cows. Auroch were still wild in Britain when Neolithic people had set about felling forest for clearings on which they grazed domesticated cattle, and grew crops from grains they'd brought with them. The cattle that Neolithic people had also brought, were descendants of auroch, which were domesticated in Asia at least twice during the Neolithic Age. By the late Bronze Age, auroch – one of the largest herbivores in post-glacial Europe, were extinct in Britain.

A warm thrilling wind rushed up the headlands, buffeting me off the path. Gulls mewled on cliff edges, fulmars and gannets wheeled. At Abercastell, stormlight doused the mortared cottages and kayaks with such theatrical drama the large-bellied men in wetsuits launching boats from the trailers of four-by-fours looked like actors in a film.

When Rob and I were last here, we'd gone for a pint up the hill, and the landlord had told us he'd run a vegetable cooperative till the 1980s. "It was all fields of cauliflowers up this coast then," he'd said, "but not any more thanks to a couple of bad winters and the supermarkets. Especially the Big T. You know who I mean. They used to invite us to their Christmas dinner, and *we* were supposed to buy *them* drinks because it was such an honour to be there. They've ruined the vegetable trade." Much of Sir Benfro was still arable. But regarding vegetables I'd only seen a few potato fields.

History shows that whenever climate or economy made arable agriculture difficult in Cymru, livestock farming has dominated, particularly in the uplands. It was dominant now, more than ever. Before post-war intensification, farmers had also grown oats and vegetables and kept pigs and poultry alongside commercial produce, but now livestock was all they had left, little wonder they clung to it. It had been fine in the Iron Age, when there were so few people, to rely on meat and dairy. But the climate is about to get catastrophically unpredictable, and the population bigger than ever.

The sky had become moodier still. Rocks like sharks pierced the water. Someone had built pebble obelisks along the storm bank at Abermawr. A single wave broke, and retreated. The Melin Tregwynt mill stream ran onto Aberbach, ripples knotting over black stones. A few sand martins flew in and out of clifftop burrows, and a man and his dogs hurried off the beach, past small upturned boats, a black shed and white cottage, set off by the light like a John Knapp-Fisher. A tractor rolled into view, and turned round.

Farmers have to feed an increasingly large population in an increasingly turbulent climate. We need protein, but meat and dairy requires significantly more land and water (subsequently producing more greenhouse gas emissions) than vegetable proteins. Dried beans and pulses, despite being largely imported, are densely packed with a long shelf life. With no refrigeration or complex packaging requirements, they are shipped rather than air-freighted, so despite the food miles, their impact is vastly lower than that of meat – especially conventionally produced meat.

A quarter of global greenhouse gas emissions come from food production, more than half of which are from animal products. Carbon dioxide equivalent (CO2e) footprints (which take into account *all* the greenhouse gases produced on the farm, factory, road and shop) put beef and lamb at the top of the table. The UK cross-government programme on food security research would publish 'The Carbon Footprint of High Protein Food' in 2017. It found 1kg of lamb was responsible for the emission of 48kg of CO2e. 1kg beef produced 32kg of CO2e, pork 6kg, poultry, eggs, tofu and Quorn all 3kg, and pulses (beans and lentils) 1kg. It takes a lot of land, water and energy to feed livestock. But for Cymru, where beef and sheep farming is not just part of the cultural and physical landscape today but has been for millennia, this is devastating. I am devastated. It is as bad as the end of coal.

History also demonstrates, (as do contemporary community enterprises and organic farms), that Cymru can produce fruit, vegetables, grains and even legumes, though not as easily (especially with the drastic whims of climate change), or cheaply (in terms of current subsidies) as livestock. But survival demands resilience. And resilience demands diversity. Change is possible, inevitable and stressful. Yet farmers, despite being hampered by regulations, being crushed by financial stress and by the accusation that they don't care about wildlife, despite pressure from consumers who want food cheaper than it costs to produce – despite all this, farmers understand what is needed. In 2018 Wyn Evans, NFU Vice Chair for Livestock would tell me "We know as livestock producers that in the future we will have to change. Though livestock will always be a prominent force in upland areas and where it has been traditionally reared, we know the ground will have to be shared with alternative foods, such as more substantial crops to feed our livestock and more locally grown fruit and vegetables to service local communities." It's easy to blame big companies, politicians, farmers. But we shoppers have the worst habits. We need to up our game too.

After being vegetarians for twenty years, Rob and I began eating meat again (but not very much). Rob, because when he'd worked for a year in Zambia, vegetarianism had been a middle-class privilege, and me to support Cymreig farmers. Our diet is mostly plant based. But now and again, we buy a bit of local mince. I'd feel better if it was organic and the animals had been able to roam freely, and browse a range of natural plants.

The birds stopped singing. The landscape grew dark but luminous. At Pwllcrochan, the path dropped into a mouth of snarling rocks. I could smell wet sheep where they'd sheltered in the gully, then the smell of the sea was more potent and the scream of gulls amplified. The sea boomed. A filthy black cloud stole in and the rain began. It felt like popping candy on my hand. I climbed, and from the top of Carn Ogof, saw scattered farms, gorse heath and brown cattle. Dead heather shone. A tarn gleamed. Pencaer lighthouse winked on a bulkhead, and disappeared as I watched, into a curtain of rain. A shroud rose from the coves and then I noticed bladder campion and sorrel at my feet.

I pitched my tent and put on dry clothes. The rain was loud on the canvas. The hills disappeared, the sea was revealed and then vanished. I snuggled in and ate lentil burgers still smoky from the fire they'd been cooked on.

Last night's rain washed my ankles. The wildness slipped away as I stepped onto the lighthouse road, though the wall was hairy with lichen. The wildness was always trying to claw its way back, and I hoped one day it would succeed.

Walking was easy on the rolling plateau. A yacht sailed east, a Stena ferry powered towards Wdig, waves from the west clashed with tides from the north, and lady's bedstraw, bugle and kidney vetch tangled the grasses. Families were heading for the lighthouse, and I lent them my binoculars to see the seals hauled up in the coves. I was close to Bae Ceredigion now, nearing home, but I didn't want to get there.

I passed Carreg Wastad, site of the last (failed) invasion of Britain in 1797, and turned onto a housing estate from which chaffinches were swarming into the coastal scrub. A sign to Garth Wen led me down an alley that petered out in a muddle of compost bins and bramble-swamped paving slabs, and there it was – a cromlech erected between 4000-2,500 BC by those first British farmers and overlooked now, by a rook-patrolled hill and a lamppost.

Light skewered my eyes as I sweltered up to Abergwaun. The cannon that had stymied the invaders was marooned on a traffic island. I ate my lunch in the graveyard and saw Rob get off the bus. He said the rain had been so bad at home Dyfi Bridge was closed to floods and our garden path lost to the stream. Now sun flickered over the boats, kayakers, and coloured buoys, but I wasn't fooled by the serenity. Abergwaun always felt feisty to me and I wasn't surprised to read that locals had allegedly rolled boulders onto Norman ships, and that cobbler Jemima Nicholas had (according to legend), rounded up fourteen of the French invaders with a pitchfork.

I'd loved being alone, but being alone with Rob was magnificent. We kissed at each stile, and gazed down on silver coves, and at Pwll Gwaelod which had a pub on the beach. We drank outside with a hairy-armed building contractor who lived next door and invited us to camp in his field. His mates, he said, were all firefighters and lifeboatmen. "The RNLI raises so much money they don't know what to do with it all," he said. "Honest to God they don't – they're all volunteers, they've got more than they can spend!" The sun burned a red trail through blue sky and big smoky clouds brought the night.

We put up our tent between diggers and tractors, neat piles of planks, and expanded foam, and ate the feast Rob had brought, of baguettes and camembert, peppers and wine. The evening grew warm. We slept with the tent open and at some point heard the death screams of a rabbit.

By morning we were naked on top of our sleeping bags, but a wind stirred the canvas and dark clouds gathered as we climbed Ynys Dinas. The horizon was ominously clear and Trefdraeth ahead veiled in rain.

The Preselau rolled roundly inland. Stone had been quarried from their north slopes throughout the Neolithic Age, including the bluestone used for the smallest and earliest of Stonehenge's stone circles. The igneous dolerite and rhyolite had formed into natural pillars which were apparently detached from the rock face with wooden wedges swelled by rain, before being lowered onto platforms of earth and stone. I found it hard to imagine until I read about the burnt hazelnuts and charcoal that quarrymen had left at the site, and then I pictured them clearly on a lunch break.

At Cwmyreglwys, graves and a single wall were all that the 1859 storm had spared of the church. Two men in long coats stood on the seawall, deep in discussion, backdropped by dark sky like spies in a film, or druids, as if we walked in uncertain dimensions. A dog called Henry hoovered our crumbs. "The coast to the north looks fabulous from the sea," said Henry's owner. "I've got a *boat,*" she added pointedly. We hurried on, following a long blue hose piping slurry between headlands, which had burst in the valley between. Slurry was pumping into the reeds and two farmers were shouting and cursing, trying and failing to stop eutrophication happening right there and then. Whether the accident was their own fault or just a result of the usual sequence of one thing leading to another, over decades, over centuries, over millennia, they were sure as hell trying to fix it. The scene seemed to encapsulate what the subsidy regime and we shoppers had resulted in – desperate farmers trying to grab what eluded them and squirted them with shit.

The rain began, but the headlands were too steep for waterproofs. We shrugged in and out of them, shouting "I love you" at intervals, feeling wild and mad. The rain got heavier. A Dad and five kids with crab buckets ran ahead to Trefdraeth. Even in this caliginous light the bay was a radiant swirl, the water a silver ghost. Rain splashed our eyes. We made for a pub. Squalls slapped the window. The barman said it was in for the afternoon but would be fine tomorrow and put the forecast on to prove it. We sat in damp clothes getting grumpy, watching rain pour onto shop canopies.

By late afternoon it had eased and our moods lifted as we stepped out. From the cliffs, we looked back at the Preselau sulking beneath funereal cloud, and the rivers spilling across the vast beach, and three windsurfers racing almost out of sight. Silver light on the sea made hoops and searchlights and spangles. The wind walloped us on. Fulmars whirled above and below. Some of the path was dry, where the rain had been whipped over it. Wind thrashed the yellow grass, hemp agrimony, ragwort and dead foxgloves. Sea mayweed shook. Tormentil and speedwell hunkered, knapweed and sheep's bit survived on short stalks like bursts of fireworks, and a waterfall of ragwort spilled down a slope.

Friesian cattle huddled in corners of large hedged fields. The cliffs were hacked blocks of Parmesan, bitten by giants. Cormorants flew far below. The path forced us over landslips and squeezed us through bracken. In places, the soil had eroded to rock, leaving bare-rooted heather. The cliffs grew even steeper, even higher. The path narrowed and teetered round them, with only stunted scrub to arrest a plunge down precipitous slopes. Our hearts raced, we shrieked and whooped as the wind gusted and changed direction, threatening to toss us into the sea. Our world was all cliff. We yelled and laughed and looked down on the terrifyingly beautiful coast.

We passed a young couple who were pale and too frightened to speak. The plateau became less steep. Barrel-bellied ponies regarded us shyly. We felt far from anywhere. Seal groans were borne on the wind, the path climbed and fell, then the cliffs broadened to a terraced plateau so we put up our tent and looked at each other, dazed. "Wow!" we said. The wind dropped. We laid out pasties, strawberries and wine, then lay on our mats and watched the blue sky, till hearing footsteps we sat up and saw seven sheep tiptoe past in a line, each one peeping at us in turn over the bracken. More clouds were summoned for sunset. They swelled and billowed, became stone angels then were suddenly engulfed in fire. "It's like the second coming," said Rob, "like the front of a Bible." Eventually an orange haze drenched the sky and the fiery sun dropped through it and sank behind a quilt on which red cursive script was written in a language we couldn't read. We wanted to stay forever.

The rocks at Ceibwr were so blasted, stressed and inky, their erosion hastened by such confused and faulted folding, that the feeling of wildness persisted, despite the people, there being a car park, where the road swung close to the coast. Despite the pigeons cosy on ledges, despite the calmness with which fulmars floated on a pool like a mirror dropped into the sea, and the gentleness with which wavelets broke. Headlands tapered to angry knolls with sharp teeth. People had set up camping chairs on the saddle of maritime grass to gaze at the chaotic geometry, the extraordinary black triangles, whorled and contorted, collapsed and elevated.

We sat by the stream to watch grey wagtails, shocked by the landscape, letting it settle within us. But an Australian National Trust volunteer found us there. Sure, he said the cliffs were great but did we know about the Red Bull sponsored diving contest at the Blue Lagoon in Abereiddi, which would be totally awesome? We pointed out the grey wagtails and he said he wanted to get a picture of an oystercatcher because that would be the money shot, right, people would go for that right, and the more he talked, the more the cliffs slipped out of our minds and raced over the sea like the clouds, and by the time he'd gone, the grey wagtails had too.

But the wildness hadn't done with us yet. The path consistently climbed. A gull flew level, and we exchanged glances. We dropped, then climbed Pen yr Afr, thrust from the ocean floor into rollercoaster arcs and perpendicular outcrops, whorled into crevices and bashed into caves. From the top we looked back along the line of grey walls, folded and hatched beneath their bronze bracken mantle, at blue-grey sea foaming around shark-fin reefs, and heard the insistence of waves meeting rock.

The cliffs were lower then, and we dropped to our bellies to watch seals contracting their heads and tails, or lying fat and still. Save for Foel-y-Mwnt, the Ceredigion coast ahead was flat, and our spirits that had flown high and wild accommodated the gentler landscape through which Afon Teifi negotiated golden sandbars and green marsh. Sand softened the spits and the cliffs became dunes at Traeth Poppit, which was crammed with people and curving long and gold to the estuary. The estuary beckoned with a salty reek. A few kids in dinghies were paddling up rivulets and a crab slunk into the tussocks, but black mud beat us back to the road, and old leafy Llandudoch.

"There's a fox down by there," said a tanned man herding his hens away from a ditch. We crossed fields lined with trees. Oats quaked in one, sheep grazed another. Hay had been harvested. It was a golden world, but strange after the cliffs, and our moods were flatter too. At the edge of Aberteifi, smells of seaweed and garbage hung with the gulls round garages, ropes and wheelie bins. We crossed Afon Teifi.

HUNTER GATHERERS

In 10,000 BC an ice sheet still covered parts of North Britain and sea levels were about 55 metres lower than today. The landscape was treeless, the climate cold and arid. As mosses, lichens and liverworts developed, organic matter accumulated, and soil began to form. Sedges, grasses, dwarf willow, juniper and birch grew on the tundra. Mammoth, woolly rhino, Arctic fox and spotted hyena roamed, and lemming, ptarmigan, bear and wolf lived on the permafrost. In summer, horses and reindeer arrived from Doggerland (an area of land now submerged between the North Sea, that connected Britain to Europe), to graze and breed. The English Channel was still dry land and Bae Ceredigion not yet submerged. The population of Britain was about 5,000 with perhaps a few dozen in Cymru. Hunter-gatherers left evidence of occupation at Goats Hole and Cathole. Remains of a human burial dating to about 10,000 BC on Y Gogarth, indicate a diet rich in fish.

Ice had sculpted Cymru. Glaciers had scoured cwms in Eryri's hard rocks and left lakes in deep hollows. They had carved deep river valleys into hills and mountains, smoothed the softer Mynyddoedd Cambria and Bannau Brycheiniog into rounded summits, plastered ancient rock with boulder clay, and ground rocks into sands and gravels which formed moraines and created the Bae Ceredigion sarnau. Ice that had deepened valleys melted, leaving hanging valleys and waterfalls. Ice hills in the tundra collapsed into boggy basins. Sea pounded coastal slopes into cliffs and caves.

As the glaciers melted, sea levels rose. Greenhouse gases were released as tundra thawed and frozen vegetation rotted. But as it grew warmer, Britain was rapidly colonised from the southeast by a thick canopy of trees which drew carbon dioxide from the atmosphere. At first it was too cold for insects, so only wind-pollinated juniper, willow and birch grew, followed by pine, hazel and alder. As the temperature increased, the lowlands became dominated by oak, elm, ash and pine. In the south, plants like bog-bean, thrift and sedge that had survived the ice in salty marshes, began to spread. Lowlying areas became marsh. Plants like meadowsweet and ragged-robin grew on the flood-plains, and others like mountain avens colonised hills. The large herds of reindeer and horses that had migrated to and from Britain throughout preceding interglacials changed migration routes and disappeared as tundra grasslands ceded to forest – though perhaps the animals disappeared first, allowing forest to grow. Roe deer, red deer, boar, and auroch arrived. Mature woodland had scrubby edges of saplings, shrubs, hawthorn, blackthorn and holly, and herbivores like auroch and deer kept the relationship between woodland and glades in a state of flux.

Lions and spotted hyena that had hunted the reindeer survived in Britain till about 9,000 BC when humans returned on foot in small groups from future France, Germany and the Iberian peninsula where they'd spent the colder years. The humans hunted the large animals to extinction. It's likely they also destroyed parts of the woodland to promote new growth and attract grazing herds. After being depressed by the weight of the ice, the north of Britain began to rise – and is rising still.

By 7,500 BC, rising sea had separated Ireland from Britain. Hunter-gatherers travelled the rivers, leaving microliths near Wrecsam, where they dug pits and erected totems. Evidence of occupation has also been found at Nab Head. By 7000 BC, Cymru had become roughly the shape it is today. People continued to slash and burn woodland. Trees in the lowland regenerated, but in the highlands, animals grazed regrowth, leading to peat developing and soil eroding to become alluvial silt. People domesticated dogs and horses. With the big animals gone, they developed smaller flint arrow-heads, spears and harpoons to hunt nimbler prey. They dried, smoked and stored food, caught fish, lobster, crabs and eel in basket traps, and foraged for eggs, shellfish, fungi, fruit and hazelnuts. They knapped flint into axes and were semi-nomadic, travelling between coastal bases and summer hunting camps. They built thatched round houses and timber walkways, used nettle and honeysuckle fibres to make ropes, netting, clothing, belts, baskets and traps, and wore fox, beaver, wolf and bear hides. They played flutes, made beads, cast tools into lakes (perhaps as offerings), and buried their dead in caves. They carved dugouts for rivers and lakes, and made hide and willow sea-going boats.

The sea was still rising. By 6000 BC Doggerland was submerged, Britain was an island, and from now on immigrants would arrive by boat. Reed-swamp, peatbog and woodland became coast. Deciduous wildwood, dominated in Cymru by oak and hazel, with some lime, elm, pine and birch, covered 60 percent of Britain. The rest was grassland, fen, moor, rocky peaks and shrubs. The climate was wet and warm. Britain's teeming biodiversity included mountain hare, brown bear, wolf, beaver, pine marten, red squirrel, corncrake, golden oriole, hazel hen, osprey, white-tailed eagle, eagle owl, grey partridge and crested lark. Bae Ceredigion was submerged. Children's footprints were left on Môr Hafren saltmarsh. Two of the post-holes at Bryn Celli Du are found to have been Mesolithic, flint scatters have been found in Bannau Brycheiniog, and a Mesolithic midden was discovered at Prestatyn consisting largely of mussel shells.

By 5000 BC, Cymru had a small migratory population who shared ideas and traded surplus food, furs, skins and precious stones with Europeans. From 5000-4550 BC, the climate became wet and cool with a shorter growing season. Tsunamis damaged shoreline communities and the population dwindled. Redistribution of glacial and fluvial sands formed dune systems at Niwbwrch, Morfa Harlech, Morfa Dyffryn, Pentywyn, Pen-bre and Cynffig. By 4000 BC, the population of Britain was about 100,000.

CEREDIGION

*C*oastal plateau rises to Mynyddoedd Cambria. Underlying rock creates acidic soil, but glacial till forms a substrate for plants. Afon Teifi harbours three species of lamprey, while Afon Dyfi's estuary is a rare combination of shingle bank, sand dune, raised bog, salt marsh, and petrified Mesolithic forest. Vestiges of temperate rainforest remain in steep valleys. Pine marten populations have been bolstered by reintroductions. Reservoirs that served the lead mines are largely acidic, but metalliferous lichen communities, and lead-tolerant plants like sweet vernal, forked spleenwort and moonwort, colonise the spoil tips.

A dockland spirit lingered beneath the silvery veneer of river tourism. Aberteifi's docks had been busier than Bristol and Liverpool before the railway snaffled its trade and the river silted up, after which the ships took emigrants to north America instead. Rob too was departing, and I felt the old sense of loss. It was Sunday and there were no buses, so we parted awkwardly, and Rob trudged down the road for a hitch.

I plodded on alone past the Market Hall, the Islam Cultural Centre, Abdul's Tandoori Spice, The Royal India and The Fishermen's Rest, and onto the riverbank. Lobsterpots were stacked outside cottages, bladderwrack glistened on gloopy mud, but though machinery pulsed in the sewage works, it was Afon Teifi I could smell, and see through horse chestnut and hazel, and oystercatchers I could hear. Glacial meltwater had carved its valley. Fields of wheat, beet, and corn stubble lined its banks. In one, finches swarmed, in another boats awaited repair. Afon Teifi ballooned before leaving the estuary, halted in its flow by the spit protruding from Patch Caravan Park over which Canada geese were flying north, perhaps to the Dyfi marshes.

Mwnt was rammed. People had spilled off the beach to sit in a row on top of the hill, and were milling around the church whose bell tower was white against blue sky like a Mediterranean chapel. White shadows fell on white walls. I looked in and saw a vintage scene – a vicar, a woman putting orders of service into prayer books, and another extracting hymns from an organ, and felt sad, thinking again of my Dad, and the things he could no longer enjoy. I left as parishioners arrived, weaving purposefully through the holidaymakers, the old men in suits, the women in frocks. The hymns followed me for a while, and I wished that I'd stayed.

But the rosy coast smelt of old summer. Through its tangled scrub I glimpsed blue water and saw two seals roll in a creek. A red kite soared above gullies eked out by glacial streams, and I camped among fragrant Himalayan balsam in which bees buzzed until dark.

"I'd love to go hiking one day," said a man looking up from his paper in Aberporth. The chip-shop staff chatted in English over Radio Cymru and surround-sound frying. "But I've got five kids," he added proudly, "I'm just grabbing ten minutes while the washing's in the spinner." My Dad had five kids too. There were things he too would like to have done and hadn't, because like this man, more than anything, he loved being a Dad.

I joined an old lady at the bus stop. "Bore da," she said, and I faltered. She was the first stranger – ever, to have begun a conversation with me in Cymraeg. "Bore da," I repeated, then told her in Cymraeg, that I was learning, and realised it was true. I'd not given up. She said (in Cymraeg!) that everyone in Aber-porth spoke Cymraeg. Except for the retired English people, she added politely.

It was Autumn when I returned. I had just three days of walking left. Waves charged up orange sand to meet the river, slate-grey with green edges. A tractor was parked on the beach, a dinghy tossed about in the bay. There were leaves on the sand and kayaks and kelp on the grass. The kayaks were full of rain.

Seed-heads danced. Hedgerows bared rosehips and elderberries. Autumn. The wind tossed my hair. Shadows darkened the sea as if whales were swimming beneath. Cormorants dived. The school holidays were over and bundled-up pensioners had replaced the families. At Tresaith I climbed and looked back. Two bottlenose dolphins broke the surface three times then were gone. The path twisted through woodland then out to gorse heath where fireweed had gone to seed and bracken was brown. Afon Saith, diverted by a glacier 10,000 years ago, sprang over the cliff. The sea was shifting metal. A hawthorn framed the toothy coast ahead.

Traeth Penbryn was empty save for a fisherman, its caves filled with white foam and light. Surf crashed onto clean sand against a splash of green woodland. I back-tracked through it, hazel and oakwood, glossy with ferns.

There were no longer statics in the farmyard where Mum and Dad had once holidayed, and I'd come to join them for a night. But there was still a farm café where I drank tea, and an old man came in to buy goat's cheese, while the fridge-freezer buzzed and throbbed.

Sea raced up yellow beaches and fell back with a roar. It wrote a clean white line on Traeth Bach, underscored with slatey scribbles. Wild empty fields ran inland, but the cliffs were thick with swarthy scrub. Herring gulls cried and bright wind chopped the sea from green to blue to grey and white. Mesolithic hunter-gatherers had camped at Llangrannog and left microliths there set in wood, long before Sant Crannog pitched up in a boat in the fifth or sixth century. Now Llangrannog was a seaside village at the end of the season, its labyrinthine hinterland of lanes no longer bottlenecked with traffic. A burly boatman leant on his gate to converse with an old woman, framed by telegraph wires, backdropped by walls drenched in sea-light. A man in pink trunks let the waves toss him about like a cork. The cliffs were contorted and folded. I ate my lunch in a crevice. The wind reached me there and scattered the sand, and a feather caught in a wind chimney touched down, then immediately lifted.

It was powerful, this wind that shook the flowers, these waves that whirled the birds and pounded the rocks, this light that painted them silver. The path cut a contour over the hillside and the views were wild, the drop precipitous. Scabious survived. Dead foxgloves clung to scree while the wind tried to tear them away. A chough swooped. A kestrel somehow held still. A raven tumbled and rosehips rode the heaving bracken ocean. I felt carefree and part of it all. But my peace was not to last.

A lithe bearded man was climbing up from Cwmtydu. He paused for breath and said he was from Shropshire, and we admired the landscape together till he said, "But what do you think of these wind turbines?" and I felt as if I'd been thumped. It was more than a year since I'd quit my job. I'd succeeded eventually, in not much thinking about all that. About environmental collapse. But caught off-guard I looked at this nice man from Shropshire and my heart crashed into the sea.

Some people didn't like wind turbines. People generally, whose wealth had allowed them to purchase a home or second-home with a view, who claimed to be countryside champions but who cherry-picked their arguments and expressed them loudly with the confidence of wealth. Others were quieter, and nice. I'd met them on the writing course in Llanystumdwy. One was a dear elderly friend. They were repulsed by these machines that sliced the air, and I sympathised. (As I did with communities who risked having local control wrested from them by multi-national energy companies.) But not in that moment I didn't. I hated them all. Their four-by-fours and enormous carbon footprints. I hated them for hampering the renewable energy industry, even as climate change became climate chaos, for planting doubt and lies in the minds of people like this man.

Information clicked through my head. Yes, turbines are noisy if you can hear them above the wind, though not as loud as traffic or planes. Yes they kill birds, hundreds maybe thousands, while cats kill 400,000 a year in Britain alone and climate change wipes out whole species. Yes, energy is used to build them – it takes about four months of operation to pay it back. Not a consideration normally applied to anything else, mind you. No, they don't work all the time, they're not designed to work in storms, or when it's not windy and yes, like anything mechanical, they sometimes need fixing. Give. Me. Strength. I mumbled "I like them," and the nice man from Shropshire looked interested. "But do they work?" he said. "Yes," I said weakly, and he walked off seeming pleased, leaving me broken.

We were catapulting into climate breakdown and our governments were scared of loud people who thought the views from their windows were more important than the degradation of the planet. I felt weak. In the job I'd quit, I'd given workshops to people who'd smiled and applauded. It had been easy to imagine I was making a difference. Now I felt I had not.

In 1824, Joseph Fourier had pointed out the danger of rising carbon dioxide emissions due to burning fossil fuels. In 1888, Charles Brush in Ohio invented the first wind turbine to produce electricity. More than a century in which we could have developed an economy powered by renewable energy and avoided climate catastrophe. But instead we bickered. And we were still arguing about fricking wind turbines. What was the point of all those scientists investigating the impacts of our greenhouse gas emissions and explaining the risks? What was the point of all those engineers and experts creating technologies, political and economic strategies in order for us to avoid catastrophe, when their solutions were met with complacency, aggression or scorn by the people who wanted only to protect their own immediate best interests? People who either did or didn't understand the urgency, but believed either way that their wealth would save them, while the poor suffered. What was the point anyway, when no-one gave a flying fuck. My chin had slumped. My eyes had closed. I reached Cwmtydu with clenched jaw and aching head. The river spilled over the beach. The rock strata collapsed in on itself.

But I did understand. In order to embrace solutions we first have to face the problems, and they're scary so we tend not to. Facing environmental problems means grieving. It takes strength. I knew how bad it was, the implications of business as usual, the chaos, floods, fires, drought, famine, conflict, disease, and death to come. It was understandable to deny them, ignore them, carry on as usual. But to do so prevents those who do have the courage, from implementing the solutions – by simply not demanding them. Not voting for them in the shops or in the ballot box. In the face of all this my impotence was excruciating.

But it wasn't my fault – or not wholly, and not so much anymore. Not now I knew. I could find solace in the remnants of this paradise. I watched rock pipits and wagtails hop over pebbles where sea campion shivered. I climbed and my spirits rose. I was glad, so glad to be here.

Over subsequent years I would still, on occasion, find myself helpless with rage. But not often. My journey through history revealed that our bad behaviour had begun thousands of years ago. We'd been causing atmospheric pollution since at least the Bronze Age and had been destroying habitats and wiping out species since the Mesolithic. No wonder it was taking so long for people to understand the crisis. We'd all just been trying to get by, without a sense of perspective. It was a sequence of decisions made one after another over millennia that had led to environmental collapse.

We flawed, fabulous humans can address the problems by working together. But with conflict being as endemic to the human race as environmental destruction, it seems unlikely. If we don't? Many of the birds, butterflies, mammals, seaweeds, crustaceans, fish, lichens, fungi and plants I had encountered surviving at Cymru's edge in nature reserves, national parks, and places where people are rare will cop it too. Any that survive will be better off without us.

Wind banged the kissing gates and tossed up the smell from the fish-processing factory. Colourful houses climbed the hills and the seafront was crammed with eateries. An old man tipped his hat, and said Ceinewydd was nicer now the holiday season was over. Waves smashed the stone pier. Boats rested on muddy sand. Two yachts smacked the waves and a rainbow shimmered over glacial boulder-clay cliffs. Cymru was beautiful.

The sun was dropping, flickering through thorn scrub like cine-reel, when

I met a farmer walking his boxer dogs. "This bit is special," he said, "I come every night." I asked, timidly, if he spoke Cymraeg and he said that he did. I was feeling a kind of circularity. I'd been brash on setting out, forcing my clumsy Cymraeg on people, sulking when they didn't respond. I didn't mind anymore.

Like biodiversity, Cymraeg survives, but only just, sustained by the farming community, championed by campaigners, enabled by legislators. A language survey in 2013-2015 found only 24 percent of the population spoke Cymraeg — but that 41 percent of 3-15 year olds did. Cymraeg was threatened but unlike biodiversity, was incrementally, painfully slowly, clawing its way back, because Llywodraeth Cymru had recognised language cannot survive in isolated pockets. I told the farmer that I'd not met many Cymraeg-speakers around the edge of Cymru. He said in English that I spoke very nice Cymraeg and asked where I lived. "Machynlleth!" he expostulated. "Well don't go speaking any of that Gog [north] stuff!" and we laughed, but I think he was only half joking.

The sun was gilding the fireweed. I reached the waterfall where Rob and I had once camped on his birthday, and set up my tent. I loved him ferociously, but had relearned to value solitude. It had helped me come to terms with the knowledge that everything passes. We humans are not exempt. Gulls whirled. Water spilled off the plateau. A spider crawled over my leg. The sky was mad and wild. Milky cloud appeared on the horizon dissolving the red sun and briefly, the cloud turned rosy, as it does on snowy mountains.

It was my penultimate day and I felt solemn. Walking in sections had diffused any sense of big achievement. It was no big deal.

Aberaeron harbour was full of leisure-craft. Ships had been built here and herrings landed. In a few years we'd encounter a bunch of kids here, looking for Pokémon on the playing field, but now I walked straight through town. The sloes were plump and dusky. Ragwort, fireweed and rosehips rocked in a northerly wind. Teasels scrubbed the dirty sky and the sea was a heaving salty beast. A sheep when it saw me, jumped clean off the cliff onto a lower plateau. Headlights on the A487 carved up the hills. I'd followed it to Ynys Môn, and now I was following it home. This land had formed under periglacial conditions in a cold dry climate and the cliffs were crumbling. One day, they'd crumble away.

Time was a fugitive thing, and I wondered what the two whiskered men in camouflage, apparently from another decade with their poles and wooden boxes, were up to. "Rabbiting," they said. They had come to a stop at a footbridge, while their dogs chased each other in the ditch. The men called and whistled in vain, till giving up, one climbed in, and after moments of comical grappling, snatched the terrier, passed it to his friend, and shooed out the whippet and spaniel. Then in Aber-arth I came upon two laughing women with dogs and sticks. They were coaxing a large pig up a narrow street of terraced stone cottages, and I wondered if I really had been caught in a time warp.

At Llanon, I stood on the pebble ridge beneath eroding cliffs that were like grassy paws, made from glacial tundra or wind-borne dust from deserts, watching waves toss seaweed onto stones. I felt dissociated – at one with the waves that rinsed and rucked with the noise of a rain-stick, sucking pebbles down, hurling them back. I felt at one with the gulls that rose and split into groups that crossed over each other, black and white wings like an Escher print. But when the path twisted round the caravan sites to Llanrhystud and the A487, I felt at one with the peopled world too. I drank coffee at the service-station café – the only customer. A draft blew the plastic tablecloths and flapped the menus taped to the window for Beef Cawl and Pork Casserole. From inside, the weather seemed inconvenient and had made the two women staff miserable.

But it was invigorating on the hills where rain drilled my face and light iced each drop. Hill followed hill, and brown hills and grey sea were all I could see. Streams ran amok and the sea smelt like rain on a river. I felt wild as the choughs exploding into the air, wild as the huge cliffs, spiralling foam, rocks like wrecks, and red kites patrolling the slopes. The choughs came full circle, squeaking like dog toys. Buzzards scattered rabbits. Brackened hills like bottoms and breasts obscured views inland, while sessile oaks clutched the cliffs, their branches mad scribbles. On the beaches below, black strata revealed the old mud and shale beds like music score. I was in a strange mood. I felt a little wild, a little fierce. I did and didn't want to finish the journey. It had meant something to me.

I was hot in my waterproofs. And then Aberystwyth was below, the familiar sprawl of colourful terraces in a slate-grey landscape, a town I knew and loved. I regarded it sternly.

These hills were where I'd scrambled between shifts at the pub and the chip-shop, the long summer after my student friends had left and I couldn't bear to. Below me was Pen Dinas, the Iron Age hillfort which had more in common with those found on the border, suggesting border-folk may have migrated here along the route that the railway now took. As I had done. Afon Ystwyth wound between Pen Dinas and the storm beach before meeting the sea. Upriver was the farm which grew organic vegetables we bought all year round, old lead mines, and Bryn Copa, the Bronze Age copper mine which had changed the geochemistry of the surrounding peat, producing the first known example of atmospheric pollution in Britain. I looked and thought I understood it all, the deforestation, pollution and urbanisation, the populations past and present, the destruction, the recovery. But I didn't. And I didn't know what would happen next, only that it would change. And change again.

I descended to Tan y Bwlch where a Mesolithic pebble mace-head had been found, left by small bands of hunter-gatherers who had camped, fished, and knapped flint deposited here by glaciers. People that had crossed the land bridge from Europe to Britain, beginning the continuous human settlement of Cymru. Millennia of refugees, farmers, saints and princes, geologists, gypsies, colliers, bards, soldiers, pilgrims, traders, and environmentalists too, ebbing and flowing like the tide. I knew it was OK to have moved here – that all Cymry had been immigrants, once upon a time. I walked on the storm beach to watch the waves, to feel their spray, to hear the rocks rumbling as they were pounded, incessantly, against the shore. But it was tiring, walking on stones that moved beneath my feet so I walked along Afon Ystwyth instead, where distinctive plant communities grew in the shingle bank, and where I too, like Mesolithic people, had camped on summer nights.

I met Rob off the train and my strange mood vanished. We bought chips in Roundabout Chippy where I'd worked in my student years, after being charmed one night, by light pooling onto the pavement. Twenty years on, Ben and Norma from the Philippines still ran it. "How are you girl?" said Ben.

We clasped hands and climbed Consti. The light was fading. The wind was strong. It inflated our souls and gave us a demon energy so that we sprinted over inlets and bowled up steep hills which rose and fell with sheer drops to the sea. Fuliginous water flickered over Sarn Gynfelyn, the 20-metre wide glacial moraine stretching offshore for several miles, left by receding ice sheets. The sarn was associated with Cantre'r Gwaelod, a legendary kingdom protected by dykes and sluice gates that were neglected the night a big storm battered the city walls. Cantre'r Gwaelod was lost to the sea. It was in the Mesolithic Age that the sea had covered Bae Ceredigion for real.

A giant hand graffitied the sky with a copper-gold aerosol and the sun left a red line stretching all the way to Ynys Enlli. It was nearly dark. We laughed and ran down to the bay where gulls screamed and the rock face was black and frightening, and up the last hill overlooking Y Borth on its flat strip of land between bog and sea, beyond which, Afon Dyfi where I'd begun, glimmered in deep blue dusk. We ran down the last hill in the wind, and it was properly dark at the bottom.

I'd lived in Y Borth for a year. On my first night, a power cut had sent me to the Friendship Inn and we went there now. Mike was still behind the bar in his colourful jumper. We watched football with the only punter, and I, remembering that noisy candlelit night full of drinking, singing, and dominos, felt the passing of time. We picked up our rucksacks. But then old friends burst in, raucous and thirsty. "Stay!" they commanded. Nothing had changed. We slept in the gypsy caravan Jono had built in Ruth's garden, and it creaked all night in the wind.

Mesolithic-age flint tools, red deer antlers and auroch bones have been found on the beach, and drowned stumps of alder, oak, birch and pine are revealed at low tides, but we weren't thinking about them as we stood on the storm bank. We looked at the sea for the last time on this journey, but we weren't thinking that either. We were hungover.

The coast path crept over Cors Fochno. We made it as far as the church before stopping to rest. The church had been built on an island of hard rock left unscoured by the glacier which had skulked down Dyffryn Dyfi at the end of the last Ice Age, squashing surrounding land and leaving a shingle spit. The glacier had deposited a layer of blue clay in shallow tidal water on which saltmarsh accumulated. The shingle spit had apparently advanced east and dunes had developed, preventing inundation from the rising sea while freshwater built up behind them. By about 6000 BC, fen vegetation had supplanted the saltmarsh, followed by marshy alder carr which was gradually colonised by a forest of oak, birch and Scot's pine. Somehow the forest had flooded – perhaps Afon Leri had burst through the shingle spit. The stumps were preserved underwater, but standing wood died, fell, and rotted into peat. Sphagnum accumulated, creating more peat, and continued to do so for 5,000 years, forming Cors Fochno – the bog.

We looked at it now. It had probably, to a greater and lesser degree, been grazed since at least Neolithic times, and its peat dug for fuel. Two thirds had become farmland, but the remainder was still bog. A mosaic of plants including cladonia lichen and white beak-sedge, still thrive on a substrate of peat. Sphagnum and bog mosses, sundew, bog rosemary, orchids, and numerous plants still nourish large heath butterflies, rare moths and crickets, otters and waterbirds. In 2005, Countryside Council for Wales staff watched the bog swallow an entire digger.

Rushes tickled our ears. A yellow brimstone fluttered by and a linnet took off from the brambles. I rubbed bog myrtle leaves, the food of rosy marsh moth larvae, and inhaled their scent. The moths were believed to be extinct in Britain for a century till one discovered in 1965 on a train at Y Bermo, was found to have boarded at Y Borth. Scabious bobbed. Rowan berries shone. Rosehips ripened. Willow leaves yellowed. Red damselflies darted and birch leaves shone like coins in black water. We collapsed on a bench, too fragile to talk. Cloud brushed Bryniau Dyfi and swallows prepared to migrate. We heard the honk and wing-beat of geese and the rattle of a keeled skimmer. The bog soothed our eyes and invited them to glide over golden grasses and vivid purple clumps. A red kite circled. A hawker zipped under my nose. Distant, almost indistinct, a large bird with floppy flight flapped over the estuary and pivoted in the air – one of the ospreys returned to breed on Afon Dyfi after an absence of eighty years. We sat so quietly a grass snake swam across the cut leaving barely a ripple, and slipped up the opposite bank.

We dragged ourselves on. Cors Fochno was breathing and living, despite drainage at its edge – a marshy maze of water-fringed vegetation, fen, heath, scrub, and grassland – active, growing, still evolving. It was a nature reserve of course, and nature reserves aren't enough – like language, wildlife can't survive in isolated pockets. But on my journey I'd seen plants push through tarmac, fishes and birds in rivers once poisoned by lead and coal, and now on my home stretch, species return that had almost been lost – pine martens, rosy marsh moths, ospreys, red kites, and in a few years time, beavers too.

A goldfinch on fireweed. A bullfinch in the ditch. A kingfisher. A heron took off in antique flight, and escorted us to the edge of the bog, and as we crossed the horse paddock, something zipped past us too fast and low to identify, something which must have been a sparrowhawk but having seen so much, was almost more than we could accommodate.

We left the A487 for hills where chirrups quenched the traffic, fireweed scribbled its seed-heads and red oaks held onto their leaves. Buzzards wheeled and corvids chuntered, beechnuts crunched, yarrow survived and a dark stream flowed with the sound of cymbals and muted applause. There were views sometimes to Afon Dyfi across which the Tarennau rose, summits in cloud. The dunes were vanishing yet brightening like steam on a window. We heard the soft honking of geese, the lowing of cattle and dull clank of farm machinery. We saw a grey squirrel in a pedunculate oak, its tail a silver lining. A flash of blue as a jay spread its wing. A frog. Afon Eifion dashing black and white over white and black stones in small cascades. Its white noise refreshed us and we saw the overhanging branches and misty space between, epiphytes growing on mossy sessile oak boughs, washed by the wet air of temperate rainforest.

What will the future bring? I imagine seaweed and shellfish cultivated on a coast busy with boats. A sea in which fish are returning. I picture poly-tunnels full of fruit and vegetables, fields bursting with arable crops full of reapers and sowers and farmers waving from machines powered by bio-fuels grown in their own fields. Herders leading small flocks of sheep and goats to remote uplands, and free roaming cattle grazing woodland pasture, like the herbivores that had browsed woodland glades when the glaciers retreated. *Real* pastures, with long root systems that store carbon, reduce soil erosion, alleviate flooding and nourish micro-organisms in the soil. Grassland with diverse flora to benefit a multitude of invertebrates, birds and mammals, as well as livestock. Pigs in the woods, foresters planting and felling trees, and the whole lot linked by wildlife-rich field-margins, hedgerows and woodland corridors. Farms full of people *and* wildlife. It can happen. If we want it to.

In 2019, signs would appear on these hills in Cymraeg and English saying 'Yes to Conservation, No to Rewilding' and I, sick of conflict, would stay quiet. But the words that I thought were the first that I'd learned in Cymraeg. Words which back in 1979, a Tywyn shopkeeper had imbued with such significance I would never forget them. Cymru am byth. Cymru forever. Come on Cymru, I would think. Enough fighting. We can do this.

We crept uphill. We could see Dyfi Bridge and Machynlleth, the small grey town just three miles from home, which rising water is predicted to drown. It began to rain very gently. The path dipped, the view was concealed, and we crossed Afon Llyfnant back into Powys.

ICE AND FIRE

Seventeen ice ages over the last 2.5 million years have alternated with periods of warm temperate climate as part of a cycle partly relating to regular changes in the Earth's orbit round the sun, and partly by changes on Earth. At least 700,000 years ago during interglacials, small groups of hominids made forays into southern Britain where they foraged, camped and hunted wandering herds. Each time the ice returned, the hominids walked to southern Europe. About 250,000-200,000 years ago, elephants and lions were at large in southern England. Neanderthals evolved from the hominids and began to use fire. A 230,000-year-old jawbone belonging to a Neanderthal boy about nine years old was found in a cave in Bontnewydd, Sir Ddinbych, the oldest known inhabitant of Cymru. Evidence of Neanderthals using coastal caves 100,000 years later, have been found at Coygan and Lacharn.

In warm periods, temperatures were higher than today and sea level isolated Britain from the continent. Woodland grew, hippopotami swam in the Thames, and straight-tusked elephants, hyenas, rhinos, giant deer, auroch, bison, lions, and scimitar cats roamed Britain. In cool periods sea level fell, glaciers grew, tundra replaced woodland, mammoth and woolly rhinoceros occupied southern Britain and migrating reindeer and horses grazed the tundra. Neanderthals left Britain for south France in a period of extreme cold 73,000 years ago, but returned when it got warmer, and pine and spruce briefly reappeared. The Neanderthals used flint axes, scrapers, arrows and spears. Their axes have been found at Coygan, and they possibly occupied caves in Pontnewydd and Ffynnon Beuno.

By 40,000 BC, homo sapiens reached Europe from Africa, and by 26,000 BC, Neanderthals were extinct. The modern humans continued to use stone tools and twist fibres together to make nets and snares. The oldest known ceremonial burial in western Europe took place in Paviland on Penrhyn Gŵyr about 26,500 BC.

Ice returned to Cymru from 19,000-11,000 BC and humans once again followed migrating herds to southern Europe. Forest bison and antelope disappeared. At its peak, the ice was a thousand metres thick over Cymru, twice as thick in Scotland, and half as thick in England. The weight of it depressed and eroded the land. But in 13,000 BC, it started to melt. By 11,000 BC, it had largely disappeared and humans started walking back to Britain, which has been occupied ever since. The temperature rose and mammoths became extinct.

We are in an inter-glacial now. The planet is supposed to be gently cooling, before heading for another Ice Age. Instead, human activity is driving the climate the other way, from icehouse towards hothouse, at a geologically furious pace.

MACHYNLLETH

Our bodies were weary but our minds free to float with the cloud. Rhododendron ponticum, which the pollen record shows as having grown in Britain before the last Ice Age, was thriving where the spruce had been clear-felled. A forestry track sliced through slate. If unhindered, the raw slate would be colonised by lichens and moss, then by herbs, shrubs and trees. The ice-sculpted Powys hills sprawled ahead like big cats. One summit was familiar, but in an unexpected position. We were close to home but had no idea where we were, till finally, after hours of turning in unexpected directions, Afon Dyfi appeared in its floodplain of alluvial gravels, silt and clay. The valley had acted as a meltwater corridor in the last Ice Age, but had been shaped in earlier Ice Ages, by earlier meltwater.

We slithered, worn out, into Machynlleth and drank a pot of tea in The White. Rob caught the bus home. I had another three miles to walk. I paused on Dyfi Bridge to watch the river on its journey to the coast, then crossed it back into Gwynedd.

EVOLUTION

Almost a billion years ago, the landmass of England and Cymru was formed close to the South Pole. Due to tectonic plate activity, it slowly advanced north across a sea full of jellyfish-like creatures, and joined Scotland approximately 420 million years ago just south of the equator, becoming part of a huge continent. Cymru's oldest minerals and rocks had already been formed and the seas were full of fish. Three million years later, when plants were widespread, Cymru was still near the equator. It had already experienced widespread volcanism, submarine and desert conditions, and now its coal and limestone were formed in tropical forest-swamps and clear warm seas respectively. Creeping north, Britain arrived at its present latitude about 66 million years ago, with palm trees and crocodiles. North Sea gas had already been trapped. Five mass extinctions had already taken place, due to cataclysmic events like enormous pollution and climate change due to massive volcanic eruptions, or impacts by large asteroids and their after-effects. The dinosaurs had come and gone.

HOME

I paused on the hill. Beneath my feet was Silurian mudstone some 433 million years old. The view dissolved in soft cloud and sound became muted. At the top, the coast path turned northwest. The larch fronds were yellowing again.

I turned northeast and walked home, where Rob was waiting, and my heart was full. My journey had been no big deal. Yet my subconscious must have registered its passing because as I drifted into sleep, silver estuaries and the calls of curlews and oystercatchers floated across my mind. But the feeling that overwhelmed me was not one of completion, but of continuity.

For my family who love caravan holidays in Cymru,
and in memory of Dad who did too.

The Rewilder and The Shepherd

I fear for my myself, that my soul is dulled by the loss of wild life.
I fear for myself, that I will lose the hills and flocks of my heart.
I fear for my children, that they will know only yoked land.
I fear for my children, that they will not know my sheep-songs.
I am in pain, that by human hands so much has been lost.
I am in pain, that my ancestors toil will fade to mist of memory.
I would protect the vixen, and the flight of the raven.
I would protect my lambs, and the rise of the skylark.
I would bring back the wolf, the mirror of our being.
I would bring back the curlew, whose song is our own.
I love this land, and the singing wind.
I love this land, and the singing wind.
We fight for what we love.
We fight for what we love.

David Bavin

Acknowledgements

For sharing their expertise in agriculture, Celtic languages, ecology, education, environment, geography, history, literature, society and statistics, very special thanks to Mike and Rosanne Alexander, Geraint Bevan, Anne Jones, Dr Elin Jones, Gareth Jones, Tobi Kellner, Tracey Lovering, Carwen Lloyd-Williams, Caroline Oakley, James Robertson, Dr Simon Rodway and John Shrouder, without whose scrutiny, corrections and advice this book would be a wishy-washy thing. Special thanks also to John Mason, Raymond Roberts and Peter Toghill for their help with the geology bits. Remaining mistakes are entirely my own.

Thanks also to suggestions on language use from Dr Manon Davies. Particular thanks to Robyn Drury for being generous with her advice and Mike Parker for putting my feet back on Cymreig ground. To the entire team at Seren for their craft, especially Sarah Johnson for so gently making marketing un-scary, and Mick Felton for his kindness, vision and care – I am so grateful.

To Mark Lloyd from Antur Busnes for his enthusiasm, and early mentors Caroline Oakley and Allan Shepherd for guidance. To Llywodraeth Cymru for the redundancy re-training grant and the writing course tutors – particularly Peter Carty, Mark Charlton, Helen Deal and Rory Maclean, Elise Valmorbida and Nick Barlay. To the editorial team at BBC *Countryfile Magazine* whose patronage kept me going – Daniel Graham, Fergus Collins, Margaret Bartlett, Maria Hodson and especially Joe Pontin, for that first commission. A Literature Wales Writer's Bursary supported by the National Lottery through the Arts Council of Wales was received to develop this book – enormous thank yous. To staff at Llyfrgell Genedlaethol Cymru (National Library of Wales), and to Carrie for getting me there, thank you. To friends and strangers for hospitality and kindness en route, particularly Melissa, Tim, Thorin, Indi and Ashanti, Gerald and Gwyneth, Sarah and Charlie, Grebo and Tracy, the Port Talbot bus driver, Martin the guard, Glenn from Diablos, Stu, Fran and Flynn (and now Jack and Ellis), and Ruth and Jono, thank you. Thanks also to Stu for the gorgeous cover photo. To Aunty Viv for reading everything I write. To all of my big fabulous family, especially Mum for waiting patiently so very long. To Rob, for everything. And to the people of Cymru, and particularly the community of Machynlleth, for welcoming me – diolch o galon.

Select Bibliography

Books

Baines, Menna, Davies, John, Jenkins, Nigel and Lynch, Peredur I, *The Welsh Academy Encyclopaedia of Wales* (The University of Wales Press, 2008)

Breverton, Terry, *Wales – A Historical Companion*, (Amberley, 2009)

Rogers, Byron, *The Bank Manager and the Holy Grail* (Aurum, 2005)

Cambrensis, Giraldus (or Gerallt Gymro, or Gerald of Wales), *The Journey Through Wales and the Description of Wales* (Penguin Classics, 1978)

Condry, William, M, *The Natural History of Wales*, (Collins, 1981)

Crane, Nicholas, *The Making of the British Landscape From the Ice Age to the Present* (Weidenfeld and Nicolson, 2016)

Dillon, Paddy, *Walking the Wales Coast Path*, (Cicerone, 2015)

Dodd, A H, Ed by, *A History of Wrexham* (Wrexham Borough Council, 1989)

Dodd, A H, *A Short History of Wales* (John Jones, 1998)

Edwards, J M, *Flintshire* (Cambridge County Geographies: Cambridge University Press, 1914)

Evans, Robin, *Immigrants in Wales During the 20th Century: Welcome to Wales*, University of Wales Aberystwyth, 2006

German, Glyn, E, *Welsh History; a Chronological Outline*, (Y Lolfa, 2015)

Henwood, Kay, *Secrets of the Gypsies*, (Piccolo, 1974)

Howell, David W, *The Rural Poor in Eighteenth-Century Wales* (Cardiff University of Wales Press, 2000)

James, David B, *Ceredigion, Its Natural History* (Cambrian Printers, 2001)

Jenkins, J. Gerallt, *Pembrokeshire its Past and Present Explored* (Carreg Gwalch, 2016)

Jones, R Gerallt, *A Place in the Mind – A Boyhood in Llŷn* (Gomer Press, 2004)

Lewis, Hugh M, *Aberdyfi: The Past Recalled Early Welsh Way of Life in the Dyfi and Dysynni Area*, (Y Lolfa, 2001)

Mason, John, *The Making of Ynyslas* (Word After Word, 2019)

Meirion, Dafydd, *Walking Anglesey's Shoreline*, (Gwasg Carreg Gwalch, 2003)

Monbiot, George, *Feral; Searching for Enchantment on the Frontiers of Rewilding,* (Allen Lane: Penguin, 2013)

Morgan, Gerald, *A Brief History of Wales*, (Y Lolfa, 2008)

Morris, Jan, *Wales, Epic Views of a Small Country*, (Viking, 1984)

Morton, H V, *In Search of Wales*, (Methuen, 1932)

Mullard, Johnathan, *Gower*, (Collins, 2006)

Parker, Mike, *Neighbours from Hell? English attitudes to the Welsh* (Y Lolfa, 2014)

Pennant, Thomas, *A Tour in Wales, Vol 1* (Bridgend: WBC Ltd, 1991)

Ramirez, Janina, Dr, *Power, Passion and Politics in Anglo-Saxon England: The Private Lives of the Saints,* (Penguin Random House, 2015)

Ray, Keith and Bapty, Ian, *Offa's Dyke: Landscape and Hegemony in 8th Century Britain,* (Windgather Press, 2016)

Rhys, Gruff, *American Interior* (Hamish Hamilton, 2014)

Roberts, Enid, *Bardsey Bound*, (Y Lolfa, 2008)

Senior, Michael Senior, *Llŷn, The Peninsula's Story* (Gwasg Carreg Gwalch, 1997)

Senior, Michael, *Meirionnydd's Story*, (Gwasg Carreg Gwalch, 1997)

Theroux, Paul, *The Kingdom By the Sea*, (Penguin, 1983)

Toghill, Peter, *The Geology of Britain; An Introduction*, (Airlife Publishing, 2003)

Toulson, Shirley, *The Drovers' Roads of Wales*, (Wildwood House, 1977)

Tree, Isabella, *Wilding: The Return of Nature to a British Farm* (Picador, 2018)

Williams, Griffith John, *The Vale of Glamorgan: Its History and Traditions* (Plaid Cymru, 1972)

Williams, Stewart *South Glamorgan, a County History* (Stewart Williams Publishers, 1975)

Organisations, reports and articles

Agriculture

Agriculture in Wales (Wikipedia) https://gov.wales/local-area-summary-statistics-1

Alamar, M.C, Psichas, A, Spence, M and Willcock, S, *The Carbon Footprint of high-protein foods; Perceptions and impact of consumer-facing information in the UK*, (Policy Lab, February 2017)

All you need to know about Welsh farming exports and the EU, (Shropshire Star, July 30th 2019) https://www.shropshirestar.com/news/uk-news/2019/07/30/all-you-need-to-know-about-welsh-farming-exports-and-the-eu/

Armstrong, Edward, *The Farming Sector in Wales*, (Research Briefing, National Assembly for Wales, September 2016)

Climate Change Food Calculator: What's Your Diet's Carbon Footprint? (BBC News, August 19th, 2019) https://www.bbc.co.uk/news/science-environment-46459714

Global Food Security, The UK cross-government programme on food security research https://www.foodsecurity.ac.uk/

Halal consumption increasingly crucial to UK sheep industry (Farmer's Weekly, 21st December 2016) https://www.fwi.co.uk/business/halal-consumption-increasingly-crucial-uk-sheep-industry

HCC Wales What is PGI? Eat Welsh Lamb and Welsh Beef https://eatwelshlambandwelshbeef.com/what-is-pgi/

'I'm constantly putting on a brave face': farmers speak out on mental health (The Guardian,

27th February 2020) https://www.theguardian.com/environment/2020/feb/27/im-constantly-putting-on-a-brave-face-farmers-speak-out-on-mental-health

Preventing water pollution, wastewater management on farms, (NetRegs) https://www.netregs.org.uk/environmental-topics/water/more-ways-to-prevent-water-pollution/preventing-water-pollution-from-farm-discharges-to-water/

Review of Land Use Climate Change: An assessment of the evidence base for climate change action in the agriculture, land use and wider foodchain sectors in Wales (ADAS UK Ltd, October 2014) https://llyw.cymru/sites/default/files/publications/2018-02/newid-yn-yr-hinsawdd-arolwg-defnydd-tir.pdf

Ridge and Furrow (Wikipedia) https://en.wikipedia.org/wiki/Ridge_and_furrow

Sheep farming in Wales (Wikipedia) https://en.wikipedia.org/wiki/Sheep_farming_in_Wales

Slurry pollution kills fish (Cyfoeth Naturiol Cymru, Natural Resources Wales, 3rd Aug 2018) https://naturalresourceswales.gov.uk/about-us/news-and-events/news/slurry-pollu-tion-kills-fish/?lang=en

Warning over poultry farm grown 'explosion' in Wales (BBC News, 15th May 2018) https://www.bbc.co.uk/news/uk-wales-44108740

Wasley, Andrew, *Deadly gas: Cutting farm emissions in half could save 3,000 lives a year* (Global Research, The Bureau of Investigative Journalism, 13th June, 2019) https://www.global-research.ca/deadly-gas-cutting-farm-emissions-half-could-save-3000-lives-year/568088 9

Biodiversity

Coastal Flora of Wales, https://beachguide.wales/flora/flora.html

Hickman, Leo '*If you want red squirrels, you have to kill greys*' (The Guardian, 5th Sept, 2012) https://www.theguardian.com/environment/2012/sep/05/red-grey-squirrels-cornwall

List of Extinct Animals of the British Isles (Wikipedia) https://en.wikipedia.org/wiki/List_of_extinct_animals_of_the_British_Isles

Living Planet Report 2016 (WWF) http://assets.wwf.org.uk/custom/lpr2016/

Marshall, Tom, *Waste can clean up polluted soil,* (Natural Environmental Research Council, 10th Feb 2011) https://nerc.ukri.org/planetearth/stories/917/#:~:text=The%20waste%20also%20aerates%20the,to%20stop%20them%20contaminating%20groundwater.

Oosthoek, K. Jan, *The origin of nature conservation in Britain – a short introduction* (Environ-mental History Resources, July 25th, 2015) https://www.eh-resources.org/origins-nature-conservation-in-britain/

Perry, Sarah, *Living Seas, Future Fisheries: The Welsh Fishing Industry* (The Wildlife Trust of South

and West Wales, 2015) https://www.welshwildlife.org/living-seas/future-
fisheries/#:~:text=Future%20Fisheries%20is%20an%20essential,pressures%20the%2
0marine%20environment%20faces.

Skomer Island Manx Shearwater Factsheet https://www.welshwildlife.org/wp-content/
uploads/2011/05/Manx-Shearwater.pdf

State of Nature, UK Report 2016, Foreword by Sir David Attenborough
https://www.rspb.org.uk/globalassets/downloads/documents/conservation-projects/
state-of-nature/state-of-nature-uk-report-2016.pdf

Summit to Sea, http://www.summit2sea.wales/

The early history of salmon and freshwater fisheries law (Canal and River Trust, 16th
October, 2017) https://canalrivertrust.org.uk/enjoy-the-waterways/fishing/related-
articles/the-fisheries-and-angling-team/the-early-history-of-salmon-and-freshwater-fish
eries-law

*The State of Natural Resources Report (SoNaRR): Assessment of the Sustainable Management of
Natural Resources. Technical Report. Chapter 3. Summary of extent, condition and trends of natural
resources and ecosystems in Wales* (Natural Resources Wales, 2016) https://naturalre-
sources.wales/evidence-and-data/research-and-reports/the-state-of-natural-resources-r
eport-assessment-of-the-sustainable-management-of-natural-
resources/?lang=en#:~:text=The%20approach%20of%20SoNaRR%20is,proactive%2
0approach%20to%20building%20resilience.

Thurstan, Ruth H, Roberts, Callum M, Brockington, Simon, *The effects of 118 years of industrial fishing on UK bottom trawl fisheries* (Researchgate, 4th May, 2010)
https://www.researchgate.net/publication/47545073_The_effects_of_118_years_of_i
ndustrial_fishing_on_UK_bottom_trawl_fisheries

Reefs; Marine, coastal, and halophytic habitats (JNCC) https://sac.jncc.gov.uk/habitat/
H1170/#:~:text=The%20Saturn%20Sabellaria%20spinulosa%20biogenic,(BMT%20C
ordah%2C%202003)

UK Seafood Industry Overview, (Seafish) https://www.seafish.org/article/uk-seafood-
industry-overview

Wales Biodiversity Partnership https://www.biodiversitywales.org.uk/

Water Vole Action Plan, (Wales Biodiversity Partnership) www.biodiversitywales.org.uk

Watson, Grieg, Polluted Legacy: Repairing Britain's Damaged Landscapes, BBC News, 26th
June, 2012, https://www.bbc.co.uk/news/uk-england-derbyshire-17315323

Watts, Jonathan, *Human society under urgent threat from loss of Earth's natural life* (The Guardian,
6th May 2019) https://www.theguardian.com/environment/
2019/may/06/human-society-under-urgent-threat-loss-earth-natural-life-un-report

Wood, Christine, Bishop, John, and Yunnie, Anna, *Comprehensive Reassessment of NNS in Welsh*

marinas (Cyfoeth Naturiol Cymru, Natural Resources Wales, 2015)
https://core.ac.uk/download/pdf/78761493.pdf

Climate Change

Adapting to Climate Change: Guidance for Flood and Coastal Erosion Risk Management Authorities in Wales (Llywodraeth Cymru, Welsh Government, December 2017)
https://gov.wales/sites/default/files/publications/2019-06/adapting-to-climate-change-guidance-for-flood-and-coastal-erosion-risk-management-authorities-in-wales.pdf

Climate Change: Oil Industry argues for maximum protection levels (BBC News, 4th September 2019) https://www.bbc.co.uk/news/uk-scotland-49565953

Coal Consumption affecting climate, (The Rodney and Otamatea Times, August 14th, 1912)

Davidson, Jordan, *Carbon Dioxide Levels in the Atmosphere Hit Highest Level in 3 Million Years*, (Ecowatch, Feb 26th, 2020) https://www.ecowatch.com/carbon-dioxide-levels-atmosphere-2645274429.html

Fossil Fuels, (EESI, Environmental and Energy Study Institute)
https://www.eesi.org/topics/fossil-fuels/description

Grasso, Marco, *Oily politics: A critical assessment of the oil and gas industry's contribution to climate change* (Science Direct, 2018) https://www.sciencedirect.com/science/article/abs/pii/S2214629618306376

History of climate change science (Wikipedia) https://en.wikipedia.org/wiki/History_of_climate_change_science

Nunez, Christina, *Fossil Fuels, Explained* (National Geographic, April 2nd 2019)
https://www.nationalgeographic.com/environment/energy/reference/fossil-fuels/#:~:text=By%20Christina%20Nunez,percent%20of%20the%20world's%20energy.

Zero Carbon Britain; Rising to the Climate Emergency, 2019 and Zero Carbon Britain; Rethinking the Future, 2013 (The Centre for Alternative Technology)
https://www.cat.org.uk/info-resources/zero-carbon-britain/research-reports/zero-carbon-britain-rising-to-the-climate-emergency/

Cymru Today

2011 Census: Key Statistics for Local Authorities in England and Wales (Office for National Statistics) https://www.ons.gov.uk/peoplepopulationandcommunity/populationandmigration/populationestimates/datasets/2011censuskeystatisticsforlocalauthoritiesinenglandandwales

Energy Generation in Wales, 2018 (Llywodraeth Cymru)

https://gov.wales/sites/default/files/publications/2019-10/energy-generation-in-wales-2018.pdf

Key Statistics for Assembly Regions, May 2010, (National Assembly for Wales)
https://senedd.wales/NAfW%20Documents/10-052.pdf%20-%2017052010/10-052-English.pdf

Local Area Summary Statistics (Llywodraeth Cymru, 17th December, 2014)
https://gov.wales/local-area-summary-statistics-1

Priority Sector Statistics: 2018 (Llywodraeth Cymru Welsh Government, 2018)
https://gov.wales/priority-sector-statistics-2018#:~:text=Just%20over%20two%20thirds%20of,10.7%25).

Summary Statistics for Wales, by region, 2020. (Llywdoraeth Cymru, Welsh Government, 2020) https://gov.wales/sites/default/files/statistics-and-research/2020-05/summary-statistics-regions-wales-2020-629.pdf

Small School Closures in Wales, New Evidence, (Institute for Welsh Affairs, 2007)
https://www.iwa.wales/our-work/work/small-school-closure-in-wales-new-evidence/

Wales in Summary; An overview of Wales from the statistics we publish (Statistics and Research, Llywodraeth Cymru, Welsh Government, 14th April 2015)
https://gov.wales/summary-statistics-regions-wales-2020

Wales; Census Profile (The Migration Observatory, March, 2014) https://migrationobservatory.ox.ac.uk/resources/briefings/wales-census-profile/

Wales, constituent unit, United Kingdom (Britannica)
https://www.britannica.com/place/Wales

Yes Cymru, Indpendence in Your Pocket https://www.yes.cymru/independence

Energy

30 years on: The impact of the Chernobyl nuclear disaster, (The Journal.ie, 24th April 2016)
https://www.thejournal.ie/chernobyl-disaster-effects-ireland-2727840-Apr2016/

Energy Wales: A Low Carbon Transition, (Llywodraeth Cymru, 2012)
https://gov.wales/sites/default/files/publications/2019-07/energy-wales-a-low-carbon-transition.pdf

Final Shipment of New Magnox Fuel, (World Nuclear News, 19th December, 2011)
https://www.world-nuclear-news.org/Articles/Final-shipment-of-new-Magnox-fuel#:~:text=The%20UK's%20Wylfa%20nuclear%20power,opportunities%20in%20the%20nuclear%20industry.

Herd, George, *Wylfa: Countdown to shutdown of nuclear power station* (BBC News, 30th December 2015) https://www.bbc.co.uk/news/uk-wales-34999951

Iwan, Telor, *Chernobyl and the north Wales sheep farmers, 30 years on* (BBC News, 26th April, 2016) https://www.bbc.co.uk/news/uk-wales-36112372

Messenger, Steffan, *Wylfa Newydd: Anglesey nuclear power station to be smaller* (BBC News, 24th May, 2017) https://www.bbc.co.uk/news/uk-wales-40013117

Magnox (Wikipedia) https://en.wikipedia.org/wiki/Magnox

Nuclear Power Debate (Wikipedia) https://en.wikipedia.org/wiki/Nuclear_power_debate

Old Reactors, Magnox Reactors (No2Nuclear Power)
http://www.no2nuclearpower.org.uk/old-reactors/

Outline history of nuclear energy (World Nuclear) https://www.world-nuclear.org/information-library/current-and-future-generation/outline-history-of-nuclear-energy.aspx#:~:text=The%20reactor%20started%20up%20in%20December%201951.&text=The%20existing%20graphite%2Dmoderated%20channel,at%20the%20FEI%20in%20Obninsk.

Springfields Nuclear Fuel Plant, (Engineering Timelines) http://www.engineering-timelines.com/scripts/engineeringItem.asp?id=1015

Uranium Mining (Wikipedia) https://en.wikipedia.org/wiki/Uranium_mining

Where Does Uranium Come From? (NEI, September 2019)
https://www.nei.org/resources/fact-sheets/where-does-uranium-come-from

World's last operating Magnox reactor closes, (World Nuclear News, 31st December, 2015) https://www.world-nuclear-news.org/WR-Worlds-last-operating-Magnox-reactor-closes-31121501.html#:~:text=The%20UK's%20Nuclear%20Decommissioning%20Authority,years%20longer%20than%20originally%20planned.

Wylfa nuclear power station and the National Assembly for Wales, (Greenpeace)

Geology

Ashbourn, Julian, *An Overview of the Geology of Britain,* (Springer)
www.springer.com/gb/book/9789048188604

British Geological Survey, Teachers Notes
https://www.bgs.ac.uk/discoveringGeology/home.html?src=topNav

The BGS Lexicon of Named Rock Units — Result Details (British Geological Survey)
https://www.bgs.ac.uk/lexicon/lexicon.cfm?pub=PMCM

Geology of Ceredigion (The Museum Collection)
https://pilgrim.ceredigion.gov.uk/index.cfm?articleid=2798#:~:text=The%20geological%20history%20of%20Ceredigion%20consists%20of%3A,water%20during%20the%20Ice%2Dage.

Geology of Wales (Wikipedia) https://en.wikipedia.org/wiki/Geology_of_Wales

Geotrails and Building Stones Walks, Geological Association,
https://geologistsassociation.org.uk/geotrails-building-stones-walks/

Nield, Ted, Gower Field Guide, The Geological Society
https://www.geolsoc.org.uk/Gower

Regional Geological Summaries, British Geological Survey,
   https://www.bgs.ac.uk/research/ukgeology/wales/home.html

Sahlin, A U, Glasser, Neil F, Jansson, Krister N, Hambrey, Michael J, *Connectivity analyses of valley patterns indicate preservation of a preglacial fluvial valley system in the Dyfi basin, Wales* (Proceedings of the Geologist Association)
   https://www.sciencedirect.com/science/article/abs/pii/S0016787809000431

The Formation of the Earth's continents, Cradle of Humankind,
   https://www.maropeng.co.za/content/page/the-formation-of-the-earths-continents#:~:text=About%20250%2Dmillion%20years%20ago,giant%20continents%2C%20Gondwana%20and%20Laurasia.

The Mineral Resource Maps of Wales, (BGS)
   https://www.bgs.ac.uk/mineralsUK/planning/resource.html

Thomas, G S P, Summers, A J, Dackombe, R V, *The Late-Quaternary deposits of the middle Dyfi Valley, Wales,* (Geological Journal, October/December 1982)
   https://onlinelibrary.wiley.com/doi/abs/10.1002/gj.3350170404

Williams, Matt, How Was The Earth Formed? (Phys Org) https://phys.org/news/2014-12-earth.html

History

The 17th Century Civil Wars, British Battlefields http://britishbattlefields.com/

Booth's Uprising (BCW Project, British Civil Wars, Commonwealth and Protectorate, 1638-1660) http://bcw-project.org/military/royalist-conspiracies/booths-uprising

Bremner, Ian *Wales: English Conquest of Wales c.1200 – 1415* (BBC)
   http://www.bbc.co.uk/history/british/middle_ages/wales_conquest_01.shtml

A Brief History of Woollen Textiles in Wales, (Sheep Tales)
   https://www.sheeptales.org/history-of-wool.html

British Migration, (Geni) https://www.geni.com/projects/British-Migration-Main-Page/16155

Bryn Eryr, Iron Age Roundhouses (Historic Buildings at St Fagans, Amgueddfa Cymru – National Museum of Wales) https://museum.wales/stfagans/buildings/bryneryr/

Burton, Janet, *The Cistercians in Wales* (Monastic Wales)
   https://www.monasticwales.org/showarticle.php?func=showarticle&articleID=2

Bryant, Arthur, *The Story of England: The End of the Saxon Kingdom* (History Today, 8th August, 1953) https://www.historytoday.com/archive/story-england-end-saxon-kingdom#:~:text=Arthur%20Bryant%20looks%20at%20how,formed%20before%20the%20Normans%20came.&text=During%20the%20century%20that%20followed,than%20in%20any%20other%20country.

Caring for Military Sites of the 20th Century (CADW)
   https://cadw.gov.wales/sites/default/files/2019-
   04/Caring_for_Military_Sites_EN.pdf

Carradice, Phil, *The Council of Wales and The Marches* (BBC Wales, 7th November 2012)
   https://www.bbc.co.uk/blogs/wales/entries/c63da957-f067-3e3a-bbcc-
   1d91dd3166d4

Carradice, Phil, *The Drovers of Wales*, (BBC Wales, 8th March, 2012)
   https://www.bbc.co.uk/blogs/wales/entries/d0214007-fead-3c68-b8cb-f4ac7b78ad3d

Carradice, Phil *A history of Welsh protest* (BBC) https://www.bbc.co.uk/blogs/waleshis-
   tory/2011/11/history_of_welsh_protest.html

Carradice, Phil, *The Quaker Movement in Wales,* (BBC, 24th August, 2012)
   https://www.bbc.co.uk/blogs/wales/entries/fcfbb662-23b6-3859-b521-
   758de2c9d08c

Carradice, Phil, *Thomas Pennant, natural history pioneer* (BBC 9th August, 2011)
   https://www.bbc.co.uk/blogs/waleshistory/2011/08/thomas_pennant_natural_histor
   y.html

Celtic Kingdoms of the British Isles, (The History Files)
   https://www.historyfiles.co.uk/KingListsBritain/CymruPrinces.htm

Christianity in Wales (Wikipedia) https://en.wikipedia.org/wiki/Christianity_in_Wales

Church in Wales, Anglicanism (Britannica) https://www.britannica.com/topic/Church-in-
   Wales

Cistercians (Wikipedia) https://en.wikipedia.org/wiki/Cistercians

Coghlan, Andy, *Ancient invaders transformed Britain, but not its DNA* (New Scientist 18th March,
   2015) https://www.newscientist.com/article/mg22530134-300-ancient-invaders-
   transformed-britain-but-not-its-dna/

Cockburn, Harry *Britons who built Stonehenge were product of ancient wave of migrant farmers,*
   DNA reveals (Independent, 16th April, 2019)
   https://www.independent.co.uk/news/science/archaeology/stone-henge-builders-
   origin-dna-migrant-farmers-a8872336.html

Confederate Ireland: A Political Overview (BCW Project) http://bcw-project.org/church-
   and-state/confederate-ireland/

Conquest of Wales by Edward I (Wikipedia)
   https://en.wikipedia.org/wiki/Conquest_of_Wales_by_Edward_I_of_England

Council of Wales and the Marches (Wikipedia)
   https://en.wikipedia.org/wiki/Council_of_Wales_and_the_Marches

David Lloyd George, BBC History
   http://www.bbc.co.uk/history/historic_figures/george_david_lloyd.shtml

David Lloyd George, History Past Prime Ministers, (Gov UK)

  https://www.gov.uk/government/history/past-prime-ministers/david-lloyd-george

Davies, Dr John, *A History of Wales*, (BBC)

  https://www.bbc.co.uk/wales/history/sites/themes/guide.shtml

Nonconformity – What is Dissent and Nonconformity? The Story of Nonconformity in
  Wales (Addoldai Cymru, Welsh Religious Buildings Trust)

  http://www.welshchapels.org/nonconformity/

Day, Graham, *The long road to Welsh devolution* (Open Learn Cymru)

  https://www.open.edu/openlearncreate/mod/oucontent/view.php?id=56099

Donnelly, Peter, *The Secret History of Britain is written in our genes* (The Telegraph, 20th March,
  2015)https://www.telegraph.co.uk/news/science/11483608/The-secret-history-of-
  Britain-is-written-in-our-genes.html

Dyfed Prehistoric Sites, Britain Express

  https://www.britainexpress.com/wales/pembrokeshire/ancient.htm

"Everywhere in Chains": Wales and Slavery (Amgueddfa Cymru, Museum Wales)

  https://museum.wales/articles/2011-03-15/Everywhere-in-Chains-Wales-and-
  Slavery/

Farming and Agriculture before the Romans (The Romans in Britain)

  https://www.romanobritain.org/11_work/raw_farming_and_agriculture.php

First World War Military Sites: Manufacturing and Research and Development, Part 1
  (Llywodraeth Cymru, Welsh Government, March 2016)

  http://www.heneb.co.uk/ww1/reports/ww1manufacturingresearch.pdf

Food in Romano-Britain (Resources 4 History)

  https://resourcesforhistory.com/Roman_Food_in_Britain.htm

French, Morvern *Flemish Migration to Scotland in the Medieval and Early Modern Periods* (University of St Andrews, 4th December 2015)

  https://flemish.wp.st-andrews.ac.uk/2015/12/04/flemish-migration-to-scotland-in-
  the-medieval-and-early-modern-periods/

Glyndŵr Rising (Wikipedia) https://en.wikipedia.org/wiki/Glynd%C5%B5r_Rising

Glwysing (Wikipedia) https://en.wikipedia.org/wiki/Glywysing

Harding, Vanessa *The Worshipful Company of Weavers* https://www.weavers.org.uk/history

History of the formation of the United Kingdom (Wikipedia)

  https://en.wikipedia.org/wiki/History_of_the_formation_of_the_United_Kingdom

Hodgman, Charlotte, *Life in the Bronze Age* (BBC History)

  https://www.historyextra.com/period/bronze-age/history-explorer-life-in-the-
  bronze-age/

Hywel Dda (Wikipedia) https://en.wikipedia.org/wiki/Hywel_Dda

Ibeji, Dr Mike (Black Death), History, (BBC)
    http://www.bbc.co.uk/history/british/middle_ages/black_01.shtml

Iron Age (Wikipedia)
    https://www.google.com/search?q=iron+age+wiki&rlz=1C1CHBF_en-
    GBGB894GB894&oq=iron+age+wiki&aqs=chrome..69i57j0l7.2435j0j15&sourceid=c
    hrome&ie=UTF-8

Johnes, Dr Martin, Bombing Raids in Wales (BBC Wales)
    https://www.bbc.co.uk/wales/history/sites/themes/periods/ww2_bombing.shtml

Johnes, Dr Martin, *Welsh Identity in Wartime* (BBC Wales)

Johnson, Ben, *History of the Wool Trade* (Historic UK) https://www.historic-uk.com/Histo-
    ryUK/HistoryofEngland/Wool-Trade/

Johnson, Ben, *Kings and Queens of England and Britain* (Historic UK) https://www.historic-
    uk.com/HistoryUK/KingsQueensofBritain/

Keaveney, Paul, *Unravelling British wool: how the local and global are intertwined in the making of
    everyday products* (The Conversation, 22nd November, 2018)
    https://theconversation.com/unravelling-british-wool-how-the-local-and-global-are-
    intertwined-in-the-making-of-everyday-products-99114

Gruffydd, Prys, *Wales, constituent unit, United Kingdom* (Britannica)
    https://www.britannica.com/place/Wales

The History of Wales, https://thehistoryofwales.typepad.com/t/pre.html

The History of Welsh Devolution (Senedd Cymru Welsh Parliament)
    https://senedd.wales/en/abthome/role-of-assembly-how-it-works/Pages/history-
    welsh-devolution.aspx

Knight, Matthew Guiseppe, *Bronze Age Hoarding in Wales, Amgueddfa Blog*, (Amgueddfa
    Cymru, National Museum Wales, 16th June, 2017) https://museum.wales/blog/2017-
    06-16/Bronze-Age-Hoarding-in-Wales/?entry=841

The Legacy of the Saints, (CADW) https://cadw.gov.wales/sites/default/files/2019-
    04/InterpplanCelticSaints_EN.pdf

Lawler, Andrew, *Kinder, Gentler Vikings? Not According to Their Slaves* (National Geographic 28th
    December 2015) https://www.nationalgeographic.com/news/2015/12/151228-
    vikings-slaves-thralls-norse-scandinavia-archaeology/

Loyn, Henry, *The Vikings in Wales* (University College Cardiff, 1976) https://www.medieval-
    ists.net/2009/10/the-vikings-in-wales/

Maltby, Mark, *The Exploitation of Animals in Roman Britain* (Geography 2016)
    https://www.semanticscholar.org/paper/The-Exploitation-of-Animals-in-Roman-
    Britain-Maltby/5c6072ef18d5aee4d2fb401e222708bd61e38410

Marcher Lord (Wikipedia) https://en.wikipedia.org/wiki/Marcher_Lord

Mesolithic Wales, Wales Prehistory,

https://sites.google.com/a/plaskynastongroup.org/walesprehistory-org/the-stone-age/mesolithic-wales

McCarthy, James *The hillforts of Iron Age Wales and why they might have been built* (Wales Online, 12th August, 2017) https://www.walesonline.co.uk/news/wales-news/hillforts-iron-age-wales-might-13452999

Ports and Harbours in North-east Wales (CPAT – Clwyd, Powys Archaeological Trust) https://cpat.org.uk/ycom/flint/flibib.htm

Prehistoric Henges and Circles (Historic England 31st October 2018) https://historicengland.org.uk/images-books/publications/iha-prehistoric-henges-circles

Prehistoric Wales (Wikipedia) https://en.wikipedia.org/wiki/Prehistoric_Wales

Prehistoric Wales, Teacher Information Pack, (CADW) https://cadw.gov.wales/sites/default/files/2019-05/151214-prehistoricresource-eng.pdf

Prior, Neil, '*Slavery: Welsh weavers 'implicated in US slave trade*" (BBC News, 16th June 2019) https://www.bbc.co.uk/news/uk-wales-48624937

Pryor, Dr Francis, History, (BBC) http://www.bbc.co.uk/history/ancient/british_prehistory/overview_british_prehistory_01.shtml

Recreating Life in Early Wales (Amgueddfa Cymru, Museum Wales, 2nd August, 2007) https://museum.wales/blog/2007-08-02/Re-creating-life-in-early-Wales/

Red Book of Hergest (Wikipedia) https://en.wikipedia.org/wiki/Red_Book_of_Hergest

Roman Conquest, Occupation and Settlement of Wales, AD 47-410 (CADW) https://cadw.gov.wales/sites/default/files/2019-04/InterpplanRomanConquestofWales_EN.pdf

Ross, David *Bronze Age Wales* (Britain Express) https://www.britainexpress.com/wales/history/bronze-age.htm

Ross, David, (Celtic Britain, The Iron Age – 600 BC – 50 AD) https://www.britainexpress.com/History/Celtic_Britain.htm

Ross, David, *Wales in the 14th Century* (Britain Express) https://www.britainexpress.com/wales/history/14th-century.htm

Round Barrow (Wikipedia) https://en.wikipedia.org/wiki/Round_barrow

Royal Welch Fusiliers (Wikipedia) https://en.wikipedia.org/wiki/Royal_Welch_Fusiliers

Ruggeri, Amanda, *The Terrifying Tsunami that devastated Britain* (BBC Earth, 29th March 2016) http://www.bbc.co.uk/earth/story/20160323-the-terrifying-tsunami-that-devastated-britain

Slate Industry in Wales (Wikipedia) https://en.wikipedia.org/wiki/Slate_industry_in_Wales

Slavery in Britain (Wikipedia) https://en.wikipedia.org/wiki/Slavery_in_Britain

Sport in Wales (Wikipedia) https://en.wikipedia.org/wiki/Sport_in_Wales

Stonehenge: Did the stone circle originally stand in Wales? (BBC News, 12th February 2021)
  https://www.bbc.co.uk/news/uk-wales-56029203

Story of Slate (National Slate Museum) https://museum.wales/slate/story-of-
  slate/#:~:text=People%20have%20been%20quarrying%20slate,Edward%20I's%20cas
  tle%20at%20Conwy.&text=In%201787%20the%20'Great%20New,of%20Dinorwig%2
  0and%20Llyn%20Peris.

Thomas Pennant (Wikipedia) https://en.wikipedia.org/wiki/Thomas_Pennant

Timeline of Conflict in Anglo-Saxon Britain (Wikipedia)
  https://en.wikipedia.org/wiki/Timeline_of_conflict_in_Anglo-Saxon_Britain

Wales and the Civil War (Spartacus Educational) https://spartacus-
  educational.com/STUwalesCW.htm

Wales History (BBC Wales) https://www.bbc.co.uk/wales/history/sites/themes/

Welsh Bible (Llyfrgell Genedlaethol Cymru National Library of Wales)
  https://www.library.wales/discover/digital-gallery/printed-material/1588-welsh-
  bible#?c=&m=&s=&cv=&xywh=-886%2C-1%2C4734%2C4026

Welsh Devolution; The Reluctant Dragon (The Economist, 24th November 2012)
  https://www.economist.com/britain/2012/11/24/the-reluctant-dragon

Welsh Liberal Democrats (Wikipedia)
  https://en.wikipedia.org/wiki/Welsh_Liberal_Democrats

Woollen Industry in Wales (Wikipedia)
  https://en.wikipedia.org/wiki/Woollen_industry_in_Wales

Worrall, Simon *British Storms unbury an Ancient Welsh Forest* (National Geographic 26th February, 2014)
  https://www.nationalgeographic.com/news/2014/2/140226-wales-borth-bronze-age-
  forest-legend/

William Morgan (Bible Translator) (Wikipedia)
  https://en.wikipedia.org/wiki/William_Morgan_(Bible_translator)

William Ewart Gladstone (Wikipedia)
  https://en.wikipedia.org/wiki/William_Ewart_Gladstone

Identity

FIFA eligibility rules (Wikipedia) https://en.wikipedia.org/wiki/FIFA_eligibility_rules

Happy Planet Index (New Economics Foundation) www.happyplanetindex.org

Language

Dafis, Cynog, What it will take to get to a million Welsh speakers by 2050, Nation Cymru,
  25th May 2019, https://nation.cymru/opinion/what-it-will-take-to-get-to-a-million-
  welsh-speakers-by-2050/

Medieval Welsh Literature (Wikipedia) https://en.wikipedia.org/wiki/
    Medieval_Welsh_literature

Starkey, Ryan, *A Brief History of British and Irish Languages*
(Starkey Comics, March 1st, 2019) https://starkeycomics.com/2019/03/01/a-brief-
    history-of-british-and-irish-languages/

Welsh language use in Wales, 2013-15, (Llywodraeth Cymru, Welsh Government)
    http://www.comisiynyddygymraeg.cymru/English/Publications%20List/Adroddiad%2
    0-%20Y%20defnydd%20o'r%20Gymraeg%20yng%20Nghymru,%202013-15%20-
    %20Saesneg.pdf

Gwynedd

Aberdaron (Wikipedia) https://en.wikipedia.org/wiki/Aberdaron

About Pwllheli (Pwllheli Cymru) https://www.pwllheli.cymru/information/

Big Train Meets Little Train; exploring on the Great Little Trains of Wales https://bigtrainlit-
    tletrain.com/downloads/BigTrainLittleTrain_Guidebook_2016.pdf

Boston Lodge (Wikipedia) https://en.wikipedia.org/wiki/Boston_Lodge

Brown M J, Evans A D *Physical and geotechnical investigations of the manganese deposits of Rhiw,
    western Llŷn, north Wales Technical Report WF/89/14* (Prepared for the Dept of Trade and
    Industry, Keyworth, Nottingham, 1989)

Cadwalader's Ice cream (Wikipedia)
    https://en.wikipedia.org/wiki/Cadwalader%27s_Ice_Cream

Caley, Arthur *On land and sea* (BBC North West Wales, 29th February 2012)
    http://downloads.bbc.co.uk/wales/archive/bbc-north-west-wales-tywyn-arthur-
    caley.pdf

Caley, Atrhur BBC North West Wales, Tywyn

Church in Wales Inquiry after rector burns bible pages, BBC News 22 July 2011
http://www.bbc.co.uk/news/uk-wales-mid-wales-14241857

Cricieth (Wikipedia) https://en.wikipedia.org/wiki/Criccieth

David Lloyd George (Wikipedia) https://en.wikipedia.org/wiki/David_Lloyd_George

Davidson, Andrew Morfa Harlech, *Archaeological Assessment Report 868* (Prepared for CADW
    April 2010)

Dinas Dinlle (Wikipedia)
https://en.wikipedia.org/wiki/Dinas_Dinlle

Dinas Dinlle Hillfort, Llandwrog, (Coflein)
    https://coflein.gov.uk/en/site/95309/details/dinas-dinlle-hillfort-llandwrog

Dinas Dinlle Iron Age fort saved from erosion (BBC News, 21st, January 2011)
    http://news.bbc.co.uk/local/northwestwales/hi/people_and_places/history/newsid_
    9369000/9369294.stm

Dinas Emrys (Wikipedia) https://en.wikipedia.org/wiki/Dinas_Emrys

Dysynni Valley, (Countryside Council for Wales, Landscape and Wildlife) Cyfoeth Naturiol
    Cymru Natural Resources Wales

Elias, Twm Glaslyn Marsh – *200 Years Since the Construction of the Cob* (Natur Cymru, Issue 50)

Ffestiniog and Welsh Highland Railways https://www.festrail.co.uk/

Ffestiniog Railway (Wikipedia) https://en.wikipedia.org/wiki/Ffestiniog_Railway

Ffynnon Fair, Uwchmynydd, Aberdaron (Well Hopper)
    https://wellhopper.wales/2013/11/01/ffynnon-fair-uwchmynydd-aberdaron/

Gwynedd (Wikipedia) https://en.wikipedia.org/wiki/Gwynedd

Historic Landscape Characterisation, Llŷn – Area 18 Llanengan and Abersoch PRN 33488
    (Gwynedd Archaeological Trust Ymddiriedolaeth Archaeolgecol Gwynedd)
    http://www.heneb.co.uk/hlc/llyn/llyn18.html

Historic Landscape Characterisation

Llŷn – Area 4 Rhiw and Penarfynydd (PRN 33485) (Gwynedd Archaeological Trust
    Ymddiriedolaeth Archaeolgecol Gwynedd)
    http://www.heneb.co.uk/hlc/llyn/llyn4.html

History of Gwynedd during the High Middle Ages (Wikipedia)
    https://en.wikipedia.org/wiki/History_of_Gwynedd_during_the_High_Middle_Ages#:
    ~:text=The%20history%20of%20Gwynedd%20in,11th%20through%20the%2013th%
    20centuries.&text=Gwynedd%20emerged%20from%20the%20Early,causing%20politi-
    cal%20and%20social%20upheaval.

Know; An illustrated guide to the history, culture and environment of Gwynedd and West
    Clwyd, TARGED, 1994, Gwasg Dwyfor

List of Scheduled prehistoric Monuments in Gwynedd (former Merionethshire) (Wikipedia)
    https://en.wikipedia.org/wiki/List_of_Scheduled_prehistoric_Monuments_in_Gwyne
    dd_(former_Merionethshire)

Llanbedrog Information – Headland and Foel Felin Wynt (Jampot)(Llanbedrog Info)
    http://www.llanbedrog.info/

Llandygai (Wikipedia) https://en.wikipedia.org/wiki/Llandygai

Llanystumdwy (Wikipedia) https://en.wikipedia.org/wiki/Llanystumdwy

Llewelyn Fawr ab Iorwerth, Prince of Gwynedd (Geni) https://www.geni.com/people/Llewelyn-
    ab-Iorwerth-Prince-of-Gwynedd/6000000003807598493

Lleyn Peninsula Hills and Mountains (The Mountain Guide) https://www.themountain-
    guide.co.uk/wales/lleyn-peninsula

Llŷn Peninsula (Wikipedia) https://en.wikipedia.org/wiki/Ll%C5%B7n_Peninsula

Meirionnydd (Wikipedia) https://en.wikipedia.org/wiki/Meirionnydd

Nant Gwrtheryn, https://nantgwrtheyrn.org/

Nant Gwrtheyrn (Wikipedia) https://en.wikipedia.org/wiki/Nant_Gwrtheyrn

Nefyn (Wikipedia) https://en.wikipedia.org/wiki/Nefyn

Our History (Rheilffordd Talyllyn Railway) https://www.talyllyn.co.uk/about/history

Owen, Dr Brian, *A Tragic Year in Nefyn* (Stories of Nefyn/ Straeon am Nefyn)
    http://www.nefyn.com/Stories/ATragicYearInNefyn.aspx

Penrhyn Castle (Wikipedia) https://en.wikipedia.org/wiki/Penrhyn_Castle

Penrhyndeudraeth (Wikipedia) https://en.wikipedia.org/wiki/Penrhyndeudraeth

Porthmadog (Wikipedia) https://en.wikipedia.org/wiki/Porthmadog

Portmeirion (Wikipedia) https://en.wikipedia.org/wiki/Portmeirion

Plas Glyn-y-Weddw History (Plas Glyn-y-Weddw)
    https://www.oriel.org.uk/en/history#:~:text=Plas%20Glyn%20y%20Weddw%20wa
    s,to%20Cardiff%20businessman%20Solomon%20Andrews.

R S Thomas Poems (Classic Poetry Series, 2004) www.poemhunter.com

Roberts, David, *Nant Gwrtheyrn* (Rhiw)
    https://www.rhiw.com/pobol/pobol_llyn/david_roberts/nant_gwrtheyrn.htm

Smith, George *Tywyn Coastal Assessment Scheme, Report 555* (Prepared for ABP Marine
    Environmental Research Ltd November 2004)

Return to the Ferry, A Pictorial history of the 15 inch gauge Fairbourne Railway,
    https://www.return2ferry.co.uk/

Roseveare, M J, *Tywyn-Dolgoch Uplands Review* (RCAHMW, May 2006)
    http://orapweb.rcahms.gov.uk/coflein/6/630110.PDF

St Tudwal's Islands (Wikipedia) https://en.wikipedia.org/wiki/Saint_Tudwal%27s_Islands

Sarn Badrig (Wikipedia) https://en.wikipedia.org/wiki/Sarn_Badrig

Stephen, Graham, *Gwaith Powdwr* (Geotopoi, July 28th, 2011)
    https://geotopoi.wordpress.com/2011/07/28/gwaith-powdwr/

The Logboat, Amgueddfa Forwrol Llŷn Maritime Museum, http://www.llyn-maritime-
    museum.co.uk/eng/cwch-boncyff.html

The academic, the minister and the schoolmaster: arson in North Wales, 1936 (Those Who
    Will Not Be Drowned, Mainly About History, June 24th 2011) https://thosewhowill-
    notbedrowned.wordpress.com/

The Village of Llanystumdwy www.llanystumdwy.com

Trefor (Wikipedia) https://en.wikipedia.org/wiki/Trefor

Trewyn, Hywel, *Suspended jail sentence for landlord in Penrhyndeudraeth pub gun row* (North
    Wales Live, 18th April 2013) https://www.dailypost.co.uk/news/north-wales-
    news/suspended-jail-sentence-landlord-penrhyndeudraeth-2651439

Vermaat, Robert, *Castel Guorthegirn* (Vortigern Studies)
    http://www.vortigernstudies.org.uk/artcit/castel.htm

Victoria Dock, Caernarfon (History Points)
    https://historypoints.org/index.php?page=victoria-dock

Visit Snowdonia https://www.visitsnowdonia.info/

Welsh seascapes and their sensitivity to offshore developments (White Consultants)
https://www.whiteconsultants.co.uk/expertise/seascape-character-assessment/welsh-seascapes-and-their-sensitivity-to-offshore-developments/

West of Wales Shoreline Development Plan 2 (February 2011, Consultation Royal Haskoning) file:///C:/Users/Jule/Downloads/Section%204_Coastal%20Area%20D_Introduction_Feb%202011_English%20(2).pdf

Wildlife (Ymddiriedolaeth Ynys Enlli Bardsey Island Trust)
https://www.bardsey.org/wildlife

William Madocks (Wikipedia) https://en.wikipedia.org/wiki/William_Madocks

Ynys Môn

American aircrew memorial, Holyhead (History Points)
https://historypoints.org/index.php?page=american-aircrew-memorial-holyhead#:~:text=This%20memorial%20commemorates%20the%20American,in%20the%20Second%20World%20War.&text=A%20few%20minutes%20later%20the,the%20sea%20off%20Holyhead%20Mountain.

Anglia anchor memorial, Holyhead (History Points)
https://historypoints.org/index.php?page=anglia-anchor-memorial-holyhead#:~:text=Anglia%20anchor%20memorial%2C%20Newry%20Beach,in%20the%20First%20World%20War.

Anglesey (Wikipedia) https://en.wikipedia.org/wiki/Anglesey

Anglesey Energy Island, (Science Café, 13th March 2012) BBC Radio Cymru Wales

Anglesey Landscape Strategy Update 2011, Cyngor Sir Ynys Môn The Isle of Anglesey County Council, https://www.anglesey.gov.uk/documents/Docs-en/Planning/Planning-policy/Local/Supporting/Anglesey-Landscape-Strategy-Update-2011.pdf

Barclodiad y Gawres Burial Chamber (Coflein)
https://coflein.gov.uk/en/site/95545/details/barclodiad-y-gawres-burial-chamber-the-giantesss-apronful-aberffraw

Beaumaris Castle, Cadw https://cadw.gov.wales/visit/places-to-visit/beaumaris-castle

Beddmanarch – Cymyran Site of Special Scientific Interest

Countryside Council for Wales
https://naturalresources.wales/media/644618/SSSI_0492_SMS_EN0014011.pdf

Belgian Promenade, Menai Bridge (History Points)
https://historypoints.org/index.php?page=belgian-promenade-menai-bridge#:~:text=During%20the%20First%20World%20War,It%20was%20rebuilt%20in%201963.

Betteley, Chris, *Locations for radioactive waste burial oonsidered* (Cambrian News, 23rd February 2019) http://www.cambrian-news.co.uk/ article.cfm?id=127517&headline=Locations%20for%20radioactive%20waste%20burial %20considered&sectionIs=news&searchyear=2019

The Bulkeley Arms and Uxbridge Square, Menai Bridge (History Points) https://historypoints.org/index.php?page=the-bulkeley-arms-and-uxbridge-square-menai-bridge#:~:text=In%20the%2018th%20century%20this,battle%20of%20Waterl oo%20in%201815.

The Cefni saltmarsh (History Points) https://historypoints.org/index.php?page=the-cefni-saltmarsh

Drama recounts life from William Bulkeley's diaries, (BBC News, 21st September, 2014) https://www.bbc.co.uk/news/uk-wales-north-west-wales-29288565

Dutch navy memorial, Holyhead (History Points) https://historypoints.org/index.php?page=holyhead-dutch-navy-memorial#:~:text=This%20memorial%2C%20created%20in%202014,during%20the %20Second%20World%20War.&text=Several%20were%20directed%20to%20serve,1 940%2C%20was%20the%20liner%20Stuyvesant.

Evans, Owen, *Anglesey must not be a nuclear waste dumping ground* (North Wales Live, 26th January 2018) https://www.dailypost.co.uk/news/anglesey-must-not-nuclear-waste-14205846

Former air-raid shelter, Holyhead (History Points) https://historypoints.org/index.php?page=former-air-raid-shelter-holyhead

Former flying boat slipway (History Points) https://historypoints.org/index.php?page=site-of-flying-boat-slipway#:~:text=The%20slipway%20at%20Llanfaes%2C%20near,which%20use%20w ater%20as%20runways.&text=In%20the%20grounds%2C%20large%20workshops,by %20the%20Royal%20Air%20Force.

Former Wylfa nuclear power station (History Points) https://historypoints.org/index.php?page=wylfa-nuclear-power-station

Geology, Anglesey http://angleseynature.co.uk/geology.html

Great Escape survivor's club, Rhosneigr (History Points) https://historypoints.org/index.php?mact=News,cntnt01,detail,0&cntnt01articleid=2 80&cntnt01category_id=1&cntnt01returnid=3900

Holyhead (Wikipedia) https://en.wikipedia.org/wiki/Holyhead

Holyhead St Cybi (Britain Express) https://www.britainexpress.com/attractions.htm?attraction=575

Llanddwyn Island (Anglesey History) https://www.anglesey-history.co.uk/places/llanddwyn/

Llys Llywelyn – Medieval Court (St Fagans Amgueddfa
Cymru Museum of Wales) https://museum.wales/stfagans/buildings/llys-llywellyn/

Malltraeth (Wikipedia) https://en.wikipedia.org/wiki/Malltraeth

Menai Bridges (Anglesey History) https://www.anglesey-history.co.uk/places/bridges/

Moelfre War Memorial (History Points)
    https://historypoints.org/index.php?page=moelfre-war-memorial

Natural History of Anglesey (Anglesey History) https://www.anglesey-
    history.co.uk/angnatur.html

Newborough National Nature Reserve and Forest, Anglesey (Cyfoeth Naturial Cymru
    Natural Resources Wales) https://naturalresources.wales/days-out/places-to-
    visit/north-west-wales/newborough/?lang=en

Newborough Warren and Llanddwyn Island National Nature Reserve, Newborough,
    Anglesey (First Nature) https://www.first-nature.com/waleswildlife/
    n-nnr-newborough.php

Newborough Warren reserve (History Points)
    https://historypoints.org/index.php?page=newborough-warren-reserve

Owen, Dr Hugh, *THE DIARY OF BULKELEY OF DRONWY, ANGLESEY, 1630-1636. Introduction
    TRANSACTIONS OF THE ANGLESEY ANTIQUARIAN SOCIETY 1937 pp. 26-172*

Penrhos Coastal Park (Woodland Trust) https://www.woodlandtrust.org.uk/visiting-
    woods/woods/penrhos-coastal-park/

Rhosneigr, (Wikipedia) https://en.wikipedia.org/wiki/Rhosneigr

Sand Dunes (Anglesey Nature) http://angleseynature.co.uk/sanddunes.html

Site of first Land Rover drawing, Red Wharf Bay (History Points)
    https://historypoints.org/index.php?page=land-rover-drawing-site

Site of HMS Thetis beaching (History Points)
    https://historypoints.org/index.php?page=site-of-hms-thetis-beaching

Site of RAF Bodorgan, Malltraeth (History Points)
    https://historypoints.org/index.php?page=site-of-raf-bodorgan-
    malltraeth#:~:text=In%201940%20work%20began%20on,use%20by%20the%20Air
    %20Ministry.&text=At%20this%20point%20the%20airfield,were%20stored%20at%20
    the%20site.

Site of wartime air tragedy, Rhosneigr (History Points)
    https://historypoints.org/index.php?page=site-of-wartime-air-tragedy-rhosneigr

Site of witches' landing, Llanddona (History Points)
    https://historypoints.org/index.php?page=site-of-witches-landing-
    llanddona#:~:text=A%20boat%20full%20of%20witches,in%20the%20early%2020th
    %20century.

Skeleton at Llanbedrgoch, Anglesey, sheds light on Viking Age (BBC News, 25th October
    2012) https://www.bbc.co.uk/news/uk-wales-north-west-wales-20072974

South Stack Lighthouse (Trinity House) https://www.trinityhouse.co.uk/lighthouses-and-
    lightvessels/south-stack-lighthouse

Stanley Embankment (Wikipedia) https://en.wikipedia.org/wiki/Stanley_Embankment

Stena Line ferry terminal (History Points)
    https://historypoints.org/index.php?page=stena-line-ferry-terminal

The Skerries, Isle of Anglesey (Wikipedia)
    https://en.wikipedia.org/wiki/The_Skerries,_Isle_of_Anglesey

Twr Mawr Lighthouse (Wikipedia)
    https://en.wikipedia.org/wiki/T%C5%B5r_Mawr_Lighthouse

Wales Nature and Outdoors, Anglesey, Surfing. (BBC Cymru Wales)
    https://www.bbc.co.uk/wales/nature/sites/surfing/pages/nw_anglesey.shtml

WRVS Volunteer in Newport and surrounding area of South East Wales
Prisoner of War helps out on farm WW2 (BBC People's War, 29th June 2005)
    https://www.bbc.co.uk/history/ww2peopleswar/stories/29/a4301029.shtml

Ynys y Moch, Menai Bridge (History Points)
    https://historypoints.org/index.php?page=ynys-y-moch-menai-
    bridge#:~:text=Ynys%20y%20Moch%20means%20%E2%80%9Cisland,rested%20on
    %20Ynys%20y%20Moch.

Conwy

Airship Repair Site, 1918, Llandudno (History Points)
    https://historypoints.org/index.php?page=airship-repair-site-1918-llandudno

Carneddau (Wikipedia) https://en.wikipedia.org/wiki/Carneddau

Codman Family Tree, Punch and Judy http://www.punchandjudy.com/codtree.htm

Colwyn Bay (Wikipedia) https://en.wikipedia.org/wiki/Colwyn_Bay

Conwy Castle (Wikipedia) https://en.wikipedia.org/wiki/Conwy_Castle

Conwy Castle (Cadw) https://cadw.gov.wales/visit/places-to-visit/conwy-castle

Conwy County Borough (Wikipedia)
    https://en.wikipedia.org/wiki/Conwy_County_Borough

Great Orme (Wikipedia) https://en.wikipedia.org/wiki/Great_Orme

The Great Orme Mines, (Historic UK) https://www.historic-uk.com/HistoryUK/
    HistoryofWales/The-Great-Orme-Mines/

John Collins Funfairs Ltd http://www.johncollinsfunfairs.com/

Kashmiri Goats The Great Orme, Llandudno http://www.llandudno.com/the-great-orme-
    kashmiri-goats/

Kinmel Camp (Wikipedia) https://en.wikipedia.org/wiki/Kinmel_Camp

Knightly's European Leisure Ltd, (Visit Wales)
  https://www.visitwales.com/attraction/adventure-or-themed-attraction/knightlys-
  european-leisure-ltd-1834663

Little Orme (Wikipedia) https://en.wikipedia.org/wiki/Little_Orme

Llandudno (Wikipedia) https://en.wikipedia.org/wiki/Llandudno

Llandudno Pier (Wikipedia) https://en.wikipedia.org/wiki/Llandudno_Pier

Lloyd George Salute Site (History Points) https://historypoints.org/index.php?page=lloyd-
  george-salute-site

Nature Reserves (North Wales Wildlife Trust Ymdderidiaeth Natur Gogledd Cymru)
  https://www.northwaleswildlifetrust.org.uk/nature-reserves

Pen Eye, Penmaenmawr https://www.theeyepenmaenmawr.org/Our-Heritage

The Simons Family – Over 130 Years as Travelling Show People (Wrexham History)
  https://www.wrexham-history.com/simons-family-130-years-travelling-show-people/

Spinnies Aberogwen Nature Reserve (North Wales Wildlife Trust Ymdderidiaeth Natur
  Gogledd Cymru) https://www.northwaleswildlifetrust.org.uk/nature-
  reserves/spinnies-aberogwen

Victoria Pier (Wikipedia) https://en.wikipedia.org/wiki/Victoria_Pier

Welcome to Victoria Pier, Colwyn Bay http://www.victoriapier.co.uk/

'We Were Annihilated': Account of Conwy WWI Captain Reveals Terror of Ypres (National
  Army Museum, 5th December 2014) https://www.nam.ac.uk/

Welcome to Conwy http://welcometoconwy.com/
  #:~:text=Welcome%20to%20Conwy%20is%20a,in%20our%20Conwy%20Business%
  20Directory.

Sir Ddinbych

Carradice, Phil *Death of Bishop Morgan, translator of the Bible into Welsh* (BBC Wales)
  https://www.bbc.co.uk/blogs/wales/entries/66107562-fddd-320b-85e5-
  af1e9e3bb0c7

Castell Dinas Bran (Castles of Wales) http://www.castlewales.com/dinas.html

Cathedral Architecture, The Diocese of St Asaph, (The Church in Wales) https://stasaph-
  cathedral.wales/

Chapman, Dr Adam, WELSH BATTLEFIELDS HISTORICAL AND DOCUMENTARY
  RESEARCH Denbigh – 1646, (RCAHMW) http://battlefields.rcahmw.gov.uk/wp-
  content/uploads/2017/02/Denbigh-Castle-siege-1646-Chapman-2013.pdf

Clywydian Range (Wikipedia) https://en.wikipedia.org/wiki/Clwydian_Range

Clywydian Range and Dee Valley AONB
  https://www.clwydianrangeanddeevalleyaonb.org.uk/

Coastal towns in cycle of poverty, says think tank (BBC News, 5th August 2013)
https://www.bbc.co.uk/news/uk-23549534

Dafarn Dywarch Llandgla (History Points) https://historypoints.org/
index.php?page=dafarn-dywyrch-llandegla

Denbighshire (Wikipedia) https://en.wikipedia.org/wiki/Denbighshire

Denbigh – Denbighshire (British History Online) https://www.british-history.ac.uk/
topographical-dict/wales/pp288-304

Denbighshire Historic Settlements (CPAT)
https://cpat.org.uk/ycom/denbigh/denbigh.htm

Foel Fenlli (The Mountain Guide Wales) https://www.themountainguide.co.uk/wales/
foel-fenlli.htm

Grant, F R, *Analysis of a peat core from the Clywydian Hills, North Wales* (Royal Commission on
the Ancient and Historic Monuments of Wales)
https://www.yumpu.com/en/document/view/37934633/analysis-of-a-peat-core-
from-the-clwydian-hills-north-wales-royal-

Historic Landscape Characterisation, The Vale of Clwyd (CPAT)
https://www.cpat.org.uk/projects/longer/histland/histland.htm

The Making of the Vale of Llangollen and Eglwyseg Historic Landscape (CPAT)
https://www.cpat.org.uk/projects/longer/histland/llangoll/vlintr.htm

The Old Smithy, Llandegla (History Points) https://historypoints.org/index.php?page=the-
old-smithy-llandegla

Park on former cemetery, Rhyl (History Points)
https://historypoints.org/index.php?page=park-on-former-cemetery-rhyl

Llandegla (Wikipedia) https://en.wikipedia.org/wiki/Llandegla

Llangollen (Wikipedia) https://en.wikipedia.org/wiki/Llangollen

Prestatyn (Wikipedia) https://en.wikipedia.org/wiki/Prestatyn

Rhyl (Wikipedia) https://en.wikipedia.org/wiki/Rhyl

Rhyl History Club https://rhylhistoryclub.wordpress.com/

Sir Y Fflint

Bagillt (Wikipedia) https://en.wikipedia.org/wiki/Bagillt

Birchall, John P The Early Industrialists in Flintshire
https://www.themeister.co.uk/hindley/flintshire_industrialists.htm

Dee Estuary (Wikipedia) https://en.wikipedia.org/wiki/Dee_Estuary

Dee Estuary Birding http://www.deeestuary.co.uk/

Flint Castle (Wikipedia) https://en.wikipedia.org/wiki/Flint_Castle

Flint Through The Ages http://www.fflint.co.uk/index.html

Former British Rail ferry, Llannerch-y-Môr (History Points)
   https://historypoints.org/index.php?page=former-british-rail-ferry-llannerch-y-mor
Historic settlements in Flintshire (CPAT)
   https://www.cpat.org.uk/ycom/flints/cpat1142int.pdf
Place, Geoffrey *This is Parkgate* (Parkgate and District Society, 1999)
Rhodes, J N *Derbyshire Influences on Lead Mining in Flintshire in the 17th Century 1968,* (Peak
   District Mines Historical Society) https://pdmhs.co.uk/
Ruabon Moor (Nature's Calendar, BBC)
   http://www.bbc.co.uk/naturescalendar/spring/moors_hills/
   worlds_end/ruabon.shtml
Ryall, Gemma *90 Year Mystery of Soldier Riots* (BBC News, 4th March 2009)
   http://news.bbc.co.uk/1/hi/wales/7923380.stm
St Tegla's Church, Llandegla (History Points) https://historypoints.org/index.php?page=st-
   tegla-s-church-llandegla
Sidoli's ice cream parlour celebrates 100 years in Rhyl (BBC North East Wales, 3rd August
   2010)
   http://news.bbc.co.uk/local/northeastwales/hi/people_and_places/history/newsid_8
   878000/8878979.stm
TSS *Duke of Lancaster* (1955) (Wikipedia)
   https://en.wikipedia.org/wiki/TSS_Duke_of_Lancaster_(1955)
The Old Quay House, Connah's Quay (History Points)
   https://historypoints.org/index.php?page=the-old-quay-house-connahs-quay
The Vale of Llangollen: *Dinbren*, Llangollen Community, Denbighshire, and Llangollen Rural
   Community, Wrexham (CPAT)
   https://www.cpat.org.uk/projects/longer/histland/llangoll/1149.htm

Border and England
Battle of Maserfield (Wikipedia) https://en.wikipedia.org/wiki/Battle_of_Maserfield
Clun Heritage Trail https://www.visitshropshirehills.co.uk/wp-
   content/uploads/2015/12/clun-towntrail.pdf
England-Wales Border (Wikipedia) https://en.wikipedia.org/wiki/
   England%E2%80%93Wales_border
Herefordshire Through Time (Herefordshire Council) https://htt.herefordshire.gov.uk/
Hilltop venue for the 'Sport of Kings' (BBC)
   http://www.bbc.co.uk/shropshire/features/places/oswestry/racecourse.shtml
John Mytton (Wikipedia) https://en.wikipedia.org/wiki/John_Mytton
Johnson, Ben Herefordshire Cider Trail (Historic UK) https://www.historic-
   uk.com/HistoryMagazine/DestinationsUK/Herefordshire-Cider-Trail/

Kington (Wikipedia) https://en.wikipedia.org/wiki/Kington,_Herefordshire

Lambert, Tim *A Short History of Shrewsbury* http://www.localhistories.org/shrewsbury.html

Mainstone (Wikipedia) https://en.wikipedia.org/wiki/Mainstone

Pengwern, Eastern Powys (The History Files) https://www.historyfiles.co.uk/KingListsBritain/BritainPengwern.htm#:~:text=Although%20its%20exact%20origins%20cannot,all%20of%20Powys'%20eastern%20territories.

Rushock, Herefordshire (Wikipedia) https://en.wikipedia.org/wiki/Rushock,_Herefordshire

Welcome to Discovering Shropshire's History http://www.shropshirehistory.org.uk/

Welsh Lost Lands (Wikipedia) https://en.wikipedia.org/wiki/Welsh_Lost_Lands

Welsh Marches (Wikipedia) https://en.wikipedia.org/wiki/Welsh_Marches

Wrecsam

Battle of Crogen (Wikipedia) https://en.wikipedia.org/wiki/Battle_of_Crogen

Chirk (CPAT) https://cpat.org.uk/ycom/wrexham/chirk.pdf

Chirk (Wikipedia) https://en.wikipedia.org/wiki/Chirk

Chirk Castle (Wikipedia) https://en.wikipedia.org/wiki/Chirk_Castle

The history of the township of Brymbo https://thefireonthehill.wordpress.com/

Pontcysyllte Aqueduct and Canal (UNESCO) https://whc.unesco.org/en/list/1303/

Wrexham (Wikipedia) https://en.wikipedia.org/wiki/Wrexham

Wrexham Countryside Strategy – Strategaeth cefn gwlad Wrecsam, Wrexham County Borough, 1998

Powys

Battle of Bryn Glas Hill, Pilleth (National Trails) https://www.nationaltrail.co.uk/en_GB/attraction/battle-bryn-glas-hill-pilleth/

Beacon Ring (CPAT) https://cpat.org.uk/beacon-ring/

Breeze, Andrew *A Welsh Poem of 1485 on Richard III* (Richard III Society) http://www.richardiii.net/downloads/Ricardian/2008_vol18_breeze_welsh_poem.pdf

Breidden Hill (Wikipedia) https://en.wikipedia.org/wiki/Breidden_Hill

Burfa Castle (Wikipedia) https://en.wikipedia.org/wiki/Burfa_Castle

Buttington (CPAT) https://cpat.org.uk/ycom/mont/buttington.pdf

Bro Trefaldwyn (CPAT) https://www.cpat.org.uk/projects/longer/histland/montgom/1074.htm

Digging For victory (Canal and River Trust) https://canalrivertrust.org.uk/enjoy-the-waterways/walking/canal-trails/montgomery-canal-trail/stop-3-digging-for-victory

Evans, Robin *The Battle of Bosworth – A Welsh Victory?* (History Review)
   https://www.questia.com/library/journal/1G1-95106398/the-battle-of-bosworth-
   field-a-welsh-victory-robin
Gladestry (CPAT) https://www.cpat.org.uk/ycom/radnor/gladestry.pdf
Gladestry (Wikipedia) https://en.wikipedia.org/wiki/Gladestry
Granner Wood (Woodlant Trust) https://www.woodlandtrust.org.uk/visiting-
   woods/woods/granner-wood/
Hay-on-Wye (CPAT) https://cpat.org.uk/ycom/bbnp/hayonwye.pdf
Hay-on-Wye (Wikipedia) https://en.wikipedia.org/wiki/Hay-on-Wye
Hay Bluff (Wikipedia) https://en.wikipedia.org/wiki/Hay_Bluff
Historic settlements in Montgomeryshire (CPAT)
   https://www.cpat.org.uk/ycom/mont/cpat1134int.pdf
Kerry Ridgeway, Ancient Trackway (Megalithic Portal)
   https://www.megalithic.co.uk/article.php?sid=15285
Knighton, Powys (Wikipedia) https://en.wikipedia.org/wiki/Knighton,_Powys
Leighton Hall and Home Farm Estate (Leighton Village)
   https://www.leightonnews.com/history/leighton-hall-and-home-farm-estate/
Llanymynech (Wikipedia) https://en.wikipedia.org/wiki/Llanymynech
Llanymynech Rocks (Montgomeryshire Wildlife Trust) https://www.montwt.co.uk/
   nature-reserves/llanymynech-rocks
Machynlleth (Coflein) https://coflein.gov.uk/en/site/96261/details/machynlleth
St Mary's Newchurch, (The Church in Wales)
   https://parish.churchinwales.org.uk/s626/churches/st-marys-newchurch/
Mid Wales and the Battle of Montgomery, 1644 (BCW Project) http://bcw-
   project.org/military/english-civil-war/wales-marches/battle-of-montgomery
Montgomery Canal (Canal and River Trust) https://canalrivertrust.org.uk/enjoy-the-
   waterways/canal-and-river-network/montgomery-canal
The Myddelton Family Home, (National Trust) https://www.nationaltrust.org.uk/
   chirk-castle/features/the-myddelton-family-home
Powys (Wikipedia) https://en.wikipedia.org/wiki/Powys
The Royal Oak, Gladestry, https://www.theroyaloakgladestry.co.uk/
River Teme (Wikipedia) https://en.wikipedia.org/wiki/River_Teme
The Vale of Montgomery (CPAT)
   https://www.cpat.org.uk/projects/longer/histland/montgom/montgom.htm

Sir Fynwy

Abbots of Tintern (Monastic Wales) https://www.monasticwales.org/person/153
Black Rock Lave Net Heritage Fishery http://www.blackrocklavenets.co.uk/

Bulmers (Wikipedia) https://en.wikipedia.org/wiki/Bulmers

Bulwark, Chepstow (Wikipedia) https://en.wikipedia.org/wiki/Bulwark,_Chepstow

Caggle Street Near Llanvertherine (History Points)
https://historypoints.org/index.php?page=llanvetherine-caggle-street

Chepstow (Wikipedia) https://en.wikipedia.org/wiki/Chepstow

Hatterall Ridge (Wikipedia) https://en.wikipedia.org/wiki/Hatterrall_Ridge

The History of Llanthony Priory (Llanthony Priory Hotel) https://www.llanthonyprioryho-tel.co.uk/the-history

More flood warnings as rivers swell (BBC News, 4th February, 2002)
http://news.bbc.co.uk/1/hi/wales/1801187.stm

Lave Net Fishery, Portskewett (History Points)
https://historypoints.org/index.php?page=lave-net-fishery-portskewett

Lave Net Fishing Season to Start (Chepstow Beacon, 27th May, 2015)
http://www.chepstowbeacon.co.uk/article.cfm?id=1092&headline=Lave%20net%20fishing%20season%20to%20start&sectionIs=sport&searchyear=2015

Llangattock Lingoed (Wikipedia) https://en.wikipedia.org/wiki/Llangattock_Lingoed

Llanthony Priory (Wikipedia) https://en.wikipedia.org/wiki/Llanthony_Priory

Monmouth (Wikipedia) https://en.wikipedia.org/wiki/Monmouth

Monmouthshire (Wikipedia) https://en.wikipedia.org/wiki/Monmouthshire

Monmouthshire Flooding Scheme Begins on Wyesham Estate (BBC News, 14th January, 2013) https://www.bbc.co.uk/news/uk-wales-south-east-wales-21008456

Monnow Bridge (Welcome to Monmouth) https://www.visitmonmouthshire.com/places-to-visit/monmouth-in-monmouthshire.aspx

Pandy, Monmouthshire (Wikipedia)
https://en.wikipedia.org/wiki/Pandy,_Monmouthshire

The Picturesque Wye Tour (Visit Monmouthshire)
https://www.visitmonmouthshire.com/picturesquewyetour.aspx

Pugh, Desmond, *Historical Disaster Averted at Commerce House* (Monmouthshire Beacon, 12th August, 2015)
http://www.monmouthshirebeacon.co.uk/article.cfm?id=1614&headline=Histori-cal%20disaster%20avoided%20at%20Commerce%20House&searchyear=2015

Rare Glimpse of Severn Tunnel Pumping Power (South Wales Argus, 5th September, 2011)
https://www.southwalesargus.co.uk/news/9232824.rare-glimpse-of-severn-tunnel-pumping-power/

Redbrook (Wikipedia) https://en.wikipedia.org/wiki/Redbrook

River Wye (Wikipedia)
https://en.wikipedia.org/wiki/River_Wye

Second Severn Crossing (Wikipedia)
   https://en.wikipedia.org/wiki/Second_Severn_Crossing

Severn Bridge (Wikipedia) https://en.wikipedia.org/wiki/Severn_Bridge

Severn Estuary (Wikipedia) https://en.wikipedia.org/wiki/Severn_Estuary

St Cadoc's Church – Llangattock Lingoed (Village Alive Trust)
   https://www.villagealivetrust.org.uk/what-to-see/churches/st-cadocs-church

Tintern (Wikipedia) https://en.wikipedia.org/wiki/Tintern

Tintern Abbey (Wikipedia) https://en.wikipedia.org/wiki/Tintern_Abbey

Tintern Abbey, Wales (Sacred Destinations) http://www.sacred-
   destinations.com/wales/tintern-abbey

West, A D, Durell S E A leV dit, Gray, C, *Severn Estuary Bird Food Monitoring* (Centre for
   Hydrology and Ecology) http://nora.nerc.ac.uk/id/eprint/3402/1/SevernScopingFi-
   nalN003402CR.pdf

White Castle (Cadw) https://cadw.gov.wales/visit/places-to-visit/white-castle

Ysgyryd Fawr (Wikipedia) https://en.wikipedia.org/wiki/Ysgyryd_Fawr

Casnewydd

The Alexandra Docks (Newport Harbour Commissioners) http://www.newportharbour-
   commissioners.org.uk/dock_history.htm

Caldicot and Wentloog Levels (Wikipedia)
   https://en.wikipedia.org/wiki/Caldicot_and_Wentloog_Levels

Ebbw River (Wikipedia) https://en.wikipedia.org/wiki/Ebbw_River

Goldcliff Priory (Wikipedia) https://en.wikipedia.org/wiki/Goldcliff_Priory

Gwent Levels (Gwent Wildlife Trust) https://www.gwentwildlife.org/

Historic Landscape Characterisation, The Gwent Levels (The Glamorgan-Gwent Archaeological Trust) http://www.ggat.org.uk/cadw/historic_landscape/Gwent%20Levels/
   English/GL_Main.htm#:~:text=The%20Outstanding%20Historic%20Landscape%20o
   f,'hand%2Dcrafted'%20landscape.

Moore Scott, Terry Medieval Fish Weirs on the Mid-tidal Reaches of the Severn River
   (Ashleworth-Arlingham) (Glevensis 42, 2009)
   http://www.glosarch.org.uk/Glev%2042%20Pt2.pdf

Morris, Stephen, *A 'Berlin Wall for Wildlife' battle looms over Gwent Levels* (Guardian, 18th
   October, 2013) https://www.theguardian.com/environment/2013/oct/18/gwent-
   levels-wildlife-motorway-plan-m4-conservation

Newport Coast Path https://www.newport.gov.uk/documents/Leisure-and-
   Tourism/Newport-Coast-Path-Map-English.pdf

Newport Docks (Wikipedia) https://en.wikipedia.org/wiki/Newport_Docks

Newport, Wales (Wikipedia) https://en.wikipedia.org/wiki/Newport,_Wales

Newport Wetlands (Wikipedia) https://en.wikipedia.org/wiki/Newport_Wetlands

Newport Wetlands Reserve (RSPB) https://www.rspb.org.uk/reserves-and-
events/reserves-a-z/newport-wetlands/

River Usk (Wikipedia) https://en.wikipedia.org/wiki/River_Usk

Transporter Bridge (Newport Museums and Heritage
Service) https://www.newport.gov.uk/heritage/Transporter-Bridge/Transporter-
Bridge.aspx

Uskmouth power stations (Wikipedia)
https://en.wikipedia.org/wiki/Uskmouth_power_stations

Caerdydd

Cardiff (Wikipedia) https://en.wikipedia.org/wiki/Cardiff

Biodiversity of Cardiff An Introduction to wildlife, habitats and conservation,
Cardiff council Environmental Advice Team on behalf of the Cardiff Biodiversity Partnership. 2008

Cardiff Bay (Wikipedia) https://en.wikipedia.org/wiki/Cardiff_Bay

Cardiff Bay Barrage (Wikipedia) https://en.wikipedia.org/wiki/Cardiff_Bay_Barrage

Cardiff Harbour Authority https://cardiffharbour.com/

Cardiff History, The Forgotten Rogue of Tudor Cardiff (The Penny Post)

Clwb Ifor Bach (Wikipedia) https://en.wikipedia.org/wiki/Clwb_Ifor_Bach

Clwb Ifor Bach History Cardiff (History Points)
https://historypoints.org/index.php?page=clwb-ifor-bach-cardiff

Discover Cardiff Bay https://www.cardiffbay.co.uk/

Flat Holm (Wikipedia) https://en.wikipedia.org/wiki/Flat_Holm

Gilbert de Clare (The Castles of Wales) http://www.castlewales.com/clare.html

Jenkins, David, *Captain Scott sails from Cardiff* (Amgueddfa Cymru, Museum Wales)
https://museum.wales/articles/2010-06-09/Captain-Scott-sails-from-Cardiff/

Lightfoot, K W B, *Rumney Castle* (The Castles of Wales)
http://www.castlewales.com/rumney.html

Lightfoot, K W B, *The Norman Invasion of Wales and Rumney Castle* (Castles of Wales)
http://www.castlewales.com/glam_rum.html

Norman / Medieval (Cardiff Castle) https://www.cardiffcastle.com/time-
traveller/normans.htm

Norwegian Church https://www.norwegianchurchcardiff.com/

Rhymney River (Wikipedia) https://en.wikipedia.org/wiki/Rhymney_River

Romani Cymru: Romany Wales Project (Culture 24, Art, History, Science)
https://www.culture24.org.uk/history-and-heritage/www70842

Steep Holm (Wikipedia) https://en.wikipedia.org/wiki/Steep_Holm

Sweet Baboo (Wikipedia) https://en.wikipedia.org/wiki/Sweet_Baboo

Y Fro Morgannwg

Aberthaw (Wikipedia) https://en.wikipedia.org/wiki/Aberthaw

Aberthaw Power Stations (Wikipedia)
   https://en.wikipedia.org/wiki/Aberthaw_power_stations#:~:text=Aberthaw%20Po
   wer%20Station%20refers%20to,of%20Gileston%20and%20West%20Aberthaw.

Ap Dafydd, Iolo, *Warning over Aberthaw Power Station emissions* (BBC News, 16th October,
   2014) https://www.bbc.co.uk/news/uk-wales-south-east-wales-29640387

Barry and Barry Island (Visit the Vale)
   https://www.visitthevale.com/en/Destinations/Barry.aspx

Barry Docks (Wikipedia) https://en.wikipedia.org/wiki/Barry_Docks

Barry Island (Wikipedia) https://en.wikipedia.org/wiki/Barry_Island

Barry Town United wins Welsh League court battle (BBC News, 9th August, 2013)
   https://www.bbc.co.uk/news/uk-wales-
   23638992#:~:text=A%20football%20club%20has%20won,running%20it%20for%20t
   wo%20seasons.

Barry, Vale of Glamorgan (Wikipedia)
   https://en.wikipedia.org/wiki/Barry,_Vale_of_Glamorgan

Bendrick Rock (British Institute for Geological Conservation) https://geoconservation-
   live.org/sites/bendrick-rock/

A Brief History of Ogmore and Ogmore-by-Sea (St. Brides Major, Southerndown and
   Ogmore-by-Sea Community)
   http://www.stbridesmajor.co.uk/Shared_pages/history/pages_history/history_obs.ht
   m#:~:text=Ogmore%2Dby%2DSea%20grew%20rapidly,Farmhouse%20was%20built
   %20in%201535.

Carradice, Phil, *Llantwit Major: seat of learning,* (BBC, 6th June 2012)
   https://www.bbc.co.uk/blogs/waleshistory/2012/06/llantwit_major_seat_of_learn-
   ing.html

Carreg Castell-y-Gwynt, Llanfynydd (Coflein)
   https://www.coflein.gov.uk/en/site/303853/details/carreg-castell-y-gwynt-cairn-
   llanfynydd

Collins, Peter, *Aberthaw Power Station under renewed threat of closure after named as one of the dirtiest in Europe* (Wales Online, 16th October, 2014)
   https://www.walesonline.co.uk/news/wales-news/aberthaw-power-station-under-
   renewed-7948573

Collins, Peter *Living on the edge! Owners of caravans left dangling over a cliff see their homes moved
   back from the brink* (Wales Online, 4th August, 2014)

https://www.walesonline.co.uk/news/wales-news/porthkerry-park-cliff-edge-caravan-owners-7561755

Cwm Colhuw, Llantwit Major Beach (Visit the Vale) https://www.visitthevale.com/en/Be-Inspired/Sea-Surf-Sand/Cwm-Colhuw-Llantwit-Major-Beach.aspx

Cwm Nash (Visit the Vale) https://www.visitthevale.com/en/Be-Inspired/Sea-Surf-Sand/Cwm-Nash.aspx

Day, Liz, *Barry Island Pleasure Park reopens: How faded memories became a vibrant fairground in just 96 hours* (Wales Online, 3rd April, 2015) https://www.walesonline.co.uk/whats-on/whats-on-news/barry-island-pleasure-park-reopens-8980053

Dyckhoff, Tom, *Let's move to Porthcawl, South Glamorgan* (Guardian, 27th March, 2015) https://www.theguardian.com/money/2015/mar/27/lets-move-porthcawl-south-glamorgan-wales

Geologists' Association South Wales Group Dinosaur footprints at The Bendricks (South Wales Geologist Association) http://swga.org.uk/wp-content/uploads/2020/01/Bendrick.pdf

Glamorgan Heritage Coast (Visit Wales) https://www.visitwales.com/destinations/south-wales/glamorgan-heritage-coast

Gileston (Wikipedia) https://en.wikipedia.org/wiki/Gileston

Lambert, Mark, *An Empty Land Pre-Norman Vale of Glamorgan* (Hidden Glamorgan, 14th October, 2015) http://glamorganhistoryandarchaeology.blogspot.com/

Lavernock (Wikipedia) https://en.wikipedia.org/wiki/Lavernock

Llantwit Major (Wikipedia) https://en.wikipedia.org/wiki/Llantwit_Major

Knapton, Sarah *800-year old monk found poking out of cliff-top* (The Telegraph, 10th March, 2014)

Mathieson, Karl, *UK lobbying to keep open one of Europe's dirtiest coal power stations* (The Guardian, 19th August, 2014) https://www.theguardian.com/environment/2014/aug/19/uk-lobbying-to-keep-open-one-of-europes-dirtiest-coal-power-stations

Ogmore Castle (Castles of Wales) http://www.castlewales.com/ogmore.html

Ogmore-by-Sea (Wikipedia) https://en.wikipedia.org/wiki/Ogmore-by-Sea

Porthkerry (Wikipedia) https://en.wikipedia.org/wiki/Porthkerry

Rhoose (Wikipedia) https://en.wikipedia.org/wiki/Rhoose

St Donats (Wikipedia) https://en.wikipedia.org/wiki/St_Donats

Sully Island (Wikipedia) https://en.wikipedia.org/wiki/Sully_Island

Vale of Glamorgan (Wikipedia) https://en.wikipedia.org/wiki/Vale_of_Glamorgan

Vale of Glamorgan, National Landscape Character, (Cyfoeth Naturiol Cymru Natural Resources Wales, 31st March, 2014)

https://naturalresources.wales/media/682624/nlca36-vale-of-glamorgan-description.pdf

Wick, Vale of Glamorgan (Wikipedia)

    https://en.wikipedia.org/wiki/Wick,_Vale_of_Glamorgan

Pen y Bont

Bridgend (Wikipedia) https://en.wikipedia.org/wiki/Bridgend

Bridgend Origins (Bridgend Town Council)

    http://www.bridgendtowncouncil.gov.uk/bridgend-origins.aspx

History Around the Area – Stormy Down (Kenfig, The Complete History, August 24th,
    2007)

The Irish Celts (The Kenfig Society – Cymdeithas Cynffig)

    https://thekenfigsociety.weebly.com/the-irish-celts.html

Kenfig National Nature Reserve (First Nature) https://www.first-
nature.com/waleswildlife/e-nnr-kenfig.php

Kenfig Pool (Wikipedia) https://en.wikipedia.org/wiki/Kenfig_Pool

Merthyr Mawr (Wikipedia) https://en.wikipedia.org/wiki/Merthyr_Mawr

Merthyr Mawr Sand Dunes (Wikipedia)

    https://en.wikipedia.org/wiki/Merthyr_Mawr_Sand_Dunes

Merthyr Mawr, Kenfig, and Margam Burrows Summary (Glamorgan and Gwent Archaeolog-
    ical Trust) http://www.ggat.org.uk/cadw/historic_landscape/
    kenfig/english/merthyr_mawr_summary.html

Merthyr Mawr Warren National Nature Reserve, near Bridgend (Cyfoeth Naturiol Cymru
    Natural Resources Wales) https://naturalresources.wales/days-out/places-to-
    visit/south-east-wales/merthyr-mawr-nnr/?lang=en

Pilgrimage and Tourism, Llandaff Cathedral, Church in Wales

Porthcawl (Wikipedia) https://en.wikipedia.org/wiki/Porthcawl

Porthcawl Elvis Festival (The Elvies) http://www.elvies.co.uk/

Scheduled Monuments in Bridgend

    https://ancientmonuments.uk/wales/bridgend#.X0Q4_8hKhdg

St Teilo's Church, Merthyr Mawr, Bridgend (The Church in Wales) https://parish.churchin-
    wales.org.uk/l545/churches-en/st-teilos_-en/

St Teilo's Church, Merthyr Mawr (Coflein)

    https://www.coflein.gov.uk/en/site/163/details/st-teilos-church-merthyr-mawr

Welcome to Porthcawl http://www.porthcawl-wales.com/

Castell-nedd

Aberavan Beach (Wikipedia) https://en.wikipedia.org/wiki/Aberavon_Beach

Baglan Bay (Wikipedia) https://en.wikipedia.org/wiki/Baglan_Bay

Baglan Bay Power Station (Wikipedia)
    https://en.wikipedia.org/wiki/Baglan_Bay_power_station

Baglan Energy Park – A Neath-Port Talbot success story http://www.npt-
    business.co.uk/2139

Briton Ferry (Wikipedia) https://en.wikipedia.org/wiki/Briton_Ferry

Brunel Dock Accumulator Tower at Briton Ferry Dock (Stay in Wales) https://www.stayin-
    wales.co.uk/wales_picture.cfm?p=4142

Evans, Edith, *Roman Roads in South East Wales* (Report for Cadw and the Glamorgan Gwent
    Archaeological Trust, September, 2004)
    http://www.ggat.org.uk/cadw/cadw_reports/pdfs/GGAT%2075%20Yr3%20Roads%
    20final.pdf

Excavating the Roman Fort at Neath (The Glamorgan Gwent Archaeological Trust)
    https://ggat.wordpress.com/2010/11/08/excavating-the-roman-fort-at-neath/

Fforest Fawr (UNESCO Geopark) https://www.fforestfawrgeopark.org.uk/

Historic Margam (Parc Gwledig Margam Country Park) http://www.margamcountry-
    park.co.uk/1253

Humphries, Mark *Welsh History Month – Is a Roman milestone the most important object in Welsh
    history?* (Wales Online, 30th April, 2013)
    https://www.walesonline.co.uk/lifestyle/nostalgia/welsh-history-month-roman-
    milestone-3312220

List of Scheduled Monuments in Neath Port Talbot (Wikipedia)
    https://en.wikipedia.org/wiki/List_of_Scheduled_Monuments_in_Neath_Port_Talbot

Margam Discovery Centre (Field Studies Council) https://www.field-studies-
    council.org/locations/margam/

Margam Stones Museum (Wikipedia)
    https://en.wikipedia.org/wiki/Margam_Stones_Museum

Neath (Wikipedia) https://en.wikipedia.org/wiki/Neath

Neath Auxiliary Fort; Nidum, Neath Roman Fort (Coflein)
    https://www.coflein.gov.uk/en/site/301350/details/neath-auxiliary-fort-nidum-neath-
    roman-fort

Neath Port Talbot (Wikipedia) https://en.wikipedia.org/wiki/Neath_Port_Talbot

Neath Port Talbot Land Map Landscape Assessment Final Development Plan (Neath Port
    Talbot County Borough Council Countryside Council For Wales, December 2004)
    https://www.npt.gov.uk/media/9005/spg_landmap_landscape_
    assessment_2004.pdf

Neath Port Talbot Landscape and Seascape Development Plan, Supplementary Planning
    Guidance (Neath Port Talbot County Borough Council, May 2018)
    https://www.npt.gov.uk/media/9004/spg_landscape_seascape_may18.pdf

Neath Roman Fort (Britain Express)
    https://www.britainexpress.com/attractions.htm?attraction=826
Port Talbot (Wikipedia) https://en.wikipedia.org/wiki/Port_Talbot
Port Talbot (Associated British Ports) https://www.abports.co.uk/locations/port-talbot/
Port Talbot Parkway Station (Great Western Railway) https://www.gwr.com/plan-
    journey/stations-and-routes/port-talbot-parkway
Rest Bay (Wales, Nature and Outdoors, BBC Cymru Wales)
    https://www.bbc.co.uk/wales/nature/sites/surfing/pages/se_rest_bay.shtml
Richard Thomas and Baldwins (Wikipedia)
    https://en.wikipedia.org/wiki/Richard_Thomas_and_Baldwins
Richard Thomas and Co (Grace's Guides)
    https://www.gracesguide.co.uk/Richard_Thomas_and_Co
River Kenfig (Wikipedia) https://en.wikipedia.org/wiki/River_Kenfig
River Neath (Wikipedia) https://en.wikipedia.org/wiki/River_Neath
Scunthorpe Steelworks (Wikipedia)
    https://en.wikipedia.org/wiki/Scunthorpe_Steelworks
Sker Grange; Blakescarre (Coflein) https://coflein.gov.uk/en/site/19971/details/sker-
    grangeblakescarre
St Tydug's Church, Tythegston (Coflein)
    https://www.coflein.gov.uk/en/site/408770/details/st-tudwgs-church-tythegston
Tata Steel in South Wales (Tata Steel) https://www.tatasteeleurope.com/en/sustainabil-
    ity/communities/south-wales-community
West, Carl *Welsh Heart with steel at its heart, casts a wary eye at the future* (The Guardian, 25th
    September, 2014) https://www.theguardian.com/uk-news/2014/sep/25/port-talbot-
    wales-steel-tata-job-cuts
Willie, Dai, *Quarella Stone* (Welsh Stone Forum, Newsletter 5, November 2008)

Abertawe
A Brief History of Gower (Gower Peninsula, your Guide to Gower)
Aldhouse-Green, Stephen, Paviland Cave, (British Archaeology, Issue 61, October 2001)
Bracelet Bay (Wikipedia) https://en.wikipedia.org/wiki/Bracelet_Bay
The Bulwark, Llanmadoc Hill (Coflein) https://coflein.gov.uk/en/site/301327/details/
    the-bulwark-llanmadoc-hill
Burry Holms, (Enjoy Gower) https://enjoygower.com/burry-holmes
Burry Holms (Wikipedia) https://en.wikipedia.org/wiki/Burry_Holms
Caswell Bay (Wikipedia) https://en.wikipedia.org/wiki/Caswell_Bay
Cathole Cave, Parkmill (Coflein)
    https://www.coflein.gov.uk/en/site/305612/details/cathole-cave-parkmill

Cil Ifor Top Promontory Fort (Gower) https://coflein.gov.uk/en/site/301311/details/cil-
  ifor-top-promontory-fortcilifor-top-promontory-fort-or-hillfort

Cockle (Bivalve) (Wikipedia) https://en.wikipedia.org/wiki/Cockle_(bivalve)

Crofty (Explore Gower) https://www.explore-gower.co.uk/crofty

Deborah's Hole, (The Wildlife Trust of South and West Wales)
  https://www.welshwildlife.org/nature-reserve/
  deborahs-hole-pilton-gower-swansea/

Exploring the Submerged Landscapes of Gower, Burry Holms (Mesolithic Wales)
  http://www.dyfedarchaeology.org.uk/lostlandscapes/burryholms.html

Gower Caves (Explore Gower) www.exploregower.co.uk

Gower Peninsula (Wikipedia) https://en.wikipedia.org/wiki/Gower_Peninsula

Gower Shipwrecks http://www.gowershipwrecks.co.uk/
  #:~:text=Gower%20Shipwrecks%20%2D%20Welcome,grief%20along%20its%20trea
  cherous%20coastline.

Hardings Down https://www.swansea.gov.uk/hardingsdown

History and Archaeology (Gower Commons) https://www.gowercommons.org.uk/history-
  and-archaeology/

Historic Landscape Characterisation, Gower (Glamorgan-Gwent Archaeological Trust)
  http://www.ggat.org.uk/cadw/historic_landscape/gower/english/Gower_039.htm

How Did Iron Age People Live? BBC Bitesize
  https://www.bbc.co.uk/bitesize/topics/z82hsbk/articles/z8bkwmn#:~:text=Around
  %20the%20walls%20were%20jars,as%20potters%2C%20carpenters%20and%20metal
  workers.

The Iron Age (Amgueddfa Abertawe Swansea Museum)
  http://www.swanseamuseum.co.uk/swansea-a-brief-history/archaeology/iron-age

Jundi, Sophia *Ancient History in Depth: Life in an Iron Age village* (BBC 28th February, 2011)
  http://www.bbc.co.uk/history/ancient/british_prehistory/
  ironage_intro_01.shtml#:~:text=The%20period%20known%20as%20the,750%20BC
  %20to%20AD%2043).&text=Due%20to%20these%20ranges%2C%20and,described%
  20in%20quite%20generalised%20terms.

Landimore Marsh (Jessica's Nature Blog) https://natureinfocus.blog/tag/landimore-
  marsh/

Langland Bay (Wikipedia)

Llanrhidian, Oldwalls and Wernffrwd, (Gower Holidays, Stay and Explore)
  https://www.gowerholidays.com/explore-gower/llanrhidian/

Mumbles (Wikipedia) https://en.wikipedia.org/wiki/Mumbles

Mumbles and Gower (Visit Swansea Bay) https://www.visitswanseabay.com/destina-
  tions/mumbles/

Mussel Gatherers at Whiteford (Jessica's Nature Blog, September 11th, 2012) https://natureinfocus.blog/2012/09/11/mussel-gatherers-at-whiteford/

Nash G H, Beardsley A *The Survey of Cathole Cave, Gower Peninsula, Swansea* (University of Bristol and Terra Measurement Ltd, 2013) http://www.ubss.org.uk/resources/proceedings/vol26/UBSS_Proc_26_1_73-83.pdf

Oxwich (Wikipedia) https://en.wikipedia.org/wiki/Oxwich

Oxwich Bay (Wikipedia) https://en.wikipedia.org/wiki/Oxwich_Bay

Penclawdd Shellfish Processing http://www.penclawddshellfish.co.uk/

Penclawdd (Wikipedia) https://en.wikipedia.org/wiki/Penclawdd

Pennard Cliffs and Burrows (Three Cliffs Bay) (Cyngor Abertawe Swansea Council) https://www.swansea.gov.uk/pennardcliffs

Pennard, Pwll Du and Bishopston Valley, (National Trust) https://www.nationaltrust.org.uk/pennard-pwll-du-and-bishopston-valley

Port Eynon (Wikipedia) https://en.wikipedia.org/wiki/Port_Eynon

Port Eynon Point (The Wildlife Trust of South and West Wales) https://www.welsh-wildlife.org/nature-reserve/port-eynon-point-port-eynon-swansea/

Prince of Wales Dock, Swansea Docks (Coflein) https://coflein.gov.uk/en/site/419501/details/prince-of-wales-dock-swansea-docks-swansea

Promontory Forts and Earthworks (This is Gower)

Rare prehistoric footprints redefined as 7,000 years old (Cardiff University, 28th February, 2017) https://www.cardiff.ac.uk/news/view/615550-rare-prehistoric-footprints-redefined-as-7,000-years-old#:~:text=In%20a%20massive%20time%2Dshift,coast%20back%20by%203%2C000%20years.

Red Lady of Paviland (Wikipedia) https://en.wikipedia.org/wiki/Red_Lady_of_Paviland

Rhossili (Wikipedia) https://en.wikipedia.org/wiki/Rhossili

Rhosili and South Gower Coast (National Trust) https://www.nationaltrust.org.uk/rhosili-and-south-gower-coast

Rhossili at the very tip of the Gower Peninsula was a favourite destination for Dylan.(Dylan Thomas) http://www.dylanthomas.com/index.cfm?articleid=359

South Gower Coast: Long Hole Cliff, Overton, Gower, Swansea https://www.welsh-wildlife.org/wp-content/uploads/2014/03/Long-Hole-Cliff.pdf

Stone Age Man on Burry Holms, (Amgueddfa Cymru Museum Wales) https://museum.wales/articles/2007-04-17/Stone-Age-Man-on-Burry-Holms-Gower-South-Wales

Swansea (Wikipedia) https://en.wikipedia.org/wiki/Swansea

Swansea Bay (Wikipedia) https://en.wikipedia.org/wiki/Swansea_Bay

Swansea Bay's £1bn tidal lagoon given go-ahead (BBC News, 9th June, 2015)
https://www.bbc.co.uk/news/uk-wales-33053003

Swansea Bay and Porthcawl, Marine Character Areas (Cyfoeth Naturiol Cymru, Natural
Resources Wales) https://naturalresources.wales/evidence-and-data/maps/marine-
character-areas/?lang=en

Swansea Bay – Tidal Lagoon Power http://www.tidallagoonpower.com/projects/swansea-
bay/

Swansea Docks (Wikipedia) https://en.wikipedia.org/wiki/Swansea_docks

Thomas, Jeffrey L, Landimore Castle (Castles of Wales)
http://www.castlewales.com/landimor.html

Thomas, Jeffrey L, Pennard Castle (Castles of Wales)
http://www.castlewales.com/pennard.html

Three Cliffs Bay (Wikipedia) https://en.wikipedia.org/wiki/Three_Cliffs_Bay

Walker, Elizabeth, *Burry Holms, Gower Early Mesolithic and later Prehistoric Site* (Amgueddfa
Cymru Museum Wales) https://museum.wales/

Weobly Castle (Cadw) https://cadw.gov.wales/visit/places-to-visit/weobley-castle

Whiteford Burrows, National Nature Reserve and Llanrhidian Saltmarsh (Cyngor Abertawe
Swansea Council) https://www.swansea.gov.uk/whitefordburrowsnaturereserve

Whiteford National Nature Reserve (First Nature) https://www.first-
nature.com/waleswildlife/sw-nnr-whiteford.php

Worm's Head, Swansea https://www.uksouthwest.net/swansea/worms-head/

Sir Gaerfyrddin

Abandoned Communities ..... Machynys
http://www.abandonedcommunities.co.uk/machynys.html

Allt Gelli Felen, Bronze Age Hoard, Myddfai (Coflein)
https://www.coflein.gov.uk/en/site/405005/details/allt-gelli-felen-bronze-age-hoard-
myddfai

Bannon, Christie *How female aviation pioneer Amelia Earhart is still inspiring people in a small
Welsh town 90 years on* (Wales Online, 19th March, 2018)
https://www.walesonline.co.uk/news/local-news/how-female-aviation-pioneer-
amelia-14428579

Bronze Age Britain (Wikipedia) https://en.wikipedia.org/wiki/Bronze_Age_Britain

Bronze Age Hoard found near Kidwelly declared treasure (BBC News, 24th February 2012)
https://www.bbc.co.uk/news/uk-wales-south-west-wales-
17156629#:~:text=A%20%22significant%20discovery%22%20of%20a,a%20spearhea
d%20and%20an%20axe.

Burry Port (Wikipedia) https://en.wikipedia.org/wiki/Burry_Port

Burry Port Lighthouse (Wikipedia) https://en.wikipedia.org/wiki/
Burry_Port_Lighthouse

Carmarthen (Wikipedia) https://en.wikipedia.org/wiki/Carmarthen

Carmarthen, St Peter's Church (Britain Express) https://www.britainexpress.com/attrac-
tions.htm?attraction=555

Carmarthenshire (Wikipedia) https://en.wikipedia.org/wiki/Carmarthenshire

Coygan Cave (Coflein) https://coflein.gov.uk/en/site/103399/details/coygan-cave

Crabs (Marine Biological Association, incorporated by Royal Charter)
https://www.mba.ac.uk/fact-sheet-
crabs#:~:text=Crabs%20belong%20to%20a%20group,often%20with%20spines%20or
%20teeth.

Cwm-Du Round Barrow (Coflein)
https://www.coflein.gov.uk/en/site/416149/details/cwm-du-round-barrowcwmdu-
round-barrow

Dylan Thomas (Wikipedia) https://en.wikipedia.org/wiki/Dylan_Thomas

Dylan Thomas https://www.discoverdylanthomas.com/portfolio-items/dylan-thomas-
birthday-walk-laugharne

Efforts to Make Kidwelly a Nature 'spectacle' gather momentum (Llanelli Star, 27th March,
2013)

Exhibition Captures an Ancient of Fishing (Carmarthen Journal, 20th July, 2011)

Ferryside (Wikipedia) https://en.wikipedia.org/wiki/Ferryside

Fishing in Carmarthenshire (Discover Carmarthenshire) https://issuu.com/discovercar-
marthenshire/docs/carmarthenshire-fishing

Geology (MOD Pendine) https://www.qinetiq.com/pendine/conservation

Gowerton (Wikipedia) https://en.wikipedia.org/wiki/Gowerton

HARRIES BUYS GILMAN QUARRY BUSINESS (Insider Media Ltd 10th November 2011)

Heritage Locations, Kymer's Canal (National Transport Trust) https://www.nationaltrans-
porttrust.org.uk/heritage-sites/heritage-detail/kymers-canal

Hudson, Paul *Blue Bird recreates land speed record attempt* (The Telegraph, 3rd June, 2015)
https://www.telegraph.co.uk/motoring/news/9324224/100-years-of-Bluebird-
record-breakers-celebrated.html

Hull, Lise, Loughor Castle (Castles of Wales) http://www.castlewales.com/loughor.html

Machynys (Wikipedia) https://en.wikipedia.org/wiki/Machynys

Key Sites Southwest Wales – Neolithic and early Bronze Age, (A Research Framework for
the Archaeology of Wales Key Sites, Southwest Wales, 22nd December, 2003)
https://www.archaeoleg.org.uk/pdf/neolithic/KEY%20SITES%20SW%20WALES%20
NEOLITHIC%20AND%20EARLIER%20BRONZE%20AGE.pdf

Kidwelly (Wikipedia) https://en.wikipedia.org/wiki/Kidwelly

Kidwelly and Llanelly Canal (Wikipedia)
   https://en.wikipedia.org/wiki/Kidwelly_and_Llanelly_Canal

Kidwelly (Bird Guides) https://www.birdguides.com/sites/europe/britain-
   ireland/britain/wales/carmarthen/kidwelly/

Kidwelly and the Gwendraeth (Discover Carmerthenshire) http://www.discovercar-
   marthenshire.com/places/kidwelly-the-gwendraeth/

Kidwelly RFC https://kidwelly.rfc.wales/

Laugharne (Wikipedia) https://en.wikipedia.org/wiki/Laugharne

Llanelli, Dyfed Bronze Age (Archi UK) http://www.archiuk.com/cgi-bin/web-
   archi.pl?PlacenameFromPlacenameFinder=Llanelli&CountyFromPlacenameFinder=Dyf
   ed&distance=10000&ARCHIFormNGRLetter=SN&ARCHIFormNGR_x=50&ARCHI-
   FormNGR_y=00&info2search4=placename_search

Llanelli (Wikipedia) https://en.wikipedia.org/wiki/Llanelli

Llanelli RFC (Wikipedia) https://en.wikipedia.org/wiki/Llanelli_RFC

Llanelli Ranked Second

Llanelli Wetland Centre https://www.wwt.org.uk/wetland-centres/llanelli

Lyn, John, Sosban Restaurant (Llanelli Community Heritage)
   https://www.llanellich.org.uk/

Morris, W Hill, Ward, Anthony H, *Antiquarian Exploration of Presumed Bronze Age Sepulchral*
   Remains on Allt Cunedda, South East Dyfed. (Extracted from The Antiquary, published and
   copyrite held by The Carmarthenshire Antiquarian Society. http://www.kidwellyhis-
   tory.co.uk/Articles/AlltCunedda/AlltCunedda.htm

Llanmiloe (Wikipedia) https://en.wikipedia.org/wiki/Llanmiloe

Llansaint (Wikipedia) https://en.wikipedia.org/wiki/Llansaint

Llansteffan http://www.llansteffan.com/category/history/

Llansteffan (Wikipedia) https://en.wikipedia.org/wiki/Llansteffan

Loughor (Wikpedia) https://en.wikipedia.org/wiki/Loughor

Loughor, Glamorgan (A Vision of Britain Through Time)
   https://www.visionofbritain.org.uk/

Marros, Carmarthenshire (A Vision of Britain Through Time)
   https://www.visionofbritain.org.uk/place/11008

Meinir Gwyr, Glandy Cross (Coflein) https://coflein.gov.uk/en/site/
   304287/details/meini-gwyr-glandy-cross

Millennium Coastal Path, Llanelli (Sustrans) https://www.sustrans.org.uk/find-a-route-on-
   the-national-cycle-network/millennium-coastal-path-llanelli

Millennium Coastal Park (Visit Wales) https://www.visitwales.com/attraction/country-
   park/millennium-coastal-park-1843140

Move to Burry Port Wales (Coast) https://www.coastmagazine.co.uk/content/move-toburry-port-wales

Mynydd Llangyndeyrn Mountain (Discovering Carmarthenshire) http://www.discovercarmarthenshire.com/

North Dock, Llanelli Waterside, https://www.llanelli-waterside.wales/development-opportunities/north-dock/

North Dock, Llanelli: Engine House, The Pump House (Coflein)
https://coflein.gov.uk/en/site/34208/details/north-dock-llanelli-engine-housethe-pumphouse-llanelli

Owen G Dyfnallt, Agriculture – The eighteenth and early nineteenth centuries, A History of Carmarthenshire (Gen UK) https://www.genuki.org.uk/big/wal/CMN/Lloyd7

Pembrey (Wikipedia) https://en.wikipedia.org/wiki/Pembrey

Pendine (Wikipedia) https://en.wikipedia.org/wiki/Pendine

Pendine (MOD Qinetiq) https://www.qinetiq.com/pendine

Pilgrims Graves by ruins of St Michael's Church (British Listed Buildings)
https://britishlistedbuildings.co.uk/300025491-pilgrims-graves-by-ruins-of-st-michaels-church-st-clears#.X0zgb8hKhdg

Pendine (Gen UK) https://www.genuki.org.uk/big/wal/CMN/Pendine/

Pembrey Country Park (Discovering Carmarthenshire) http://www.pembreycountry-park.wales/

River Gwendraeth (Wikipedia) https://en.wikipedia.org/wiki/River_Gwendraeth

River Loughor (Wikipedia) https://en.wikipedia.org/wiki/River_Loughor

River Taf (Wikipedia) https://en.wikipedia.org/wiki/River_Taf

River Tywi (Wikipedia) https://en.wikipedia.org/wiki/River_Tywi

Sandy, Carmarthenshire, (Wikipedia)
https://en.wikipedia.org/wiki/Sandy,_Carmarthenshire

Sawyl Penuchel (Wikipedia) https://en.wikipedia.org/wiki/Sawyl_Penuchel

St Clear's (Wikipedia) https://en.wikipedia.org/wiki/St_Clears

St Lawrence's Church, Marros (Coflein)
https://coflein.gov.uk/en/site/413036/details/st-lawrences-church-marros

Stunning gold relic unearthed in Gwynedd (Amgueddfa Cymru, Museum Wales, 26 April 2007) https://museum.wales/blog/2007-04-26/Stunning-gold-relic-unearthed-in-Gwynedd/

Tappenden, Roz, *Carmarthenshire Cairn Reveals Links With Bronze Age Scotland* (Culture 24, 17th February, 2006) https://www.culture24.org.uk/history-and-heritage/archaeology/art34334

Thomas, Jeffrey L, Laugharne Castle (Castles of Wales)
http://www.castlewales.com/laugharn.html

The Rebecca Riots (BBC History) https://www.bbc.co.uk/wales/history/sites/themes/
society/politics_rebecca_riots.shtml

The Valleys Regional Park (Llywodraeth Cymru)
https://gov.wales/sites/default/files/publications/2018-12/181203-valleys-regional-
park-prospectus.pdf

Thomas, Jeffrey L *Kidwelly Castle* (Castles of Wales)
http://www.castlewales.com/kidwelly.html

Thomas, Jeffrey L St Clear's Castle (Castles of Wales)
http://www.castlewales.com/stclears.html

Turner, Robin *Villages Row over Earhart Landings Wales* Online 19th February, 2008
https://www.walesonline.co.uk/news/wales-news/villages-row-over-earhart-landing-
2196852

Welcome to Machynys Golf Club https://www.machynys.com/

Sir Benfro

Abereiddy (Wikipedia) https://en.wikipedia.org/wiki/Abereiddy

Abermawr (Wikipedia) https://en.wikipedia.org/wiki/Abermawr

Alderson, Alf, British Beach of the Week – Abermawr (Telegraph, 3rd September, 2007)
https://www.telegraph.co.uk/travel/destinations/europe/uk/wales/738179/
British-beach-of-the-week-Abermawr.html

Alderson, Alf, Beach of the Week – Freshwater West (Telegraph, Monday 24th August, 2020)
https://www.telegraph.co.uk/travel/737627/Beach-of-the-week-Freshwater-
West.html

Amroth (Wikipedia) https://en.wikipedia.org/wiki/Amroth

Angle Pembrokeshire (Wikpedia) https://en.wikipedia.org/wiki/Angle,_Pembrokeshire

Barafundle Bay (Wikipedia) https://en.wikipedia.org/wiki/Barafundle_Bay

The Bitches Rocks, (Voyage of Discovery) https://www.ramseyisland.co.uk/the-
islands/the-bitches-rocks/

The Blue Lagoon, Abereiddi (National Trust) https://www.nationaltrust.org.uk/abereiddi-
to-abermawr/features/the-blue-lagoon-abereiddi

Broad Haven (Wikipedia) https://en.wikipedia.org/wiki/Broad_Haven

Broad Haven South (Wikipedia) https://en.wikipedia.org/wiki/Broad_Haven_South

Caerfai Bay (Wikipedia) https://en.wikipedia.org/wiki/Caerfai_Bay

Caldey Island (Wikipedia) https://en.wikipedia.org/wiki/Caldey_Island

Carreg Samson (Wikipedia) https://en.wikipedia.org/wiki/Carreg_Samson

Carradice, Phil, *The Welsh 'Whisky Galore!'* (BBC Wales)
https://www.bbc.co.uk/blogs/wales/entries/91ed4f4d-28c0-3fce-b1f7-
b9180385d567

Castle Point, Old Fort, Fishguard Fort (Coflein)
https://www.coflein.gov.uk/en/site/276025/details/
castle-point-old-fort-fishguard-fort

Castlemartin Firing Range Information, Milford Marina
https://www.milfordmarina.com/about/accessing-the-marina/castlemartin-range

Castlemartin Training Area (Wikipedia)
https://en.wikipedia.org/wiki/Castlemartin_Training_Area

Ceibwr Bay (Wikipedia)
https://en.wikipedia.org/wiki/Ceibwr_Bay

Ceibwr Beach, (Bluestone)
https://www.bluestonewales.com/pembrokeshire/beaches/ceibwr

Chapel of St Non (Wikipedia) https://en.wikipedia.org/wiki/Chapel_of_St_Non

Coetan Arthur Dolmen (The Megalithic Portal)
https://www.megalithic.co.uk/article.php?sid=423

Cook, Nikki, Prehistoric funerary and ritual sites in Pembrokeshire (Pembrokeshire Historical Society)
http://www.pembrokeshirehistoricalsociety.co.uk/prehistoric-funerary-ritual-sites-pembrokeshire-nikki-cook/

Cwm Yr Eglwys Beach (Visit Pembrokeshire) https://www.visitpembrokeshire.com/explore-pembrokeshire/beaches/cwm-yr-eglwys

Dale Beach (Visit Pembrokeshire) https://www.visitpembrokeshire.com/explore-pembrokeshire/beaches/dale

Dale Fort (Field Studies Council) https://www.field-studies-council.org/locations/dalefort/

Denholm-Hall, Rupert Wales welcomes one of the world's first tidal energy generators at Ramsey Sound in Pembrokeshire, 7th August, 2014 https://www.walesonline.co.uk/business/business-news/wales-welcomes-one-worlds-first-7578186

Dinas Fach Promontory Fort (Megalithic Portal)
https://www.megalithic.co.uk/article.php?sid=17221

Dinas Island (Wikipedia) https://en.wikipedia.org/wiki/Dinas_Island

Dinas Island Spectacular Walk (National Trust) https://www.nationaltrust.org.uk/strumble-head-to-cardigan/trails/dinas-island-spectacular-walk

Dockyard and Industry – Pembroke Dock History
http://www.pembrokedockhistory.co.uk/dockyarddindustry.htm

Druidston Beach (Visit Pembrokeshire) https://www.visitpembrokeshire.com/explore-pembrokeshire/beaches/druidston-haven

Dyfed Prehistoric Sites (Britain Express) https://www.britainexpress.com/attraction-search.htm?AttractionType=Prehistoric&County=Dyfed

East Angle Bay and Beach (Visit Pembrokeshire) https://www.visitpembrokeshire.com/
explore-pembrokeshire/beaches/east-angle-bay

Fishguard (Wikipedia) https://en.wikipedia.org/wiki/Fishguard

Fishguard Port (Fishguard Port Authority) http://www.fishguardport.com/

Fishguard and Goodwick (Wikipedia) https://en.wikipedia.org/
wiki/Fishguard_and_Goodwick

Freshwater East Beach (Visit Pembrokeshire) https://www.visitpembrokeshire.com/
explore-pembrokeshire/towns-and-villages/freshwater-east

Freshwater West Beach (National Trust) https://www.nationaltrust.org.uk/features/fresh-
water-west-beach

Friends of Friendless Churches https://friendsoffriendlesschurches.org.uk/

Gateholm (Wikipedia) https://en.wikipedia.org/wiki/Gateholm

Gateholm Dig Report (Time Team, Channel 4) https://www.channel4.com/
programmes/time-team/articles/all/gateholm-dig-report/377

Gateholm Island Ancient Village or Settlement (Megalithic Portal)
https://www.megalithic.co.uk/article.php?sid=7344

Gelliswick Bay (Pembrokeshire Beaches)

The Harbour in Lower Town Fishguard (Pembrokeshire Council)
https://www.pembrokeshire.gov.uk/harbours/the-harbour-in-lower-town-fishguard

Historic Barracks Put up for Sale Wales Online, 13th August, 2010 https://www.waleson-
line.co.uk/news/wales-news/historic-barracks-put-up-sale-1902762

Iggulden, Amy, The South Wales Missile Crisis (The Telegraph, 3rd May, 2006)

Johnston, Chris, Deal to save Milford Haven oil refinery collapses (The Guardian, 5th
November, 2014) https://www.theguardian.com/uk-news/2014/nov/05/milford-
haven-oil-refinery-deal-collapses-jobs#:~:text=Hundreds%20of%20jobs%20in%20Wal
es,Gary%20Klesch%20for%20several%20months.

The Last Invasion of Britain (Historic Britain) https://www.historic-
uk.com/HistoryUK/HistoryofWales/The-Last-Invasion-of-Britain/

Lydstep Cliffs and Caverns Walk (National Trust) https://www.nationaltrust.org.uk/tudor-
merchants-house/trails/lydstep-cliffs-and-caverns-walk

Manorbier (Wikipedia) https://en.wikipedia.org/wiki/Manorbier

Marine Energy Test Area https://www.marineenergywales.co.uk/meta/

Marloes (Wikipedia) https://en.wikipedia.org/wiki/Marloes

Marloes Peninsula Pembrokeshire Coast National Park LCA 9 – MARLOES PENINSULA
https://www.pembrokeshirecoast.wales/
wp-content/uploads/2019/04/LCA9FinalJune11E.pdf

Marloes and St Bride's Community https://www.marloes.org.uk/

289

Marloes Sands and Mere (National Trust) https://www.nationaltrust.org.uk/
    marloes-sands-and-mere

Martins Haven Beach (Bluestone) https://www.bluestonewales.com/
    pembrokeshire/beaches/martins-haven

Milford Haven (Wikipedia) https://en.wikipedia.org/wiki/Milford_Haven

Milford Haven Refinery https://en.wikipedia.org/wiki/Milford_Haven_Refinery

Mill Haven (Beach Guide Wales) https://beachguide.wales/pembrokeshire/mill-haven.php

Monk Haven Beach, (Bluestone) https://www.bluestonewales.com/
    pembrokeshire/beaches/monk-haven

Monkstone Beach (Visit Pembrokeshire) https://www.visitpembrokeshire.com/
    explore-pembrokeshire/beaches/monkstone

Murco Refinery in Milford Haven bought by Singapore Company (Wales Online, 13th
    March, 2015) https://www.walesonline.co.uk/business/business-news/
    murco-refinery-milford-haven-bought-8837707

National Trail Officer's Survey Castlemartin Trail https://www.nationaltrail.co.uk/
    en_GB/short-routes/castlemartin-range/

Nevern Estuary (Newport Pembs) http://www.newportpembs.co.uk/articles/
    nevern-river-newport-pembs.php

New Sandy Haven Crossing welcomed by local communities, Pembrokeshire Coast National
    Park https://www.pembrokeshirecoast.wales/?PID=67&NewsItem=1564

Newgale Beach, Bluestone,
    https://www.bluestonewales.com/pembrokeshire/beaches/newgale

Newgale Beach (Visit Pembrokeshire) https://www.visitpembrokeshire.com/
    explore-pembrokeshire/beaches/newgale

Newport Pembrokeshire (Wikipedia) https://en.wikipedia.org/wiki/
    Newport,_Pembrokeshire

Neyland Marina and Attractions (Visit Pembrokeshire)
    https://www.visitpembrokeshire.com/explore-pembrokeshire/towns-and-
    villages/neyland

Neyland (Wikipedia) https://en.wikipedia.org/wiki/Neyland

Pembroke Castle https://pembrokecastle.co.uk/about-us/history

Pembroke Dock (Wikipedia) https://en.wikipedia.org/wiki/Pembroke_Dock

Pembroke, Pembrokeshire, (Wikipedia)
    https://en.wikipedia.org/wiki/Pembroke,_Pembrokeshire

Pembroke Refinery (Wikipedia) https://en.wikipedia.org/wiki/Pembroke_Refinery

Pembroke Yeomanry (Wikipedia) https://en.wikipedia.org/wiki/Pembroke_Yeomanry

Pentre Ifan (Wikipedia) https://en.wikipedia.org/wiki/Pentre_Ifan

Pierpoint, Chris, *Harbour porpoise (Phocoena phocoena) foraging strategy at a high energy, near-shore site in south-west Wales, UK* (ResearchGate, September, 2008)
   https://www.researchgate.net/publication/231775829_Harbour_porpoise_Phocoena_
   phocoena_foraging_strategy_at_a_high_energy_near-shore_site_in_south-
   west_Wales_UK

Popton Fort (Wikipedia) https://en.wikipedia.org/wiki/Popton_Fort

Port of Milford Haven (Milford Haven Port Authority) https://www.mhpa.co.uk/

Porthclais (Wikipedia) https://en.wikipedia.org/wiki/Porthclais

Porthgain (Wikipedia) https://en.wikipedia.org/wiki/Porthgain

Preseli Hills (Wikipedia) https://en.wikipedia.org/wiki/Preseli_Hills

Prestage, Michael, *Texaco offers to buy village,* (The Independent, 9th August, 1992)
   https://www.independent.co.uk/news/uk/texaco-offers-to-buy-village-1539321.html

Pwll Gwylog (National Trail) https://www.nationaltrail.co.uk/en_GB/attraction/pwll-gwylog/

Pwllgwaelod (Wikipedia) https://en.wikipedia.org/wiki/Pwllgwaelod

Ramsey, Pembrokeshire Coast National Park,
   https://www.pembrokeshirecoast.wales/things-to-do/pembrokeshires-islands/ramsey/

Ramsey Island (Wikipedia) https://en.wikipedia.org/wiki/Ramsey_Island

Ramsey Island Nature Reserve (RSPB)
   https://community.rspb.org.uk/placestovisit/ramseyisland/b/ramseyisland-blog

Rise, Brian, Edward Saint Carannog, Encyclopedia Mythica,
   https://pantheon.org/articles/c/carannog.html

Rhoscrowther (Archaeology in Wales)
   http://www.dyfedarchaeology.org.uk/HLC/milford/area/341.htm

Saundersfoot (Wikipedia) https://en.wikipedia.org/wiki/Saundersfoot

Seascape Character Assessment, Pembrokeshire Coast National Park Authority,
   https://www.pembrokeshirecoast.wales/wp-content/uploads/2019/04/
   Seascape-SPG-Final-English-Dec-2013.pdf

Skomer National Nature Reserve, Marine Nature Reserve https://www.first-nature.com/waleswildlife/sw-nnr-skomer.php

The Shed Bistro Porthgain http://www.theshedporthgain.co.uk/

Solva (Wikipedia) https://en.wikipedia.org/wiki/Solva

St Ann's Head Lighthouse (Trinity House) https://www.trinityhouse.co.uk/lighthouses-and-lightvessels/st-anns-head-lighthouse

St David's Head (Wikipedia) https://en.wikipedia.org/wiki/St_David%27s_Head

St David's Pembrokeshire Coast National Park LCA 18 – ST. DAVID'S HEADLAND
   https://www.pembrokeshirecoast.wales/wp-
   content/uploads/2019/04/LCA18FinalJune11E.pdf

St David's Peninsula (National Trust) https://www.nationaltrust.org.uk/st-davids-peninsula

St Dogmael's Abbey (Wiki) https://en.wikipedia.org/wiki/St_Dogmaels_Abbey

St Govan's Chapel (Wikipedia) https://en.wikipedia.org/wiki/St_Govan%27s_Chapel

Stack Rock Fort (Wikipedia) https://en.wikipedia.org/wiki/Stack_Rock_Fort

Stackpole (National Trust) https://www.nationaltrust.org.uk/stackpole

Standing stones and hill forts in St David's (National Trust)
https://www.nationaltrust.org.uk/st-davids-peninsula/features/standing-stones-and-hill-forts-in-st-davids#:~:text=Standing%20stones%20and%20tombs,dates%20back%20to%20around%204000BC

Stonehenge 'bluestone' quarries confirmed 140 miles away in Wales (UCL, 7th December, 2015) https://www.ucl.ac.uk/news/2015/dec/stonehenge-bluestone-quarries-confirmed-140-miles-away-wales#:~:text=Stonehenge%20'bluestone'%20quarries%20confirmed%20140%20miles%20away%20in%20Wales,-7%20December%202015&text=Excavation%20of%20two%20quarries%20in,they%20were%20quarried%20and%20transported.

Strumble Head Lighthouse (Wikipedia)
https://en.wikipedia.org/wiki/Strumble_Head_Lighthouse

Stackpole National Nature Reserve (Natural Resources Wales)
https://naturalresources.wales/days-out/places-to-visit/south-west-wales/stackpole-warren-national-nature-reserve/?lang=en

Stackpole Wildlife Walk (National Trust) https://www.nationaltrust.org.uk/stackpole/trails/stackpole-wildlife-walk

Tenby (Wikipedia) https://en.wikipedia.org/wiki/Tenby

Tidal Energy, Ramsey Sound https://tethys.pnnl.gov/project-sites/ramsey-sound

Trefin (Wikipedia) https://en.wikipedia.org/wiki/Trefin

Whitesands Beach (Visit Pembrokeshire) https://www.visitpembrokeshire.com/explore-pembrokeshire/beaches/whitesands

Wisemans Bridge and Stepaside (Visit Pembrokeshire)
https://www.visitpembrokeshire.com/explore-pembrokeshire/towns-and-villages/wisemans-bridge-and-stepaside

Ceredigion

Aberaeron (Wikipedia) https://en.wikipedia.org/wiki/Aberaeron

Aberarth (Wikipedia) https://en.wikipedia.org/wiki/Aberarth

Aberporth Airport (Wikipedia) https://en.wikipedia.org/wiki/Aberporth_Airport

Aberystwyth (Wikipedia) https://en.wikipedia.org/wiki/Aberystwyth

Aberystwyth (Coflein) https://coflein.gov.uk/en/site/33035/details/aberystwyth

Aberystwyth and Tregaron Bank (Wikipedia) https://en.wikipedia.org/wiki/Aberystwyth_and_Tregaron_Bank

The Benefice of Cardigan with Mwnt, Y Ferwig, and Llancoedmor in the Diocese of St Davids, (The Church in Wales) https://parish.churchinwales.org.uk/d841/churches-en/

Borth (Wikipedia) https://en.wikipedia.org/wiki/Borth

Cardigan and St Dogmael's http://cardigan-stdogmaels.co.uk/st-dogmaels-village/

Cardigan, Ceredigion (Wikipedia) https://en.wikipedia.org/wiki/Cardigan,_Ceredigion

Clarach Bay (Wikipedia) https://en.wikipedia.org/wiki/Clarach_Bay

Cors Fochno (Wikipedia) https://en.wikipedia.org/wiki/Cors_Fochno

Cors Fochno (JNCC) https://sac.jncc.gov.uk/site/UK0014791

Cymtydu Beach (Cardigan Bay Coast and Country) https://www.cardigan-bay.com/cwmtydu-beach-cardigan-bay/

Discover Ceredigion http://www.discoverceredigion.wales/

Discover Mwnt (National Trust)
    https://www.nationaltrust.org.uk/mwnt/features/discover-mwnt

Drovers, The Museum Collection
    https://pilgrim.ceredigion.gov.uk/index.cfm?articleid=2246

Dyfi National Nature Reserve – Borth Bog (Cors Fochno) and Ynyslas Dunes, Borth, Southwest Wales (First Nature) https://www.first-nature.com/waleswildlife/sw-nnr-dyfi.php

Dylan Thomas, his life, and New Quay https://www.newquay-westwales.co.uk/dylan_thomas.htm

EVENTS AND PROCESSES THAT HAVE HELPED SHAPE THE HISTORIC LANDSCAPE OF UPLAND CEREDIGION, Dyfed Archaeology
    http://www.dyfedarchaeology.org.uk/HLC/uplandceredigion/_uplandceredigionhistorical.htm

Everything Aberystwyth http://www.everythingaberystwyth.co.uk/

Felin Cwm Tydu Felin Huw (Coflein) https://coflein.gov.uk/en/site/417702/details/felin-cwm-tydi-felin-huw

Y Ferwig, Cardiganshire, A Vision of Britain through time,
    https://www.visionofbritain.org.uk/place/4095

Furnace, Ceredigion (Wikipedia) https://en.wikipedia.org/wiki/Furnace,_Ceredigion

Gjerlov, Charlotte, CORE MANAGEMENT PLAN INCLUDING CONSERVATION OBJECTIVES FOR CORS FOCHNO SAC, Countryside Council For Wales, 14th February, 2011,
    https://naturalresources.wales/media/671544/Cors%20Fochno%20SAC%20management%20plan.pdf

Gwbert (Wikipedia) https://en.wikipedia.org/wiki/Gwbert

The Life of Taliesin the Bard (BBC Themes)
    https://www.bbc.co.uk/wales/history/sites/themes/society/myths_taliesin.shtml

Llangrannog (Wikipedia) https://en.wikipedia.org/wiki/Llangrannog

Llangranog – Traeth yr Ynys Lochtyn Grid Reference: SN 310542 – SN 317550 (Geology
    Wales) http://www.geologywales.co.uk/central-wales-
    rigs/PDFs/llangranog_traeth_yr_ynys_lochtyn.pdf

Llanon, Ceredigion, Tourist Information https://www.aboutllanon.co.uk/

Llanrhystud (Wikipedia) https://en.wikipedia.org/wiki/Llanrhystud

LLANSANTFFRAED PARISH CHURCH, http://www.llanon.org.uk/jimweb/church-
    home.HTM

The Lost Lands of our Ancestors, Exploring the Submerged Lands of Prehistoric Wales
    (Dyfed Archaeology) http://www.dyfedarchaeology.org.uk/lostlandscapes/

Marine Special Areas of Conservation SACs, Ceredigion County Council
    https://www.ceredigion.gov.uk/resident/coast-countryside/conservation-and-
    wildlife/marine-conservation/

Mobbs, Paul, & MEIR, The Quiet Militarisation of West Wales' Skies
    http://www.fraw.org.uk/meir/drones.html

MOD Aberporth (Qinetiq) https://www.qinetiq.com/aberporth/about

Mwnt (Wikipedia) https://en.wikipedia.org/wiki/Mwnt

New Quay (Wikipedia) https://en.wikipedia.org/wiki/New_Quay

Pen Dinas Hill Fort http://www.aberystwyth.org.uk/attractions/pen-dinas.shtml

Penbryn (Wikipedia) https://en.wikipedia.org/wiki/Penbryn

Pine Marten Recovery Project (Vincent Wildlife Trust) https://www.vwt.org.uk/projects-
    all/pine-marten-recovery-project/

Plas Tanybwlch mansion's secrets, BBC Mid-Wales, 21st October, 2009,

RAF Aberporth http://www.rafaberporth.org.uk/

Rowlands, Daryl Aberporth, a very different kind of air traffic control (NATS, 30th July,
    2014) https://nats.aero/blog/2014/07/different-kind-air-traffic-
    control/#:~:text=Based%20on%20the%20West%20coast,military%20air%20to%20ai
    r%20engagement.

Sarn Gynfelyn (Wikipedia) https://en.wikipedia.org/wiki/Sarn_Gynfelyn

Spirit of the Miners, Discover Ceredigion http://www.spirit-of-the-
    miners.org.uk/uploads/sotm_booklet_final_eng.pdf

Taliesin (Wikipedia) https://en.wikipedia.org/wiki/Taliesin

http://news.bbc.co.uk/local/midwales/hi/people_and_places/history/newsid_8308000/
    8308654.stm

St Ina's Church, Llanina, (Coflein) https://www.coflein.gov.uk/en/site/
    105619/details/st-inas-church-llanina

Strata Florida Ystrad Fflur, https://www.stratafloridatrust.org/

Tresaith (Wikipedia) https://en.wikipedia.org/wiki/Tresaith

Welcome to Aberaeron https://www.aberaeron-wales.com/

Welsh language rally marks 50 years since Trefechan bridge protest, BBC News,
2nd February, 2013, https://www.bbc.co.uk/news/uk-wales-mid-wales-
21290118#:~:text=Welsh%20language%20campaigners%20have%20staged,standstill
%20with%20its%20first%20protest.&text=The%20bridge%20protest%20was%20the,
Cymdeithas%20over%20the%20following%20decades.

Wetlands Margin Survey 2008-10 (Cadw, Welsh Government, Dyfed Archaeology)
http://www.dyfedarchaeology.org.uk/projects/margins.htm

Winter, Rudi (Afon Ystwyth from source to Cardigan Bay) www.geograph.org.uk

Ynys Lochtyn, Ancient Village or Settlement, The Megalithic Portal,
https://www.megalithic.co.uk/article.php?sid=17612

Ynyslas (Wikipedia) https://en.wikipedia.org/wiki/Ynyslas